DICKENS STUDIES ANNUAL
Essays on Victorian Fiction

DICKENS STUDIES ANNUAL
Essays on Victorian Fiction

DICKENS STUDIES ANNUAL

Essays on Victorian Fiction

VOLUME
22

Edited by
Michael Timko, Fred Kaplan,
and Edward Guiliano

AMS PRESS

NEW YORK

DICKENS STUDIES ANNUAL
ISSN 0084-9812

International Standard Book Number
Series:0-404-18520-7
Vol. 22:0-404-18542-8

Dickens Studies Annual: Essays on Victorian Fiction welcomes essay and monograph-length contributions on Dickens as well as on other Victorian novelists and on the history of aesthetics of Victorian fiction. All manuscripts should be double-spaced, including footnotes, which should be grouped at the end of the submission, and should be prepared according to the format used in this journal. An editorial decision can usually be reached more quickly if two copies are submitted. The preferred editions for citations from Dickens' works are the Clarendon and the Norton Critical when available, otherwise the Oxford Illustrated or the Penguin.

Please send submissions to the Editors, *Dickens Studies Annual*, Room 1522, Graduate School and University Center, City University of New York, 33 West 42nd Street, New York, N.Y. 10036: please send subscription inquiries to AMS Press, Inc., 56 East 13th Street, New York, N.Y. 10003.

Manufactured in the United States of America

Contents

List of Illustrations

Preface

The editors continue to be grateful for the services of the members of the editorial and advisory boards. Special thanks go to those who wrote the comprehensive review essays. We also thank the participants in the annual Santa Cruz Dickens Conference, especially John Jordan. Alicia Carroll and Fred Kameny, the editorial assistants from CUNY, and Jack Hopper, AMS Press, deserve special commendation.

We note and express our gratitude to those in administrative posts in different institutions who continue to provide supports of various kinds: Chancellor Anne Reynolds, CUNY; President Frances Horowitz; former Provost Stephen Cahn; Executive Officer, Ph.D. Program in English, Joseph Wittreich, The Graduate School and University Center, CUNY; Vice President King Cheek, The New York Institute of Technology; President Shirley Strum Kenny, Dean John Reilly, and Chair, English Department, Charles Molesworth, Queens College, CUNY; and Gabriel Hornstein, President, AMS Press, whose encouragement has always been a constant source of strength.

—THE EDITORS

Notes on Contributors

MARGARET FLANDERS DARBY is an Assistant Professor in the Department of Interdisciplinary Writing at Colgate University, where she teaches composition, Victorian studies, and women's studies.

EDWIN M. EIGNER is a Professor of English at the University of California, Riverside. He has published three books on nineteenth-century fiction, two of them on Dickens, and has co-edited an anthology of Victorian criticism of the novel. The current essay was first delivered as a paper at the University of California's Dickens Universe, which Professor Eigner helped to found.

JOHN GLAVIN is a playwright and Associate Professor of English at Georgetown University. He has published on a variety of nineteenth- and twentieth-century British subjects, and is currently completing a book on Dickens' theatricality: *A Book in Company: Dickens, Grotowski and Adaptation.*

JASMINE YONG HALL is an Assistant Professor of English and Women's Studies at Elms College, Chicopee, Massachusetts. She is currently working on a study of the interplay between professionalism, consumerism, and gender identity in the Victorian and modern British novel. An article on *Dracula* which is part of this research is forthcoming in *The New Nineteenth Century,* edited by Barbara Harman and Susan Meyer.

MARK M. HENNELLY, JR. is Vice-Chair of the English Department at California State University, Sacramento, and has written numerous articles on Victorian fiction. His most recent work includes a discussion of liminality in *Jane Eyre* (forthcoming in *Victorian Literature and Culture*) and study of the "origins" of and in *Tess of the d'Urbervilles* (forthcoming in *The Thomas Hardy Year Book*). He is currently finishing a lengthy reading of five competing (but often complementary) critical play codes in *Oliver Twist:* romance, carnivalesque, liminal, psychoanalytic, and deconstructive—and the way each may be differently opened by a feminist response.

GERHARD JOSEPH, Professor of English at Lehman College and the Graduate School, City University of New York, has published widely on 19th century matters and is the author of two books on Tennyson. He is currently working on a book concerning legal and illegal copying in the 19th century entitled *The Guilty Art of the Copy*.

JOSS LUTZ MARSH is Assistant Professor of Literature at Stanford University, specializing in Victorian Studies and early cinema. She has published widely on film issues and current cinema; academic articles include studies of Dickens' *Dombey and Son*, the novels of George Meredith, *The Great Gatsby*, and the growth and imaging of Victorian London. Her forthcoming book, *Word Crimes: Blasphemy, Vulgarity, and Victorian Fiction*, will be published in 1995.

SCOTT MONCRIEFF is Associate Professor of English at Andrews University. He has previously written on the connections between autobiography and fiction in Dickens and Trollope, and is currently studying Sir Henry Rider Haggard's "imaginary" Africa.

WILLIAM J. PALMER is a professor in the English department at Purdue University. As a literary critic he has published numerous articles on Dickens and other British, American and Continental novelists as well as *The Fiction of John Fowles* (1975). As a film historian, he has published *The Films of the Seventies: A Social History* (1987) and *The Films of the Eighties: A Social History* (1993). As a novelist, he has written *The Detective and Mr. Dickens* (1990) and *The Highwayman and Mr. Dickens* (1992).

TREY PHILPOTTS is Assistant Professor of English at Arkansas Tech University in Russellville, Arkansas. He has published in *Dickens Quarterly* and *The Dickensian* and is currently working on the *Companion to Little Dorrit* for Edinburgh University Press.

ANNY SADRIN is Professor of English at the University of Burgundy in Dijon, France. She is the author of *L'être et l'avoir dans les romans de Charles Dickens* (Paris, 1988), *Great Expectations* (London, 1988), *Dickens ou le Roman-Théâtre* (Paris, 1992) and *Parentage and Inheritance in the Novels of Dickens* (forthcoming, Cambridge University Press). She has also published essays on Dickens, H. G. Wells, Darwin, and Carroll and is currently working on monsters and monstrosity in nineteenth-century art and fiction.

EFRAIM SICHER teaches at Ben-Gurion University of the Negev. He has published a number of books and essays on British and comparative literature and is currently working on a study of the representation of space in the Victorian novel.

KENNETH M. SROKA is Professor of English and Chair of the English Department at Canisius College in Buffalo, New York. His studies of nineteenth-century fiction have appeared in such journals as *Essays in Literature, Studies in English Literature, Studies in Scottish Literature,* and *The Wordsworth Circle.*

JULIAN WOLFREYS was Elizabeth Middleton Fellow with the Department of English at the University of Southern California between 1990-1992. Since then, he has been completing a study on national identity and Englishness in the nineteenth century at the University of Sussex. He has previously published on George Eliot, Anthony Trollope, James Joyce and feminist film theory.

Pickwick on the Wrong Side of the Door

John Glavin

Sales item in lieu of an epigraph: In the winter of 1990–91, the gift shop of the Metropolitan Opera offered for sale an intriguing beach towel. The top of the towel announced: The Original Ending of Verdi's "Aida." The middle showed a pyramid, some palm trees, and two figures in Egyptian dress, one male, the other female, peeking through an opening in the structure. And at the bottom: "Who would have thought there was a back door to this place?"

This essay asks: can we do for Dickens' Mr. Pickwick what the Metropolitan did for Verdi's Aida?

Even a cursory review of Phiz's original illustrations reveals scene after scene of the Pickwickians found, even caught, on the wrong side of doors.[1] What happens if, cued by the Verdian beach towel, we identify *wrong* with *back*, and then elide *wrong side* simply into *wrong*? What happens, that is, if we start looking for Mr. Pickwick and his Club on the wrong side of the critical door?[2] Obviously, a back/wrong door to *Pickwick* would offer Dickens' characters, like Verdi's Aida and Radames, an exit from the text. They could depart not so much the plot as the "arbitrary" and "despotic" characterizations enshrined in the procession of readings of *Pickwick* as Temple-text: a novel that "fulfills that vision . . . of the ideal possibilities of human relations in community and which, in the fulfillment, extends our awareness of the limits of our humanity" (Marcus 17).[3] But that liberation in turn requires that I suggest for readers, trapped in a different way *outside* the Novel-as-Temple, a back-way in; that I propose a mis-reading of the novel, since a reading, clearly, would go in through the numinous spaces the text itself marks Entrance, spaces that have already seen a considerable amount of critical circling about. This paper then not only mis-reads, it actually

1

delights in mis-reading *Pickwick Papers*. (After all, misreading is what Pick-wick himself—BILST / UM / PSHI / S.M. / ARK—does, not only habitually but best [1:137–39]). Like the novel's famous Fat Boy, "I wants to make your flesh creep," by offering in what follows a boldfaced, and colossal, candid transgression of Dickens' text.

1. FRONTISPIECE

A good way to misread a novel starts by ignoring the text, and, of course, keeps on ignoring it as long as possible. So instead of reading what Dickens wrote I begin on the wrong side, or "outside," of the book with the first illustration—*the frontispiece*. The frontispiece provides a likely place to start misreading not only because it surfaces outside the text—the scene is in the book but not in the plot—but also because it reveals a scene of silenced reading. Sam points Mr. Pickwick to a particularly poignant or pregnant but unspeakable space on the page. We can't tell which book that is on the round table. We can therefore only, inevitably, mis-read it. The helmet and shield atop the wardrobe suggest Cervantes, supporting the important parallel be-tween Mr. Pickwick and Don Quixote. A more conventionally Anglophile error might propose Fielding, Smollett, Sterne, Goldsmith or any of the other key progenitors of Mr. Pickwick's many sources, all probably housed in the bookcase to the side of the room. Or, if one were feeling more Franco- than Anglophile, and therefore habituated to the vertiginous joys of *myse en ab-yme*, one could suggest that a book which leaves Sam and his master looking at the same time both so amused and self-satisfied must be their own adven-tures. They are misreading *Pickwick Papers*.

They are indeed laughing because they are reading about themselves. In my ignorance I'm certain of that. And yet, despite the prestige of any reading that I can by a sort of back-formation attribute to Francophile criticism, I have to believe that the book they are reading, the book that causes them so much pleasure and laughter is, can only be, James Kincaid's *Dickens and the Rhetoric of Laughter* (Oxford: Clarendon, 1971).

In fact, I know exactly the passage in *Dickens and the Rhetoric of Laughter* that Sam and Pickwick are reading—and why it makes them laugh.

They're reading pages 14–15. And I know that because my mis-reading insistently thrusts out through the little crevice or gap between the two pages. On page 14 Professor Kincaid starts to talk about Falstaff: "if we could always laugh at Falstaff . . . we are . . . providing ourselves with a way of

glorying in his display of the primacy of the libido.'' And then on page 15
he talks about Pickwick and ''the wonderful social group assembled at the end
of *Pickwick* . . . constituting a society.'' Even in these elliptical quotations,
Falstaff figures here the comedy of liberty, or, just as well, the liberty of
comedy: libido's antithesis to law. And Mr. Pickwick figures as the other
pole of comedy, the gatherer of a ''wonderful social group,'' albeit a group,
Professor Kincaid recognizes, we can scarcely imagine functioning in any
sort of fact.[4]

And that's why Sam and Pickwick are laughing as they read Professor
Kincaid's book. Because, despite his affection for them, and of course their
very real fondness for him, they know in a very real way, at least in a
way that French criticism would understand—which may not be a *very* real
way—that Pickwick derives not only fron Don Quixote, and Uncle Toby,
and the Vicar of Wakefield, and Parson Adams, and all the rest of those key
predecessor figures, but that he also miscarries from Falstaff. Not the Falstaff
of the Henry IV plays—and, to be fair, that is the Falstaff to whom Professor
Kincaid refers—but certainly the Falstaff of *The Merry Wives of Windsor*. As
Elizabeth I may or may not have requested: Sir John in Love. Or, as the play
was retitled when John Dennis revised it in the eighteenth century: *The Comical Gallant*. A not bad description, you may allow, of Mr. Pickwick.

So there it is: the first and founding outrageous claim of this misreading: I
mislocate Falstaff as an enormous back door to *Pickwick*, an exit that ties
laughter not only to the grotesque but to libido and, to the ''contrast between
Desire and Restraint'' (Chase 39), or between desire and, a term closer to
my own argument, the severe repression of the libido: shame.

2: PICKWICK AND FALSTAFF

You see why this has to be a misreading. Mr. Pickwick is nothing like Sir
John Falstaff. Any *good* reader of the novel sees that clearly. Not even like
the Falstaff of *The Merry Wives of Windsor*. Pickwick is an ''angel in tights
and gaiters,'' Sam insists, ''a reg'lar thoroughbred angel'' (45:641). So what
if each comic hero, alike corpulent and late-middle-aged, leads a band of
three merry men through the English provinces, routinely enduring persecu-
tion from cowardly duelers and incompetent provincial justices? No right-
thinking reader is going to make much of that. Nor of the fact that it is to the
Fleet prison that both Falstaff and Pickwick are sent by the self-righteous
agents of the law, for their amelioration. Obviously, balancing superficial

similarities against fundamental differences, Mr. Sergeant Buzfuz gets it dead wrong when he insists that the Court should read Pickwick as Falstaff: that is, as a "covert, sly, underhanded" (34:473) encroacher on the liberties of the respectable wives of England. I'm not going to point out here that the Arden editor claims that Falstaff's henchman Bardolph is pronounced Bardol; I will, as Cicero says, pass over that in silence.[5] To mis-read Pickwick as Falstaff risks emulating those "howling, sadistic crowds" that assail Pickwith "wherever he turns" as though, Christopher Herbert suggests, "in obedience to some undisclosed paranoiac fantasy" (12).

What fantasy? That Pickwick, like Falstaff, whose name itself [fall-staff] eventually seems to code a phallic nonperformance, continually offers himself to women in erotically suggestive situations, which they variously read as proffer and/or threat, and in which he, again like Falstaff, fails to perform.

1. Think how he sneaks into the garden of the girl's school after dark (ch. 16), where he's found out as "the man-the man—behind the door!" that "ferocious monster" (223) who must be bound "hand and leg" and locked up "in a closet" (223);

2. Recall his voyeuristic eye-balling of Miss Witherfield at the intimacies of her toilette (ch. 22), almost fainting "with horror and dismay" but also finding it "quite impossible to resist the urgent desire to see what was going forward" on her side of the bed (309);

3. And then return to the cries of the Eatanswill electors as he kisses his hand to the lady in the box opposite the hustings (ch. 13). "Oh you wicked old rascal . . . looking arter the girls are you?" "Oh you wenerable sinner." "Putting on his spectacles to look at a married 'ooman!" "I see him a winkin' at her, with his wicked old eye." All of these taunts of course "accompanied with invidious comparisons between Mr. Pickwick and an aged ram" (171). It's not just Dodson and Fogg's clerks who spot him, that is mis-read him, as "the supposed trifler with female hearts and disturber of female happiness" (20:265). As Sam himself moralizes: "Always the vay vith these here old 'uns hows'ever, as is such steady goers to look at" (28:246).

And all this even without Mrs. Bardell's accusations.

Elaborating from parts to the whole, from paranoia into dementia, I can now misread the entire novel along a template of *The Merry Wives*. A big-bellied, grandiose narcissist insistently violates the erotic expectations of a contemporary (primarily female) order. He repeatedly offers himself as a suitor/besieger to women, raising expectations which he is unable to fulfill. For this failure to conform to both female-male and male-male models of behavior, he is repeatedly humiliated, until toward the end he is exposed and remorselessly punished for his most egregious "breach of promise." At last, he publicly submits to the narrow, exacting and conventional regime of contemporary libidinal regulation. After which, the plot displaces him by the conventional erotic structure of a young marriage. There his class replacement (Winkle/Fenton) marries against a father's will but with the father's ultimate approbation. Patriarchy thus transfers itself, without violating the norms of the bourgeois family, from an older model of masculine superiority to a newer one, adapted to the conventions of the time.

You can hear from that thumbnail sketch—probably to true Pickwickians more like a thumbnail scratched across a blackboard—that I'm not merely trying to do violence to W. H. Auden's notion that "Sex . . . is no temptation to" Pickwick (459). I want to be completely objectionable and argue exactly the reverse: that sexuality, specifically the problematics of male sexual identity and appetite, obsesses both Mr. Pickwick himself, and his Papers. And I want to compound my error by arguing that male identity is problematic for Dickens because he (in common with a significant portion of the population of New Guinea) conceives masculinity as a mode of performance, that is, as a role acquired and/or learned rather than innate and instinctive, a role, moreover, the performance of which generally poses a quandary and frequently a menace.[6]

3: PICKWICK, SEX, AND SHAME

Now here is where Falstaff, the booster with which I started this lunatic trajectory, begins to fall away from Mr. Pickwick's progress. Sir John, that priapic picador, goes after women, in exactly the same uncomplicated way he goes after the fat purses of traveling merchants on Gad's Hill (a not entirely un-Dickensian topos). Pickwick, however, is driven as much by shame as by libido, or rather shame has arrested libido in this novel, a shame rooted in a sense of the virtually indomitable and humiliating demands of male sexuality, and the equally powerful need to regulate that libido by humiliating/ameliorating the man who persists in expressing its demands. Here are the Winkles discussing the younger Winkle's run-away marriage:

> "You are ashamed of yourself, I hope, sir?" said the old gentleman.
> Still Mr. Winkle said nothing.
> "Are you ashamed of yourself, sir, or are you not?" inquired the old gentleman.
> "No, sir," replied Mr. Winkle, ... I am not ashamed of myself, or, of my wife either.   (56:793)

Throughout *Pickwick* relations with women tend always to bring men to similar scenes of shame, even in those youthful romances it espouses. But shame also censors the text so powerfully that libido can't be located except by misreading: " 'No; it ain't "dammed",' observed Sam, holding the letter up to the light, 'it's "shamed," there's a blot there—' " (33:452). In fact shame actually prompts Sam's Valentine: "I feel myself ashamed," he begins, composing the elaborate Valentine he prefers to the "normal" card of skewered hearts and scantily-clad Cupids for sale in the stationer's window.

Following Sam here, let's define misreading, then, as going behind the blot (or plot), reading what the text has tried by writing to erase. And let us look again at the frontispiece, this time along with its companion, the facing vignette title page. What are we looking at here? In the frontispiece, two men easily make a spectacle of their private lives as lively imps pull back the curtains to display a voyeuristic fantasy of untrammeled exhibitionism. In the contrary panel, an exhibitionist's nightmare: one man makes a spectacle of another, watched by a third. The psychoanalyst Andrew Morrison would tell us, I think, that we have uncovered a paradigmatic diptych of shame.

You can see the shame in the vignette. "The elder Mr. Weller" savagely beats "the red-nosed" Mr. Stiggins until he is "half suffocated" "in a horse-trough full of water" (51:739). But the shame we are watching belongs properly to Weller, not to the Shepherd. Tony is acting out his shame, reclaiming his masculinity from the "blind trust" of his second marriage by projecting his victim's status onto his rival, the Shepherd. As a result, he can reenlist in the ranks of real manhood, supervised by and imaged in the comparably big-bellied, heroic general, the Marquis of Granby, surveying the scene above. In Morrison's terms, here the hitherto failed self, which has felt "inferior in competition or in comparison with others" (12), relying on a combination of anger, rage, and contempt, converts "lack of absolute control over an archaic environment" into narcissistic inflation through a watched or mirrored grandiosity (102). Typically for this sort of fantasy, the victim does not resist, accepting projected unworthiness entirely into himself. And at the same time, to consolidate the transformation, a family member, here Sam, the son, not only witnesses but intensifies the scene, fixing the achieved difference between the successful self and its flawed, despised, dismissed alterego.

But the doubled presence of Sam connects the vignette back to the frontispiece, helping us to misconstrue one as a fantasied Pickwickian defense against the other. We can thus misread the opening iconic diptych as claiming that successful male-male bonding defends a man against the shame inevitable to any male position available in the scenarios of heterosexuality, that is: against the kinds of shaming illustrated in that series of Pickwickian misadventures with which we began. Remember that in the frontispiece and the vignette we encounter not only the first images we see starting the book, but also virtually the last moments in the novel's contrasted endings to its two major plots of bonding. The younger Weller, by devoting his life to the love of Mr. Pickwick, arrives finally at a cozy and safe *homosocial* union. But for his father, married and remarried, the farce at the horse-trough represents merely the most violent outcome for heterosexual desire and relationship in a novel in which women regularly, as Doreen Roberts argues, "deceive, bully, trap and terrorize men" (304), in which the sovereign "Dragon (called by courtesy a woman)" is always "uppermost" (2:18).

Heterosexuality enters the novel with Jingle, the novel's perfectly *self-possessed* "whole man" (2:10). Starting his career as a deracinated, plebeian intellectual, Dickens at first sides with Jingle's fun. He mocks the bourgeois dilettanti by pairing Pickwick and Jingle as the two halves of a classic clown act. Pickwick performs as *auguste*, the white-faced clown, the "epitome of culture" who "behaves elegantly and authoritatively" (Bouissac 164). Against him, the novel pits Jingle as *faire-vouloir*, the ugly clown always wearing a "suit either too large or too small . . . and eccentric in other respects" (165), who "lightheartedly violates" the cultural regime *auguste* maintains. But what is that culture?

It's the dead end, I think, of something J. G. A. Pocock has called the ideology of "commercial humanism," the counter-civic bourgeois ideal: eighteenth-century mercantile life, the Merchant's Tale that succeeded the Knight's Tale. Commercial Humanism promises to compensate the refined and polished representative of commercial society "by an indefinite and perhaps infinite enrichment of his personality, the product of the multiplying relationships, with both things and persons, in which he became progressively involved" by traveling around on business or meeting foreign businessmen (Pocock 49). That is, of course, the initial agenda of the Pickwick Club: with its "lively sense of the inestimable benefits which must inevitably result" to an individual "from extending his travels, and consequently enlarging his sphere of observation, to the advancement of knowledge, and the diffusion of learning" (1:1). And at story's end, despite his defeats, we still hear Commercial Humanism echoing in Mr. Pickwick's apology for the "pursuit of novelty" that drove his earlier travels. They were directed, he claims, in the best commercial humanist tradition: "I hope to the enlargement of my mind, and the improvement of my understanding" (57:796–97).

Early on, grand claims like Pocock's notwithstanding, Jingle spots the Pickwickian version of Commercial Humanism as merely archaic grandiosity, complacent insensitivity. Insistently trumping the white clown, the ugly clown imposes on this representative of outworn elitist culture, culture's contrary, nature, vividly displayed in what Steven Marcus calls Jingle's "qualities of free inventiveness, of active, spontaneous creativity" (192). Qualities which clearly echo his similarly marginated and talented creator. The question for our misreading then becomes: Why does the novel change? Why does Pickwick move from being the butt of satire to a hero of "principle"?

Part of the answer lies in the way Jingle, the actor, also intrudes, not only wit, but inescapably, the male body. The first time we see him his body is *escaping* clothing which cannot contain or cover him. And almost the first thing he tells us about himself is that he's Don Giovanni: remember the pseudo-Mozartian arioso of Donna Christina and the stomach pump (2:12). As the Stroller insists, on performers' "bodily energies . . . alone they . . . depend for their subsistence" (3:35). A dependence out of which the ensuing plot makes antic hay, as the seductive Jingle cuts his easy swath through the gentry's assembled widows and daughters, threatening both patriarchal Dingley Dell and the homosocial Club.

Committing the novel's social satire to Jingle the satyr has thus trapped the *Papers*, quite close to their start, in a sort of magdeburg sphere of contrary voyeuristic impulse, pulled upon simultaneously to exhibit and repress the phallus. And that may be exactly where, perhaps, the newlywed Dickens needed the novel to go, writing these early numbers while negotiating for the first time in his life a sustained and fully realized sexual encounter.[7] However liberating Jingle's linguistic energies may be, the ongoing serialization also discovers that the dangerous and disruptive energies of male libido must be denied and if possible evicted—as the Rachel Wardle escapade makes clear. This awareness, and the reconstruction it enforces, change *Pickwick* fundamentally. The satiric miscellany, a quarter of the way through its serial publication, starts to become a novel.

To see that change, we can overlay Falstaff with a different sort of Joker and re-misread *Pickwick* to say something like this. *New misreading*: We start with an original, intensively and excusively male quartet, the Pickwick Club. A triangle emerges. Pickwick passionately pursues a teasingly furtive Jingle, while Dodson and Fogg, spurred on by the spurned Mrs. Bardell, in turn pursue Pickwick. Gradually, however, Pickwick's obsessive interest in the "jaunty" and self-possessed Jingle (10), specifically in Jingle's threatened exploits with women, turns into the higher because mutual pairing—from quartet to triangle to pair—between Pickwick and an attractive but lower-class young man, Sam Weller. In the second half of the book, society forces Pickwick into prison because he has chosen Sam instead of a heterosexual alliance with Mrs. Bardell. True to himself, he goes, in this case not to Reading Gaol, but to the Fleet. Eventually, however, he is persuaded to pay the law's price to protect a retired life with Sam, at the same time enabling the now repentant Jingle to pair off permanently with his friend Job, in the Caribbean.

4: THE REGULATION OF THE PHALLUS

Now that is an almost good misreading. It gets at the way in which the novel deploys homosociality to evade the dreaded necessity of encounter with the other sex. But the problem is, it's rather "sunny" (Sedgwick 165). And I mistakenly insist that this novel not only has erotics, but that they are not just dusky but very dark indeed. Despite my considerable and obvious debt to Eve Kosofsky Sedgwick, I can't locate in Pickwickian homosociality something "affectively intense, but profoundly inexpressive; and . . . clean, clean, clean" (186). I prefer to insist perversely that those erotics are anxious, anxious, anxious. And I root that anxiety in the novel's sense that heterosexuality is inescapable. Look for a moment at Pickwick's dilemma in Miss Witherfield's bedroom: the beginning of a kind of dress rehearsal for the Bardell episode, and a key moment for any misconstruction of desire in *Pickwick Papers*.

> "Wretch," said the lady, covering her eyes with her hands, "what do you want here?"
> "Nothing, Ma'am; nothing, whatever, Ma'am;" said Mr. Pickwick earnestly.
> "Nothing!" said the lady, looking up.
> "Nothing, Ma'am, upon my honour"   (22:310)

Clearly, Mr. Pickwick wants nothing from the site of heterosexual encounter. Yet, just as clearly, he finds it "impossible to resist the urgent desire" (309) to enter the heteroerotic scene. Why not? Well, if he backs out, what happens? Outside the lady's bedroom, he finds himself "alone, in an open passage" (311), simultaneously terrified, isolated, and vulnerable. But if he backs into the bedroom—as he repeatedly must, and does—he finds himself equally terrified and ashamed. Think of the suggestively metonymic description of his night-cap: "The very idea of exhibiting his night-cap to a lady overpowered him, but he had tied those confounded strings in a knot, and, do what he would, he couldn't get it off. The disclosure must be made" (309). As the similarly terrified Peter Magnus babbles, "in a state of utmost excitement and agitation" (322) about proposing to the same Miss Witherfield: "I do not see why a man should feel any fear in such a case as this, sir. What is it, sir? There's nothing to be ashamed of" (322). But being repeatedly shamed by others and ashamed of oneself seems to be precisely what heterosexuality must mean for Pickwick and his fellows.

From the Inn at Ipswich to the Fleet the Pickwickian journey constantly threatens to devolve from homosocial progress to heterosexual labyrinth, "the best idea" of which is "losing myself" (22:308). Labyrinth here suggests prisons in general and the Fleet in particular, and so it might be useful to pause for a moment to remind ourselves that Pickwick, like other Dickensian prisoner-heroes—Clennam, Manette, Darnay—doesn't go to any of his various "jails" because of what he's done. Or even because of what he's desired to do. But because he has no desire to do what's demanded of him. The hero experiences conventional desire in all these cases as the threatened dissolution of the innocent self. In the endlessly repackaged Pickwickian ordeal of "humiliation, embarrassment, and mortification" (Morrison 57) we encounter not guilt, i.e., desire experienced as transgression against the other, but shame, desire envisioned as transgression against the self.

The novel does attempt, especially in the early parts we glanced at a moment ago, to defuse this sexual circuit of fear and shame by fantasizing a patriarchal counter-circulation of women between benevolent fathers and pliant sons-in-law. Within the make-believe of the interpolated tales, the grandfatherly chair bestows the landlady on the filial Tom Smart. In the main plot, supremely, Dingley Dell's weddings work without any need for a mother of the bride. They represent ways of imagining marriage for "individuals who are ultimately afraid of intimacy with women, terrified as they are of being united with them" (Ross 53). These fantasies depend on a kind of magic matrimony. A man enters the full power of patriarchy, possession of women and property, production of children, without the use of the phallus. In fact, the novel finally finds a way to fulfill that fantasy in granting Pickwick his last request: "I wish, if my friend Wardle entertains no objection, that his daughter should be married from my house, on the day I take possession of it" (57:796). But throughout the monthly serialization such fantasies tend to pale before the recurring matrimonial paradigm of castrated husbands and devouring wives, like Mrs. Pott and Mrs. Raddle.

So here is the worst misreading yet: in *Pickwick Papers*, yielding to sex makes men either mad, as in the Madman's Manuscript, or bad, like the perfidious Jingle, or unspeakable, like Messrs. Potts, Raddle, and Hunter. The admirable man, in contrast, finds a way to behave like a child. And so the novel heaps praise on Pickwick for remaining "juvenile," a male with a penis but not a phallus. Misread, *Pickwick Papers* might seem, then, not so much to enlarge our sense of "the highest kind of freedom," as Steven Marcus suggested ("Language into Structure" 201), but to idealize a retreat from the complex challenges of fully adult life: "the Pickwickian ideal is achieved at the cost of a dramatic circumscribing of human sensibility, the avoidance of sexuality and kinship, and the suspension of time and memory" (Rogers 35).

Emphasizing this problematic side of Pickwick's juvenility also points to why it does not really help to "out" the novel, as we did a moment back. Reading the book as a closet homosocial romance tends, ultimately, to reinscribe the erotic categories on which conventional bourgeois sexual scenarios depend. In these scenarios, heterosexual, homosocial, homosexual, the desiring subject typically takes identity from the sort of person desired. But in Dickens' novels, as in most of Dickens' life, a protagonist's primary object of desire always turns out to be the ego ideal, re-born, Freud argues, out of "the lost infantile sense of primary narcissism, when the infant took itself to be its own ideal" (Morrison paraphrasing Janine Chasseguet-Smirgel, paraphrasing Freud's "On Narcissism"; Morrison 59). The Dickensian male, from Pickwick to John Jasper, yearns not for another but narcissistically for the self, or rather "for absolute uniqueness and sole importance to someone else . . . for whom the self is uniquely special or who offers no competition or barriers to the self in meeting needs for sustenance" (Morrison 48). Romanticized, that inescapable narcissism inevitably fastens on pallid, uninteresting romantic heroines like David Copperfield's Agnes Wickfield—even her name reflects him—or Sydney Carton's and Charles Darnay's, and indeed Doctor Manette's, and Mr. Lorry's, limp but never ludic Lucie. Demonized, this narcissism becomes, variously, Dombey's love for his son Paul; Magwitch's for Pip; Quilp's passion for Little Nell. Throughout all these very different sorts of novel, the supreme object of desire remains the self in all in its fantasied perfection. The ideal pairing in *Pickwick* is, thus, neither man and woman, nor man and man, but the self and its servant. Samuel and Samivel: a specular romance.

5: SAM'S STORY

The good *Sam*/aritan looms for us now as *Pickwick*'s hero. Forget Falstaff.
It's Sam who gets rid of Jingle and points to that back door which thwarts
appetite from pressing Pickwick to death, as it did Aida. In this resurrection
of desire from the tomb of the body, Sam functions not as a stone rolled away
but as a kind of man-sized prophylactic, guaranteeing that not a drop of
Dickens' most precious psychic commodity, male narcissism, will be spilled
or squandered. Taking on Sam as his shield against a matron's claims, the
grandiose, archaic, idealized hero preserves himself intact from the infection
threatened in the needs or measurements of the other. The "compromise
formation" of their nonphysical bond thus "salvages sexual pleasure" from
"normal" and normative sexual relations everywhere "filled with anxiety and
conflict" (Stoller 39–40).[8] Sam thus ensures the comic promise implicated not
only in the Pickwick icon but in the cult of Dickensian comedy that starts
with Pickwick. (It is of course with his comic grotesques that popular culture
establishes Dickens' enduring reputation.) Downgrading new-comic romance
to the dubious dignity of subplot, that cult celebrates the eccentric solitary's
autoerotic triumph, a victory that the texts insist we read as at once both
aberrant and healthy. And thus, to an enormously anxious Victorian and
post-Victorian audience, stunned by the all-inclusive erotics of patriarchy,
Dickens' comedy repeatedly promises that one can indeed enjoy richly his
(or her: see Sairey Gamp or Mrs. Jarley) sexuality without ever having to
suffer through sex.[9]

This brings me uncomfortably close to a reading of the novel. But since
I'm all for the Pickwickian comfort of mis-reading, I'll pose two questions
instead. First, how does Sam manage to carry off this heroic service to his
master? And, more significantly for us as readers, are we really glad that he
does what he does?

For the first: how does Sam save Pickwick from the vicissitudes of other-
directed desire, from the laughing heteroerotic (Winkle and Arabella) and the
lachrymose homoerotic (Jingle and Trotter) alike? We can begin to frame an
answer by suggesting that, against the novel's intrapsychic anxieties, Sam
protects his master by setting up a sort of phallic arbitrage.[10] Like any good
arbitrageur (and surely that's an oxymoron) Sam enjoys masculinity, not only
for his own use, but in order to get it back into circulation among other men,
for Winkle, and, most importantly, for Pickwick. As the novel develops,
Sam and Pickwick enter into an erotically charged dyadic relation: "between
[Sam] and his master there exists a steady and reciprocal attachment, which

nothing but death will terminate'' (57:801)—the final words of the novel. But the presence of Mary and the "Two sturdy little boys'' (801) complicates any simplistically homoerotic reading of this structure. In effect, Sam makes it possible for neither and both simultaneously to "possess'' the phallus. From the heterosexuality that threatens to engulf them, Sam delivers himself and Pickwick by reinventing himself as the eternal son to Pickwick's pre-Oedipal father: "affectionate, supportive, noncompetitive and facilitating'' (Meyers and Schore 246). Sam lets Pickwick and the novel keep all his many faults without ever having to confront their consequences. He thus produces Pickwick as a heroic male text, rather than himself enact the experience of that text. Pickwick: master of the house. Sam: father of the family. We can think about their relation along the lines some psychologists call "phallic narcissism''—a son who has identified himself early on with a weak father repairs the "shame of being weak'' through a fantasied union with an idealized male parent (described in Morrison 58). (An experience with obvious affinities to Dickens' own early life.) Sam metamorphoses Pickwick from the butt of Jingle's satire to—not merely a good man—but an angel, that is a male with no conceivable use for a penis.

6: VILLAINS

But even Sam can't save Pickwick from Dodson and Fogg. Nowhere do we have to work harder to retrieve the meanings that accumulate on the wrong side of the door than when we insist on remembering that the bad buddies win big in this book.

> "Do you know that I have been the victim of your plots and conspiracies?'' continued Mr. Pickwick. "Do you know that I am the man whom you have been imprisoning and robbing? Do you know that you were the attorneys for the plaintiff in Bardell and Pickwick?''
> "Yes, sir, we do know it,'' replied Dodson.
> "Of course we know it, sir,'' rejoined Fogg, slapping his pocket—perhaps by accident.   (53:750)

If Jingle embodies the novel's source of intrapsychic anxiety, Dodson and Fogg represent the counter extrapsychic threat, what sociology calls 'hegemonic masculinity,'' the organized male socioeconomic structure which in any society dominates all women and most men (Carrigan, Connell, and Lee 90–91). (In Bouissac's terms, Dodson and Fogg, all masculine hegemons, parallel the circus's MC, the non-quiche-eating real men who function as "the warden of a set order" [Bouissac 164]). This notion of hegemonic masculinity allows us to reformulate the different anxieties embodied in Jingle and in Dodson and Fogg as the distinction between masculinity defined as libido and masculinity defined as law, and more pointedly, for our argument, as the difference between heterosexuality and hegemony.

Of course, if law in this novel were *L.A. Law*, that distinction would make no sense. But all the lawyers in *Pickwick* are extravagantly homosocial. Their offices in the Inns of Court empty easily at dusk into the snuggeries of the George and Vulture or toward "agreeable little part[ies]" like Perker's for "Mr. Snicks the Life Office Secretary, Mr. Prosee the eminent counsel, three solicitors, one commissioner of bankrupts, a special pleader from the Temple, [and] a small-eyed peremptory young gentleman, his pupil, who had written a lively book about the law of demises" (47:657). Indeed, as Mrs. Bardell learns to her chagrin, lawyers' power roots in equal imperviousness to men's and women's claims. It is in their apparently inviolable security from any feeling even bordering on erotic desire that the Pickwick lawyers root their superiority to other and lesser men. Pleasure in their world equals power. Hegemony assigns the novel from fantasy to history.

The lawyer pair cap a professional male hierarchy, starting with the Rochester soldiery, for whom the Pickwickians and Jingle are both unspeakably beyond the hegemonic pale (2:43), and who frequently leave Pickwick, not to our surprise, feeling "ashamed" (44). And now we pick up Commercial Humanism again. With these bodies of professional men, the novel witnesses the early nineteenth century's crucial transfer of male hegemony from an earlier to a later form of capitalist ideology, from a culture of "commercial humanism" to the ideology of administration: lawyer-land (Pocock 50). If Pickwick comes into the novel believing this Edmund Burke that "Manners . . . are of more importance than laws (quoted by Pocock 49); he, like the even less fortunate Jingle, learns from Dodson and Fogg, and the Fleet, the impossibility of resisting the ruthless inefficiencies of administration. The Trial and its aftermath, the Fleet, subordinate him to the new utilitarian masculinity formed to master "face-to-face class conflict and the management of personal capital" (Carrigan, Connell, and Lee 99). This new hegemony controls through management not possession of capital. When Pickwick, both far richer and far less powerful than Dodson and Fogg, purchases his freedom on their terms, manhood as the expression of feeling gives way to masculinity as the instrument of force.

But the novel wants us to blot this defect, to somehow read this loss as a win. Consequently, for the better part of the three installments after the Fleet, it insistently resituates Pickwick in the goofy and powerless world of the early excellent adventures, this time as companion to Sawyer and Allen, the Bill and Ted of their day. Pickwick leaves the Fleet to secure the elder Winkle's consent to the marriage (and not, as is often suggested, because he has forgiven Mrs. Bardell and thus secured happiness through compassion. This is *Merry Wives* not *Measure for Measure*; Pickwick is no nun). But it also insists that Pickwick fail in his quest to Birmingham. The wharfinger turns him down flat, echoing at the novel's end the initial insulting condescension of the officers of the 97th. We can't escape from the novel's repeated assertion that hapless, frivolous, ineffectual Pickwick can't make a difference in the world. That is the novel's final and happy "point," and Sam's central achievement. To save Pickwick the man from the deepest anxieties within, the novel has had to sacrifice him to the powers without. He is good, we are assured, because he is impotent.

And here we suddenly find ourselves returning to Falstaff, and Professor Kincaid's antithetical comic pair. Falstaff, the small seigneur of old family, now in every way bankrupt, banished in *Henry IV, Part 2* from the new national bureaucracy, at the end of *The Merry Wives* is similarly exorcised from the burgher precincts of bustling Windsor. We can read Sir John as the Oedipal father demonized. Only by rendering that old man grotesque for persisting in sexuality and impotent in performance can the young man guilt-lessly make his own erotic comedy. Pickwick, the pre-Oedipal father, is also at the end rendered historically and sexually impotent, in this case to secure the male psyche from the shame of sexuality itself. Sam has rescued Pickwick by infantilizing him. But by insisting that infantilism embodies the highest sort of virtue he and the novel also leave Pickwick defenseless against the worst sorts of virility.

7: CODA

Which brings me to my second question, and my final paragraphs. Are we really glad that Sam does what he does? Sam's elision of idealism into infantilism, turning *Pickwick Papers* from satire into comedy, is what tempted me toward this farrago of mis-readings. It raises for me a disturbing question about our culture's fond allegiance to the book. Is the otherwise reliable

Karen Chase correct to read this conclusion as a triumph of ''moral conscious-ness'' (44). Or is it closer to a more momentous, big and disturbing win for narcissism? I think of Dickens' essay on childhood: "Where We Stopped Growning." Do we stop growing if, to idealize, we infantilize ourselves or another? When, as readers, we accept and revel in this happy ending as an alternative to the complexities of fully adult existence. Or do we stop growing if we don't or can't somehow idealize, even if that means we must, at the same time, infantilize?

In a sense, of course, all happy endings idealize, just as all happy endings are infantile.[11] They restore us momentarily to that sense of power over the ordinary vicissitudes of existence, that imaginary omnipotence we renounce to become mature. And they do so by conferring imagined, idealized goodness on those figures who stand in for ourselves and for those structures and relations we need to retrieve as perfect, or at least perfectible. Cleverly done happy endings merely disguise these infantile origins.

But, then, as Joseph Westlund has argued about the effect of Shakespeare's comedies, "we need to believe in what can never be quite there" (94). On that belief depends our capacity to love others (impossible without idealiza-tion) and also to repair the daily damage life does to our selves. The answer may depend finally on how we read what we admire. The satiric or merely critical spectator,—someone who, shall we say, reads lovelessly—who stands outside of and thus sees all the illusion involved by participating in any sort of field or text, may suffer in exchange what Pierre Bourdieu calls "the misery of men without social qualities" (197), the (putative, private) misery of men like Dodson and Fogg. On the other hand, investment in any social text, and supremely investment in comedy, certainly involves illusions like Sam's. But perhaps we might agree that a "well-founded illusion," my final definition of misreading, may procure for us a great deal more than it costs. Especially nice—this is again Bourdieu—"one can always join the game without illusions." It seems to depend on what you mean by the wrong side of the door.

Notes

I am delighted to acknowledge here my un-Fleet-ing debt to John Jordan and Murray Baumgarten, the founders and directors of the Dickens Project at the University of California at Santa Cruz, where this paper was originally deliv-ered (July 1990).

NOTES

1. The most egregious instances would include, but by no means be limited to, the following. Pickwick squeezed by Cook behind the back door of Westgate House in "The Unexpected Breaking Up of the Ladies' Seminary" (ch. 16). After his day of hunting and boozing the inebriated yokels hoot at "Mr. Pickwick in the Pound" (ch. 19). The pendant illustration to the pound, "Mr. Pickwick in the Attorney's Office," exhibits Pickwick outside the swing-door of the clerks' room at Dodson and Fogg, once more the subject of superior sneers (ch. 20). At Ipswich, in "The Middle-Aged Lady's Room" the horrified Pickwick peers between bed-curtains, trapped on the wrong side of the door in a lady's bedroom (ch. 22). Later in the novel, "Mr. Winkle's Situation When the Door 'Blew-To' " exposes Winkle in a night shirt, trapped between the firmly locked door of his inn and the inappropriately open door to Mrs. Dowler's sedan chair (ch. 36). Behind prison doors "Mr. Pickwick Sits for His Portrait" to the Fleet keepers (ch. 40). Finally, Pickwick vainly attempts to clamber out the cab door to escape "Mr. Bob Sawyer's Mode of Travelling" (ch. 50).
2. The novel uses the phrase "On The Wrong Side of the Door" as a running title for the episode in chapter 36, in which Mr. Winkle is trapped in a compromising situation with Mrs. Dowler outside the Inn at Bath.
3. Dickens himself imbricates pyramid, tyranny, writing, characterization, and even plotting in that passage in *David Copperfield* where the narrator-hero describes his efforts to master shorthand: "When I had groped my way, blindly, through these difficulties, and had mastered the alphabet, which was an Egyptian Temple in itself, there then appeared a procession of new horrors, called arbitrary characters; the most despotic characters I have ever known; who insisted, for instance, that a thing like the beginning of a cobweb, meant expectation, and that a pen-and-ink sky-rocket stood for disadvantageous" (609; ch. 38).
4. Before I go on to compound my error, I need to point out that Professor Kincaid continues almost immediately after page 15 to erase the liberty-law distinction he had just made, to probe a crucial connection between laughter and the grotesque. The Falstaff-Pickwick axis represents merely a moment in his extensive exploration of the nature of Dickensian comedy. I, however, go on to deflate his witty globule into a pedantic anthill.
5. "BARDOLPH" Probably to be pronounced 'Bardle' (it is spelt 'Bardol' in the Q of *1H4*, II. IV. 329)." (Shakespeare 2)
6. My description of Dickens' attitude toward male sexuality borrows heavily from David Gilmore's description of the men of the Sambia (Gilmore 147).
7. It is worth recalling, if only in passing, the circumstances of the novel's creation: Charles Dickens, in 1836, publishing his first novel, *The Posthumous Papers of the Pickwick Club*, returns from the honeymoon of his longed-for marriage to Catherine Hogarth. And almost immediately he starts revising that novel in a radically new way. The new husband now has his protagonist, Mr. Pickwick, explore the possibilities of breach of promise. Indeed, from now on the novel works out obsessively how to fight breach of promise until the lady quits all claims to the gentleman. One senses the beginning here of that increasingly obsessive Dickensian agenda, to unwrite in radical fiction the bourgeois normalcy his marriage forced him to live. An agenda that collapsed under his passion for Ellen Ternan, to open the way to the very different (guilt-, not shame-obsessed)

novels of the 1860s. See Claire Tomalin's invaluable *The Invisible Woman* for the history of that romance.

8. I rely in this discussion of aberration on Robert J. Stoller's illuminating and enlightened distinction between *variants* and *perversions*. Both are classes of what he calls *aberration*: "an erotic technique or constellation of techniques that one uses as his complete sexual act and that differs from his culture's traditional, avowed definition of normality." A *variant* refers to "an aberration that is not primarily the staging of forbidden fantasies, especially fantasies of harming others." The term *perversion* he limits exclusively to "a habitual, preferred aberration necessary for one's full satisfaction, primarily motivated by hostility." Because variant only makes sense within Stoller's larger nomenclature, my argument prefers to collapse the distinction into two opposing terms: aberration (non-normative, erotic technique free of hostility and hatred) and perversion (non-normative, erotic technique dependent on hostility and hatred). See Stoller's *Perversion* (passim), for the definition of terms pages 3–5.

9. Evelyn Waugh inverts Dickens' point at the end of *A Handful of Dust*: the corruption of heterosexuality at home reduces Tony Last to the ultimately Pickwickian vignette of endlessly rereading Dickens to Mr. Todd in the Amazonian jungles. But where Dickens, at the beginning of the nineteenth century, can locate the comic release in such a pairing, Waugh's high modern satire, at a comparable point in the twentieth, can only find Todd's death. I think we have yet to appreciate the impressive success with which the Victorians used eccentricity as a prodigious defense against the encompassing threat of bourgeois sexuality.

10. The plot invents this arbitrage at the moment when Pickwick in Bath splits Sam in two, as it were, and sends him off to minister to Winkle. Thereafter, as Pickwick and Winkle parallel each other's stories through the latter parts, the novel ensures its apparent compliance with the demands of a hegemonic heterosexuality while at the same time constructing the pairing of its preferred narcissism. The last third of the novel thus perfectly emulates Freud's description in "The Splitting of the Ego in the Process of Defence": "On the one hand, with the help of certain mechanisms he rejects reality and refuses to accept any prohibition; on the other hand, in the same breath he recognizes the danger of reality, takes over the fear of that danger . . . and tries subsequently to divest himself of the fear" (275). In the novel's plot, Pickwick rejects the reality of bourgeois sexual hegemony by his reckless behavior before, during, and after his imprisonment. At the same time, he does everything possible to establish his charge, Winkle, in a respectable marriage, as Freud comments: this splitting achieves a "very ingenious solution of the difficulty"—both sides "obtain their share: the instinct is allowed to retain its satisfaction [narcissism] and proper respect is shown to reality [marriage]" (278).

11. The richest contemporary reading of Victorian comedy remains Robert Polhmus' *Comic Faith*. I find particularly suggestive his reading of Sairey Gamp as a figure who shares "the novelist's addiction to what is not": "Dickens's fantasy confronts us with the depth, the amoral perversity, and the glee of our rebelliousness against what is" (120). I am in equal parts rallied and chilled by this unimprovably apt summation.

WORKS CITED

Auden, W. H. "Dingley Dell and the Fleet" (1962). *Charles Dickens: A Critical Anthology*. Ed. Stephen Wall. Baltimore: Penguin, 1970. 458–68.

Bouissac, Pierre. *Circus and Culture*. Bloomington: Indiana UP, 1976.

Bourdieu, Pierre. *In Other Words: Essays towards a Reflexive Sociology*. Stanford: Stanford UP, 1990.

Carrigan, Tim, Bob Connell, and John Lee. "Toward a New Sociology of Masculinity." *The Making of Masculinities: The New Men's Studies*. Ed. Harry Brod. Boston: Unwin, 1987. 63–100.

Chase, Karen. "Personality in a Pickwickian Sense." *Eros and Psyche: The Representative of Personality in Charlotte Brontë, Charles Dickens, and George Eliot*. New York: Methuen, 1984. 25–46.

Dickens, Charles. *David Copperfield*. Ed. Trevor Blount. New York: Penguin, 1966.

———. *The Posthumous Papers of the Pickwick Club*. Introd. Bernard Darwin. London: Oxford UP, 1959.

Fogel, Gerald I., Frederick M. Lane, and Robert S. Liebert. *The Psychology of Men: New Psychoanalytic Perspectives*. New York: Basic, 1986.

Freud, Sigmund. "The Splitting of the Ego in the Process of Defense" (1940). *Standard Edition* 23:275–78. London: Hogarth , 1953.

Gilmore, David. *Manhood in the Making*. New Haven: Yale UP, 1990.

Herbert, Christopher. "Converging Worlds in *Pickwick Papers*." *Nineteenth-Century Fiction* 27 (1972):1–20.

Kincaid, James. *Dickens and the Rhetoric of Laughter*. Oxford: Clarendon, 1971.

Marcus, Steven. *Dickens from Pickwick to Dombey*. New York: Simon, 1968.

———. "Language into Structure: Pickwick Revisisted." *Daedalus* 101 (1972):183–202.

Morrison, Andrew P. *Shame: The Underside of Narcissism*. Hillsdale, NJ: Analytic, 1989.

Meyers, Donald I., and Arthur M. Schore. "The Male-Male Analytic Dyad: Combined, Hidden, and Neglected Transference Paradigms." Fogel 245–61.

Pocock, J. G. A. "Virtues, Rights, and Manners." *Virtue, Commerce, and History*. Cambridge: Cambridge UP, 1985. 37–50.

Polhemus, Robert. *Comic Faith*. Chicago: U of Chicago P, 1980.

Roberts, Doreen. "*The Pickwick Papers* and the Sex War." *Dickens Quarterly* 7 (1990):299–311.

Rogers, Philip. "Mr. Pickwick's Innocence." *Nineteenth-Century Fiction* 27 (1972):21–37.

Ross, John Munder. "Beyond the Phallic Illusion: Notes on Man's Heterosexuality." Fogel 49–70.

Sedgwick, Eve Kosofsky. *Between Men: English Literature and Male Homosocial Desire*. New York: Columbia UP, 1985.

Shakespeare, William. *The Merry Wives of Windsor*. Ed. H. J. Oliver. London: Routledge, 1990.

Stoller, Robert J. *Perversion: The Erotic Form of Hatred*. New York: Random, 1975.

Tomalin, Claire. *The Invisible Woman*. New York: Knopf, 1991.

Westlund, Joseph. "Expanding The Method." *Poetics* 13 (1984):421–32.

Fragmentation in *The Pickwick Papers*

Anny Sadrin

In his 1847 preface to *Pickwick*, Dickens explains that when William Hall approached him with the "Nimrod Club" project, what he agreed to collaborate on was a mere "something," a something to be "published in shilling numbers," "a monthly something" meant to be "a vehicle for certain plates to be executed by Mr SEYMOUR" (43-44). This was by no means an ambitious scheme: the *Papers*, as he wrote in a later preface (1867), "were designed for the introduction of diverting characters and incidents; . . . no ingenuity of plot was attempted, or even at that time considered very feasible by the author in connexion with the desultory mode of publication adopted" (49).

All Dickens had to do, therefore, after agreeing to Hall's proposition, was to think of a means of coordinating the various episodes so that "the different incidents" should be "linked together by a chain of interest strong enough to prevent their appearing unconnected or impossible" (41) and he "thought of Mr Pickwick" (44). Mr Pickwick, thus, was a pre-text in both senses of the word: he came before the text and he came as a justification of the text. He was to be the leading, or rather the linking figure, the camera eye, the innocent Quixotic observer of the world around him. There was no need for the author to think any further, no need to plot, organize or write "mems." What was at stake was not the serialization of a story but of stories, self-contained instalment numbers, new "Sketches by Boz."

Quite naturally, the book was perceived by Dickens' contemporaries as fragmentary: "it is rather fragmentary," Miss Mitford wrote to a correspondent; Forster called it "a succession of actual scenes" and an anonymous reviewer for the *Athenaeum* described it as a "periodical (for such it is)." But these early readers liked the book for what it was, an "extravagant," "laugh-provoking" piece of writing in the great English tradition that reminded them of Fielding, Sterne, Smollett, and, more recently, Pierce Egan and Surtees.[1]

Later generations were much more critical: "Dickens," said Chesterton, "tries to tell ten stories at once . . . sticks in irrelevant short stories shamelessly, as into a scrapbook" (16). But he was none the less enthusiastic about the book in his own inimitable way, finding in it "a sense of the gods gone wandering in England" (19).

It was only in fairly recent years that fragmentation began to be considered by the critics as a capital sin, an antiliterary gesture and a good reason for dismissing the book as rubbish, as did some critics in 1967 on the grounds that it appeared "to have been written in a series of jerkily spasmodic bouts of inane euphoria" (19).

Such dismissals are fair enough after all and less detrimental by far to the Pickwickian spirit than the generous but wrong-minded attempts made by others to salvage the book, rescue it from the hands of the profaners and, by demonstrating its coherence and complex thematic organization, make sure that it will remain for ever and ever on the shelves of our University Libraries: for the danger would be to keep it there for the wrong reason. The interpolated stories, we are told, are relevant to the whole thing, they are not mere padding but contribute to underscoring the main themes of the book: which they do, of course, in that they deal with Dickens's favorite subjects—prison, death, revenge, unrequited love—but then they might just as well be inserted in any Dickens novel. Pickwick's journeys are also presented as a Pilgrim's Progress, his education and enlightenment as a new version of the Fall:[2] personally, I must say that I find Pickwick more like Parson Adams than like the old Adam of Genesis and, for all his kindheartedness, more like the pagan gods of Chesterton than like Bunyan's Christian, more rambling than pilgriming.

The trouble with these well-intentioned defenders of Dickensian unity is that they moralize art: unity is good, fragmentation is bad, they seem to say. Of course, we, modern readers, prefer unity; we like a plot; we like consistency; and, especially for critical purposes, we are all very fond of symbolism and messages and decoding; and we all find it rather frustrating to have to concede that "Chops and Tomata sauce" means no more—and no less—than "Chops and Tomata sauce"!

Dickens himself, as we have seen, writes almost apologetically about this question in his various prefaces; but he never tries to conceal the fact that he enjoyed the fun of it or to disguise desultoriness as purposive organization. And I would even argue that fragmentation suited him and that serialization was more than merely circumstantial, that it corresponded to some deeper urge in him: otherwise, he would not have stuck for life to this not only "desultory" but "trying" mode of publication. It meant taking risks, it required an adventurous attitude to literary creation and implied the acceptance of imperfection, accidents, change, finitude, death.

I: A STROLLER'S TALES:
NARRATIVE FRAGMENTATION

When he wrote *Pickwick*, Dickens was only twenty-four, but even at this early age, he had learned from cruel experience that life was unpredictable. He had plotted his life, as we all do, and things had come out differently. He had plotted to become "a learned and distinguished man" and possibly go to Cambridge (a remark in the "Autobiographical Fragment" suggests no less), but at the age of twelve he was sent to work in the Strand (Forster 21-22). He had later intended or plotted to become an actor, but on the day when he was appointed to be interviewed by George Bartley and Charles Kemble at Covent Garden, he was in bed with a bad cold. He had long expected and plotted to marry Maria Beadnell and one of the reasons why he agreed to the Nimrod Club proposal was that he needed money for his approaching marriage to another girl. The very publication of *Pickwick* was disturbed and interrupted on two occasions by the unexpected and untimely deaths of Robert Seymour and Mary Hogarth. Seymour's suicide necessitated urgent reorganization and the selection of a new partner, and the sudden death of Mary so grieved and perturbed him that Dickens was unable to produce the fifteenth installment in time. These, among other reasons, probably account for the acute sense of the "mutability of human affairs" (79) that the *Papers* convey in spite of their lightness of tone.

In the later novels the theme was to be dealt with much more dramatically, becoming even really tragic: with Dickens' growing obsession with dust, decay, and vanity, these "dark" novels often read like variations on Ecclesiastes. Here tragedy—madness, revenge or death—is confined to the inset tales which, to use Heinz Reinhold's felicitous expression, provide "tragic relief" to a fundamentally humorous book where mutability is generally accepted as a life principle, like breathing, or as a law of nature, like the alternation of night and day (146). "The sun rises and the sun goes down," says Ecclesiastes, but in *Pickwick* we are told more about dawn than about nightfall. The opening lines of the book give the tone with "The first ray of light which illumines the gloom'' and converts obscurity ''into a dazzling brilliancy'' (67), and the natural fragmentation of time remaining throughout the major ordering principle of the story, a great many chapters open on a new day, a new month, a new season. Chapter 2 in this respect is quite characteristic: ''That punctual servant of all work, the sun, had just risen, and begun to strike a light on the morning of the thirteenth of May, one thousand eight hundred and twenty-seven, when Mr Samuel Pickwick burst like another sun from his slumbers, threw open his chamber window, and looked out upon the world beneath'' (72–73). We might go on quoting many such episodes beginning with Pickwick ''contemplating nature, and waiting for breakfast'' (128) or springing ''like an ardent warrior from his tent-bedstead'' (155) or with the Pickwickians rediscovering the beauties of spring or looking forward to the Christmas festivities. Ordering in *Pickwick* is more or less synonymous with chronology.

Similarly, the narrative syntax for each episode follows the ''and then'' pattern that this extract from chapter 6 illustrates to perfection:

> *Meanwhile* the round game proceeded right merrily. Isabella Wardle *and* Mr Trundle ''went partners,'' *and* Emily Wardle *and* Mr Snodgrass did the same; *and even* Mr Tupman *and* the spinster aunt established a joint-stock company of fish and flattery . . . *and when* the old lady looked cross at having to pay, they laughed louder than ever; *on which* the old lady's face gradually brightened up, *till at last* she laughed louder than any of them. *Then . . . till . . . whereupon . . .*
>
> The evening glided swiftly away, in these cheerful recreations; *and when* the substantial though homely supper *had been* despatched, *and* the little party formed a social circle round the fire, Mr Pickwick thought he had never felt so happy in his life, and at no time so much disposed to enjoy, and make the most of, the passing moment.   (143–44; my italics)

A passage like this one, celebrating the ''passing moment,'' is typical of the book's awareness of mutability and of the author's and characters' acceptance of it. The book ends on similar considerations: ''Let us leave our old friend in one of those moments of unmixed happiness, of which, if we seek them, there are ever some, to cheer our transitory existence here'' (896). We have indeed, throughout the book, moved from one scene of ''unmixed happiness'' to another, from one day to another, from one season to another, and no more. Pickwick's wisdom has excluded plotting.

This exclusion is quite explicit, quite deliberate. When, by taking action against him, Mrs. Bardell gives Pickwick a chance of becoming the hero of a proper story, he simply declines the offer and refuses to let himself be caught in the trap of plot: ''let me hear no more of the matter,'' he says,

"And now . . . the question is, Where shall we go next?" (578). Not even the Fosterian question "What is going to happen next?" and certainly not Christian's "What shall I do to be saved?" but simply "Where shall we go next?" which expresses this sense of immediacy that so characterizes the book.

And so, they go to Bath; and there, they entirely forget about Mrs. Bardell and Dodson and Fogg. Not a word is said of the lawsuit during the Bath chapters and neither readers nor characters worry about the outcome. Nobody cares.

Even when, on his return to London, Pickwick is imprisoned in the Fleet, he does not seem to care about what is going to happen to him and whether he will stay there for ages or not. He just looks about him. The present makes him sad, but the future does not worry him. In fact, Pickwick has no future; except, of course, the simplest of futures, which is death, as the narrator makes a point of emphasizing in the very last words of his chronicle: "on this, as on all other occasions, he is invariably attended by the faithful Sam, between whom and his master there exists a steady and reciprocal attachment which nothing but death will terminate" (898).

The certainty of death has been felt throughout the *Papers*. For Pickwick, as for all of us, death is from the start known to be the inevitable outcome, but, meanwhile, he behaves like an easygoing stoic, taking things as they come. And so do we, as the readers of a plotless story. Our reading involves no interpreting, no speculating, no predicting, no expectations. Pickwick has always known what it will take Rick Carstone a lifetime to learn that "we must not expect," that it is far wiser to wait and see, which is also Sam's conviction, and the narrator's: "Sam . . . meditated, at first, on the probable consequence of his own advice, and the likelihood of his father's adopting it. He dismissed the subject from his mind, however, with the consolatory reflection that time alone would show; and this is the reflection we would impress upon the reader" (457).

These are the reflections that many later novels would impress upon the reader. In fact, Dickens' best-plotted stories paradoxically aim at no less than the destruction, or, to use a more fashionable word, at the deconstruction of plot, especially the deconstruction of the hero's plot. *Dombey and Son* and *Great Expectations* are undoubtedly the most outstanding instances of this strategy of irony, which consists in simultaneously encouraging and undermining wish-fulfillment dreams. The author, in both cases, goes to great lengths to mislead the hero into building castles in the air, dreaming the wrong dream, placing himself in the wrong novel, even hoping against the odds, the better in the end to demolish his mental constructions and thereby subvert the expectations raised by the title in the reader's mind. But in *Pickwick* there is no deconstruction for the simple reason that there never was any construction in the first place. Or what construction there is is purely formal and stylistic, entailing purely stylistic deconstruction.

II: BROKEN ENGLISH:
LINGUISTIC FRAGMENTATION

It is the task of the so-called "editor" to sort out the enormous amount of notes that he is supposed to start from and organize them into coherent sequences. His many references to his editorial duties, besides making it clear that he is in fact the author of these sketches, aim at underscoring the conventions of the genre. For instance, he writes:

> whatever ambition we might have felt under other circumstances to lay claim to the authorship of these adventures, a regard for truth forbids us to do more than claim the merit of their judicious arrangement and impartial narration.
>
> (115–16)

Part of the game also consists in complaining that the task is rendered difficult by the overabundance of notes—he speaks of "multifarious documents" (67) and of "voluminous papers" (236)—by their lack of consistency, even, occasionally, by their unreadability:

> Mr Snodgrass, as usual, took a great mass of notes, which would no doubt have afforded most useful and valuable information, had not the burning eloquence of the words or the feverish influence of the wine made that gentleman's hand so extremely unsteady, as to render his writing unintelligible, and his style wholly so. By dint of patient investigation, we have been enabled to trace some characters bearing a faint resemblance to the names of the speakers; and we can also discern an entry of a song . . . in which the words "bowl" "sparkling" "ruby" "bright," and "wine" are frequently repeated at short intervals. We fancy too, that we discern at the very end of the notes, some indistinct reference to "broiled bones;" and then the words "cold" "without" occur: but as any hypothesis we could found upon them must necessarily rest upon mere conjecture, we are not disposed to indulge in any of the speculations to which they may give rise. (169)

Clearly, one of his major editorial difficulties is to make sense of such fragments. Another is to have to comply to the rules of serial publication or chapter division: "But bless our editorial heart," he writes at the end of chapter 28, "what a long chapter we have been betrayed into! We had quite forgotten all such petty restrictions as chapters, we solemnly declare" (480).

Fragmentation is constantly presented by the narrator as a necessary evil, unsuited to his own taste for stylistic decorum and high-flown rhetoric. For he knows what good writing is; he knows it implies coordinating, subordinating, syntaxing, shaping. In this respect, the very first paragraph of the book, which like all first paragraphs is a kind of "ars poetica," is exemplary:

> The first ray of light which illumines the gloom, and converts into a dazzling brilliancy that obscurity in which the earlier history of the public career of the immortal Pickwick would appear to be involved, is derived from the perusal of the following entry in the Transactions of the Pickwick Club, which the editor of these papers feels the highest pleasure in laying before his readers, as a proof of the careful attention, indefatigable assiduity, and nice discrimination, with which his search among the multifarious documents confided to him has been conducted.

The style is ideally periphrastic, adjectival, florid, Micawberish. Dickens in fact overdoes it, so that the paragraph reads—and is clearly meant to read—as a parody of the lofty style. On the one hand, we have a narrator who is most conspicuously a linguistic conformist, on the other, we have a writer who is, as Roland Barthes says of Raymond Queneau, "at war with literature" (125; my translation). And this is the reason why a whole army of unconventional, singular narrative voices are soon introduced in the book and entrusted with the task of experimenting with style, even for some of them of deconstructing the English "langwidge" (582).

These deconstructors, mainly Jingle and the two Wellers, are better remembered for what they say than for what they do. They are linguistic performers, "with . . . the gift o' the gab wery gallopin" (353), intruders, uninvited interpolators, always with a ready story. But their stories are very different in length, style, and purpose from the nine officially interpolated ones. They break not only the thread but also the tone of the main narrative. They come unexpectedly, when the others are well advertised and given titles. They are improvisations, when the others are either read or "repeated." They are told at a stretch, in spoken and broken English, with no regard for spelling, or grammar, or syntax, or paragraph division or tense sequence, when the others are logically constructed, well provided with introductions and conclusions, divided into neat paragraphs, and properly, albeit conventionally told. But, because of their very unconventionality, they strike us as poetic and they point out the artificially constructed nature of the other narrators' style.

Jingle's disjointed rhetoric is even, paradoxically, a fantastic form of articulateness, inventiveness and artistry. Not, however, the unconscious inventiveness that James Kinsley has in mind when he writes that "Jingle is the first sustained attempt by Dickens at free-association monologue," paving the way for characters like Mrs. Nickleby and Flora Finching.[3] The comparison is unfair on him: these talkative women indisputably belong to the category of "inefficient" tellers that Barbara Hardy describes as "unprofessionally out of control, involved, naïve, and floundering," whereas he never flounders and is well in control of his eccentric "system of stenography" (163). How else could it be? This "system of stenography" is all too obviously the private joke of the "professional" novelist who is fast rising above his condition as a hack journalist and shorthand reporter. Dickens is having fun playing a clown's verbal playfulness and telegraphic style against the overblown rhetoric of such windbags as Pott, the ludicrous representative of stereotyped journalistic verbosity. As a creative artist, he is free now to experiment with narrative discourse and even to turn stenography into a modern, almost Joycean form of poetic diction.

Jingle is also—in which he again reminds us of his creator—a professional actor who "performs" language, that is uses language as a performative, knows "how to do things with words." Each of his verbal utterances is literally a "speech-act", a pure act of creation of the "Let there be light, and there was light" type; but, paradoxically, it is also an act that cannot survive itself. His dramatic mode of expression creates a sense of immediacy, a sense of intense, yet short-lived illusion. His stories are not intended to be recorded or repeated like the "officially" interpolated ones. They are, so to speak, "disposable stories," requiring only instantaneous suspension of disbelief: "I should like to see his poem," says Snodgrass (83), but he never asks Jingle to show it to him, never tries to verify its existence. "I should like to have seen that dog," says Winkle wistfully, wisely using the modality of regret. Jingle is a cheap-jack whose cheap merchandise can be produced on request: "Will you allow me to make a note of it?" Pickwick asks after hearing the story of the dog. "Certainly, sir, certainly—hundred more anecdotes of the same animal," Jingle replies. "Will you allow me to make a note of that little romance down, sir?" asks Snodgrass, deeply affected by the story of Donna Christina. "Certainly, sir, certainly,—fifty more if you like to hear 'em" (81).

We are told that Snodgrass and his friends fill their notebooks "with selections from his adventures" (82), but few notes ever come to life again under the editorial hand of Boz. Jingle's adventures have no endurance. They have no future, and they have indeed no past to speak of. All are undated: they occurred "once," "one day," even "other day" (*sic*, 79), which sounds like "sometime, never," as in Lewis Carroll's "jam every other day". Such timelessness entails verblessness: Jingle clearly prefers nouns or verbal nouns to verbs ("operation," "consent," 81), or adverbial particles ("head off," 79), or onomatopeias ("crash," "knock," 79). This man from "No Hall, Nowhere" (167) is also a man from "Nowhen." Significantly, toward the end, when he is in the Fleet and "delivers" a "singular summary of his prospects in life" (690)—the prospect in fact being death—he never uses the future, but a sort of a-temporal present, what Aragon would call "an absent," "a language of what is not":

> Nothing soon—lie in bed—starve—die—Inquest—little bone-house—poor prisoner—common necessaries—hush it up—gentlemen of the jury—warden's tradesmen—keep it snug—natural death—coroner's order—workhouse funeral—serve him right—all over—drop the curtain.   (116; my translation)

For Jingle the world is a stage and he a mere strutter.

III: BITS AND PIECES:
FRAGMENTATION AS A THEME

Jingle's fragmented diction is well suited to his subject, which itself is no other than fragmentation. His stories are all stories of death, the most extreme form of disintegration: the death of Donna Christina, the death of Don Bolaro, the death of the mother of five, his own death, the death of King Charles I, the near death of the dog, the death of civilization. Very appropriately, his first journey with the Pickwickians brings him to Rochester, which offers him a splendid opportunity of celebrating the magnificence of ruins with his deconstructed sentences: "Ah! fine place . . . glorious pile—frowning walls—tottering arches—dark nooks—crumbling staircases—Old cathedral too—earthly smell— . . . old fellows, with great red faces, and broken noses . . ." (82). There is no discrepancy between style and subject matter. Here again, we are reminded of Barthes writing about Queneau's *Zazie dans le Métro*: "the noble fabric of the written style still holds together, but worm-eaten and flaking off . . . ; this deconstruction, kept well under control, is like the beauty of ruins" (125; my translation).

The "attraction of repulsion" for the beauty of ruins, dismemberment, decapitation, amputation, and death is not only Jingle's but Dickens' favorite subject. Throughout his work, language, people and objects are mutilated or threatened with mutilation. Jingle, Sam, and Sarah Gamp are undoubtedly his most famous specialists of linguistic amputations and distortions, though by no means the only droppers of h's or word-twisters. For words are never safe in Dickens' world; they rather seem, like Miss Tox's plants, under the constant threat of being clipped, "reduced to their simplest expression." And so are the name-bearers: poor Tupman finds himself shortened (or castrated?) into "Tuppy" by his rival in love, Pickwick is split asunder into "Pig Vig" by Count Smorltork (or "Smalltalk"?) and the "Merrikins" can hardly claim full citizenship to America. Which, of course, is nothing to the many instances of physical or bodily fragmentation that we are told about. The medical students in *Pickwick* do not seem to have any other function than to talk idly of operations, amputations, and dissection. Here are a few examples of their "table talks": "Nothing like dissecting, to give one an appetite," declares Bob Saywer at breakfast. "I've put my name down for an arm, at our place," says Benjamin Allen, ". . . We're clubbing for a subject, and the list is nearly full, only we can't get hold of any fellow that wants a head. I wish you'd take it." "No," replies Bob, "can't afford expensive luxuries" (494). "Took a boy's leg out of the socket last week," explains Hopkins, another sawbones, ". . . exactly two minutes after it was all over, boy said he wouldn't lie there to be made game of, or he'd tell his mother if they didn't begin" (526).

Tearing apart, smashing to smithereens, disintegrating, maiming, dissecting is such commonplace practice in Dickens that the world of his novels is full of fragments: tumbledown houses, "remnants of loaves and pieces of cheese, . . . and scrags of meat, . . . and mutilated crockery, and bellows without nozzles, and toasting-forks without prongs" (this is in the Fleet, 683), "the . . . fragment of an inscription . . . to be deciphered" (Pickwick's famous discovery, 217), and, of course, a whole crowd of one-eyed, one-handed, one-legged characters, fragmented people oddly reconstructed: the missing eye has been replaced by a glass eye, the missing hand has been replaced by a hook, the missing leg has been replaced by a peg.

The fascination wooden legs in particular hold for Dickens was long ago pointed out by John Carey: "Dickens's most popular lifeless bit," he writes, "is the wooden leg, about which he has a positive obsession" (91). A closer look at the "lifeless bit" might help us to a closer understanding of the "obsession."

First, it should be observed that wooden legs in Dickens' novels are a male prerogative. This is quite justifiable on historical grounds. Men were more exposed than women to mutilation, especially in wartime. During the Napoleonic wars, hundreds of men returned from the battlefield maimed for life and, as a child, Dickens must have come across many ex-soldiers with artificial legs limping along the streets, whereas a woman with a wooden leg must have been a rarity. But I am personally convinced that if no Miss Killmansegg ever entered his fictitious world it is for a reason that has little to do with verisimilitude: the reason is simply that the male prerogative is also, in a very strict sense, a male appendage.

Dickens selects his victims carefully: either old bachelors, or henpecked or otherwise incompetent husbands. In *Barnaby Rudge*, when there are "gusts of bad weather" in the Tappertit household and Sam has "correct[ed] his lady with a brush, or boot, or shoe," his wife retaliates by "taking off his legs," leaving her poor "Samson" totally helpless (630-31). The wooden leg of Mrs. Gamp's late husband is eloquently reported to have been "quite as weak as flesh, if not weaker" (*Martin Chuzzlewit* 625). More striking still: whenever there is a wedding, phallic pegs are sure to be in attendance, though whether it be for better or for worse is a debatable matter. During the ceremony of Florence Dombey's wedding, "A man with a wooden leg chewing a faint apple and carrying a blue bag in his hand, looks in to see what is going on; but finding it nothing entertaining, stumps off again, and pegs his way among the echoes out of doors" as if he felt unequal to the performance (807). Most entertaining, on the contrary, seems the spectacle in *Our Mutual Friend* of Bella and John walking arm in arm toward Greenwich Church where they are about to be married: the onlooker, a gruff and glum old pensioner, is admittedly better equipped than the *Dombey* helpless voyeur, having no fewer than *two* wooden legs. At the sight of the happy pair, the old man is "stricken by so sudden an interest that he perk[s] his neck . . . as if he were trying to stand on tiptoe with his two wooden legs," which soon has a remarkably rejuvenating effect on his "lifeless bit":

> Some resemblance of old Valentines, wherein a cherub . . . had been seen conducting lovers to the altar, might have been fancied to inflame the ardour of his timber toes . . . For years the wings of his mind had gone to look after the legs of his body; but Bella had brought them back for him . . . and they were spread again.
>
> He was a slow sailer on a wind of happiness, but he took a cross cut for the rendezvous, and pegged away as if he were scoring furiously at cribbage. When the shadow of the church-porch swallowed them up, victorious Gruff and Glum likewise presented himself to be swallowed up.   (664-65)

This sounds very much like active voyeurism!

Wooden legs in Dickens may be useless instruments, but they are never "unnecessary details." And when, with these texts in mind, we return to earlier and less explicit ones, we can detect associations that we had not noticed before. Let us consider for instance the scene in *Pickwick* that takes place at the White Hart in the early morning following Rachael's elopement with her seducer. Jingle is in a hurry to go out and get a marriage licence and Sam Weller on being told that "number twenty-two" "wants his boots directly" reacts as follows:

> Look at these here boots—eleven pair o' boots; and one shoe as b'longs to number six, with the wooden leg. The eleven boots is to be called at half-past eight and the shoe at nine. Who's number twenty-two, that's to put all the others out? No, no; reg'lar rotation, as Jack Ketch said, when he tied the men up. Sorry to keep you a waitin', sir, but I'll attend to you directly.   (198)

This outburst, of course, is fundamentally comic and gratuitous. Yet, at some unconscious level of meaning, it threatens and disturbs and forebodes no good. And indeed, a moment later, the arrival of Pickwick and Wardle brings the love affair to an end. The incongruous wooden leg was not of very good omen. Nor was the further reference to Jack Ketch!

At this stage, admittedly, we should not make too much of a young author's whimsical ramblings. But, over the years, as less and less was left to chance, the network of associations was to gain in complexity and structural significance. And by the time he came to write *Our Mutual Friend*, Dickens had learned to build his obsessions into coherent meaning, even turning fragmentation into a unifying theme. The Gruff and Glum scene comes at the happy end of a novel whose hero has long been self-divided, cut off from his past and his origins, fragmented into various personalities under various pseudonyms, and is at long last recovering his integrity and his true identity. The novel was, even more generally, about fragmentation: the fragmentation of society into classes, the fragmentation of decayed objects into dust, the whole theme being, so to speak, "embodied" in Silas Wegg, the most memorable character with a wooden leg in Dickens.

Wegg is, metaphorically speaking, both castrated and castrating: his body has lost its integrity: his leg has been amputated, his name is no more than a portmanteau word, the reduction of two words, "wooden" and "leg," which have undergone surgical treatment. He has no family; he is a bachelor of the anal type, thrifty, unwilling to "spend" (Marcus 22). And he does to words and things and people what he has done to himself: his stall is described as "sterile"—"the hardest little stall of all the sterile little stalls in London."

Everything about him is associated with rottenness, decay, and dryness: "the stall, the stock, and the keeper, were all as dry as the Desert" (45). He also decapitates and circumcizes words, dislocates his sentences, twists and sprains the English grammar, intrigues and plots and tells tall stories, and might well be described as "a latter-day Jingle . . . with a wooden leg." He actually describes himself as a "literary man *with* a wooden leg," a definition far more disturbing than mine, for, inevitably, our attention is drawn by the conspicuously italicized *"with"* to the literary man most closely related to him, that is to say his creator (49). This, again, sounds very much like a private joke, even a double-barreled one: at the time when he conceived this grotesque figure of an incompetent reader, Dickens who, short of a wooden leg, had a very bad foot and walked wih a limp, devoted much of his energy to his own public readings. An ageing man, he was, besides, less productive than in former days: his last-born child was already twelve, and three years had elapsed between the completion of his previous novel and the first install- ment of the new one, which, ironically, was to be followed by a mere fragment of a book. So that the portrait of the "literary man *with* a wooden leg" came to be, somehow, his testament on vanity, the vanity of writing and of plotting, and perhaps even of being. "I have a prospect of getting on in life and elevating myself by my own independent exertions," Wegg ex- plains to Venus, while inquiring after his leg, "and I shouldn't like—I tell you openly I should *not* like—under such circmstances, to be what I may call dispersed, a part of me here, and a part of me there, but should wish to collect myself like a genteel person" (82). Dickens had spent a lifetime trying to collect himself into a genteel person and I have a feeling that he now realized in a more tragic way than in the days of *Pickwick* that he would never achieve this integrity, that ultimate fragmentation was to be the inevitable outcome of all his undertakings whether personal or professional. But the change between the two books is in the main a mere matter of degree. Wegg, when he has to face his own failure as a fiction-maker, expresses the same sense of loss as the narrator of *Pickwick* had done thirty years before, though in a more pathetic tone: "There was, further, Miss Elizabeth, Master George, Aunt Jane, and Uncle Parker. Ah! When a man thinks of the loss of such patronage as that . . ." (790). Less gushingly sentimental, the earlier narrator was more of a fatalist: "It is the fate of most men who mingle with the world, and attain even the prime of life, to make many real friends, and lose them in the course of nature. It is the fate of all authors or chroniclers to create imaginary friends, and lose them in the course of art," he wrote in his closing chapter (896). Still, even in the "prime of life," Dickens had this awareness, that losing is the common lot and that "all is vanity and striving after wind."

NOTES

This article is based on a paper read by the author at the annual conference of the University of California Dickens Project in Santa Cruz, 4 to 10 August 1991.

1. See Philip Collins, ed. *Dickens: The Critical Heritage* (London: Routledge, 1971) 30–41, and Robert L. Patten's introduction to the Penguin edition of *Pickwick* 19–20.
2. Discussed by Patten in his introduction, 21–31.
3. Introd. to the Oxford edition of *Pickwick* xxvii.

WORKS CITED

Aragon, Louis. *Je n'ai jamais appris à écrire ou les incipit.* Geneva: Skira, 1969.

Barthes, Roland. *Essais critiques.* Paris: Le Seuil, 1964.

Carey, John. *The Violent Effigy.* London: Faber, 1973.

Chesterton, G. K. *Appreciations and Criticisms of the Works of Charles Dickens.* London: Dent, 1911.

Collins, Philip, ed. *Dickens: The Critical Heritage.* London: Routledge, 1971.

Dickens, Charles. *Barnaby Rudge.* London: Oxford UP, 1961.

———. *Dombey and Son.* London: Oxford UP, 1960.

———. *Martin Chuzzlewit.* London: Oxford UP, 1959.

———. *Our Mutual Friend.* London: Oxford UP, 1963.

———. *The Pickwick Papers.* Ed. and with an introd. by Robert L. Patten. Harmondsworth: Penguin, 1986.

———. *The Pickwick Papers.* Ed. James Kinsley. Oxford: Clarendon, 1986.

Forster, John. *The Life of Charles Dickens.* London: Dent, 1966.

Hardy, Barbara. "Dickens's Storytellers." *Dickensian May 1973.*

Marcus. Steven. *The Other Victorians.* London: Corgi, 1971.

Reinhold, Heinz. " 'The Stroller's tale' in *Pickwick*." *Dickensian* Sept. 1968.

Dickens' Metafiction: Readers and Writers in *Oliver Twist, David Copperfield*, and *Our Mutual Friend*

Kenneth M. Sroka

Dickens' fifteen novels are filled with readers and writers, characters for whom specific moments of reading and writing, either as isolated or repeated acts, become important clues to character, signals of development, or means of self-discovery and renewal. For example, in *Great Expectations* (1860–61) Pip's adult ability to name himself confidently in the novel's first sentence is immediately linked to his earlier childhood reading of his parents' tombstones to conjure up an image of his family's physical appearance. On the other hand, many characters who are nonwriters, nonreaders, or what we might call "misreaders" (readers who view reading merely functionally or undervalue it) are depicted as shallow, selfish, and small-minded. The miserly Smallweeds in *Bleak House* (1852–53), for instance, pride themselves on being nonreaders: "We have never been readers in our family. It don't pay. Stuff. Idleness, Folly. No, no!" (ch. 21). As the interpretive tools of human experience, reading and writing unlock the mystery of the self and keep alive the imaginative sense of human wonder in a world that had become increasingly demythologized, more "functional," literal, and mechanistic, and therefore hollow and meaningless. The many instances of "nonfunctional" reading and writing in Dickens' novels are valuable exercises of "Fancy" which remythologize the world and give their fictional readers and writers access to "the secret opening through which the inexhaustible energies of the cosmos pour into human cultural manifestation" (Campbell 3).

Generally, "Fancy" for Dickens meant every experience which nurtured the imagination. He included in it "anything from colourful jollity and fun, to that imaginative sustenance which should nourish in both children and adults a wisdom of the heart, as well as provide an escape from present sorrow.'' The readers and writers in Dickens' novels specifically place reading and writing within that definition and subtly illustrate how they contribute to that wisdom of the heart. The implicit manner in which the nonfunctional literacy motif operates is consistent with Dickens' view of the implicit workings of Fancy: ''Dickens saw in Fancy a moral as well as a recreative function: not, however, a designedly didactic one. . . . Fancy, for Dickens, operates not through . . . clumsy moralising . . . but in a way more akin to Wordsworth's memories of those moments which proved the 'hiding places of man's power,' 'the anchor of my purest thoughts . . . And soul of all my moral being' '' (Collins 191–92).[1] Though Dickens rarely engaged in theoretical discussions of his works, his fictional readers and writers within the novels become unconscious theorists who offer us valuable insights into the silent workings of Fancy catalyzed by books.

Dickens' numerous fictional readers and writers dramatize the implicit aesthetic function of reading and writing. They define and defend the role of author and reader as guardians and transmitters of private and public myth in a culture which often viewed fiction as self-indulgent idleness and fiction writers as mere entertainers. In other words, Dickens' novels can be viewed as examples of Victorian metafiction, fiction whose matter is the nature of fiction, the phenomenon of reading and writing, and the interrelationship of writer, text, and reader. Although literacy as metafiction is an important motif in many of Dickens' novels, three major works spanning his career amply illustrate its importance and suggest Dickens' sense of the progressive devaluation of Fancy in his age—*Oliver Twist* (1837–39), *David Copperfield* (1849–50), and *Our Mutual Friend* (1864–65). The reading scenes in *Oliver Twist* suggest the wonder and the unconscious workings of childhood Fancy. Reading and writing in *David Copperfield* extend their influence to the self-conscious but positive stages of early adulthood. In *Our Mutual Friend* the harshness of a ''literary dark age'' dominates the novel's readers, reduces the potency of nonfunctional literacy, and threatens to stifle Fancy.

Oliver Twist (1837–39) contains several reading scenes which regularly associate reading books with visions or dreams—mostly anxiety dreams, but wish-fulfillment dreams and even daydreams as well. Most of these reading scenes elicit powerful memories of the past, or feelings of fear and guilt in the character doing the reading. They often explicitly link the reading moment with a dreamy state of semiconsciousness which blurs the experience and blends imaginative vision with waking reality (Miller, *Charles Dickens*

73–76).[2] In other words, the reading scenes in *Oliver Twist* catalyze in the fictional reader the common cathartic effects significant reading experience might have on us when we read. Although the reading scenes in this early Dickens novel are not always skillfully rendered, their frequency demands our attention. The most important reading scenes in *Oliver Twist* involve Oliver, Nancy, and Mr. Brownlow.

When Oliver Twist reads, the scenes take on extraordinary magic qualities associated with childhood innocence and powerful imagination. Oliver mysteriously knows how to read despite his lack of education as a workhouse orphan. He is a "miracle child," immune to evil, even while in the underworld power of the satanic Fagin, who gives him books to read on the lives and crimes of famous criminals. The intensity of the reading terrifies Oliver: "The terrible descriptions were so real and vivid, that the sallow pages seemed to turn red with gore; and the words upon them, to be sounded in his ears, as if they were whispered, in hollow murmurs, by the spirits of the dead. In a paroxysm of fear, the boy closed the book, and thrust it from him." Despite Oliver's innocence and immunity to evil, he comes face to face with it intensely: "he stood alone in the midst of wickedness and guilt" (ch. 20). While Oliver's magic literacy reflects the distance between him and evil, it also reveals the power of books as windows onto the knowledge of good and evil, vicarious dream experiences that impress the reader imaginatively, but leave him unharmed. Ironically, immediately after Oliver closes the book and completes a prayer for deliverance, Nancy arrives to deliver him to Sikes, who will use Oliver in the attempted burglary of the Maylies. Oliver's vicarious experience of crime in books is to be transformed into and contrasted to harmful reality when he is forced to participate in a crime and is left wounded and abandoned by Sikes.

After the attempted burglary, when Oliver is taken in by the Maylies, his recuperation from his gunshot wound is generally presented as an idyllic time, filled with dreamy intimations of some once and future paradise: "The memories which peaceful country scenes call up, are not of this world . . . there lingers . . . a vague and half-formed consciousness of having held such feelings long before. . . ." These dreamy, ideal, healing moments are described in terms of positive, even religious reading experiences. A white-headed gentleman "taught him to read better, and to write." He would walk with Mrs. Maylie and Rose and listen to them "talk of books; or perhaps sit near them . . . and listen whilst the young lady read: which he could have done, until it grew too dark to see the letters." At night Oliver "read a chapter or two from the Bible, which he had been studying all the week, and in the performance of which duty he felt more proud and pleased, than if he had been the clergyman himself'' (ch. 32). Such wish-fulfillment reading moments contrast greatly with the earlier reading scene in Fagin's den, but they are rare in *Oliver Twist* and short-lived.

Two chapters later (ch. 34), while he is still at the Maylies', Oliver falls asleep one evening at "twilight" (appropriately), while he is "intent upon his books . . . poring over them for some time." The narrator describes Oliver's state as one in which "reality and imagination become so strangely blended that it is afterwards almost matter of impossibility to separate the two." Oliver's "books were lying on the table before him . . . And yet he was asleep." The former idyllic moments linked with the earlier reading during Oliver's recovery change again. In this half-sleep, Oliver sees Fagin and then wakes to find Fagin gazing at him through the window. Oliver leaps "from the window into the garden" and calls for help. The scene echoes and contrasts Adam's two dreams in book 8 of *Paradise Lost* (292–11, 460–80). Oliver dreams and wakes to find it true, but unlike Adam's positive dreams (one of earthly inheritance and the other of his helpmate, Eve), Oliver's dream is, once again, an anxiety dream of a threat to his inheritance and to his life, a dream linked both to his intense reading (one type of "window") and to the devilish reality of Fagin in the "garden" outside the literal window.[3] Though Oliver has indeed seen Fagin and Monks at the window, the scene has an ambiguity about it, even after Oliver awakes. The search party can find no traces of intruders: " 'It must have been a dream, Oliver,' said Harry Maylie" (ch. 35). The ambiguity of the scene is central and appropriate because it echoes what the reader of *Oliver Twist* experiences generally as well: the novel is a hybrid creation with roots in both the dark, surreal world of private dreams and the harsh, public realities of the Victorian underworld. Though the dream rhythm of Oliver's reading scenes is punctuated with wish-fulfillment, fear and anxiety dominate.

Less immune to the consequences of evil, Nancy relates a reading experience she has had to Mr. Brownlow when they meet on London Bridge: "Horrible thoughts of death, and shrouds with blood upon them, and a fear that has made me burn as if I was on fire, have been upon me all day. I was reading a book to-night, to wile the time away, and the same things came into the print." Brownlow minimizes her fear by attributing it to "Imagination," but Nancy believes her fanciful fears to be more serious than real ones and connects them, somewhat shakily, with her reading: "I'll swear I saw 'coffin' written in every page of the book in large black letters,—aye, and they carried [an unreal] one close to me, in the streets to-night." Dickens links to her reading Nancy's guilt over her betrayal of Sikes and her fear of his retaliation (ch. 46).

Two more important reading scenes in *Oliver Twist* illuminate Mr. Brownlow's character and his relationship with Oliver. Brownlow's first accidental encounter with Oliver and our first introduction to him as a character occur at a book-stall where Brownlow's deep involvement in the book he is reading makes him ignorant of the fact that the Artful Dodger and Charlie Bates have picked his pocket. From the beginning of the scene until its end in the next chapter when he takes Oliver into his care, Brownlow has a book in his hand. Moreover, Dickens takes unusual pains to tell us about Brownlow's reading at the book-stall, a detail which ordinarily might be disposed of more quickly:

> He had taken up a book from the stall, and there he stood, reading away, as hard as if he were in his elbow-chair, in his own study. It is very possible that he fancied himself there, indeed; for it was plain, from his abstraction, that he saw not the book-stall, nor the street, nor the boys, nor, in short, anything but the book itself: which he was reading straight through: turning over the leaf when he got to the bottom of a page, beginning at the top line of the next one and going regularly on, with the greatest interest and eagerness. (ch. 10)

Brownlow appears to be a "misreader" whose reading in this case is primarily escapist since it causes him to see nothing of the reality around him. In fact such an introduction to Mr. Brownlow is entirely appropriate since his early role in the novel is rather passive. He is a well-to-do old bachelor who later will characterize himself as a "solitary, lonely man" since the death, years ago, of his fiancée (ch. 49). Brownlow lives a rather neutral, escapist existence, but Oliver's sudden entrance into his life will transform him into a vigorous man of action who rescues Oliver, pursues the villains, and reveals Oliver's past and thus his identity to him. The changes Oliver effects in Brownlow's life begin immediately during this extended reading scene. Oliver's parents, Edwin Leeford and Agnes Fleming, were Brownlow's close friends, and his aunt (Leeford's sister) was Brownlow's fiancée. Brownlow vaguely and unconsciously sees in Oliver's features a resemblance that summons up vivid memories. Brownlow moves away from his initial role as "misreader" when Dickens once again links a powerful emotional moment with reading.

"Book in hand," Brownlow joins the mob pursuing Oliver after mistaking him for the pickpocket. When Oliver is caught, locked up, and awaiting his appearance before the local magistrate Mr. Fang, Brownlow "turned with a

sigh to the book, which had been the innocent cause of all this disturbance''
(ch. 11). Brownlow's earlier, absent-minded concentration at the book-stall
now takes a different shape: noticing something familiar in Oliver's face, he
"called up before his mind's eye a vast amphitheatre of faces over which a
dusky curtain had hung for many years. 'No,' said the old gentleman, shaking
his head; 'it must be imagination.' '' As with Nancy later in the scene on
London Bridge, Brownlow overhastily dismisses the valuable intuitions he
has, but their power over him reasserts itself and stirs a mixed sense of both
loss and hope within him:

> He wandered over them again. He had called them into view, and it was not
> easy to replace the shroud that had so long concealed them. There were the
> faces of friends, and foes, and of many that had been almost strangers peering
> intrusively from the crowd, there were the faces of young and blooming girls
> that were now old women; there were faces that the grave had changed and
> closed upon, but which the mind, superior to its power, still dressed in their
> old freshness and beauty, calling back the lustre of the eyes, the brightness of
> the smile, the beaming of the soul through its mask of clay, and whispering of
> beauty beyond the tomb, changed but to be heightened, and taken from earth
> only to be set up as a light, to shed a soft and gentle glow upon the path to
> heaven.

Brownlow fails to match Oliver's features with the faces of his reverie, so he
"buried them again in the pages of the musty book." Later in the scene Mr.
Fang asks Brownlow accusingly: "The prosecutor was reading, was he? . . .
Oh, that book, eh? . . . Is it paid for? . . . I consider, sir, that you have
obtained possession of that book, under very suspicious and disreputable
circumstances; and you may think yourself very fortunate that the owner of
the property declines to prosecute. Let this be a lesson to you, my man, or
the law will overtake you yet.''

Brownlow's "guilt" is more subliminal than that suggested by Mr. Fang's
charge. It has to do more with regret over his own lost past summoned up by
Oliver's face in the amphitheater of faces Brownlow sees in his vivid recollection. When Brownlow leaves Fang's office, he takes the unconscious Oliver
from the street and brings him home. Brownlow is a more involved person
than he was at the beginning of the scene, and he still has the book in hand:
"Dear, dear! I have this unhappy book still!" Similar to the rendering of
Nancy's reading scene discussed above, the association of books and their
effects is accomplished rather loosely, by physical juxtaposition, but it is
nonetheless evident despite their relatively weak connection. Dickens sets

Brownlow's intense recollection in a reading scene, and thus implicitly drama-
tizes another elementary power of books, namely to fix and enable us to see
the constant truths of our past beyond the accidents of mutability.

The second reading scene involving Mrs. Brownlow and Oliver occurs in
Brownlow's study, which, like the room at the Maylies', has a "window"
overlooking "gardens." Oliver finds himself in "a little back room, quite
full of books, with a window, looking into some pleasant little gardens. There
was a table drawn up before the window, at which Mr. Brownlow was seated
reading." When Oliver enters, Brownlow "pushed the book away from him[-
self], and told him to come near the table, and sit down." With Oliver and
Brownlow facing the window, surrounded by books, what follows is a simple
and humorous literary critical discussion about the relative desirability of
reading, writing, and selling books, with Oliver opting for reading or selling
books rather than writing them (ch. 14). This is the single humorous reading
scene in the novel. Dickens jokes with the reader through his characters'
suggesting that authorship is the least desirable of experiences with books.
He may be alluding to the financial problems he was experiencing at the time
due to his overcommitments to publishers and his relatively small financial
returns on his writings.

At other points in the discussion, Oliver marvels at "where the people
could be found to read such a great number of books as seemed to be written
to make the world wiser." The narrator responds, "Which is still a marvel
to more experienced people than Oliver Twist, every day of their lives." The
comment may be implying that there aren't in fact many serious readers
though there are a lot of books, or it may be cautioning that books do not
necessarily make the world wiser nor diminish its evil. Ironically, shortly
after this discussion, Oliver is recaptured by Sikes and Nancy (ch. 15) while
he is returning some books for Mr. Brownlow. Oliver's errand in the dangerous streets of London so soon after escaping Fagin and serious illness is a
rather careless mistake on Brownlow's part, especially since he sends him
merely to prove to Mr. Grimwig that Oliver is trustworthy. At this point,
Brownlow's books have not made him wiser nor more effective than Oliver's
enemies, as he and Grimwig sit passively staring at a watch while Oliver is
hauled off again to Fagin's den.

The reading scenes in *Oliver Twist* function much like a child's reading of
fairy tales. For the most part they depict innocent readers gazing safely into
a looking glass and seeing in various degrees the reality of evil in the world.
At the end of the novel, Oliver, like the child reader, remains innocent and
safe, but more aware of a darker truth beyond his immediate experience.

Victorian readers of *Oliver Twist* likewise looked with relative innocence at an evil they had been less conscious of previously. As Sir Francis Burdett, an experienced M. P., wrote: "Whether anything like it exists or no I mean to make enquiry for it is quite dreadful, and, to Society in this country, most disgraceful" (Fielding 40).

The many reading scenes in *Oliver Twist* are evidence of an important motif in Dickens' novels which had not quite worked itself out as yet in his art. In a later novel such as *David Copperfield* (1849–50), however, literacy becomes a richer, more complex key to experience and self-knowledge, and Dickens' realization of the motif is much more artful and polished. In *David Copperfield* writing combines with reading to explore the powerful and beneficial influence books have upon the reader's and the writer's Fancy.

Late in *David Copperfield* when David has become a successful author, Aunt Betsey Trotwood says to him: "I never thought, when I used to read books, what work it was to write them." David modestly answers, "It's work enough to read them, sometimes" (ch. 62). The exchange echoes the earlier humorous discussion between Oliver and Brownlow. Oliver's preference for reading books is consistent both with his more passive nature and with the predominance of reading scenes in *Oliver Twist*. David, however, is primarily an author, so writing has equal importance with reading in *David Copperfield*. Literacy in *David Copperfield* deals with fear, healing, and the resurrection of the past as it did in *Oliver Twist*, but these effects of reading are extended to the act of writing as well. The unpolished motif in *Oliver Twist* has become richer and more artistically realized in *David Copperfield*.[4]

David Copperfield consciously writes his past, a memory book ("this narrative is my written memory" [ch. 48]), so that "these pages" might show whether he is the hero of his own life, as the famous first sentence says. So the real action of *David Copperfield* is David's writing. Moreover, it is a private experience, a solitary burden to be stuck with oneself and to solve the mystery of that self: "this manuscript is intended for no eyes but mine" (ch. 42). To read *David Copperfield* is to eavesdrop, to look over David's shoulder as he writes and to discover with him through his writing who he is. It is a more intimate relationship than even that which Dora has with him when she enthusiastically sits at his side and hands him his pens. David's writing and our reading give meaning and substance to what he calls "the ignorant present" (ch. 33).

Although there are several "authors" in *David Copperfield*, David is the central writer and the creator of the others in his pages. His training for authorship is based in his love for words, for David has been a voracious reader all his life, from the earliest crocodile book read with Peggotty and remembered as a precious relic of his youth to the collection of novels left him by his father: "This was my only and my constant comfort. When I think of it, the picture always rises in my mind, of a summer evening, the boys at play in the churchyard, and I sitting in my bed, reading as if for life" (ch. 4). As a child at church, David puts life into the memorial verses he reads on the wall tablets:

> I look up at the monumental tablets on the wall, and try to think of Mr. Bodgers late of this parish, and what the feelings of Mrs. Bodgers must have been, when afflictions sore, long time Mr. Bodgers bore, and physicians were in vain. I wonder whether they called in Mr. Chillip, and he was in vain; and if so, how he likes to be reminded of it once a week. (ch. 2)

For David, books themselves, like real experiences, make up valuable memories. At Salem House, he retells to Steerforth the plots of the novels he has read, but worries that he has disrupted their fixed, written order in his oral rendition:

> What ravages I committed on my favorite authors in the course of my interpretation of them, I am not in a condition to say, and should be very unwilling to know; but I had a profound faith in them, and I had, to the best of my belief, a simple earnest manner of narrating what I did narrate; and these qualities went a long way. (ch. 7)

Although telling stories at Salem House risks distorting them, it also forces David to recreate them in his own words and thus constitutes the beginning of his own authorship. The greater danger of relying on unwritten memory alone is the possibility of forgetting entirely. One of David's great fears at the warehouse of Murdstone and Grinby is that his "old readings . . . were fast perishing out of my remembrance" (ch. 11). An earlier clue to David's sense of the tendency of oral expression to slip away comes when he recites his lessons under the glaring eyes of the Murdstones: ". . . I begin to feel the words I have been at infinite pains to get into my head, all sliding away, and going I don't know where. I wonder where they *do* go, by-the-by?" (ch. 4).

When David serves his legal apprenticeship with Spenlow and Jorkins, his reading shifts to the "immense manuscript Books of Evidence taken on affidavit, strongly bound, and tied together in massive sets, a set to each cause, as if every cause were a history in ten or twenty volumes" (ch. 23). In on instance, David's work in court is extended because "the evidence was just twice the length of Robinson Crusoe'' (ch. 26). David's legal apprenticeship and his work as a parliamentary reporter convince him of the abuse of words inherent in political writing:

> Night after night, I record predictions that never come to pass, professions that are never fulfilled, explanations that are only meant to mystify. I wallow in words. Britannia, that unfortunate female, is always before me, like a trussed fowl: skewered through and through with office-pens. . . . (ch. 43)[5]

By comparison, David renders his own cause and history in a single, rich, narrative volume. Story refines the raw data of experience and organizes it more concisely than the encyclopedic tomes of the law, which often raise more problems than they solve.

David finds more truth in the words of fiction and so returns to his early love by becoming a novelist himself and lets his story-telling skill spill over into the record of his own life. Although writing can't literally bring back the past, writing his own story peoples David's past by substituting ink and paper existences for what were David's flesh and blood realities. If words cannot be made flesh, we have the consolation that flesh may be made into words. As a boy David was terrified by the biblical story of Lazarus rising from the dead; as an author, David resurrects the specters of his own past and those who shared his experience. Dickens, too, speaks of his books as people, as his children. In the ''Preface'' to *David Copperfield* he writes:

> Of all my books I like this the best. It will be easily believed that I am a fond parent to every child of my fancy, and that no one can ever love that family as dearly as I love them. But like many fond parents, I have in my heart of hearts a favorite child. And his name is DAVID COPPERFIELD.

Just as Dickens compares his books to children, Mr. Micawber compares parenthood to authorship when, speaking of his children, he refers to himself as ''The Author of their being'' (ch. 52). Books—like people—are creations whose mysteries we seldom exhaust. David's book, whose title, for most people, is his name, comes alive as an ink-and-paper clone of himself, an amiable and revealing body-snatcher, a living memory to give substance to David's ignorant present. In likening books to people, *David Copperfield* underscores the value of authorship and implicitly argues for the power of words and the psychic benefits of reading and writing.

In the famous last paragraph of *David Copperfield*, David reiterates his sense of the resemblance of life and the real people of our memories to the characters of a fiction. He says, apostrophizing Agnes, ''. . . so may I, when realities are melting from me like the shadows which I now dismiss, still find thee near me . . .' '' (ch. 64). David's reality, like all reality, melts into the shadows of the past. The shadows of fiction, too, resurrect and reincarnate the past and pass it on to the reader in the present. David's act of writing vividly fixes in words the past that is himself and saves it from slipping into the oblivion of unconscious memory.

For the most part, David's written memories are intense recreations of the past: "I see and hear, rather than remember, as I write about it" (ch. 45).[6] Often David explicitly links his act of remembering past experience with his present act of writing. For example, he describes a surprise meeting with Dora early in their relationship: "I had not been walking long, when I turned a corner, and met her. I tingle again from head to foot as my recollection turns that corner, and my pen shakes in my hand" (ch. 26). David's consciousness of his shaking hand calls attention to the vividness of the memory, but it also reminds us of his real present action, namely writing, not meeting Dora. At times, present writing makes the memory of an experience more real than the experience itself because some other emotion interfered with the initial event. When David is courting Dora, his emotions are too focussed on her to notice the affection he feels for Traddles. However, writing about Traddles redresses the balance somewhat by acknowledging what went unnoticed earlier: "His honest face, as he looked at me with a seriocomic shake of his head, impresses me more in the remembrance than it did in the reality, for I was by this time in a state of such excessive trepidation and wandering of mind, as to be quite unable to fix my attention on anything" (ch. 41). In this case David adjusts what had been for him an instance of his ignorant present.

The vitality of David's writing reveals his courage as his own historian. When he remembers the most painful experiences of his past, he writes on though the writing brings him agony. This is especially true of his recounting Steerforth's seduction of Emily and Steerforth's own death. In a manner typical of the Victorian writer's shying away from sexual matters, David's account of Emily's seduction is secondhand; he's not present at her flight but hears the story from Ham and by way of Emily's letter. The pain of this memory is less because of David's distanced account of it. Although he hesitates to write of it, when he approaches the topic he allows the writing to work out the pain:

A dread falls on me here. A cloud is lowering on the distant town, towards which I retraced my solitary steps. I fear to approach it. I cannot bear to think of what did come, upon that memorable night, of what must come again, if I go on.

It is no worse, because I write of it. It would be no better, if I stopped my most unwilling hand. It is done. Nothing can undo it; nothing can make it otherwise than as it was.   (ch. 31)

This is a curious instance of how a writing convention affects the writer-hero's sense of himself. David's distanced account of sexual indiscretion enables him to resign himself more easily to the pain of its memory. However, the account of Steerforth's death is painted more boldly since, if anything, Victorian writers tended to overstate rather than distance their death scenes. The result is that the more detailed memory of Steerforth's death lingers in David's memory, more painful than any other memory and unreconciled in his mind until the very moment he writes of it:

> I now approach an event in my life, so indelible, so awful, so bound by an infinite variety of ties to all that has preceded it, in these pages, that, from the beginning of my narrative, I have seen it growing larger and larger as I advanced, like a great tower in a plain, and throwing its fore-cast shadow even on the incidents of my childish days.
>
> For years after it occurred, I dreamed of it often. I have started up so vividly impressed by it, that its fury has yet seemed raging in my quiet room, in the still night. I dream of it sometimes, though at lengthened and uncertain intervals, to this hour. . . .
>
> As plainly as I behold what happened, I will try to write it down. I do not recall it, but see it done; for it happens again before me.   (ch. 55)

In these instances, seeing David work at his writing enables us to understand the influence of a common writing convention on his coping with the past. In both cases, however, David remains the courageous self-historian.

David likens his composing process to an elaborate and dangerous sea journey whose outcome, like David's own heroism, is uncertain despite David's being born with a caul, the good-luck charm of sea-voyagers. Dickens himself equated writing *David Copperfield* with crossing the sea: when he had almost completed the novel, he wrote, "I am within three pages of the shore" (Kincaid, 197). David's voyage, like Dickens', is amidst a sea of word memories, a "sea of remembrance" (ch. 53) which is elusive and protean, a verbal ocean which brings death and life alike.

The sea brings death to Steerforth and Ham, as it did earlier to Ham's and Emily's fathers. It also brings nearly as effective a separation as death when Dan Peggotty and Emily emigrate to Australia. David reports their ship's departure as if they had died: "Surrounded by the rosy light, and standing high upon the deck, apart together she clinging to him, and he holding her, they solemnly passed away" (ch. 57). After David's mother dies, he visits Yarmouth. Thinking to himself while he lies in his familiar bed at the boat-house, David shifts the meaning of the word "sea" from a literal to a figurative one: "I lay down in the old little bed in the stern of the boat, and the wind came moaning on across the flat as it had done before. But I could not help fancying, now, that it moaned of those who were gone; and instead of thinking that the sea might rise in the night and float the boat away, I thought of the sea that had risen, since I last heard those sounds, and drowned my happy home" (ch. 10).

The sea is a life source as well, however, as Dan Peggotty's explanation of Barkis's impending death suggests: " 'People can't die along the coast . . . except when the tide's pretty nigh out. They can't be born, unless it's pretty nigh in—not properly born, till flood. . . .' " Similarly, the description of the incongruous legal functions of Doctors Commons links the sea with life's basic business: "It's a place that has an ancient monopoly in suits about people's wills and people's marriages, and disputes among ships and boats" (ch. 30).

The sea is the most appropriate symbol for David's written memory, therefore, because like words and remembrance it conveys the sense of the simultaneous vitality and mortality of human experience. It is significant that Steerforth's servant, whose presence always embarrasses David into a consciousness of his youth and inexperience, is named Littimer, which might mean "seashore," while Mr. Omer, whose name suggests "sea," is a coffin-maker. Experience remains "drowndead" until it is resurrected by David's writing.

The triple paradox of the sea, words, and memory being simultaneously vital and mortal is perhaps best illustrated by David's account of his last view of Steerforth. David remembers seeing Steerforth's drowned body on the shore: "I saw him lying with his head upon his arm, as I had often seen him lie at school" (ch. 55). The words David uses repeat almost verbatim his earlier description of the living Steerforth asleep at home: "He was fast asleep; lying easily, with his head upon his arm, as I had often seen him lie at school" (ch. 29). The repetition of words reveals the awakening power of memory to please us by making the past alive while it frustrates us with the certainty of the past's irrevocability.[7]

While David is the primary author in *David Copperfield*, there are also several "minor authors" who, by contrast, reinforce David's writing achievement. The minor authors—Julia Mills, Mr. Dick, Dr. Strong, and Mr. Micawber—fail largely because, unlike David, they cannot face the past courageously or because they write merely to escape the present. As Mr. Brownlow was a "misreader," the minor writers in *David Copperfield* are its "mis-writers."

Julia Mills, Dora's companion and intercessor with David, mistakes her masochistic nourishment of the memory of an unsuccessful love affair for worldly wisdom:

> "I speak," said Miss Mills, "from experience of the past—the remote irrevocable past". . . . Miss Mills sang—about the slumbering echoes in the caverns of Memory; as if she were a hundred years old. . . . That sagacious Miss Mills . . . that amiable, though quite used up, recluse; that little patriarch of something less than twenty, who had done with the world, and mustn't on any account have the slumbering echoes in the caverns of Memory awakened. . . .
>
> (ch. 33)

Like David, she composes a journal, but reads aloud from it itemizing Dora's daily actions while slipping in parenthetical bits of her own observations: "Are tears the dewdrops of the heart?" David easily sees through Miss Mills's self-indulgence: "I could not help feeling, though she mingled her tears with mine, that she had a dreadful luxury in our afflictions" (ch. 38). As an author, Julia exaggerates the tyranny of the past, and in fixing experience in her book, she unrealistically stops the clocks of her own life (preceding Miss Havisham by ten years).

Mr. Dick, Dr. Strong, and Mr. Micawber are much more interesting as minor authors. Mr. Dick's past is filled with real, unexaggerated suffering: ill-usage by his family causes him to drop his real name, Richard Babley; a sister's bad marriage and a brother's unkindness bring on a fever which leaves Mr. Dick simple-minded. To function in the world, Mr. Dick requires the protection of someone as kind and strong-willed as Aunt Betsey. While his brother called him mad and would have him institutionalized, Aunt Betsey considers him eccentric and insists he has a memory. Mr. Dick's efforts at authorship reveal the pain he feels in remembering his past.

For ten years Mr. Dick has been writing a "Memorial" for an indefinite Lord Chancellor, but the work fails to progress because he cannot keep King Charles I out of it. When King Charles lost his head in 1649, his troubles somehow found their way into Mr. Dick's head and have since been an obstacle to his writing.[8] Aunt Betsey interprets, as a literary critic might: " 'That's his allegorical way of expressing it. He connects his illness with great disturbance and agitation, naturally, and that's the figure, or the simile, or whatever it's called, which he chooses to use.' " Mr. Dick creates a fiction, as authors do, to capture indirectly and come to terms with disturbing human truths. Both David and Mr. Dick take flights of fancy, but Mr. Dick's carries his beyond the page into literal action. To escape the problems of authorship, Mr. Dick flies his kite, which is made up of pieces of his Memorial manuscript: " 'When it flies high it takes the facts a long way,' " he remarks (ch. 14). David sees Mr. Dick's kite-flying as a sign of his blissful ignorance: "it lifted his mind out of its confusion and bore it . . . into the skies" (ch. 15).

For Mr. Dick the truth is too painful. As an author flying his kite, he is happy, but the Memorial remains unfinished. Unlike Mr. Dick, David faces his painful past and completes his own "Memorial." In fairness to Mr. Dick as a writer, it must be said that he succeeds in copying legal documents for Tommy Traddles. Writing has, in that case, a stabilizing influence upon him, though it involves merely copying. In his limited way Mr. Dick's work for Traddles and his influence on another would-be author, Dr. Strong, make him the hero of his own life.

Dr. Strong labors at a dictionary, which, like Mr. Dick's Memorial, won't ever be completed. The head boy at Dr. Strong's school tells David: "it might be done in one thousand six hundred and forty-nine years, counting from the Doctor's last or sixty-second birthday" (ch. 16). By the end of the novel, the dictionary has progressed to "somewhere about the letter D" (ch. 64), whereas David has managed to spell out his whole name narratively. While walking, Dr. Strong reads sections of his dictionary aloud to Mr. Dick, who "believed the Dictionary to be the most delightful book in the world" (ch. 17). Later, Mr. Dick sends Dr. Strong's name up on his kite: " 'The kite has been glad to receive it . . . and the sky has been brighter with it' " (ch. 45).[9] Dr. Strong's dictionary is a questionable enterprise, however, which does not resolve the uneasiness he feels about the difference in age between him and his wife, Annie. David's book, on the other hand, enables him to sort out his relationships with the women in his life, from his infatuation with the elder Miss Larkins to his more serious love for Dora and Agnes.

Micawber's writing is primarily transactional, not poetic, but his flair for the dramatic elevates, though comically, his otherwise purely informational prose. Micawber is an indefatigable letter-writer, an author of a petition for debtors, and a legal clerk to Uriah Heep. All Macawber's writing, especially the letters, deals not with the fixed past but with the transient present, usually in the area of economic difficulties. At times the current financial crisis is solved by a turn of events between the beginning and end of the letter. In other instances a letter which at first brings good news ends with a postscript in which Micawber contemplates suicide, usually by means of his shaving gear. Thus writing for Micawber reflects his mercurial nature and is generally an unstable affair rather than the stabilizer it is for David and, in its small way, even for Mr. Dick. Micawber's letters reflect his inability to seize his present and be responsible for his past. Unrealistically, Micawber uses his pen as a magic wand to exorcise past debts: in Micawber's mind, to write an I.O.U. is to pay the debt.

He redeems himself, however, in his best letter, a lofty indictment of Heep which Micawber performs rather than reads, as if it were a dramatic script, and thus an important instance of nonfunctional writing for him. His exposure of Heep's embezzlement results in the restoration of Aunt Betsey's property and Mr. Wickfield's business. Later, as an emigrant to Australia, he works hard as a farmer, cancels his debts, and makes Mrs. Micawber's wish come true that their past financial crises "be buried in oblivion" (ch. 54). Micawber's new personal stability is marked by his new success as a writer: he becomes a newspaper correspondent in Australia and publishes a volume of his letters. Mr. Micawber's role as a minor author, therefore, develops from failure to relative success. Like David's, Micawber's writing reflects his maturation, his new ability to face the present responsibly.

The minor authors in *David Copperfield* emphasize by contrast the value of David's authorship. David's completed pages define his heroism, the courageous and meticulous sorting out of his own life. As the novel ends, David shows that he has heeded Aunt Betsey's earlier warning: "It's in vain, Trot, to recall the past, unless it works some influence on the present" (ch. 23). He unites his past to his present in linking his writing to his life with Agnes, who comes to represent the real external present which saves David from wallowing in words and introspection.[10] She is the vehicle by which he relates his internal verbal quest to the reality outside himself, the vehicle by which he raises his eyes "upward" (the last word David writes) from the world of words to the world of flesh and blood around him. That linkage puts memory and writing in their proper places and brings David harmony: "She touched the chords of my memory so softly and harmoniously, that not one jarred within me; I could listen to the sorrowful, distant music, and desire to shrink from nothing it awoke" (ch. 60).

David Copperfield is central among Dickens' works not only because it was the eighth of his fifteen novels, but because in it alone does Dickens defend so thoroughly the function and value of writing and reading as the raw materials of memory. Unlike Oliver, David becomes a successful author who finds his identity not in his passive knowledge of his biological parentage, but in actively writing his own story. As we read *David Copperfield* and watch David write, we overshoot the boundaries of nationality and time and can sense within ourselves the shaping of a human past, a new experience and a new memory of something we feel we have always known.[11]

Edgar Johnson calls *Our Mutual Friend* "the darkest and bitterest of Dickens' novels . . . *The Waste Land* of Dickens' work" (1043). Similarly, J. Hillis Miller regards the world of *Our Mutual Friend* as demythologized by an avaricious society that has reduced people to "their worth in pounds, shillings, and pence" and the natural world to "the sheer, massive inertia of matter—heavy, impenetrable, meaningless, alien to man." Fire, wind, dust, mud, and river are no longer "symbols . . . of some reality which transcends them, and for which they stand." They have become, instead, less than what they are because all of life has been redefined as "money, money, money, and what money can make of life" (*Charles Dickens* 172, 175–76, 169). In such a hollow world, Fancy is impoverished much more than in the worlds of *Oliver Twist* and *David Copperfield*. For the readers and writers in those earlier novels, reading and writing serve as interpreters of and mediators between reality and consciousness, but the readers in *Our Mutual Friend* enjoy little or no such direct interpretation or mediation.

In *Our Mutual Friend* readers and reading scenes abound, but literacy is redefined in three ways. In the worst cases, it is reduced, as all experience has been, to a pragmatic, lifeless, money-making activity, illustrated in the characters of Silas Wegg, Charley Hexam, and Bradley Headstone. For these mercenary readers, literacy is merely a part of their inert world. On the other hand, for minor characters such as Young Blight, Miss Peecher, and Jenny Wren, reading and writing are escapes, in varying degrees, from the unpleasantness of the real world instead of keys to unlock its mystery. Finally, in its most positive redefinition, reading is an indirect, secondary instrument for the fictional reader, a talisman of sorts, which affects the character, but depends, in turn, upon that character's direct action to effect a catharsis in some other character. Noddy Boffin's reading and his subsequent role in the transformation of Bella Wilfer illustrate how much more in *Our Mutual Friend* than in *Oliver Twist* and *David Copperfield* reading experience depends on direct human action to actualize its potential.[12]

Silas Wegg is the most mercenary of the readers in *Our Mutual Friend*. He hires himself out to Noddy Boffin as "a literary man" who will read to him from the "Decline-and-Fall-Off-The-Rooshan-Empire" and from the various lives of misers Boffin will later collect. Wegg, of course, is a con-artist who fleeces Boffin by pandering to his desire for reading and impresses him with his repeated misquotations of poetry:

" 'A literary man . . . and all Print is open to him!' That's what I thought to myself, that morning" pursued Mr. Boffin, ". . . and yet all print is shut to me. . . . Now, it's too late for me to begin shoveling and sifting at alphabeds and grammar-books. . . . But I want some reading—some fine bold reading, some splendid book. . . . How can I get that reading, Wegg? By . . . paying a man truly qualified to do it, so much an hour (say twopence) to come and do it."

Wegg raises his price to half a crown per week, doubles it, and suggests that poetry would be still more expensive; " 'For when a person comes to grind off poetry night after night, it is but right he should expect to be paid for its weakening effect on his mind' " (I, ch. 5).

Like Mr. Boffin, who in his innocence feels that reading comes with the territory of his new social position, Charley Hexam hungers for reading in his aspiring to become a Pupil-teacher. When we first meet him delivering a message about John Harmon's "drowning" to Mortimer Lightwood at the Veneerings, Charley's desire for literacy wins our sympathy. He meets Lightwood in the Veneering library with its "bran new books, in bran new bindings liberally gilded." Looking at the painting of Chaucer's pilgrims on the library wall, Charley resembles Chaucer's young Clerk, who would gladly both learn and teach: ". . . he glanced at the backs of the books, with an awakened curiosity that went below the binding. No one who can read, ever looks at a book, even unopened on a shelf, like one who cannot." Although Charley attends school where he is learning to read and write and teaches his sister, Lizzie, her letters, both he and Lizzie feel guilty about their attempts at literacy because they view them as a betrayal of their father, Gaffer Hexam, the waterside character who earns his living by scavenging from the dead bodies he finds in the river:

"I was all in a tremble [Lizzie tells Charley] . . . when you owned to father you could write a little."
"Ah! But I made believe I wrote so badly, as that it was odds if any one could read it. And when I wrote slowest and smeared out with my finger most, father was best pleased, as he stood looking over me."

Like Charley, Lizzie equates ignorance with fidelity and chooses, so long as her father lives, to be content with her "library" in the fire, where she gazes and reads the future for her brother:

"Well! There am I, continuing with father, and holding to father, because father loves me, and I love father. I can't so much as read a book, because, if I had learned, father would have thought I was deserting him, and I should have lost my influence". . . .

"You said you couldn't read a book, Lizzie. Your library of books is the hollow
down by the flare, I think."
"I should be very glad to be able to read real books. I feel my want of learning
very much, Charley. But I should feel it much more, if I didn't know it to be
a tie between me and father."   (I, ch. 3)

The fear of reading which Charley and Lizzie share illustrates what is true
generally about reading in *Our Mutual Friend*: to actually read (as opposed
to merely owning books as the Veneerings do), to pursue knowledge and the
ideals that spring from it, to nurture Fancy, is to challenge the powerful
inertia of ignorance or to ignore the hollow "voice of Society," both of which
dictate that all worth comes only from money.

Charley Hexam quickly loses our earlier sympathy when he develops into
the image of his mentor, Bradley Headstone, and advances Headstone's suit
to win Lizzie in the hopes of raising himself in Headstone's estimation.
Headstone's reading knowledge is purely mechanical and mercenary:

He had acquired mechanically a great store of teacher's knowledge. . . . From
his early childhood up, his mind had been a place of mechanical stowage. . . .
There was a kind of settled trouble in the face. . . . He always seemed to be
uneasy lest anything should be missing from his mental warehouse, and taking
stock to assure himself.   (II, ch. 1)

The "settled trouble" in Headstone's face is the emotional repression he
suffers because of his monomaniacal and acquisitive view of learning and the
resultant imbalance in his ability to cope with reality. His book knowledge
affords him no wisdom, no comfort, no healing mediation between his mind
and the world. When his passion for Lizzie Hexam and his jealousy of Eugene
Wrayburn grow, his learning offers him no remedy. His passions ride him in
the night like evil spirits, and the narrator suggests that a written version of
his sufferings would have taxed the interpretive powers of the best scholars:
"He had been spurred and whipped and heavily sweated. If a record of the
sport had usurped the places of peaceful texts from Scripture on the wall, the
most advanced of the scholars might have taken fright and run away from the
master" (III, ch. 11). Like Silas Wegg and Charley Hexam, Bradley Headstone has devalued and disabled literacy by making it merely his inert
property.

Two reading moments late in the novel raise but do not exorcise the demons
of jealousy for the last time within Bradley Headstone. In the first, Riderhood
visits Headstone's schoolroom unexpectedly, asks him to write his name on
the blackboard, and has the class read the name aloud: " 'I ain't a learned

character myself,' said Riderhood, surveying the class, 'but I admire learning in others. I should dearly like to hear these young folks read that there name off, from the writing.' " The rest of Riderhood's "lesson" to the class is, in effect, an indictment of Headstone's name, an inadvertent prophecy for it, and a hint that Riderhood intends to blackmail Headstone. Riderhood associates Headstone's name with the suit of clothes he wore during the attack on Wrayburn. Before Riderhood leaves the classroom, Headstone "turned his face to the black board and slowly wiped his name out." It is the last straw for Headstone, who, in an earlier reading moment, has seen a newspaper story reporting that Wrayburn has survived the attack, married Lizzie Hexam, and intended to let Headstone suffer privately rather than turn him in.

The simple scene both ignites the violent anger in Headstone and foretells his approaching death. Riderhood's "reading lesson" so affects Headstone that it brings to the surface before his observing pupils the rage hidden within him: "he fell into the fit which had been long impending." Two days later Headstone carries both himself and Riderhood to their watery deaths (IV, ch. 15).

Three minor characters in *Our Mutual Friend*—young Blight, Miss Peecher, and Jenny Wren—escape the dissatisfaction of reality by creating fictional characters and scenarios as compensations. While Wegg, Charley, and Headstone equate literacy with material gain, these "escapists" diminish it by detaching it from the world altogether. Young Blight, the clerk of Lightwood and Wrayburn, invents fictional clients and enters them into his employers' Appointment Book and Callers' Book in order to ignore the disgrace of their lack of clients and thereby maintain his own self-esteem (I, ch. 8). Like young Blight, Miss Peecher, an innocent schoolmistress hopelessly in love with Bradley Headstone, escapes the pain of her unrequited love through the fanciful creations of her mechanical writing:

> [She was] a little book. . . . She could write a little essay on any subject, exactly a slate long, beginning at the left-hand top of one side and ending at the right-hand bottom of the other, and the essay should be strictly according to rule. If Mr. Bradley Headstone had addressed a written proposal of marriage to her, she would probably have replied in a complete little essay on the theme exactly a slate long, but would certainly have replied yes.   (II, ch. 1)

Headstone's thwarted passion for Lizzie spills over into real violence, but Miss Peecher's love for him expresses itself harmlessly in the innocent fantasies which she shapes in her imaginary writings and readings both inside and outside her classroom:

If her faithful slate had had the latent qualities of sympathetic paper, and its pencil those of invisible ink, many a little treatise calculated to astonish the pupils would have come bursting through the dry sums in school-time under the warming influence of Miss Peecher's bosom. For oftentimes when school was not, and her calm leisure and calm little house were her own, Miss Peecher would commit to the confidential slate an imaginary description of how, upon a balmy evening at dusk, two figures might have been observed in the market-garden ground round the corner, of whom one, being a manly form, bent over the other, being a womanly form of short stature and some compactness, and breathed in a low voice the words, "Emma Peecher, wilt thou be my own?" after which the womanly form's head reposed upon the manly form's shoulder, and the nightingales tuned up. (II, ch. 11)

Both young Blight and Miss Peecher let their literary Fancy burn the bridge to reality, whereas Headstone's learning affords him no bridge to use at all. In all these cases—mercenary or escapist—literacy fails to serve as mediator or interpreter between the self and the outside world.

Jenny Wren stands out among the "escapists" in *Our Mutual Friend*, for, despite her minor role, she comes closest of any of the characters in the novel to resembling "the artist." Jenny illustrates the diminished power of the artist in a pragmatic and painful world and the artist's subsequent retreat from it. Jenny leads a double life, a life of "sorrowful happiness," to use her term for the view she has of the world from Mr. Riah's rooftop. At best her art and her reading lessons offer her temporary relief from her suffering, and her preference for their pleasure over the unsatisfactory truth of daily life makes her the most serious escapist in the novel.

Although Jenny Wren is neither a writer nor an avid reader, her artistry as a dolls' dressmaker very much resembles that of the artist-novelist. Jenny takes great pains in observing the life around her and transforming her human models into her dolls. Her work, like the novelist's, begins in real life:

"[I]t's the hardest part of my business. . . . I have to scud about town at all hours. If it was only sitting at my bench, cutting out and sewing, it would be comparatively easy work. . . . There's a Drawing Room, or a grand day in the Park, or a Show, or a Fete, or what you like. Very well. I squeeze among the crowd, and I look about me. When I see a great lady suitable for my business, I say, 'You'll do, my dear!' and I take particular notice of her, and run home and cut her out and baste her."

When she completes her work, she takes pride in the panorama she has created of little, make-believe people who fill a miniature world. Looking in a toy-shop window, Jenny says, " 'Now look at 'em. All my work!' This referred to a dazzling semi-circle of dolls in all the colours of the rainbow, who were dressed for presentation at court, for going to balls, for going out driving, for going out on horseback, for going out walking, for going to get married, for going to help other dolls to get married, for all the gay events of life'' (III, ch. 2).[13]

The "gay events of life," however, are confined to the imaginary lives of Jenny's dolls and are nearly nonexistent for Jenny herself. She is a dwarfed, crippled, and misshapen young woman burdened with the care of her drunkard father and carrying with her the image of a fantasy lover who will come to court and marry her. In fairy-tale fashion, she expresses three wishes to her friend Mr. Riah, her "fairy godmother" who calls her "Cinderella": she wishes for a coach and six, for her father's reformation, and for a normal back and legs. None of the wishes comes true, of course. Jenny's life is for the most part filled with labor and pain, relieved somewhat by her friendship with Riah and Lizzie Hexam and by the promise of love when she meets Mrs. Sloppy late in the novel. The other solace Jenny enjoys, namely the reading lessons Eugene Wrayburn provides for her and Lizzie, similarly removes her from the flurry of the world. Most appropriately, it is during one of her reading lessons with Lizzie that Jenny best articulates the separation between the two halves of her life—the pleasure of her artistry and the suffering of her day-to-day life.

Jenny and Lizzie devote as much time as they can to the "book-learning" paid for by Wrayburn. On Riah's rooftop the reading time allows her to escape the troubles of everyday life which continue in the streets beneath them:

> They both pored over one book. . . . Another little book or two were lying near. . . . "We are thankful to come here for the rest, [Jenny says]. . . . It's the quiet and the air. . . . [Despite the City noise and the pollution,] it's so high. And you see the clouds rushing on above the narrow streets, not minding them, and you see the golden arrows pointing at the mountains in the sky from which the wind comes, and you feel as if you were dead. . . . Oh, so tranquil! . . . Oh, so peaceful and so thankful! And you hear the people who are alive, crying, and working, and calling to one another down in the close dark streets, and you seem to pity them so! And such a chain has fallen from you, and such a strange good sorrowful happiness comes upon you!"

More like one of Tennyson's Lotos-Eaters than Oliver reading idyllically at the Maylies', Jenny washes her hands of the real world and prefers the rooftop-reading world of "death." When Riah leaves the roof temporarily, she calls out: " 'Don't be long gone. Come back and be dead!' " Jenny's siren-like invitation impresses even Riah's master, the money-lender Fascination Fledgeby: ". . . the call or song began to sound in his ears again, and, looking above, he saw the face of the little creature looking down out of a Glory of her long bright radiant hair, and musically repeating to him, like a vision: 'Come up and be dead! Come up and be dead!' '' (II, ch. 5).

The mercenary and the escapist readers in *Our Mutual Friend* threaten the power of nonfunctional literacy to revitalize human experience, though they do not stifle it entirely by themselves. Well-intentioned teachers also contribute to the failure of book learning because they are often blind to both the street wisdom and the deficiencies of the learner. Charley Hexam, for instance, first learns from the streets, "the great Preparatory Establishment in which very much that is never unlearned is learned without and before book." The narrator condemns the reading instruction at the Ragged School which Charley attends because the texts were ineffectual or meaningless to students seasoned by city street life or too ignorant to understand what they were reading:

> [A]ll the place was pervaded by a grimly ludicrous pretence that every pupil was childish and innocent. This pretence . . . led to the ghastliest absurdities. Young women old in the vices of the commonest and worst life, were expected to profess themselves enthralled by the good child's book, the Adventures of Little Margery. . . . Contrariwise, the adult pupils were taught to read (if they could learn) out of the New Testament; and by dint of stumbling over the syllables and keeping their bewildered eyes on the particular syllables coming round to their turn, were as absolutely ignorant of the sublime history, as if they had never seen or heard of it. (II, ch. 1)

In *Our Mutual Friend* the weakened power of literacy depends more and more upon human agency to rekindle its force, yet the readers capable of acting seem largely absent from the novel.

For literacy to stir the Fancy in the great dust-heap of the world of *Our Mutual Friend*, the readers within the novel must first redefine "reading" more directly in terms of human experience, to restore for themselves the lost recognition of the value and power of a mythologized world. Eugene Wrayburn's casual remarks suggest such a redefinition during a discussion with Mortimer Lightwood:

> "You charm me, Mortimer, with your reading of my weaknesses. (By-the-bye, that very word, Reading, in its critical use, always charms me. An actress's Reading of a chamber-maid, a dancer's Reading of a hornpipe, a singer's Reading of a song, a marine painter's Reading of the sea, the kettle-drum's Reading of an instrumental passage, are phrases ever youthful and delightful.)"
> (III, ch. 10)

The use of "reading" to mean the interpretation of a real experience instead of a book experience surfaces often in *Our Mutual Friend*.[14] Gaffer Hexam is illiterate, but he "reads" the "BODY FOUND" notices which paper the walls of his house by their position in the collage: "Gaffer read them as he held the light. . . . 'I can't read, nor I don't want to it, for I know 'em by their places on the wall. . . . They pretty well papers the room, you see; but I know 'em all. I'm scholar enough!' " (I, ch. 3). Mr. Riah learns his instructions from reading Fledgeby's face: "he read his master's face, and learnt the book" (III, ch. 13); and Fledgeby himself reads the world only in terms of pounds, shillings, and pence: "there is no animal so sure to get laden with it [money], as the Ass who sees nothing written on the face of the earth and sky but the three letters L.S.D." (II, ch. 5). Of all the readers in *Our Mutual Friend*, Mr. Boffin is the only character who is depicted explicitly as combining his reading of books with his reading of experience, a process which helps to convert the mercenary Bella Wilfer into a more sympathetic character.

The effect on Mr. Boffin of Silas Wegg's reading from *The Decline and Fall of the Roman Empire* is to frighten him: " 'Wegg takes it easy, but upon-my-soul to a old bird like myself these are scarers. . . . I didn't think this morning there was half so many Scarers in Print. But I'm in for it now!' " (I, ch. 5). Boffin's fear of what he hears of the decadence of Rome and of what he later learns of the fates of several famous misers spurs him on to his plan to save Bella Wilfer. In other words, reading works its magic as a mediator and interpreter of the real world on the innocent, ignorant, good-hearted man. Mr. Boffin, in turn, becomes a fictional enactment of what he reads: he pretends to imitate the misers he has learned about and thereby opens Bella's eyes to her own faults. Reading works its catharsis on Bella indirectly, through the agency of Boffin's role-playing.

Boffin's innocent deception begins in a reading scene which interweaves Bella's reading a book with Mr. Boffin's pretending to tyrannize over his secretary, John Rokesmith:

> Bella took her book to a chair in the fireside corner, by Mrs. Boffin's work-table. Mr. Boffin's station was on the opposite side.
> "Now, Rokesmith," said the Golden Dustman, so sharply rapping the table to bespeak his attention as Bella turned the leaves of her book, that she started; "where were we?"

After "humiliating" Rokesmith sufficiently, Boffin dismisses him:

> The Secretary rose, gathered up his papers, and withdrew. Bella's eyes followed him to the door, lighted on Mr. Boffin complacently thrown back in his easy-chair, and drooped over her book. . . .

Bella felt that Mrs. Boffin was not comfortable, and that the eyes of that good creature sought to discover from her face what attention she had given to this discourse, and what impression it had made upon her. For which reason Bella's eyes drooped more engrossedly over her book, and she turned the page with an air of profound absorption in it. . . .

Bella ventured for a moment to look stealthily towards him under her eyelashes, and she saw a dark cloud of suspicion, covetousness, and conceit, overshadowing the once open face. . . .

A deceiving Bella she was, to look at him with that pensively abstracted air, as if her mind were full of her book, and she had not heard a single word!

The scene begins Bella's "war with herself," her concern about the new "illegibility" of Mr. Boffin's face, and her repeated self-questionings in her mirror (III, ch. 5).

Bella also becomes the sole companion to Mr. Boffin on his morning book-buying excursions in search of volumes on the lives of misers. The books they purchase remain hidden from Bella and are substituted for by Boffin's acting out the selfish lives they recount:

It very soon became unnecessary to tell Bella what to look for, and an understanding was established between her and Mr.Boffin that she was always to look for Lives of Misers. Morning after morning they roamed about the town together, pursuing this singular research. . . . It was curious that Bella never saw the books about the house, nor did she ever hear from Mr. Boffin one word of reference to their contents. . . . But beyond all doubt it was to be noticed, and was by Bella very clearly noticed, that, as he pursued the acquisition of those dismal records with the ardour of Don Quixote for his books of chivalry, he began to spend his money with a more sparing hand.   (III, ch. 5)

Boffin's deception, rooted in his reading, acts as a touchstone for Bella and eventually proves her to be "the true golden gold." Bella marries John Rokesmith and comes to interpret what she had read in Boffin's actions:

"When you saw what a greedy little wretch you were the patron of, you determined to show her how much misused and misprized riches could do, and often had done, to spoil people; did you? Not caring what she thought of you . . . you showed her, in yourself, the most detestable sides of wealth, saying in your own mind, "This shallow creature would never work the truth out of her own weak soul, if she had a hundred years to do it in; but a glaring instance kept before her may open even her eyes and set her thinking."
(IV, ch. 13)[15]

Mr. Boffin has performed an exorcism of sorts, a vicarious purgation with the help of the instruments of Fancy, his books and his acting.

The Boffins, John Rokesmith and Bella, Lizzie and Eugene Wrayburn, and a small number of minor characters add some light and hope to the generally dismal world of *Our Mutual Friend*, but the predominant effect of the novel remains bleak, and the last chapter is given over to "The Voice of Society" where the Podsnaps and Lady Tippins still reign. If we wish to find further cause for hope, perhaps it comes in Dickens' "Postscript," in which he mentions the railway accident he had been involved in the previous June. He fancifully describes the recovery of parts of the manuscript of *Our Mutual Friend* by treating the characters as passengers rescued from the wreckage. Moreover, he connects his life with his fiction by speaking of "The End" of each:

> On Friday the Ninth of June in the present year, Mr. and Mrs. Boffin (in their manuscript dress of receiving Mr. and Mrs. Lammle at breakfast) were on the South-Eastern Railway with me, in a terribly destructive accident. When I had done what I could to help others, I climbed back into my carriage . . . to extricate the worthy couple. . . . I remember with devout thankfulness that I can never be much nearer parting company with my readers for ever than I was then, until there shall be written against my life, the two words with which I have this day closed this book: —The End.

The "Postscript" has a Copperfieldian ring to it because it reminds us, maybe with a bit of desperation this time, of the relationship between reading and living, of literacy's power to help us make sense of our stories no matter how bleak they may be, of the need to keep Fancy alive. Finally, associating life with story, Dickens reminds us that we too are among the readers of *Our Mutual Friend*, whose reading of the novel may stir within us the fear of its vision, as Mr. Boffin's reading did for him. Like *Oliver Twist* and *David Copperfield*, *Our Mutual Friend* remythologizes the world, but we leave Dickens' last complete novel with a more tempered optimism that we felt when we left those earlier works.[16]

The readers and writers in *Oliver Twist*, *David Copperfield*, and *Our Mutual Friend* reveal a gradual demythologizing of the world over nearly three decades of Dickens' writing career. In late decades, the writings of Victorian aesthetes such as Oscar Wilde and Walter Pater celebrate the imagination, but witness as well the disjunction of imagination from its integrating function among the wonders of the self, the physical world, and the world of human relationships. In the darkening vision of metafiction in his novels, Dickens mirrors the diminished role of Fancy in Victorian England and foreshadows the continued division between the sacred and the profane in the twentieth century. Amidst the gloom of such a world view, however, Dickens' art reaffirms the value of nonfunctional literacy and offers the individual reader and writer an option for renewal and the rediscovery of the natural wonder of experience which mankind has tried so hard to conceal.

NOTES

1. I am grateful to my colleague and former teacher Dr. Thomas Fitzsimons for his lecture to the Buffalo chapter of the Dickens Fellowship on Dickens' attitudes toward education and for introducing me to Professor Collins' work.
2. Miller explains that the significance of this half-waking state lies not in the fact "that it links a real state to an imaginary state, but that it links a *present* state to a *past* state." Miller's argument stresses the importance of the scenes as instances of Oliver's experience of "affective memory" rather than their function as aesthetic moments.
3. A similar scene occurs in the first chapter of Charlotte Brontë's *Jane Eyre* (1847): Jane sits reading in an enclosed window seat, "shrined in double retirement . . . the clear panes of glass, protecting, but not separating me from the drear November day." Steven Marcus discusses the "hypnagogic" moments in *Oliver Twist* biographically, linking them psychologically to moments in Dickens' personal history: "[F]or the window and the book we recur to the scene in the window at the blacking factory, and behind it, perhaps, to Dickens's earlier recollection of himself as a small boy on 'a summer evening . . . sitting on my bed, reading as if for life' " (371–73).
4. Earl B. Brown, Jr., likewise discusses David as an author: "Through the process of writing he finally can dissassociate himself from his past and face his future" (1). "Authorship" as a theme in the novel, however, moves to second place in Brown's study and is viewed as a frame for the treatment of David's maturation. My discussion will focus more on the process and nature of authorship rather than their effect.
5. In ch. 52, David digresses into a speech about the tendency of men to tyrannize over words in legal matters:

Again, Mr. Micawber had a relish in this formal piling up of words, which, however, ludicrously displayed in his case, was, I must say, not at all peculiar to him. I have observed it, in the course of my life, in numbers of men.

6. J. Hillis Miller calls attention to the vividness of David's memories, but maintains that there is no "transcendence of time through a merger of past and present. . . . The past is, for Dickens, definitely past, and lost in the ocean of things that once were, and are no longer . . ." (*Charles Dickens* 154). Miller seems to diminish unnecessarily the imaginative presentness of David's recollections. Later he qualifies his view by citing examples of "experiences of *déjà vu*, the strange sensation of autohypnosis in which one feels oneself to be reenacting a scene which has occurred before, long ago in the past, or in another life" (158).
7. Alfred Tennyson called this "the passion of the past, the abiding in the transient" (Houghton and Stange 43). Tennyson himself uses the image of the sea in his "Tears, Idle Tears," a lyric poem published in *The Princess* (1847). Tennyson's verse, like David's book, captures the double nature of memory as both a vital and a mortal sea journey:

Fresh as the first beam glittering on a sail,
That brings our friends up from the underworld,
Sad as the last which reddens over one
That sinks with all we love below the verge;
So sad, so fresh, the days that are no more.

(Houghton and Stange, 43)

E. Pearlman connects the paradox of the sea in *David Copperfield* to the double nature of sexual passion as both generative and destructive: "Drowning is not only a way of dying—it is the plunge into the sea of passion; its ineluctable corollary is that sex and sexual passion are dangerous and destructive. Therefore Dora dies of the consequences of miscarriage—she dies of the love that is 'wrung out of' David. The association between water and passion permeates the novel" (3949.

8. The detail of associating King "Charles" with Mr. "Dick" suggests a new candidate for what Steven Marcus has called the biographical alphabet game in Dickens' novels, the suggestion that the initials of certain characters link them more closely to their author, "C.D."; for example, Charles Darnay, or David himself (D.C.) (289–92, 346). It is at least interesting that all three—David, Mr. Dick, and Dickens—are authors in varying degrees of "imagination all compact." Stanley Tick first links Mr. Dick's name to John Dickens, Dickens' father, and points out that "Dick" was a nickname given to Dickens by his friend, Clarkson Stanfield. Micawber calls Mr. Dick "Mr. Dixon," which sounds like "Dickens," and Peter Ackroyd reminds us that "Dick" was George Cruikshank's nickname for Dickens (294). Tick's argument, however, that Mr. Dick is primarly a metaphor for Dickens overshoots Mr. Dick's more immediate function as a contrast to David's authorship: the "principal 'truth' of Mr. Dick . . . [is] that he is an image of the author himself" (143). Earl B. Brown, Jr., suggests that Mr. Dick as a failed author is a major foil for David (83–85).

9. Tick briefly mentions that Dr. Strong and Mr. Dick are "two unsuccessful word men" (151), perhaps missing the further suggestion of the phrase, namely that they are both men made of words through David's writing. E. Pearlman links Dr. Strong and Mr. Dick as authors who parody both David's autobiography and Dickens' *roman à clef*. Pearlman also calls attention to the curious and subtle coincidence that the number of years which Dr. Strong's student speculates it will take for the completion of the dictionary—1,649—is the same as the date of the execution of Charles I, the event which repeatedly delays the completion of Mr. Dick's "Memorial" (399).

10. J. Hillis Miller discusses Agnes' function as a symbol of fate who guides David's actions more than he is aware of: only "in the perspective of his total recollection of his life . . . can he see that it is not so much his own mind as the central presence of Agnes which organizes his memories and makes them whole." Despite Agnes' influence, Miller does not view David as "a mere puppet, manipulated by his destiny": with the aid of Agnes' guidance, "David, then, has both made himself and escaped the guilt which always hovers, for Dickens, over the man who takes matters into his own hands" (*Charles Dickens* 157–59).

11. Janet H. Brown discusses David's "single organizing consciousness," the narrative web which "itself becomes indistinguishable from its spinner," and the call of the novel to readers to "recognize in David Copperfield the same precious creature they cherish in themselves" (197, 199).

12. Stanley Friedman's excellent study of the reading motif in *Our Mutual Friend* explains how reading contributes to the two main strands of the novel's plot, the

Bella-Rokesmith and the Lizzie-Eugene storylines. Boffin's concern for literacy and his pretended mania for books about misers lead to the hiring of Rokesmith, the warning of Bella about her mercenariness, and the testing and punishment of Wegg (38–53). Similarly, Lizzie Hexam's illiteracy and the reading lessons which Eugene Wrayburn provides subsequently enable her to write to the Boffins and link her with Bella (53). Friedman also shows how the reading motif reveals character through the attitudes that several characters (Charley Hexam, Rogue Riderhood, and Bradley Headstone among them) have toward reading (54–56). Richard D. Altick offers a brilliant sociological perspective in his linking of the literacy motif in *Our Mutual Friend* with education, print, and paper in 1865 England. Paper and its associations with reading, books, and the topical concern with education become the focus for "the author's sense of the *Zeitgefühl*, the elusive, intangible, often largely undefined quality of the moment": "Just as the railway defines the contemporaneity of *Dombey and Son* . . . so the more diffuse and variegated references to education, print, and paper are Dickens's expression of the special tone of urban England twenty years later. . . . His allusions to printed matter and the ability to read are, on the whole, period color rather than commentary; their function is sociological, not symbolic except insofar as they are connected with the theme of education" (247, 253).

13. The toy-shop window modifies somewhat the earlier window metaphors in the reading scenes in *Oliver Twist*. It still suggests the transparent barrier which both separates and allows association between the real world and the imaginative one. The major difference, however, is that in *Oliver Twist* the windows suggest that books look out onto the real world, whereas the dolls in the window are there primarily because they are to be sold—most appropriate for *Our Mutual Friend*.

14. Stanley Friedman points out the double import of Wrayburn's remark: in referring to various "artists," "Eugene uses 'reading' in its figurative senses of acting and interpreting. . . . Boffin and John 'read' Bella and Wegg, while the latter 'misreads' Boffin. But Eugene's banter also reminds us of the literal meaning of 'reading' and helps us to recognize the significance in this novel of the image and the idea of literacy" (60). Similarly, Richard Altick sees Wrayburn's remark in its "parenthetical embroidery on the theme of the word 'reading' " as an instance of Dickens' "free-associational storehouse" which "contributes to our sense of the importance of reading—the ability, the act—in this novel" (248–49).

15. John Rokesmith-John Harmon aids Boffin in the transformation of Bella, but it is Boffin's action, not Rokesmith's, which is associated with the reading motif. Rokesmith himself is often associated with books and reading, as Stanley Friedman points out, because "Dickens wants us to see Rokesmith as an educated, well-read man" (57), but the link between Rokesmith's reading and his actions is not so clearly evident as in Boffin's case. Perhaps we are to think that Rokesmith's success at role-playing is an extension of his earlier reading, a talent which we witness in Boffin as it develops simultaneously with his increased reading. After Bella's marriage to Rokesmith, she too becomes an avid reader, but her reading contributes primarily to her image as another of Dickens' domestic saints, a portrait that would probably find few admirers among modern readers:

Mrs. J.R., who had never been wont to do much at home as Miss B.W., was under the constant necessity of referring for advice and support to a sage volume entitled The Complete British Family Housewife, which she would sit consulting, with her elbows on the table and her temples on her hands, like some perplexed enchantress poring over the Black Art. . . . Another branch of study claimed the attention of Mrs. John Rokesmith for a regular period every day. This was the mastering of the newspaper, so that she might be close up with John on general topics when John came home. (IV. ch. 5)

Friedman sees Bella's postnuptial reading as a sign of her increased seriousness (56–57).

16. Miller defines the qualified positive experience of the reader of *Our Mutual Friend* when they enter the novel's "world of verbalized consciousness": "[I]n describing Bradley and all the other characters in the novel, in making a verbal image of their lives and of the world they live in, Dickens produces a gap between the reader and this world, a gap which suffices to liberate at least the reader from it. The reader at least is able to recognize these lives as null, and therefore to escape from the situation which traps the characters if we imagine them as real" (1959, 303–04). In another excellent discussion of the benefits one derives from reading *Our Mutual Friend*, Rosemary Mundhenk explains how the novel's complex narrative structure educates the reader: "By learning of his limited powers of perceiving and knowing, the reader becomes engaged actively in the thematic concerns of the novel. . . . Although given clues, the reader must often form his own pattern of the fragments, resolve for himself the contradictions and participate actively in the process of discovery that he shares with the characters" (51, 57). As Miller and Mundhenk suggest, readers of *Our Mutual Friend* earn the tempered optimism they enjoy when they've completed the novel.

WORKS CITED

Ackroyd, Peter. *Dickens*. New York: Harper, 1990.

Altick, Richard D. "Education, Print, and Paper in *Our Mutual Friend*." *Nineteenth-Century Literary Perspectives*. Ed. Clyde de L. Ryals et al. (Durham: Duke UP, 1974). 237–54.

Brontë, Charlotte. *Jane Eyre*. New York: Houghton, 1959.

Brown, Earl B., Jr. "The Rhetoric of Charles Dickens: A Study of *David Copperfield*." Diss. Emory U, 1971.

Brown, Janet, H. "The Narrator's Role in *David Copperfield*." *Dickens Studies Annual* 2 (1972):197–207.

Campbell, Joseph. *The Hero with a Thousand Faces*. Princeton: Princeton UP, 1949.

Collins, Phillip. *Dickens and Education*. London: Macmillan, 1963.

Dickens, Charles. *Bleak House*. Baltimore: Penguin, 1971.

———. *David Copperfield*. London: Oxford UP, 1981.

———. *Oliver Twist*. Baltimore: Penguin, 1966.

————. *Our Mutual Friend*. Baltimore: Penguin, 1971.

Fielding, K. J. *Charles Dickens: A Critical Introduction*. Boston: Houghton, 1965.

Friedman, Stanley. "The Motif of Reading in *Our Mutual Friend*." *Nineteenth-Century Fiction* 28 (1973):38–61.

Johnson, Edgar. *Charles Dickens: His Tragedy and Triumph* 2 vols. New York: Simon, 1952.

Marcus, Steven. *Dickens: From Pickwick to Dombey*. New York: Simon, 1965.

Miller, J. Hillis. *Charles Dickens: The World of His Novels*. Cambridge: Harvard UP, 1959.

————. "Our Mutual Friend." *Dickens: A Collection of Critical Essays*. Ed. Martin Price. Englewood Cliffs: Prentice, 1967. 169–76.

Mundhenk, Rosemary. "The Education of the Reader in *Our Mutual Friend*." *Nineteenth-Century Fiction* 34 (1979):41–58.

Pearlman, E. "David Copperfield Dreams of Drowning." *American Imago* 28 (1971):391–403.

Tennyson, Alfred. "Tears, Idle Tears." *Victorian Poetry and Poetics*. Ed. Walter E. Houghton and G. Robert Stange. Boston: Houghton, 1968.

Tick, Stanley. "The Memorializing of Mr. Dick." *Nineteenth-Century Fiction* 24 (1969):142–53.

Carnivalesque "Unlawful Games" in
The Old Curiosity Shop

Mark M. Hennelly, Jr.

I

If the official version of Truth lies passively at the bottom of a well in *The Old Curiosity Shop* (1840–41), unofficial, carnivalesque varieties of truth swirl potently inside a magic cauldron of tripe stew. In Dickens, as in Rabelais and the entire carnivalesque tradition of play, whatever lies in repose self-definitively adopts the posture of untruth, while whatever swivels in a grotesque round dance alternatively adapts itself to the profound fullness of cornucopious life. In this sense, if we accept Forster's view that the novel was only "taking gradual form, with less direct consciousness of design on [the author's] part than I can remember in any other instance throughout his career" (I:133), it is because Dickens did not adapt his hitherto improvised tale to the carnivalesque model of *Gargantua and Pantagruel* until chapters 15–19, when Nell and her Grandfather flee London and begin their picaresque pilgrimage with the strolling players. On the other hand, if Dickens had Rabelais somewhere in mind from the very beginning, it is because the playful carnivalesque essentially believes that life is eternally "taking gradual form." In either case, the curious result is as different from the *jeu d'esprit* of *Pickwick* as Quilp is from Jingle or Dick Swiveller from Sam Weller; and conversely, if the angel in tights and gaiters seems finally more carnivalesque than angelic little Nell, it is only because Pickwick journeys underground in Fleet, while she never experiences underground treasures but must even sanctify (or sanitize) the tripe by officiously saying grace over it before the impromptu play symposium can begin.

Adopting Forster's lead, most readers have felt that the apparent formlessness of *The Old Curiosity Shop* suggests, in fact, that it is even more of a *jeu d'esprit* than *Pickwick*, not realizing that it is actually Dickens' most philosophically consistent (and paradoxically curious) novel precisely because it is a carnivalesque game of spirits. Following Rabelais' model, *The Old Curiosity Shop* is a grotesque if not gnostic quest for the life-meaning of the Holy Bottle, which meaning seems personified in the carnivalesque nature of Quilp, that prodigious feeder-drinker appearing downside up in coaches and Nell's bed—the inside out spirit of what most of us conceal, the virtual incarnation of the *mundus inversus*. In his relevant introduction to the four essays in *The Dialogic Imagination*, Michael Holquist discusses Bakhtin's theory of the developing novel form as a kind of "heterglossia" or "polyphony," that is, not a panegyric like the monologic funeral oration commemorating Nell, but a *pangenre* or "carnivalization" (xix) of genres like the salmagundi tripe itself or the pastiche of literary forms playing for control of *The Old Curiosity Shop* in chapters 15–19.[1]

The magic potion of tripe first appears in the "large iron cauldron" in the "ancient" Jolly Sandboys Inn as a special example of the many instances of treasure chambers stocked with motley curiosities—here golden brown bouillon—in the novel. When the lid is initially raised, even that "misanthropical" philosopher and Punch showman Mr. Codlin responds in a way that illustrates Rabelais' repeated point that lamenting and laughing philosophies—"democritizing" and "heraclitizing"—are dialogically interdependent, much like playing and praying: "there rushed out a savoury smell, while the bubbling sound grew deeper and more rich, and an unctuous steam came floating out, hanging in a delicious mist above their heads— . . . Mr. Codlin's heart was touched." But the landlord's specific catalogue description of this "delightful steam" more clearly identifies the tripe as a carnivalesque flow of the primary processes of life as well as a potpourri of all genres liquid enough to adapt to these protean forms of life's playful display: " 'It's a stew of tripe,' said the landlord smacking his lips, 'and cow-heel,' smacking them again, 'and bacon,' smacking them once more, 'and steak,' smacking them for the fourth time, 'and peas, cauliflowers, new potatoes, and sparrow-grass, all working up together in one delicious gravy.' "[2] No wonder that when the cover is again removed for serving, "the effect was electrical," especially since the ensuing meal is liberally refreshened with "warm ale" and "the happy circumstances attendant upon mulled malt" (18:136–38). Thus, the cauldron of tripe even significantly prefigures the later "great pot, filled with some very fragrant compound, which sent forth a grateful steam, and was indeed [the] choice purl" (57:427), which Dick Swiveller concocts to re-freshen the Marchioness and which makes their cribbage games more joyfully carnivalesque.

Of all the many references to tripe in Rabelais, perhaps the most famous and certainly the most relevant is the first which occurs when pregnant Gargamelle attends a feast that serves an "abundance of tripes" (I:4, 19), and then after "eating too many tripes," she discovers that her responsive little giant Pantagruel "sprung up and leapt" from her womb. And with a somewhat curious notion of obstetrics, he then "issued forth at her left eare," all the while shouting "Some drink, some drink, some drink, as inviting all the world to drink with him" (I:6, 24, 26).[3] Bakhtin begs Rabelais' reader to "pay special attention" to such playful tripe imagery and its particular "role in grotesque realism." For Bakhtin, "tripe, stomach, intestines are the bow-els, the belly, the very life of man. But at the same time they represent the swallowing, devouring, belly. Grotesque realism played with this double image, we might say with the top and the bottom" of the cosmos. Again, "the belly does not only eat and swallow, it is also eaten, as tripe. . . . Further, tripe is linked with death, with slaughter, murder, since to disem-bowel is to kill. Finally it is linked with birth, for the belly generates." Bakhtin's relevant conclusion deserves full citation:

> Thus, in the image of tripe life and death, birth, excrement, and food are all drawn together and tied in one grotesque knot; this is the center of bodily topography in which the upper and lower stratum penetrate each other. This grotesque image was a favorite expression of the ambivalence of the material bodily lower stratum, which destroys and generates, swallows and is swallowed, The "swing" of grotesque realism, the play of the upper with the lower sphere, is strikingly set into motion; the top and the bottom, heaven and earth, merge in that image. (162–63)

In this sense, carnivalesque tripe, reinforced by the analogous but more familiar, improvised "versions of the great drama of Punch" potentially hidden away in his thesaurus "temple" (18:141), helps clarify "all the roar and riot" (19:148) in these chapters, just as the repeated image of "oyster shells, heaped in rank confusion" (15:115)—here and elsewhere in the novel imagistically linked with *grottoes* (see 39:295)—promises a valuable pearl (one almost hears the suppressed pun *purl*) of grotesque, hidden spirit and insight.[4] After seeing that the food chain of tripe suggests the cyclic links between life and death, the reader discovers that the pastoral herds of "sleepy cows" and the "beautiful pastures and fields of corn" (15:117–18) no longer imply the confusing if not disturbing ascendancy of the *idyll* genre in the

novel—one nearly hears another pun in that very name—but rather prepare
naturally for their bloody and bloodless harvesting or "cropping" in the tripe.
In the same way, the unplayful allusions to *Pilgrim's Progress* with their
implied condemnation of the "Fair [at the town Vanity where] there is at all
times to be seen jugglings, cheats, games, plays, fools, apes, knaves, and
rogues, and that of all sorts" (Bunyan 125) prepare for the compensatory
"unlawful games" of the "jugglers or mountebanks" here, especially again
that "merry outlaw" the "beaming Punch" who is finally uncovered and
"displayed in the full zenith of his humour" (17:130, 132; 19:150) like some
dark sun. In other words, the carnivalesque "unlawful games" repeatedly
compete with formal, official genres, just as in Punch, "a favorite character
in the play . . . was held to be a libel on the beadle" by the official "authorities" (17:133).[5] Nell's problem in this episode is really, then, the inherent
limitation of the "classical" or monologic response to multifarious life. For
her, the motley, strolling players "were not the fittest companions she could
have stumbled on," and Codlin, in fact, is indecently drunk on ale. Thus she
feels disoriented rather than delighted by stimuli like the magical steam of
tripe: the "sickening smells from many dinners came in a heavy lukewarm
breath   upon   [her]   sense."   Any   "delirious"   or   carnivalesque
"scene . . . frightened and repelled" Nell (19:146, 148).

Consequently, Steven Marcus' assertion that "*The Old Curiosity Shop* is
a frustrated or failed idyll" (135) surely misses the spirit of carnivalesque
success and fulfillment in the novel. Admittedly, there are many echoes, in
fact ludic laments, of Dickens' favorite idyll, Goldsmith's *The Deserted
Village*, including "the village preacher" and "village [school] master" and
even a grandfatherly "good old sire" who wishes for "worlds beyond the
grave" and "his lovely daughter" who "left a lover's for a father's arms."[6]
In fact, the most subtle idyllic notes in Goldsmith are haunting, ambivalent
lyrics of the relevant *Et in Arcadia Ego* motif, in which *Ego* can be variously
translated as playing Pan, mocking King Death, or even that greatest bane of
all arcadias—pining and disillusioning Self-Consciousness:

> Sweet smiling village, loveliest of the lawn,
> Thy sports are fled and all thy charms withdrawn;
> Amidst thy bowers the tyrant's hand is seen,
> And desolation saddens all thy green.   (11.35–38)[7]

Surely, it is not that all "sports are fled" in these five central chapters of
The Old Curiosity Shop. The nostalgic and regretful tone of *ubi sunt?* complains only that pastoral play and piping seem to flee when the dawning "light

[of Divine] creation's mind" surrenders to the dusky Demiurgic vision of creative Misrule's "eyes in which old forests gleamed" (15:114). As Nell and her Grandfather "penetrated very far into the labyrinth" of primitive-popular play forms, the transitional twilight portentously unveils its own liminal guardian: "The freaks of Punch . . . perched cross-legged upon a tombstone. . . . all loose and limp and shapeless" (16:122) with full carnivalesque play potential, which Bakhtin has traced through Pulcinella's many historical transformations (251–52).[8] And the ambivalence of the dance of death motif here playfully persists throughout the novel, as for example when "some young children sported among the tombs, and hid from each other, with laughing faces" (53:394), while Nell begins one of her several brief pilgrimages to the "deep, dark echoing well" (396), which stagnates in moribund contrast to the deeper play of the echoing cemetery green. Even the word *limp* associated with Punch suggests antistructural rites of passage as diagnosed in Victor Turner's concepts of the *liminal* and *liminoid*, besides recalling all the significant limping limbs in this episode and throughout Dickens.[9] Reversing and even subverting the expected priapic connotations of lusty Punch, this particular carnivalesque sense of *limp* suggests that the improvisational potential of the puppet play remains open and adaptable to all being-altering processes, whereas erect rigidity would suggest self-paralysis before possible threshold transformations like the inviting tripe bowl and Punch curtain.

Even though Dickens' carnivalesque Punch is clearly identified with his Quilpian Apollyon, still "the burden of that same Punch's temple" (17:132) is as heavy for the picaresque Codlin as his own different burden is for the pilgrim Christian. And both questers beat Death—one with prayer, the other with play. For Christian, "the miseries of Earth . . . show the way to Heaven" and validate the sacrifice of having "given up the game" of life (15:115) to insure his soul's eternal rest; for Punch, on the other hand, Earth's the right place for love, as Frost would put it, and there can be no progression without the playful strife of contraries, as Blake would say. Punch's graveyard seems haunted by "last Sunday's text that this was what flesh came to" as ironically illustrated by a horse "cropping the grass," and such carnal or carnivalesque folly suggests the Psalm of Fools (Psalm 14, old Psalm 13) with its sanctimonious reading of the "heart" of "the fool." But this official condemnation of going "astray" and growing "perverse," as Sandra Billington describes it (41–43), in the unofficial, popular tradition conjures not the artificial court fool but a dancing natural fool like Swiveller later in the novel. Illustrated Psalters even depict a dancing, playing, merry outlaw like

Dick or Punch. Accordingly, the performing "dog in disgrace" at the end of chapter 18 must fast and play "Old Hundredth" (Psalm 100) on the organ, while his more favored fellows feast themselves on "unusually large pieces of [tripe] fat," implying perhaps the carnivalesque version of a reward-punishment process. At the same time, Old Hundredth itself is a "Processional Hymn" or "joyful song" praising the Good Shepherd "to all generations," just as the repeated image of fooling "bells" which proclaim games often harmonizes with the church bells knelling Nell's premature demise in the novel.[10]

Again, all such confusion is clarified by the paradoxical processing of tripe, which involves feeding livestock to kill, growing corn to pick, swallowing stew to celebrate and survive, defecating or producing fertilizer to grow new corn and cows for the next cycle of "cropping," and thus working to play and playing to work. This same process of eternal becoming and refreshening informs Nell's subsequent encounter in the graveyard with the old woman who serially transforms from crone to mother to wife to maid as she magically seems to grow young before Nell's very eyes and thereby dramatically demonstrates the primary identity between graves and gardens. Nell tries repeatedly to practice this good earth mother's model of metamorphosis but never fully understands that just as we plant bulbs in gardens to grow flowers to harvest, we plant bodies in graveyards to harvest their spirit as well as to provide more growing space for new live bodies. Life eats life as the trickster Codlin eats tripe. And when little Nell compulsively picks flowers in graveyards, like Proserpine in the vale of Enna, she fails to realize, as the related Pan mythology suggests (Hillman 43–44), that she too must be at least symbolically deflowered to complete the natural process.[11] Here "the Pan's pipes" (16:126) play *all*, especially "saying things and then contradicting 'em" (18:138), as life revolves between 'the clock and . . . the cauldron" (19:144). And the carnivalesque *gay time* of "the delights of the present" indeed "beguiled time" (19:144), to repeat one of Dickens' favorite play tropes which appears prominently in *Pickwick*, before time itself can fly irretrievably away. In fact, the owner of the central clock, Master Humphrey, is himself a poor, deformed creature of "awkward and ungainly sports" (*Master Humphrey's Clock* I:9), but one who at least knows that hiding curious art away inside his clock can playfully beguile time just as processing tripe can. To invoke the repeated pun in both Rabelais and Dickens, *gammon* reminds us that food and play are analogously related to natural processes, to the recurring rhythms of life and death.

II

With this extended example of the carnivalesque in mind, we can now document more fully the specific nature of Rabelais' influence on Dickens. Many readers have noted in passing a Rabelaisian element in the Inimitable. Chesterton's brief remarks are more or less representative: "Rabelais did not introduce into Paphlagonia or the Kingdom of the Coqcigrues satiric figures more frantic and misshapen than Dickens made to walk about the Strand and Lincoln's Inn." And "satire like that of Rabelais" and Dickens is playfully energetic if not violent "satire that juggles with the stars and kicks the world about like a football" (220). For our purposes, it may certainly seem crucial that the *Gargantua* famously enumerates 217 games played by that young giant after dinner (I:22, 63–66), and as Bakhtin relevantly points out, this catalogue prompted translators to join the fun and lengthen the list by adding various play forms native to their own language and country (231–32). And yet such an encyclopedic approach to play represents only a tiny taste of the Rabelaisian play spirit that generally flavors all Dickens' novels, but seasons *The Old Curiosity Shop* more richly and satisfyingly than any other.

Dickens owned an 1838 edition of Sir Thomas Urquhart's original 1653 English translation of *Gargantua and Pantagruel*, complete with Theodore Martin's "Introductory Notice and Life of Rabelais" (Stonehouse 96), which itself "increased the list of recreations by adding English games" (Bakhtin 231). More to the present point, Dickens' 16 November 1838 letter to Richard Bentley reports that in his capacity as editor of *Bentley's Miscellany*, he is forwarding "The Rabelais article" of P. W. Banks for his publisher's approval or at least reaction (*Letters* I:455). And finally, a second letter of 23 November recounts that Dickens is forced to cancel a morning appointment with Bentley in order to be available "to Mr. Bankes [*sic*] for the purpose of going over his Rabelais paper" (*Letters* I:459). Thus, a year and a half before the appearance of *The Old Curiosity Shop* Dickens is engaged in a fairly extensive study of Rabelais. This conclusion is warranted not merely from the above correspondence but from the finally published text of Banks, which unaccountably was not published in *Bentley's*, but did appear—or at least some version of it did appear—in three lengthy installments (more than forty double-column pages altogether) titled "Of Rabelais" in *Fraser's Magazine* (November 1839, February and July 1840).[12]

The finally published piece, plagued as it is with interminable digressions and a coyly familiar tone, still remains intriguing evidence of Dickens' familiarity with Rabelais' life and work and thus challenges us to see the impact of this familiarity on his next novel *The Old Curiosity Shop*. In fact and as implied already, without an understanding of Dickens' Rabelaisian model, especially as explained as the jewel of the playful carnivalesque tradition by Bakhtin, I feel that no reader can completely appreciate the true virtue and enduring vitality of *The Old Curiosity Shop*. When understood as part of that carnivalesque tradition, however, the entire novel becomes more than just a literary *curiosity*, or better, that repeated term itself (and the related concept of the *uncanny*) achieves enriched thematic resonance. Moreover, Quilp's mysteriously indeterminate role in the novel itself becomes more satisfying even while remaining paradoxical and indeterminate when viewed as a personification of the carnivalesque energy field. In this context, the novel again rightly appears as a carnivalesque fairground upon which life games are contested between "official" or academic genres like the idyll, pastoral romance, elegy, and progress novel and "unofficial," popular, and playful traditions like the Trickster, Wild Man, Punch and Judy drama, *Danse Macabre*, and Our Lady's Tumbler. Finally, the "carnivalesque grotesque," reinforced by Turner's insights on liminal phenomena, enlightens the specific antics of Dick Swiveller. The carnivalesque particularly clarifies Dick's apparently eccentric movements, gambling, drinking, and his courting and educating the Marchioness. Consequently, these two mutually renewing figures ascend literally from the wine cellar and figuratively from the dissolution of Quilp and Nell to produce our final vision of them drinking life to the lees and "playing many hundred thousand games of cribbage" seemingly forever in present time.

As I have suggested in "Dickens's Praise of Folly: Play in *The Pickwick Papers*," it would seem that Dickens achieved a uniquely transcendent play perspective in his first novel, one which appears shaped generally by his own acquired love for the picaresque and, more inherently, by his related, idiosyncratic passion for all play motifs. But then his (re)reading of Rabelais helped to give more folk-traditional form and substance to his play motifs and thereby to pit the popular fair play of the village green and town square against the perverse foul play of educational, ecclesiastical, and especially civil or generally "official" legal and literary systems. Dickens' personal grave thoughts at this time about the death of Mary Hogarth and the most comforting way to mourn her passing (including the morbid desire to be buried alongside her) surely complicated—some might even argue compromised—his appraisal of the carnivalesque in *The Old Curiosity Shop*, just as the salutary effect of "ancient games" conversely perplexed Tennyson's grief during the second Christmas sequence of *In Memoriam* and caused him to ask if "grief can be changed to less" (st. 78).[13]

In Rabelais, the answer to this great, deep question is invariably an eternal yea as, for instance, when Gargantua, on "the one side, seeing his wife Badebec dead, and on the other side his sonne Pantagruel borne, so fair and so great," cries "Shall I weep?" After some natural vacillation, he decides rather to drink from his wine cellar and celebrate his playful infant (II:3, 182–83), creating what Bakhtin calls the characteristic carnivalesque motif of "pregnant death." Tennyson's grief naturally takes longer to assuage, but ultimately wedding bells replace funeral knells as "the feast, the speech, the glee," "the dance," and even "the foaming grape of eastern France" all conspire to rejoice in "the perfect rose" of his sister Emily on her marriage or deflowering day (Epilogue). And the much more clearly carnivalesque context of *The Old Curiosity Shop* likewise seems ultimately to affirm the gay ascendant power of "the rosy" and the cribbage game over the grave collective death wishes of Nell and her maudlin mourners. Thus, Dickens seems to say, the greatest pity is sorrowful rejection of a playful universe; the greatest prize (in almost Buddhist fashion) is playful participation in a sorrowful universe. And it is almost as if that miraculous invocation in Rabelais' Prologue, "hearken joltheads . . . or dickens take ye," becomes a time capsule dedicated to Dickens three hundred years later, one provoking him to revive the carnivalesque spirit for his own renewal as well as for the renaissance of his Victorian culture.[14]

Turning to Banks's essay, we should note at the outset that his introductory appraisal of Rabelais' "illimitable" personality could just as easily have been written about the equally fun-loving Inimitable Dickens: "No man had a keener sense of ridicule—a more discursive habit of fun. The one was mentally electric: it only required that his eye should touch the object. The other was illimitable. Neither could the world or reality chill it, nor the world of imagination exhaust it. Everything his intellect chose to magnetise became fun" (Nov. 529). And although Banks's description of Rabelais' readership is meant to be exclusive because of the author's erudition (and "grossest" indecency), his various categories of uncommon readers (Nov. 520–21) ironically attest to the popularity of both Rabelais and Dickens with uncommon and common readers alike.[15] Banks further argues that Rabelais played the role of "mere prattling buffoon" to avoid "popular resentment" against his radical ideology: "the monstrous buffoonery with which some of the noblest passages of sublimest truth are surrounded was necessary for his protection" (517). Bakhtin conversely argues, as one could also argue about Dickens, that the very buffoonery, which is intimately aligned to the "popular" world, itself creates the "passages of sublimest truth."

For instance, Banks cites Rabelais' general emphasis on "bodily refection,—that is . . . eating and drinking" and his specific (and crucial) highlighting of "that dialogue of Plato's which is entitled 'The Banquet' " (516) in the very first sentence of *Gargantua and Pantagruel*. The complete reference is significant not only for its introduction of the motif of *curiosities*, but also for its relevant celebration of the theme of philosophic feasting or table talk, which is so meaningful in Rabelais and *The Old Curiosity Shop*.[16] In fact, the dramatics and dialogics of *The Symposium* and its grand debate on love seem clearly and repeatedly echoed in both Rabelais' and Dickens' mutual devotion to feast days. Thus, of particular interest is the allusion in chapter 8 of book 1 to a specific curiosity, Gargantua's prized medallion "wherein was portrayed a man's body with two heads, looking towards one another, foure armes, foure feet, two arses, such as Plato, in *Symposio*, sayes was the mystical beginning of mans nature" (31–32). In *The Symposium* itself, Aristophanes initially misses his turn to philosophize on love because he has eaten too much and too quickly and is thus temporarily afflicted with the hiccups and must wait until after Eryximachus has delivered his turgidly technical and logical analysis of love—even though the satirist's eating disorder itself ironically prefigures his own more earthy and carnal approach. Aristophanes' somatic perspective involves, of course, the myth of the original "circle men" or androgynes: "each human being was a rounded whole, with double back and flanks forming a complete circle," which image itself, captured on the medallion in Rabelais, playfully suggests an elemental creature—we might even call it *Quilpnell*—like the primitive coupling of the female beauty and the male beast in Henry Fuseli's "The Nightmare."[17] One may blame Descartes' dualism for originally splitting Eros and Logos, but Aristophanes implies that the rupture came earlier and was perhaps due to hair-splitting logic like that of Eryximachus.[18] At any rate, the primal-circle men represent no dreadful nightmare but only delightful disorder, if not elemental harmony, which is why the newer dispensation of Olympians so feared them. Modern cultures, however, can only discover the latent legacy of the circle men in the leapfrogging somersault or cartwheel so dear to both Rabelais and Dickens: "when they wanted to run quickly they used all their eight limbs, and turned rapidly over and over in a circle, like tumblers who perform a cart-wheel and return to an upright position" (Plato 59).

Banks's lengthy section on Theleme provides several examples of Rabelais' love of leaping, and Bakhtin repeatedly sees this paradigmatic act as the inversive-subversive essence of life-integrating and death-transcending carnivalesque play. Like the juggling and acrobatics in *Hard Times*, the simply spellbinding game of red and black in *Nicholas Nickleby*, or Dickens' repeated motif of leapfrogging tombstones, the cartwheel is a microcosmic game miming cosmic harmony:

> [The] simplest expression [of] the primeval phenomenon of popular humor [is] the cartwheel, which by the continual rotation of the upper and lower parts suggests the rotation of earth and sky. This is manifested in other movements of the clown: the buttocks persistently trying to take the place of the head and the head that of the buttocks. . . . All these gay leaps and bounds are as ambivalent as the underworld itself. Harlequin's somersaults are topographical; their points of orientation are heaven, earth, the underworld, the top and the bottom. They represent an interplay, a substitution of the face by the buttocks; in other words, the theme of descent into hell is implicit in this simple acrobatic feat.   (353, 396–97)

The Old Curiosity Shop, of course, is replete with strolling (and even spelunking) players who double as cartwheeling whirling dervishes. Thus Punch, Whisker the pony, Kit, Quilp, and Swiveller all particularly enjoy "the ecstasy of sommersets on the pavement" (49:365). But this seems especially true of little Tom Scott, the curious wharf boy who always stands on his head, thereby frustrating and fascinating his dwarfish master until the end of the novel, when he relapses to his "natural taste for tumbling" (5:41) and "began to tumble for his bread" happily ever after. In fact, "he assumed the name of an Italian image lad, with whom he had become acquainted; and afterwards tumbled with extraordinary success, and to overflowing audiences." Ever subversive as well as inversive, ludically loyal Tom is indeed all alone in "shedding tears upon the inquest" of Quilp and betraying "a strong desire to assault the jury," whereupon he is dismissed by that most unplayful "court" and must be content with "standing on his head upon the [outside window] sill, until he was dexterously tilted upon his feet again by a cautious beadle" (Chapter the Last 549). And though Tom's tumbling, circular kinetics prefigure the Swiveller's replaying of the legend of "Our Lady's Tumbler," for Aristophanes, the "circular shape" and the "hoop-like method of progression" of the cartwheeling androgynes illustrate the truly playful source (and model) of human love: "It is from this distant epoch, then, that we may date the innate love which human beings feel for one another, the love which restores us to our ancient state by attempting to weld two beings into one and to heal the wounds which humanity suffered (Plato 60, 62).[19]

But to return to Banks's essay, he at least footnotes the "*in vino veritas*" (July 64) motif which figures so centrally in Rabelais and Dickens and which seems significant in Quilp's and Swiveller's pantagruelism. In emphasizing Gargantua's exemplary education at Theleme, Banks also quotes the cardinal commandment of that (mis)rule: "DO WHAT THOU WILT" (Nov. 520), which of course Quilp, much like Panurge, embodies even though as imp of the perverse he will also act "contrariwise" like some Wonderland creature. For example, he characteristically chides his mother-in-law, Mrs. Jiniwin, because she and her crone cronies engage in a carnivalesque *caquet* (Bakhtin 105–06), cackling the forbidden feminist doctrine that Mrs. Quilp "has a right to do as *she* likes" (4:35, emphasis added). At any rate, in Banks's final installment, he quotes generously from the Theleme episodes dramatizing Gargantua's education or re-education away from the grave, academic theorizing of his former scholastic pedagogues. These lengthy citations (July 77–80) all deal with the central role of feasting and frolic—"so many gammons" of both bacon and ball-playing—in one's educational growth, which documents that Rabelais, like Dickens, promotes a theory of playful education because it integrates town and gown, the life of the academy with the ludic action of life itself. And as the mentorship of *Gymnast* implies, the etymological link between the European *gymnasium* and the classroom is literally realized in Gargantua's seemingly endless series of scholastic somersaults: "at one leap he would skip over a ditch, spring over a hedge, mount six paces upon a wall, ramp and grapple after this fashion up against a window" (79) as a Rabelaisian precursor of Tom Scott.

The five different schools in *The Old Curiosity Shop* provide relevant variations on this education trope, ranging from the conventional connections between reading and writing on the one hand, to something like what Carroll's undersea, carnivalesque curriculum terms "Reeling and Writhing" (129) on the other. Except for the probable pun on its "dumb-bells," the Wackles' "Ladies' Seminary" is decidedly uncarnivalesque with its "corporal punishment, fasting, and other tortures and terrors"—though Sophy's class on "general fascination" (8:63) would have possibilities for Carroll. The "Boarding and Day Establishment" of Miss Monflathers severely frowns upon all "gymnastic exercise" (27:201) as a dangerous surrender to carnivalesque "impulse" over scholastic "decorum," even though it pompously preaches "healthful play" after Dr. Watt's verses. For the man-hating Monflathers, strenuous physical exercise, much like laboring in a wax museum, is "very naughty and unfeminine, and a perversion," so that it is little wonder that "the brightest glory of Miss Monflather's school" resembles "some extraordinary reversal of the Laws of Nature" (31:235–37). The student-athlete dying young at Mr. Marston's first school, on the other hand, had developed "in his learning and his sports too" (24:184). But the "half-holiday" granted his classmates in his honor, even though they dream of "plunging into the woods, and being wild boys and savages," is finally unlike Kit's and Barbara's holiday at Astley's Circus because it actually terminates in the elegiac twilight vision of "the boys at play upon the green" (25:188–92). This image reads more plaintively than the desertions in Goldsmith and rather recalls the increasing sense of lament over lost play fields and feelings in Blake's "The Ecchoing Green" and "Nurse's Song" of Experience, where twilight play portends the bittersweet demise of innocence and the reasonable realization that inevitably "our sports have an end." Blake's envious Nurse teaches her wards that "Your spring & your day are wasted in play," and the tone here is different than the essential Rabelaisian spirit and really much closer to Carroll's playfully and plaintively curious "dream child moving through a land / Of wonders wild and new" in his disjunctive framing verses. In fact, tiny Alice's universal dreams so fear a rude awakening to reality that, echoing major tropes associated with tiny Nell, they appear "Like Pilgrim's withered wreath of flowers / Pluck'ed in a far-off land" (23).

Thus, most of the literal educational motifs in *The Old Curiosity Shop* seem to remind us of little Nell among her curiosities and the way she finally shuns the playful, peripatetic value of these strolling, grotesque realities, just as the small boy from Marston's second school vows "to forsake his playmates and his sports to bear her company" (55:413). Nell's pilgrimage "towards the West" (43:321), like Pantagruel's toward the western underworld concealing the Holy Bottle, finally arrives at this parish school.[20] Even though it appears alive with gymnastic "leapings, scufflings, or turnings" (52:393), Marston's academy still suffers from the Bachelor's regressive identification with the play motifs he feels are denied to adults and from his patronizing belief that education regrettably must replace play learning with book learning rather than trying to accommodate if not reconcile both skills as at Theleme. Unlike Rabelais' utopian gymnasium, Marston's seems simply and nostalgically to lament the death of the play impulse rather than understand that play can survive to expand Life and can even, as Punch's tumble with the Skeleton illustrates, teach Death a hard lesson. Thus, like Mrs. Jarley's wax Grimaldi who transforms into a famous grammarian, gymnastic Panurge and Punch are each play docents teaching us that games both entertain and educate, while Schoolmaster Marston and the administrative Bachelor can only mourn the fact that their brand of pedagogy must preclude play.

Dickens' educational ideal is clearly his final and presumably antic academy, the nameless "school of his selection" where, "in redemption of the vow he had made upon his" near deathbed, Dick Swiveller enrolls the Marchioness. In fact, he enrolls her under the mysterious name of "Sophronia Sphynx," which seems somehow to recall and redress his earlier staggerers with Sophy Wackles and "the sphinx" Sally Brass. Though "the expenses of her education" are dear, Dick sacrifices; and his dear Marchioness matriculates marvelously, like Gargantua at Theleme, "as she soon distanced all competitors" in her gymnasium, raising herself repeatedly to "a higher grade." Though there is no real description of this "establishment" of higher learning, it becomes a bona fide finishing school for the Marchioness, who emerges from it resplendent at nineteen, "good-looking, clever, and good-humoured." Further, its well-rounded curricular care prepares its graduate to become Dick's bride, "looking more smiling and fresh than ever." It may even be that its liberal education, like that at Theleme which also prepared studymates to "entertain that mutual love till the very last day of their life, in no less vigour and fervency, then [sic] at the very day of their wedding" (I:53, 164), finally instructed the Marchioness in 'the mysteries of cribbage" since happily ever after the newlyweds "played many hundred thousand games of cribbage." Such unbounded play recalls Rabelais and the carnivalesque's infinite delight in infinite digits (Rabelais and His World 464–65). No wonder "that upon every anniversary of the day on which he found her in his sick-room," Dick—the Marchioness's first play mentor—and his star player-pupil enjoy "great glorification" (Chapter the Last:551–52) together. Thus, to paraphrase Dickens' educational views more as a carnivalesque process than as a categorical proposition, we can conclude that the Teacher must become a Trickster, just as the student must become "silly." Indeed, Robert L. Pelton's study of the Trickster shares much with Bakhtin's heuristic non-theory of the carnivalesque and with Dick Swiveller's educational "nonsense": "the trickster incarnates in every culture the oxymoronic imagination at play, literally 'fooling around' to discover new paradigms and even new logics. As such he reveals man's freedom to shape the world just because it actively offers itself to him—even if he must trick it to make it come across" (272).

III

Such imaginative free play represents, of course, *curiosity*, and Banks's article repeatedly and significantly invokes this term. For example, Banks celebrates the process of what Bacon dubs " 'the pleasure of curiosity' " (July 72) and what he himself admires as "the torch of Arabian curiosity" (68), which helped illuminate the pyramids for Europe.[21] Rabelais clearly typifies what again Bacon terms " 'circle-learning,' " which " 'gives the mind a freedom' " and promotes " 'exercising the understanding in the several ways of inquiry and reasoning' " so as to follow " 'dexterously . . . the bents and turns of [a] matter in all its researches' " (note*, 65–66). Consequently, Arnold's more celebrated discussion of playful curiosity in "The Function of Criticism at the Present Time" (1865) presumably itself benefited from what might now be called the tacit Rabelais-Banks-Dickens collaboration. At least, Arnold's Victorian attack on "the practical English nature" recalls the scholarly contest of signs in Rabelais between Thaumast, "a great Scholar of England," and the ludimagister Panurge as both vie to plumb "the bottom of that undrainable Well, where Heraclitus says the truth lies hidden," which image, as suggested above, also figures prominently in *The Old Curiosity Shop*. In the novel, many curious questers "would strip fair Truth" and so drown in "the waters of her well" (54:400) without, I think, discovering that, like the myth of the divine child, the Heraclitean notion of Time is "the playing boy . . . who possesses the supreme power in the universe" (Bakhtin 82). In the opening chapter of *Master Humphrey's Clock*, the good Master himself plays trickster "as a whet to the curiosity of his neighbors" (7), and yet ironically the last trick seems to be played against men like this same "single gentleman" and Nell's other celibate male mourners who are gratuitously glad that for once perfect innocence can be perpetually frozen: "We are alchemists who would extract the essence of perpetual youth from dust and ashes, tempt coy Truth in many light and airy forms from the bottom of her well" (11).

No, the unholy trinity of Quilp, Swiveller, and Kit—a disjunctive example of the carnivalesque *farce jouée à trois personnages* (Bakhtin 467)—surely practices the truth of its game gospel more perceptively and persuasively than the pulpiteering, tiresome trinity of the Schoolmaster, Sexton, and Bachelor preaches its grave gospel, just as Panurge's creatively complicated design of what the cockney Mr. Chuckster might call "taking a sight" or even "cocking a snook" (38:283) completely disarms all "the Lepers of Britanie."[22] When Panurge "began to shake his faire Codpiece, shewing it to Thaumast," this playful pièce de résistance signals his certain semiotic victory, and the out-played Englishman is courteous enough to admit that Panurge's "signification of the signes" or better "fooleries" has "discovered the very true Well, Fountain, and Abysse of the Encyclopedia of learning" (II:18–20, 251–62). In the same way, the ever "curious" Dick Swiveller figuratively finds his truth in the wine cellar with the Marchioness, where it is also invariably discovered in Rabelais, which demonstrates the etymological if not abyssal truth that just as *antique* and *antic* share the common semantic heritage of being fantastic and grotesque, so too *curiosity* is related to *courtesy* and hence *courting* since all three take great care (*cura*) in their common play with truth. And Arnold's related discussion of "the word *curiosity*" and the peculiarly English "disparaging" of the "free play of the mind upon all subjects" (407), like Bakhtin's treatment of the carnivalesque, suggests that literary criticism has mistakenly neglected this form of play, and yet to be successful, criticism must not only understand curiosity, it must also practice it.[23]

At Theleme Abbey, Rabelais plays ambiguously with these same concepts as he seems to identify *instinct* with "vertuous actions" and *honour* with "vice" so that the Humanity courses in what we might call this *Panversity* all demand a prerequisite in Curiosity, "for it is agreeable with the nature of man to long after things forbidden, and to desire what is denied us." There-fore, "if any of the gallants or Ladies should say, Let us drink, they would all drink: if any one of them had said, Let us play, they all played" (I:57, 163). Further, it would seem that added units in Curiosity are required for a major in Literary Criticism since the lengthy and bedeviling "Prophetic Rid-dle," which was significantly "found under the ground . . . ingraven in a copper plate" and which heads Rabelais' next chapter, reads infernally or at least indeterminately like so many Proverbs of Hell. This cameo inset piece seems in no way as clearly allegorical as the paired invitations and invectives traced by *"The Inscription set upon the great Gate of Thélème"* comprising all of chapter 54. In other words, though Bakhtin is generally correct in believing that "Thélème is the opposite of a monastery; that which is forbid-den in the monastery is permitted and even prescribed in Thélème" (412), the problem still remains of determining just what is prescribed and what is proscribed by the underground inversive-subversive text. The encoded "DO WHAT THOU WILT" may even suggest "READ WHAT THOU WILT" and yet REMEMBER that your reflections are always self-reflections. Thus, Gargantua honestly yet regretfully reads "this aenigmatical monument" as a warning against "carnal nature and depraved nature" or doing what you wilt. On the other hand, the presumably wiser monk replies, "make upon it as many grave allegories and glosses as you will, and dote upon it you and the rest of the world as long as you please: for my part, I can conceive no other meaning in it, but a description of a set at tennis in dark and obscure termes,'' which really isn't a bad way to approach the carnivalesque in Dickens as long as one recalls the play "meaning" of a set at tennis. The monk then proceeds in mock scholastic style to pursue the play allegory in this dark conceit—Rabelais' version of Jabberwocky. However, after eventually deducing that "the Globe terrestrial is the tennis-ball,'' he concludes with a model reading that suggests that games may not be life and cannot be critically enjoyed, but life certainly is a curious game and the best literary criticism of *Gargantua and Pantagruel* (and of *The Old Curiosity Shop*) is a form of playful curiosity which accepts the related mysteries of life and literature with a nonjudgmental joie de vivre: "After playing, when the game is done, they refresh themselves before a clear fire, and change their shirts: and very willingly they make all good cheer, but most merrily those that have gained: And so, farewell'' (167–68).

One of the comparable subjects curiously if not hermeneutically played with in *The Old Curiosity Shop* is the *Gothic* (and indeed all *grotesque* forms) whose spirit is particularly symbolized in that "monument of ruin" (53:397), the church which seems the enshrined goal of Nell's pilgrimage and whose architecture is so memorably illustrated in the text by George Cattermole. In fact, this Gothic decor seems an elaboration of the first illustration of Nell among the curiosities, the vision of which had initially sparked Dickens' imagination and which lingers as a curiously haunting reminder of the apparent dualisms energizing this novel. In Dickens' words, "in writing the book, I had it always in my fancy to surround the lonely figure of the child with grotesque and wild, but not impossible, companions, and to gather about her innocent face and pure intentions, associates as strange and uncongenial as the grim objects that are about her bed when her history is first foreshadowed'' (Preface xii). Ruskin's apt commentary "On the Nature of the Gothic" (1853) itself curiously recalls much of Dickens' novel and reminds us how intimately Gothic dualisms of light and dark or monstrous gargoyle and gentle madonna depend upon each other. Ruskin, even more than Dickens, is enamoured of Quilpine "Grotesqueness," that is, "creations of ungainly shape and rigid limb, but full of wolfish life, fierce as is the winds that beat, and changeful as the clouds that shade them" (366).[24] In fact, Ruskin's dramatization of Gothic curiosity recalls the same primary if not primal process in Dickens and suggests how central this *Sehnsucht* is to the ultimate meaning of *The Old*

Curiosity Shop and its Rabelaisian 'philosophy of dreams,'' which Swiveller associates with the real "mysteries of cribbage" (64:475):

> It is that strange *disquietude* of the Gothic spirit that is its greatness; that restlessness of the dreaming mind, that wanders hither and thither among the niches, and flickers feverishly around the pinnacles, and frets and fades in labyrinthine knots and shadows along wall and roof, and yet is not satisifed, nor shall yet be satisfied.   (382–83)

Significantly, Ruskin's commentary on medieval cosmological architecture anticipates Bakhtin's discussion of Rabelais' *theatrum mundi* "in architectural terms," especially "towers and subterranean passages" (318) and the prevalent motif of "the carnivalesque upside down" or "reconstruction of space," which like the somersault reverses established values as the Gothic also strives to do in its analogous if not identical celebration of grotesque or concave grotto energies.[25] In *The Old Curiosity Shop*, Quilp of Tower Hill appears as "some monstrous image" or the dream incarnation of an "old statue" fallen from a city arch, and yet he is also the "demon" of the pit if not ironically the true genius of the well which so fascinates Nell. She even experiences "a mingled sensation of curiosity and fear" when Quilp appears as the gargoyle or *gay monster* and then dreams she is "hemmed in by a legion of Quilps" (27:207–08). Stranger still, Quilp is not just associated with heights and depths. He is also linked to another apparent nightmare opposite when her Grandfather invades Nell's bedroom, "creeping along the floor" with "wandering hands" as she is "troubled by dreams of falling from high towers" and strange "murmurs" haunt "the walls and ceiling" (30:228–29), which uncannily replays the image of Quilp so curiously asleep in Nell's bed "that he seems to be standing on his head" (12:96). Both of these dream images curiously reconstruct and perversely valorize space.

The mysterious point here is crucial to the reader's experience of the novel and the way Rabelais helps clarify this experience. It is not simply that Dickens and Rabelais are kindred spirits with kindred familiars and that Banks's citation of the list of curiosities or "wanton toyish figures," especially the "capricious" jeweled boxes (Nov. 516) appearing in Rabelais' opening paragraph, reappears in *The Old Curiosity Shop* as the sexton's other art ("miniature boxes, carved in a homely manner," 53:396) and as Mr. Chuckster's "snuff-box" ("Ornamented with a fox's head curiously carved in brass," 53:416), though like the cauldron of tripe all three sets of curious enclosures reflect grotesque play motifs. It is not even that the entire carnivalesque epic of Rabelais revels in literal curiosities like the "several curiosities" Pantagruel sends Gargantua, which make up the subject of the fourth chapter of book 4, or that Bakhtin suggests that the *curiosité* itself is a kind of subgenre (246), that Rabelais himself delighted "in curiosities, in rare and unusual objects" (445) related to the medieval fascination with the "grotesque concept of the body" and its "relics" (349), or that the curious "motley" motif of the Wild Man army reflects the theme "of the inside-out and turn-about" or "gay monster" like Quilp, who helps exercise and exorcise the terror of time, death, and hell (391).[26] Ironically, Bakhtin summarily dismisses what is perhaps his most pertinent and perceptive lead. After relevantly discussing "curiosities" in the neglected literature of folk culture, he simply notes his fellow Russian, O. Freidenberg, and his insight that such "antique specimens" significantly reflect "the spirit of prelogical thought," which seems so crucial to Dickens' sense of the *uncanny*, but which Bakhtin neglects as irrelevant to folk humor, even though it "remains almost unexplored" (54).

In this sense, most commentators on *The Old Curiosity Shop* have emphasized the significance of the *principle of contrast* in the novel but have not examined its literary, philosophical, and psychological relationships to the *process of curiosity* or to Bakhtin's point that "Rabelais continually used the traditional folklore method of contrast, the 'inside out,' the 'positive negation' " (403) to reinforce his primary belief in "the dual-bodied world of becoming" (420). And Dickens himself significantly reinforced this theme of curious contrasts in the 1841 single-volume edition of the novel by adding a pivotal statement linking Nell's observation of the sexton and his curiosity boxes to her vertical tour of the Gothic church: "Everything in our lives, whether of good or evil, affects us most by contrast" (Penguin edition 53:493). Initially, such a proposition seems simply but accurately to reflect what Northrop Frye calls the endemic *allegro* and *penseroso* "contrast of cadences in romance" (83–84). And if read quickly (just as a hurried reading of *The Old Curiosity Shop* might also suggest), Frye's clearly relevant commentary in *the Secular Scripture* seems to depend upon a very simple if insightful contrast between polar oppositions reminiscent of Nell and Quilp:

> The characterization of romance is really a feature of its mental landscape. Its heroes and villains exist primarily to symbolize a contrast between two worlds, one above the level of ordinary experience, the other below it. There is, first, a world associated with happiness, security, and peace; the emphasis is often thrown on childhood or on an "innocent" or pre-genital period of youth, and the images are those of spring and summer, flowers and sunshine. I shall call this world the idyllic world. The other is a world of exciting adventures, but adventures, which involve separation, loneliness, humiliation, pain, and the threat of more pain. I shall call this the demonic or night world.

Because of the powerful polarizing tendency in romance, we are usually carried
directly from one to the other.   (53)

Yet Frye's subsequent discussion of the relevance of play to romance's
apparent binary structure (56), especially his notation that "cards and dice
are common in descent narratives, because of their overtones of fatality and
chance" (124; see also 156), his treatment of Quilpine "*forza* and *froda*,
where violence and guile are coiled up within each other like the yin-and-
yang emblem of Oriental symbolism" (87), and particularly his elaboration
of the centrality of the Proserpine myth with its attendant motifs of demon
lover, food, death, and health (86–87) and the related significance of the link
between the value of the Heroine's virginity and a "well-adjusted sexual life"
(79–80) all suggest how unstable the apparently contrasting worlds of romance
are in a work like *The Old Curiosity Shop*. Such genre instability, as introduced earlier, is not only compatible with Bakhtin's particular notion of
dialogic structure but reinforces the relevance of Rabelais to *The Old Curiosity
Shop*. For Bakhtin, in fact, the dialogic pairs of apparent contraries in *Gargantua and Pantagruel* reflect "one of the folkloric roots of the novel and of its
specific dialogue," and these same pairs often appear "in circus sideshows,"
suggesting that the motley carnival figures in Dickens replay the origins of the
novel itself and, for Bakhtin (434), its essentially polyphonic or *pangeneric*
structure.

As a (generally) carnivalesque and (particularly) Gothic romance, *The Old
Curiosity Shop* text is an old curiosity shop where the buying reader must
beware discovering himself or herself among the merchandise. Thus reading
window shoppers are actually peering through the looking glass at a wonderland of interdependent metaphysical and mental projections. What we perceive are apparently polarized contrasts: Quilp-Nell, Codlin-Short, dwarfs-
giants, gardens-graves, light-dark, innocence-experience, love-death, dream-
reality, play-work. But again the process of curiosity teaches us that actually
what we see self-reflected, in what Frye calls this "mental landscape," are
primary identities. And the curious dialogic play between these elusive and
delusive contrasts establishes protean relationships, like the old giants waiting
upon the dwarfs, which flicker from the equivocal, to the analogous, to the
univocal. In other words, though we may tend to think of (a) *curiosity* as a
permanent state rather than a processual desire or *Sehnsucht*, it is actually
both at the same time. Nell famously enjoys "a curious kind of pleasure in
lingering among [the] houses of the dead" (17:128), and yet (or consequently?) children see this "wax-work child" (31:235) herself as "an important item of the curiosities" (28:211) of Mrs. Jarley. Thus, she who is

curious is herself a curiosity—at least to the object of her curiosity as Alice relevantly learns from the Unicorn or as Carroll more explicitly suggests when he notes that "this curious child was very fond of pretending to be two people" (33). In other words, we are all most curious about those strange things which are secretly most familiar to us, which insight becomes almost conventional wisdom in Gothic literature where a curious demon like Dracula "may not enter anywhere at the first, unless there be some one of the household who bid him to come; though afterwards he can come as he please" (Stoker 264). When her Grandfather peers at the face of Nell's corpse "as if impelled by some momentary recollection or curiosity" (71:534), one profound implication is that curiosity ambiguously represents *both* primal memory and desire. Every *Sehnsucht* actually re-presents a homesickness.

Consequently and finally, then, curiosity is analogous if not synonymous with Freud's notion of the *uncanny*.[27] In his essay on "The Uncanny" (*"Die Unheimlich"*), Freud relevantly diagnoses this kind of curiosity which occurs when "the fear of death" conjures the appearance of haunting yet curiously fascinating doubles like Quilp. He posits that "this invention of doubling as a preservation against extinction has its counterpart in the language of dreams" (141), as it also clearly does in the language of romance and carnivalesque literature. Thus, "many people experience the feeling [of uncanny curiosity] in the highest degree in relation to death and dead bodies, to the return of the dead, and to spirits and ghosts" (149), as Dickens may have in his fascination with the Paris Morgue—which fascination he even self-definitively labels as "inimitable" (Forster I:513, 517–18). For Freud, when one represses "home-sickness," or *heimlich* curiosity about prenatal existence in the womb, such curiosity reasserts itself in a "morbid anxiety" about posthumous existence in the tomb, or more particularly an *unheimlich* curiosity over harbingers of death who appear to be strangely familiar (148).

Paradoxically, then, nostalgic curiosity or *heimlich* desires for the paradisal beginnings of life and a curious dread of the infernal end of life subliminally overlap. And through an unconscious "repetition-compulsion," the curious personality projects contrasting doubles, like Nell and Quilp, whose *allegro* and *penseroso* impulses represent life and death simultaneously. "Thus *heimlich* is a word the meaning of which develops toward an ambivalence, until it finally coincides with its opposite, *unheimlich*" (131), just as the word *daimon* or alter ego developed into *demon*.[28] After his haunting vision of Nell asleep among the curiosities, Old Humphrey, *lying awake* back in his bedroom, muses that "it would be a curious speculation . . . to imagine her in

future life, holding her solitary way among a crowd of wild grotesque companions; the only pure, fresh, youthful object in the throng. It would be curious
to find———.'' Then he suppresses this curiosity about an uncanny ''region
on which I was little disposed to enter'' and so goes to sleep to ''court
forgetfulness,'' but finally finds himself compulsively repeating in dream
oblivion these ''same images'' of the uncanny curiosities playfully ''grinning
from wood and stone'' and the familiar ''beautiful child in her gentle slumber,
smiling through her light and sunny dreams'' (1:13–14). Thus, his uncanny
curiosity ultimately bids both of these contrasting familiars to enter the family
household of his mind and achieve some sort of carnivalesque reintegration,
the process of which unfolds as the rest of the novel develops.[29]

IV

Quilp, the plastic and playful shapeshifter, becomes the uncanny personification of this reflexive energy field of curiosity. More simply he represents
Otherness: the entire range of the unconscious (and of the ''carnivalesque
grotesque'' itself): ''the prime mover of the whole diabolical device''
(64:495). Indeed, with his ever ''comical expression of curiosity'' (50:373),
Quilp, ''the small lord of the creation'' (4:37), is not just a demiurgic prime
mover, but his repeated elementalism suggests he is grotesquely playful *prima
materia* itself: ''the evil genius of the cellars come from underground upon
some work of mischief'' (48:356). Consequently, in trying to evaluate Quilp
who is figuratively ''grottoed at the seams'' (15:115), one must always bear
in mind the blessing of Bacbuc, Rabelais' Priestess of the Holy Bottle, when
she glorifies ''the Subterranean Ruler'' and the ''excellent Things'' he provides for Proserpine: ''the greatest Treasures, and most admirable Things,
are hidden under Ground, and not without reason'' (V:48, 422–23).[30] If, then,
the reader is confused or disturbed that so many characters seem cursed by
the monstrous mark of Quilp—Punch's nose and hump, Old Humphrey's
hunchback, the Garlands' congenital clubfoot, Nell's diminutive size, and the
Marchioness's very bloodline, Rabelais reveals that such monstrosities may
be miraculous blessings in disguise. This is especially true insofar as Swiveller
inherits Quilp's playfully magic motion, magic potion, and particularly his
magical, gaming ''Genie'' (64:475) of a daughter who, like Proserpine, rises
from ''somewhere in the bowels of the earth'' (36:271) just as all Pantagruelian treasures are ''hid within the Bowels of the Earth'' (V:48, 423). In this

sense, E. A. Dyson is clearly insightful in asking, "isn't Quilp, after all, a game with the reader?" (115).[31]

Though Quilp is often associated with the word *mystery* (besides *monster* and *grotesque*) so that "any index to his mood or meaning" remains "a perfect blank" (48:357), his carnivalesque origins imply that he may ultimately be no more indeterminate than the Wild Man of folklore or Dame Nature herself—*Physis* in Rabelais, who eventually absorbs "Antiphysis, who ever was the Counterpart of Nature" (II:32, 188). Replaying the Wild Man figure, Quilp "likes a little wildness. I was wild myself once" (23:175) and seems to project his own priapic power onto Swiveller, "being pretty well accustomed to the agricultural pursuits of sowing wild oats" (33:249). "In an instant" the dwarf can even transform into an "uproarious, reckless little savage" (51:384), especially at the Wilderness tavern. And the famous illustration captioned "Quilp's Grotesque Politeness" particularly captures the paradox of the Wild Man's many transformations as the hirsute but humble bowing figure almost cons Dickens' favorite "Grimaldi reflex," all the while flanked on the left by the words *MAN/BEAST* over the scrawled cartoon of a king (or is it the "mystery devil" *Erl-King*, parent of "the carnivalesque figure of the Harlequin"? Bakhtin 266–67) and on the right by a carved game board and the phonetic or natural spelling *SKITLS* (facing 447), recalling the Wild Man's essential roots in the world of play.[32] The dancing forest fool is traditionally a "size shifter" or Trickster who "may assume the guise of both dwarfs and giants" (Berenheimer 44–47), just as Quilp characteristically capers in "a kind of demon dance" (21:165), and his "forbidding aspect" seems "so low in stature as to be quite a dwarf, though his head and face were large enough for the body of a giant" (3:22). Even his first home on Tower Hill and his repeated associations with protean fire link this playful pyromaniac with the firework displays of the Wild Man since Strutt indicates that in the eighteenth century Tower Hill was famed for its "grand firework" festivities (297).

Further, Quilp playfully incarnates Nature in a triple carnivalesque sense: as physical, bodily nature, as the external, natural world, and as a kind of universal, pantheistic reality; and together all of these function in a type of satyr play to criticize and correct everything that is unnatural or "Antiphysis," that is, both the self-proclaimed and the secret enemies of the life force of Pan or Eros. Bakhtin devotes a lengthy chapter of his book on Rabelais to "The Grotesque Image of the Body and Its Sources" (303–67), and his main points here are that carnal-carnivalesque cavities and protuberances, like the mouth and nose, demonstrate the topsy-turvy correspondences which integrate the upper and "lower stratum" of the body (anal mouth and phallic nose), which link the human body with the geological corpus of caves and mountains, and which ultimately reflect the cosmic relationships between the processes of death and those of birth. Quilp's prodigious tongue and cavernous mouth may not contain tennis courts (and indeed entire echoing greens) like Pantagruel's gullet-gorge (I:2, 32), but his "horribly grotesque and distorted face with the tongue lolling out" repeatedly bears *lower body* connotations, particularly when he smokes cigars in Nell's bed or vehemently protests about the exact shape of his curious nose.[33] And like Life's voracious appetites, his are truly gargantuan:

> he ate hard eggs, shell and all, devoured gigantic prawns with the heads and tails on, chewed tobacco and watercresses at the same time and with extraordinary greediness, drank boiling tea without winking, bit his fork and spoon till they bent again, and in short performed so many horrifying and uncommon acts that the women were nearly frightened out of their wits, and began to doubt if he were really a human creature.   (5:40)

Analogously, then, Quilp is associated not only with the Wild Man and all animal forms but with the complete range of natural phenomena because, as Bakhtin explains,

> the grotesque body is cosmic and universal. It stresses elements common to the entire cosmos: earth, water, fire, air; it is directly related to the sun, to the stars. It contains the signs of the zodiac. It reflects the cosmic hierarchy. This body can merge with various natural phenomena, with mountains, rivers, seas, islands, and continents. It can fill the entire universe.   (318)

At no time are Quilp's ties with the playful natural elements more meaningfully apparent than at the moment of his apparent death, which ultimately seems more triumphantly transcendent than terminal, especially when compared with the narrator's later dispassionate recollection of Trent's drowning or with Nell's static death scene. In fact, this scene parodies the conventional deathbed bromide *as in life so in death* as it reprises Quilp's carnivalesque qualities with his "yell," his "wild" eyes, the repeated emphasis on his "corpse" or "carcass," and the fact that in true Pantagruelian, "all-thirsty" fashion, "the strong tide filled his throat" when his act of drowning seems to drink in the entire universe symbolized by each "element"—"mud," "gust of wind," "hundred fires," and "the resistless water" itself. And yet like Quilp the elements seem to be in a process of eternal and interchangeable becoming—"slippery," "slimy," and culminating in a "swamp" as the "sky was red with flame, and the water . . . tinged with the sullen light as it flowed along" (in Hablot Browne's illustration *"The End of Quilp"* facing 67:503, the entwined Quilp and elements are almost indistinguishable). Finally significant is the repeated play imagery, as the elements "toyed and sported" with Quilp's body, and significantly, "the hair, stirred by the damp breeze, played in a kind of mockery of death—such a mockery as the dead man himself would have delighted in when alive" (67:510).[34]

The key sense here is playing in "mockery of death" since the phenomenology and meaning of death have been crucial topics throughout the novel—personified, in fact, in "the freaks of Punch . . . perched cross-legged upon a tombstone"—and Quilp himself had earlier played in "mockery of death" after the false reports of his drowning. In some versions of the Punch drama, the mocking puppet is even reported drowned, but later of course he himself kills Death, the Skeleton. In Rabelais, Pantagruel relevantly discusses with Macrobius and Epistemon the natural lamentation that ensues upon the deaths of heroes: "both the Continent and adjacent Islands are annoyed with great Commotions; in the Air, Fogs, Darkness, Thunder, Hail; Tremblings, Pulsations, Arietations of the Earth; Storms and Hurricanes at Sea" (IV:26, 174). But again, Panurge's playful art helps Epistemon return from death where he "had spoken with Lucifer familiarly, and had been very merry in hell," for much like Quilp, all "the devils were boone companions, and merry fellowes." In fact, Epistemon even quotes a verse written as Epictetus' motto which suggests that the ability "To leap and dance, to sport and play" (II:30, 295–300) seems to cure or at least simply contain and control the condition of death.[35] For Bakhtin, such "gay and free play" is ever "full of deep meaning" (207), which here could suggest the inevitable rising of Quilp as spring always follows winter, or it could imply the resurrection of Quilp's spirit in another who delights in spirits, or the resurrection of another, like the almost dying Swiveller, through the agency of Quilp personified in his daughter.[36] As James Hillman relevantly puts it in his "Essay on Pan," the "death of Pan supposedly coincided with the rise of love" (57). Or as Bakhtin argues, Death is always "pregnant death": "the dead body, blood as seed buried in the earth, rising for another life . . . is one of the oldest and most widespread themes" (327) of the carnivalesque as well as of many other ritualistic traditions.[37] When he enlarges upon Pascal's describing the Trickster as the " 'glory and refuse of the universe,' " Pelton wisely reminds us that renewal is particularly and relevantly part of this archetypal player's mythology. For Pelton the Trickster affirms the doubleness of the real and denies every one-dimensional image of it. If he struggles with the High God and causes pain and death to enter the world, spoiling primordial bliss, his quarrel is not with the divine order as such, but with a false human image of the sacred, one that cannot encompass suffering, disorder, and the ultimate mess of death. . . . [But when the Trickster demonstrates that death is subservient to life], then death's absoluteness of movement will guarantee life's eternal reirruption. . . . He uses death to stop death—social stasis or breakdown, cosmic rivalry and noncommunion.

(262–63)

In *Gargantua and Pantagruel*, "the Great God Pan" is "our All" and appropriately appears everywhere both linguistically in the *Pan*-prefix and literally, especially playing and piping the role of "the loving Shepherd" (IV:28, 179). In *The Old Curiosity Shop*, Quilp too plays this role and represents "all nature healthy" (69:524), though he also descends in the form of a *panic* attack upon characters as diversely unhealthy as Nell, Mrs. Jiniwin, and Sampson Brass. As Trickster he is "always cheating at cards" (23:177), and yet paradoxically he "plays a fairer game than" (9:73) most characters and readers imagine unless we recall Bakhtin's pertinent discussion of the carnivalesque's characteristic "single two-faced image" for the *unus mundus* (286) and the fact that, as personified in Pan, all of Rabelais' "ambivalent images are dual-bodied, dual-faced, pregnant" (409) like all of life itself. In the words of Pantagruel, "oftentimes the Angel of Satan is disguized and transformed into an Angel of Light" (III:14, 379), and consequently the reader must wonder whether the angel of light does not adopt the opposite mask in Quilp. Like all the puzzles in Rabelais, however, mercurial Quilp actually demands that we abandon reductively contrasting allegories of life altogether, and see rather that, like Pan, all life is manifold, pure process or becoming and thus wears diverse masks indiscriminately as Time devours us, or, like Heraclitus' boy, plays with us. Consequently, the only appropriate response to life must be to play back with it rather than to preach about it, or as the Sacred Bottle ultimately prophesies, to "Drink!" life to its fullest, remaining true to the meaning of Pantagruel's name—"All-Thirsty."

To pursue the relevant Pan mythology a moment longer, we should note here other relevant insights from James Hillman's monograph "An Essay on Pan" and from Edgar Wind's chapter on "Pan and Proteus" in *Pagan Mysteries in the Renaissance*, which particularly clarify Quilp's *Panurgic* role in the novel. For instance, Hillman discusses Pan's reincarnation as the playful "*kobold*, or little demon," who is "phallic, dwarf-like, fertile, both lucky and fearful" and linked with "concepts like hunch, intuition, uncanny feeling, or even prophecy" (59-60), much like Quilp. This association between intuition and *hunch*backs even recalls the old superstition that touching a hunchback's hump brings good luck. Further, as a nightmare incubus, Pan is associated with "hypermotor activity" (62), both as the strangling burden that depresses the dreamer and as the manic "cure" that casts off and exorcises the delusion in a paradoxical version of "like cures like" (50). Pan is also the perpetual *"observer"* of life's play, like the spying Quilp and his daughter forever at her keyhole, and this voyeuristic role is linked to his natural *curiosity* and the self-reflexive insight that finally "we are the observing Pan" (52). Moreover, "In every nymph there is a Pan, in every Pan a nymph" because "rawness and shyness go together" (54), like "instinct and inhibition" (55), which has already been suggested of the relationship between Quilp and his fleeing nymph Nell. In fact, Pan's natural habitat revolves between "mountain-top and grotto" (47–48) in the same way that the carnivalesque seeks playfully to neutralize all such false dichotomies. Thus, official systems treat Pan somewhat the way that Bakhtin believes critical canons have treated carnivalesque forms. Pan may be "turned into a Christian devil" (53) or sublimated into an uninformed preview of Christ, but for Hillman "all education, all religion, all therapy that does not recognize the identity of soul with instinct as presented by Pan, preferring either side to the other, insults Pan and will not heal" (62), just as any attempt to divorce carnivalesque play forms from literary criticism denies the fullness of (literary) life itself.

In somewhat related fashion, as Wind implies, the Humanists who repeatedly compare God to Pan as "an infinite sphere whose circumference is nowhere and whose center is everywhere" (183) actually adopt the trope of "The Concealed God," just as the Priestess of the Holy Bottle will adopt it later. And this image is dramatically captured in the relationship between Pan and Eros and between Pan and Proteus, as it is in the relationship between Quilp and Swiveller. Thus on the one hand, Hillman suggests that the "long tradition of wall and vase paintings [that] shows Eros and Pan wrestling" like Dick and Quilp has been wrongly interpreted to reinforce orthodox morality: "The contrast between the clean stripling Eros and the hirsute awkwardness of rustic paunchy Pan, with victory to Eros, was moralized to show the betterment of love to sex, refinement to rape, feeling to passion. Moreover, the victory of Eros over Pan could be philosophically allegorized to mean Love conquers All" (57). Such a monologic response creates, really, a false adversarial relationship between the two gods and their dialogic interplay, or as Hillman argues, "To go on judging our Pan-behavior in the light of love continues a suppression of instinctual qualities and an enmity towards nature that cannot but have psychopathological results" (57). It may even be that

Dickens falls partial victim to this kind of confusion since he clearly suggests the unique victory of Dick's creative power—and yet still, Quilp's natural resiliency perhaps finally does conquer all.

On the other hand, another way to envision the relationship between Quilp and Dick is in terms of that between Pan and Proteus. As Wind puts it, quoting Pico's "Orphic *Conclusiones*: 'He who cannot attract Pan, approaches Proteus in vain.' The advice to seek for the hidden Pan in the ever-changing Proteus refers to the principle of 'the whole in the part,' of the One inherent in the Many" (158). In other words, "The doctrine that Pan is hidden in Proteus, that mutability is the secret gate through which the universal invades the particular, deserves credit for a peculiar philosophical achievement" (176) whose Renaissance origins link it generally with the carnivalesque tradition and particularly with the fact that we cannot fully understand Quilp's spirit without understanding his playful manifestations in Swiveller. In fact, by linking upper and lower worlds, such "hybrid gods" were grotesque *curiosities*—"monsters and abnormal portents" (167)—whose Rabelaisian and Dickensian meaning always subordinates monologic Scholasticism, Little Bethel, and self-serving Law to a more "pagan" sense of the paradox of dialogic Life itself.[38]

Indeed, in order to understand such a mysterious paradox, the Renaissance created special serious games, like the invisibly swiveling "*manens moveor*, an emblem for the coincidence of motion and rest" (182), that is, "the spinning of a top which, when it comes to a stand, combines a state of rest with the greatest speed of rotation" (180). Such real toys, like Dickens' own play metaphors, suggest that the hidden god is never really absent, just as Quilp is always somehow and somewhere present in the ever-spinning Swiveller: "These serious games (*serio ludere*) consisted in finding within common experience an unusual object endowed with the kind of contradictory attributes which are difficult to imagine united in the deity. The motionless eye of God, for instance, is said to follow us everywhere. But can an eye stay at rest while it moves?" (179). And since "the hybrid gods of Orphic theology consistently follow a logic of their own, which is the logic of concealment" or "infolding" (168), a work like Cusanus' *De ludo globi* demands a new kind of play hermeneutics from its audience, just as the full heuristic satisfactions of *Gargantua and Pantagruel* and *The Old Curiosity Shop* are available only through an awareness of the carnivalesque tradition. Without such a playful awareness, the reader may find that Pantagruel is only an obscene giant, Quilp a sadistic dwarf, and Swiveller a hyperactive and alcoholic poetaster.

Thus, whether personifying carnal nature, the physical world, or metaphysical reality, Quilp creates panic and a kind of carnivalesque pansophy at the same time. Such a reading leads naturally to his role of satirizing the unplayful and famished enemies of feast and frolic, that is, those killjoys who oppose the protean life force even like Nell's pathetic grandfather paralyzed in his "time-worn room" where "the solitude, the wasted life, and gloom, were all in fellowship. Ashes, and dust, and ruin!" (71:533). Quilp's rampant vitality more playfully mocks the celibacy of all the bachelors in the novel, just as the "artless sports" of his prior paramour Sally Brass—that cross-dressing, snuff-taking, "amiable virgin"—have transformed "her life in[to] a kind of legal childhood" and "state of lawful innocence" in carnivalesque mockery of virginal, innocent Nell (36:269–70).[39] In fact, playboy Quilp conjures his own "bachelor hall" and enjoys a "free and gipsy mode of life" in "agreeable freedom from the restraints of matrimony" (50:371–72) as "a devil-may-care bachelor." And this kind of playful, dialogic approach to the marriage question (and the related value of virginity) recalls similar debates in *Gargantua and Pantagruel*, especially over whether or not Panurge should wed. Pantagruel's dialogic advice to his indecisive friend relevantly anticipates many of Quilp's "Quips," for it banters back and forth "not unlike to the Song of Gammer Yeabynay; it is full of Sarcasms, Mockqueries, bitter Taunts, nipping Bobs, derisive Quips, biting Jerks, and contradictory Iterations, the one part destroying the other" (III:10, 356). In other words, Quilp practices the "praise-abuse" pattern, which Bakhtin sees as so central to the carnivalesque tradition since it helps "form an indissoluble whole" by reinforcing "ambivalent fullness" (421), just as the dwarf, "bowing with grotesque politeness," achieves when he confronts an inn chambermaid: "he first made faces at her, and then wanted to kiss her" (48:356). Quilp, then, becomes the most prominent image of "saying things and then contradicting 'em," in other words, a virtual incarnation of Dickens' beloved game "called Yes and No" (*Christmas Books* 55).

Bakhtin's explanation of such "ambivalence" perceptively suggests Quilp's role in the novel and links it again with *curiosity*: "It is a gay and free play with objects and concepts, but it is a play that pursues a distant, prophetic goal: to dispel the atmosphere of gloomy and false seriousness enveloping the world and all its phenomena, to lend it a different look, to render it more material, closer to man and his body, more understandable, and lighter in the bodily sense" (380). Thus, Quilp cries " 'I hate your virtuous people' . . . throwing off a bumper of brandy, and smacking his lips, 'ah! I hate 'em every one!' " which in carnivalesque terms reveals that paradoxically he plays a normative reality principle. He not only repeatedly emphasizes the fleshly needs of "chubby, rosy Nell" (48:360), but also corrects the related woodenness of Kit, as for example when the dwarf chastizes the gigantic Kit doll with "his usual weapon," the "infallible poker" (67:507, 505), which playfully resembles the conjuror's wand, Punch's phallic baton, and the satirist's pen all at the same time. Indeed, Robert Leach relevantly sees Punch himself as "a fierce assertion of disobedience and a refusal to accept good manners, good order, good sense, or even goodness itself" (165).

"The accustomed grin" of this "sly little fiend" also gaily exorcises the gloomy "solemnities of Little Bethel" (41:306, 309). In fact, Kit's mother Mrs. Nubbles finds a direct relationship between her carnivalesque experience at Astley's Circus and the eruption of the grotesque Quilp into that dismally dissenting chapel: "Mr. Quilp did in his own person represent and embody that Evil Power, who was so vigorously attacked at Little Bethel, and who, by reason of her backslidings in respect of Astley's and oysters, was now frolicsome and rampant" (48:361). But somewhat unexpectedly, Quilp's most antic animus turns against that "white-livered man of law" (67:508) Sampson Brass, whose own hypocritical solemnities are decidedly unplayful and, in fact, serve as an eerie precursor of Mrs. Clennam's Sabbitarian jeremiad against play in *Little Dorrit*:

> I am of the law. I am styled "gentleman" by Act of Parliament. I maintain the title by the annual payment of twelve pound sterling for a certificate. I am not one of your players of music, stage actors, writers of books, or painters of pictures, who assume a station that the laws of their country don't recognize. I am none of your strollers or vagabonds.   (60:449)

It is therefore quite fitting that Quilp employs what Bakhtin terms "tricks of causing thirst, . . . provoking jokes and curses" (326) in correcting Sampson's dry-as-dust legality by repeatedly forcing him to drink red-hot *punch*. In fact, the only two characters that Quilp does not really punish are the two "backsliding" acrobats—the tumbling Tom Scott and pirouetting Swiveller who himself both pummels and enjoys a potation with Quilp, which may recall the popular belief that Punch's " 'namesake' " was that delightful concoction of " 'rum, lemon and sugar' " (Leach 57).[40]

V

Before our concluding discussion of the pivotal carnivalesque role of Dick Swiveller, the extremely pertinent insights of Victor Turner in *From Ritual to Theatre: The Human Seriousness of Play* and their relevance to processual reality in the novel deserve attention. Although Turner never mentions Bakhtin, he too highlights Rabelais' "ludic capacity," that is, his curiosity or tendency "to 'play' with . . . possibilities of form and meaning"—especially when "Rabelais' disorderly, scatological heaps of symbolic forms standing for the disorderly deeds and attributes of Gargantua and Pantagruel challenged the neatness of scholastic theological and philosophical systems" (23). In fact, Turner's account of the originally West African (hence the similarity with Pelton's insights) but really universal "Trickster deity of the Crossroads," the two-headed *Exu*, reinforces much that we have already suggested about the Rabelaisian nature of Janus-faced Quilp, himself buried "in the centre of four lonely roads" (Chapter the Last 549):

> one face is that of Christ, the other, Satan's. *Exu*, whose ritual colors are black and red, is the Lord of the Limen and of Chaos, the full ambiguity of the subjunctive mood of culture, representing the indeterminacy that lurks in the cracks and crevices of all socio-cultural "constructions of reality," the one who must be kept at bay if the framed formal order of the ritual proceedings is to go forward according to protocol. He is the abyss of possibility; hence his two heads, for he is both potential savior and tempter. He is also destroyer, for in one of his modes he is Lord of the Cemetery.   (77)

As Turner very significantly and relevantly advances his hypothetical distinctions between *liminal* and *liminoid* experiences (like "the carnival," 43), he suggests, I think, the fate of the play impulse in a culture experiencing *deliminalization*, that is, wasteland industrialization, as in the Black Country in *The Old Curiosity Shop*, and the consequent displacement of its old ritualistic play values into the new, less stable liminoid forms which generally characterize modern life. Again, for Turner "liminality is peculiarly conducive to play, where it is not restricted to games and jokes, but extends to the introduction of new forms of symbolic action, such as word-games or original masks." But with increased technology and emphasis on rational logic and abstraction, such ritualistic play retreats into the grotesque underground like those "terrible spectres, who lie at all . . . times in the obscene hiding-places of London, in archways, dark vaults and cellars" (Chapter the Last 549) besides in more glorious "hiding-places" like Punch temples and tripe cauldrons. Consequently, Turner rhetorically asks "whatever happened to liminality, as societies increased in scale and complexity, particularly Western industrial societies? With deliminalization seems to have gone the powerful *play* component." In fact, this repressed but "powerful *play* component" resurfaces and returns in more ambivalent *liminoid* or carnivalesque forms like Exu and Quilp. Thus, what is in fact spawned underground is a new creative grab-bag of protean symbolic forms—what we may even term *curiosities*: "Eros may sport with Thanatos, not as a grisly Danse Macabre, but to symbolize a complete human reality and a Nature full of oddities" (85).

In this sense, culture itself in Dickens' novels beginning with *The Old Curiosity Shop* seems to be at a crossroads, at a transitional period somewhere between the liminal and liminoid (indeed Rabelais perhaps represents the first act or even prelude in this lengthy stage of historical play) so that much of what Turner writes of the liminal, which is always pregnant with liminoid possibilities, also sharpens our response to the novel. Thus, although the liminal *inverts* while the liminoid *subverts* the standard Cartesian or binary way of thinking, both " 'play' with the elements of the familiar and defamiliarize them. Novelty emerges from unprecedented combinations of familiar elements." And again, the results of such uncanny play are themselves curiosities: the "free or 'ludic' recombination in any and every possible pattern, however weird, that is of the essence of liminality, liminality *par excellence*" (27–28). In the transitional world of *The Old Curiosity Shop*, Quilp and Sampson Brass even heatedly debate the significance of "combinings together" (62:462). For Turner, such liminoid combinations actually realize the full, latent potential of the liminal and, in fact, often accomplish this fulfillment by what Fagin (and contemporary ritual theory) might call self-sacrificial "deep play" (26:188) and what in *The Old Curiosity Shop* amounts to a paradoxical practice of *alterations* or transformations like Dick Swiveller's: "a transformative self-immolation of order as presently constituted, even sometimes a voluntary *sparagmos* or self-dismemberment of order, in the subjunctive depths of liminality." This "authentic reordering comes about" because "subjunctivity is fittingly the mother of indicativity, since any actualization is only one among a myriad possibilities of being" (83–84). Finally, for Turner a kind of participational theater, much like Bakhtin's expansive, festive carnival or like a ritualistic Punch drama (Leach 173), becomes one of the most enriching liminoid experiences because, recalling the action of *The Old Curiosity Shop*, it unmasks and amends "the hypocrisy of all social structure which shape human beings, often by psychical and even physical mutilation (foot-binding, corsets, indigestible foods), in the image of abstract social status-roles." This *remedial* function of the performing arts is particularly crucial in correcting sanctimonious, official formalities such as little Nell's funeral, which is no *funferall* wake like Finnegan's: "This has been especially the case as religious ritual has been stripped of its flexible, ludic components, its sacred clowns, masked tricksters, riddling narratives, to make way for rigorous solemnity, serious and official discourse about privileged or transcendental 'meanings' " (116).

For Bakhtin, these performing arts are also plastic arts because carnivalesque forms pantomime "the dual-bodied world of becoming" with "free and gay" popular play motifs, which, as in *The Old Curiosity Shop*, are finally more representational than the frozen standard forms and genres (including the pastoral) which mask themselves as realistic and descriptive rather than delusive prescriptive modes. Thus, carnivalesque transformations "fuse and combine elements that the mind is accustomed to divide strictly and even to oppose to each other" (420–21). The result is something like the Platonic universe of delusive fallen forms, and yet the golden key for playful philosophers like Rabelais, Dickens, and Bakhtin is finally not to the kingdom of heaven but to the heaven of an earth characterized by fluid, ludic reality (and liminality): "the extremely fanciful, free, and playful treatment of plant, animal, and human forms" (Bakhtin 32). In *Gargantua and Pantagruel*, this metaphysical "flow" is registered on almost every page, but perhaps the more than eighty "very strange," antic alterations Epistemon discovers in the underworld most closely prefigure the transformations in *The Old Curiosity Shop*. For example, Piso becomes "a clownish swaine," "Ulysses, a haymower," "Hannibal, a Kettlemaker and seller of eggeshels," "Lancelot of the lake . . . a flayer of dead horses," and "Pope Alexander, a rat-catcher" (II:30, 295–99), just as Mrs. Jarley conciliates Miss Monflathers "by altering the face and costume of Mr. Grimaldi as clown to represent Mr. Lindley Murray as he appeared when engaged in the composition of his English Grammar, and turning a murderess of great renown into Mrs. Hannah More" (29:216), among many other playful alterations.

Thus, even though in the first chapter Master Humphrey tries to conjure "strange tales" to "find one adapted to this mystery" of the "extraordinary contradiction" between the "innocence of the child" Nell and the "nightly absence" of her doting Grandfather (12) and on the very last page, Kit similarly finds that all the "alterations [around the old curiosity shop] were confusing" (555), nevertheless the Rabelaisian model illustrates that apparently contrasting alterations are naturally both realistic and renewing. In fact, the novel discloses at one point that "the uncertainty of human life" even demands that "human nature" likewise practice "a good and merciful adjustment" (53:397), and such adjustments or adaptive alterations, if they prove to be salutary, are invariably playful in the text.[41]

Like the fire that "roared and leaped" and shared "play days" with the figurative fire god who tends it and shelters Nell (44:332), experience in the novel resembles a "democritizing" kiln or "heraclitizing" crucible (again, Rabelais links the equally "fiery" laugher and weeper) with whose processing flux one must dance in order to be converted to life.[42] But as is usual with Dickens, life's playful alterations are extremely "warious." Shapeshifting tricksters like Quilp can alter "his countenance by twisting it into all imaginable varieties of ugliness" (48:358), recalling all the various were-creatures who haunt folklore, and Quilp can also creatively adapt his tricks for different varieties of game as the dwarf has "man-traps, cunningly altered and improved for catching women" (50:377). On the other hand, Grandfather, the deluded gambler, is so "wrapt in the game of chance" that he cannot creatively control appearing "like another creature in his shape, a monstrous distortion of his image" (31:230), while the perversely inflexible "Miss Monflathers improvis[es]" Watt's "healthful play" into "work alway" to the detriment of poor children (31:236).[43] The poet Mr. Slum, conversely, prides himself on his "convertible" verses which allow him playfully (and in terms of Dickens' past, profoundly) "to alter the acrostic" for Warren's Blacking, so that it becomes "a positive inspiration for Jarley" (28:213). And Mrs. Jarley herself practices the mental equivalent of such linguistic somersaults by altering her anxiety-ridden mental construct for "Miss Monflathers, who, from being an object of dire vexation, [now] became one of sheer ridicule and absurdity" (32:239).[44]

Perhaps the most singularly carnivalesque symbol of such hocus-pocus is another curiosity container, the "kind of temple" in which the single gentleman mixes an egg, coffee, raw steak, and water so that, with the aid of "a spirit-lamp" and "some wonderful and unseen agency," it blends a whole breakfast feast (35:266). "Punch's temple," still another "dark box," creates a similar transubstantiation with its artfully improvised "fire of wit" and "cheerful rattle" (17:132) constantly changing to fit the various moods of various audiences.[45] Dickens himself (not, I think, the forgotten narrator Humphrey), of course, plays the ultimate creative Trickster here when, for example, he punningly alters language like *Buffon* and *Buffoon* (51:383), establishing a kind of Rabelaisian link between natural history and the carnivalesque, or when he invokes the prototypical Rabelaisian pun on *spirit* by having Sampson Brass congratulate Quilp's "extraordinary spirits! His humour is so extremely playful!" not realizing that Quilp will momentarily force him to play Pantagruel and "drink off all the spirit": " 'Moisten your clay, wet the other eye, drink, man!' cried the dwarf" (62:460–64). But Dickens' creative tricks appear most impressive when he alternates a lugubrious elegiac tone as Nell "descended the narrow steps which led into the

crypt'' at the end of chapter 55 with ludic Dick Swiveller at the beginning of
the next chapter posturing in that "pestiferous old slaughter-house," the Brass
legal office, with "a small parcel of black crepe" commemorating his loss
of Sophy Wackles. Dick's own ludicrously lachrymose "soliloquy" here
performatively alters Nell's prayerful elegy with its own playful repertoire
replete with self-conscious self-satire and washed down, if not baptized, with
an uplifting modest quencher:

> Mr. Swiveller did not wind up with a cheerful hilarious laugh, which would
> have been undoubtedly at variance with his solemn reflections, but . . . being
> in a theatrical mood, he merely achieved that performance which is designated
> in melodrama "laughing like a fiend,"—for it seems that your fiends always
> laugh in syllables, and always in three syllables, never more or less.

Lest we completely forget *Nell*, however, Dickens' punning rhyme immediately recalls the tone of his prior alteration or adaptaton: "The baleful sounds
had hardly died away, and Mr. Swiveller was still sitting in a very grim state
in the clients' chair, when there came a ring—or, if we may adapt the sound
to his then humour, a knell—at the office bell" (413–15).

VI

It is Dick, of course, who finds himself "utterly aghast at [every] unexpected alteration of circumstances," which he affectionately dubs "staggerers": "Under an accumulation of staggerers, no man can be considered a free
agent." Nevertheless, Dick is eternally a free agent, one whose carnivalesque
practice and participation in life counter all official "systems of moral philosophy" by playing like "a clown in pantomime" or a carnivalesque high priest
of perpetual motion which out-staggers the staggerers (13:102, 34:254–55).[46]
Although Dick can shape-shift with the best of them by altering "himself
into as flat a shape as possible" (35:264), his real transformative virtuosity,
like Sam Weller's, is linguistic. His carnivalesque art grounds chaotic life
with the "extemporary adaptation of a popular ballad to the distressing circumstances of his own case" (50:374) or that of others as he repeatedly
improvises and integrates literature with life: " 'Begone dull care: ' fan that
sinking flame of hilarity with the wing of friendship; and pass the rosy wine,"
which consecrates a Rabelaisian trinity of laughter, mutuality, and festive
spirits. Such transformative talent provides Dick with an almost inexhaustible
fund of pious frauds and "pleasant fictions" like miraculously transubstantiat-
ing bedsteads into bookcases, "gin-and-water" into countless cups of "rosy

wine,'' and a one-room flat into ''lodgings,'' which conjures a carnivalesque ''notion of indefinite space'' and cornucopious ''plural number'' (7:53).[47] Consequently, this ultimate ''single gentleman'' is polymorphous and *polymetis* like Quilp (and Odysseus). But Swiveller finally proves more polysemous than the dwarf with his multiple dirty tricks because Dick's sense of what Turner would term *communitas* is finally *human*, which never means ''single'' in Rabelais or Dickens, while double-dealing Quilp remains an isolated carnivalesque mask even as he transforms from married man to gaily grotesque bachelor.

Thus, after a literally fitful beginning, Swiveller turns *real* in a more identifiably human sense than Quilp does because for all his pleasant fictions, Dick celebrates the value of suffering and loving as well as the more explicitly playful dimensions of reality. Without Quilp's inchoate carnivalesque energy, there really could be no Swiveller, and the dwarf appropriately calls Dick ''my pet, my pupil, the apple of my eye'' (50:373) and even asks, ''let me be a father to you'' (23:171). But Quilp finally remains the pure, unrevealed potential of the universal and collective Pan experience, while Dick is the fully individuated act, or better play, of becoming. In a sense, then, Swiveller is even the incarnation of his future father-in-law almost as the liminoid humanizes the potential of the liminal, as the ''trickster god'' unleashes the ''trickster hero'' (Kérenyi in Radin 189), or as Pan is revealed in the flashing metamorphoses of Proteus. Though Dick uniquely also plays Eros to Quilp's Pan and Punch to the dwarf's Judy by raining ''staggering blows'' on his *daimon* while ''performing a kind of dance round him'' (13:99) and though he promises the unjustly arrested Kit that if he amends his ways, the Swiveller ''would connive at his kicking Sampson Brass on the shins and escaping [with Kit] up a court'' (59:442), Dick is finally more peacemaker than troublemaker. And, of course, he is also a playmaker who can ''perform the serious pantomime'' in ''dumb show'' or verbally communicate ''the gay and festive'' by abjuring blood sports for what Drew Hyland calls the ''responsive openness'' (52) of the ludimagister: ''feeling, as a mutual friend, that badgering, baiting, and bullying, was not the sort of thing calculated to expand the souls and promote the harmonies of the contending parties'' (3:24). As soon as the Brass siblings desert the legal atmosphere of their office, Dick compensatorily *alters* their awful officialdom with his own ''unlawful games'': a ''performance of maniac hornpipe . . . in the fulness of his joy'' (34:253), and he anticipates Frederick Dorrit's plaintive clarinet solos by repeatedly ''playing the flute'' when staggerers are too much with him.

Dick is still enough of a grotesque realist, however, to know that such performances must not become too formulaic as maudlin or even masochistic set pieces. After playing cribbage with the Marchioness, he recalls that "Chegg's wife plays cribbage; all fours likewise. She rings the changes on 'em now. From sport to sport they hurry her, to banish her regrets, and when they win a smile from her, they think that she forgets—but she don't." Here the final emphatic and expanded spondee realistically corrects the formal iambic versifying, just as his perpetual cribbage play with the Marchioness realistically corrects the iambic dirge of the official funeral oration for Nell. Even more, Dick's performed necrolatry itself dissolves when the pleasure becomes too painful, and his altered play prop again attests to his incarnate, fluid realism: "Melting from this stern and obdurate, into the tender and pathetic mood, Mr. Swiveller groaned a little, walked wildly up and down, and even made a show of tearing his hair, which, however he thought better of, and wrenched the tassel from his nightcap instead" (58:432). Indeed, after he suffers the carnivalesque staggerer of a "plain cook of three feet high appearing mysteriously from under ground" (34:258), Dick "makes it more real and pleasant" (57:427) by calling her "Marchioness." Then, after performing a dazzling series of "theatrical conventionalities," Dick "felt it necessary to discharge his brigand manner for one more suitable to private life" (58:429) out of compassion for the all too unlettered but eminently human Marchioness—he has already "applied himself to teaching her the game" of cribbage, but her course in literary allusion remains ahead. Also remaining ahead are still more alterations: especially Dick's symbolic illness when he is "Dead, all but" (64:476) and the subsequent process of his becoming even more "happily adjusted" (66:492) to his phenomenological staggerers. As Pelton, borrowing Turner's own terminology, characterizes this Trickster role, "He reassures precisely because he reveals how human vulnerability at moments of radical change is, in truth, liminal openness. Through it dissolution itself is dissolved, and formlessness becomes the passage to new form" (269).

Finally, we need to be clearer about Dick's profound but often perplexing relationship with the carnivalesque in general and *Gargantua and Pantagruel* in particular, especially since one of the "theatrical conventionalities" he graces the Marchioness with is " 'Some wine there. Ho!' He illustrated these melodramatic morsels, by handing the tankard to himself with great humility, receiving it haughtily, drinking from it thirstily, and smacking his lips fiercely" (58:429). The paradoxical combination of Dickens' own playfully imitative praising-abusive adverbs, especially when further combined with prandial or banquet imagery, exemplifies Bakhtin's repeated carnivalesque belief that "laughter, food, and drink defeat death" (299). The even more specifically relevant "images of food, wine, love, and gambling are manifestly linked with popular-festive forms" so that this kind of "grotesque symposium travesties and debases the purely idealistic, mystic, and ascetic victory over the world" like "the Last Supper" (295–96) or Nell's joyless funeral valediction in chapter 72 with its abstract emphasis on "the blank that follows death—the weary void—the sense of desolation" (545). Such world famine must be compared with Dick's and the Marchioness's First Supper, almost apropos of which Bakhtin writes that "it is as if the ancient marketplace comes to life in closed chamber conversation. Intimacy begins to sound like the familiarity of bygone days, which breaks down all barriers between men" and women (421). And we might recall that during their Barmecide feasts after Dick's rebirth, a communion service of toast and tea becomes an "Arabian Night" under the magic of Dick's waking play vision of the Marchioness transformed into "the Princess of China" or divining "Genie": "playing cribbage with herself at the table. There she sat, intent upon her game, . . . shuffling the cards, cutting, dealing, playing, counting, pegging—going through all the mysteries of cribbage as if she had been in full practice from her cradle!" (64:475–76). Later, "a mighty hamper" with "some giant load" of "delicate restoratives" magically fills Dick's flat, and "all that abundance" becomes a carnivalesque confirmation of his renewed commitment to life (66:492–93). Such scenes confirm both his earlier official title as "Perpetual Grand Master" of that "select convivial circle called the Glorious Apollers" (13:103) and Dick's ability "to be merry under any circumstances" (7:54). Thus he reflects all outstanding members of the carnivalesque "Buffoon societies," especially the " 'Carefree Lads' " (97), which Bakhtin sees personifying "popular laughter." This notion further recalls Dick's repeated role as clown or harlequin, which Bakhtin also links with the carnivalesque when he discusses Justus Moser's "Harlequin, or the Defense of the Grotesque-Comic," published in 1761: "this defense was placed in Harlequin's own mouth" (see 35 ff.), just as it often is with Dick.

Dick's carnivalesque replay of the twelfth-century Franciscan tradition of "Our Lady's Tumbler" seems to be especially resonant in *The Old Curiosity Shop* with its apparently conflicting moods of playing and praying, and in this sense perhaps the legend was even a vehicle for resolving Dickens' tonally opposing feelings for Swiveller and Mary Hogarth.[48] As he wrote Forster apropos of Nell's death and the Schoolmaster's stoicism, "I can't preach to myself the schoolmaster's consolation, though I try. Dear Mary died yesterday, when I think of this sad story" (I:139); yet in response to Forster's fascination with Dick, his creator also wrote 'I *mean* to make much of him" (I:135, Dickens' emphasis). Bakhtin mentions " 'God's jugglers' (*ioculatores Domini*)" as an example of "a carnivalesque Catholicism" (57) and later reminds us that "Rabelais himself was a Franciscan" (261) and so was presumably quite familiar with this French legend. At any rate, D. H. Dooling's retelling of the story, curiously in connection with Trickster mythology, beautifully captures the mood of nostalgic play and laughing bittersweetness that riddles Dick's role in the novel.

"Once long ago in France," begins Dooling, "the legend tells us, there was a minstrel who wandered from here to there throughout the land, earning his living by dancing and tumbling to entertain whoever would gather to watch him on the village greens and in the fairs." The tumbler eventually settles down in a monastery, but feels ashamed of his irreligious, "foolish trade" until he decides to offer his play itself as a prayer to "the holy Virgin": "The skill to leap and tumble and dance is all I have; will you allow me to offer it to you?" He then performs his devotional dance in the crypts beneath the abbey, but one day he "began his dancing, his leaping and praying until he fell at last in a faint." Our Lady seems so moved by this staggering fall that she performs a miracle: "the image of the Virgin stirred and came to life," just as the Marchioness does under Dick's similar devotion, and thus we are even tempted to believe that Nell might have come to real life had Dick fulfilled his plan to court her. In any event, like the Marchioness, Mary then "ministered to him," and the Abbot officiously accepts the minstrel's somersaulting play as a genuine form of prayer, at which real miracle the tumbler "was so overcome with joy [and] his heart leaped up with such a bound that it began to break." Thereupon, "the Holy Virgin and her angels came . . . to receive the soul of her minstrel as it departed from his body, and to bear it with her to Heaven" (35, 37). And yet how dead-sounding, finally, is this last official valediction when read alongside the Marchioness's comparable ministering to Dick: "she laved his face and hands, brushed his hair, and in short made him as spruce and smart as anybody under such circumstances could be made." Under the spell of "her laughing joy," in fact, "Mr. Swiveller submitted in a kind of grateful astonishment beyond the reach of language" (66:490). Significantly, our last vision of this somer-saulting minstrel and his Marchioness pictures them enjoying *this* world with "many hundred thousand games of cribbage" rather than the *next* world with the virginal Nell and her ministering angels.

One of the implicit purposes of the foregoing discussion of Dick has been to document how an awareness of the carnivalesque play tradition clarifies Swiveller's role in ways that have been significantly neglected even by past brilliant treatments of him, like Garrett Stewart's in *Dickens and the Trials of Imagination.*[49] And Dick's place in this tradition is nowhere more crucial than in its connection with the "suspicious" play forms of mobility, gambling, and particularly drinking. In this sense, the carnivalesque key to Dick appears in his glorious surname *Swiveller* and the Marchioness's benevolent malapropism *Liverer* (64:478). In *Nicholas Nickleby*, appropos of the less glorious "Snow Hill," Dickens writes "The name is such a good one" in "picturing to us" a "double association of ideas" (4:29), but *Swiveller-Liverer* pictures at least *four* associated ideas in its "carnivalesque game of names" (Bakhtin 461). The primary one is captured in Stewart's now-often-repeated metaphor of "The Pivotal Swiveller." And yet just as Stewart's contention that the only reason Quilp is "made a dwarf" is so that he can fit "snugly into Nell's tiny bed" (112) is unfortunate from a carnivalesque perspective, so too his actual analysis of Dick's mobility unfortunately neglects the carnivalesque and even more general play traditions: "there is surely something in 'Swiveller' that catches his directionless vitality, that willingness to take the prevailing wind which often makes him seem as though he is merely going in circles" (106). In the carnivalesque and for Dickens there is almost no such thing as "merely going in circles"![50] And as Stewart provocatively demonstrates, Dick is certainly much more important than the rotary horse in *Pickwick* or the equally rotary Whiskers in this novel, even if that "dancing" pony, as it characteristically "wheeled round," becomes a prototypical example of carnivalesque "gorgeous liveries" (19:150): "the freest animal in creation" (65:485). No, Dick's tendency "to revolve rapidly . . . in the sudden fury of his spirits" (56:417) seems geared, like his use of spirits themselves, "rather for protracting and spinning out the time to the very utmost limit of possibility" (57:425). Consequently, his beloved "small servant" likewise "flutters round and round" (65:484), imitating her mentor's playful act of "beguiling time" like some *manens moveor* by practicing the carnivalesque motif of what Bakhtin calls "gay time."

Thus besides prefiguring the *Ringmaster* Sleary with his "swivel eye," Dick also resembles another familiar Trickster figure, the Whirling Dervish who, as Peter J. Awn explains, swivels and 'proceeds to pivot in measured, fluid movements" to "the mournful lament of the reed pipe . . . the metaphor of the soul's longing" (again like Dick with his magic flute). Also suggesting

Dick's rosy source of inspiration, the spherical harmony of the Dervish approximates "the image of the burgeoning rose" as it follows the "path to the center"—the "*axis mundi*, the spiritual center of the universe" (94–95). And analogously the Pantagruelists learn that the Great God Pan himself, like his world, is an oval "Breviary or Flask" (V:46, 416). In the words of the Priestess of the Holy Bottle: "Now, my Friends, you may depart, and may that Intellectual Sphere, whose centre is every where, and Circumference no where, whom we call GOD, keep you in his Almighty Protection" (V:48, 422). Dick's own "mazy dance" featuring a full repertoire of "such spins and twists as filled the company with astonishment" (8:64) at the Wackles' Ladies Seminary perhaps best illustrates his Dervishness. But no previous or subsequent body language communicates the boundless energy of this miraculous motion man like the playful blur he becomes in the Brass law office, which seems almost to alter if not dissolve the natural laws of time and space, besides defying the atmosphere of penal "confinement":

> Mr. Swiveller burst in full freshness as something new and hitherto undreamed of, lighting up the office with scraps of song and merriment, conjuring with inkstands and boxes of wafers, catching three oranges in one hand, balancing stools upon his chin and penknives on his nose, and constantly performing a hundred other feats with equal ingenuity; for with such unbendings did Richard, in Mr. Brass's absence, relieve the tedium of his confinement.   (36:270)

In this sense, it is significant that *liverer* in the *OED* signifies one who is "free from restraint in motion; active, nimble," which itself suggests the second meaning of Dick's name, its associations with gambling in the sense of the spinning wheel of fortune, which in the novel appears in reference to the correspondences between human and cosmic "revolutions." Even "the magic reel" (547) featured in the last chapter implies that the artist not only choreographs the magical circle dance or reel of his characters but also games with their fortunes. Thus, although Dickens ordinarily would agree with Mrs. Sparsit that "It's immoral to game" because, as Bitzer adds, "the chances are against the players" (*Hard Times*: II:1, 122), Dick's spirited turning of the wheel of fortune suggests that he heroically gambles on life and love, just as in the carnivalesque tradition "wine and gambling, were combined in a single ritual" implying "free play with the sacred" (Bakhtin 295–96). And in Rabelais the image of *alea judiciorum* or the divining dice of judgment is a repeated motif, especially notable when Panurge and Pantagruel haggle over whether dice, already forbidden by Gargantua, should be used to foretell Panurge's future marital status—coincidentally, the merry outlaw Panurge

arrives secretly equipped with "a whole Bag full" of the curious cubes
(III:11, 360–61).

In Turner's relevant etymological discussion of "play," he emphasizes the
" 'gambling' character of divination" in tribal societies and its relation to
the German *gammeln*—"to sport, make merry" (*From Ritual to Theatre*
33–34). And this, of course, is just Dick's notion of gambling with the
Marchioness. Although Isaac List and other gamesters cheat Grandfather and
although Grandfather himself is right in one sense when he vows "I never
played . . . for love of play" (9:74), Dick compassionately combines their
desire "to play for money" with his own desire "to play for love" (29:222).[51]
As is also true in *Our Mutual Friend*, the repeated word *fortune* in the novel
here relevantly recalls the familiar Renaissance iconography of Love, Death,
and Fortune, the blind hunters, all gambling for human souls. Dick, though,
gambles to save the Marchioness's spirit by sharing his stakes with her in
their famous cribbage game; presumably his "loss of three sixpences" was
willed freely and not by chance (see chapters 57–58). G. Cordery's perceptive
contrast of this match with Grandfather's compulsive gambling still misses
the carnivalesque context of this *popular festive form*, as Bakhtin would call
it, in which laughing Democritus and "Old King Cole" merge in the person
of the happily gaming Swiveller: "Merriment, Marchioness, is not a bad or
degrading quality. Old King Cole was himself a merry old soul, if we may
put any faith in the pages of history" (58:430).[52]

Thirdly, *Swiveller* also suggests a *swiller*, the significance of which is
relevant to Eaten*swill* in *Pickwick* and is also personified in the name of Little
Swills the barroom crooner in *Bleak House*. Dickens' own attitude toward
drinking seems ambivalent. On the one hand, alcoholism pathetically debilitates characters like Mr. Wickfield and even Mrs. Tony Weller, not to mention
the literally liquidated Krook. On the other hand, magic potions, especially
the motley ingredients of punch, at least partially typify the joie de vivre
of Sam Weller, and Dickens famously spoofed cautionary Cruickshank's
teetotaling fairy tales in "Frauds upon the Fairies." Further, he likened
Temperance Societies to other Sabbatarian causes opposing playful and promoting prayerful holidays in the unsigned *Examiner* article "Demoralisation
and Total Abstinence" (1849).[53] One might like to be officiously circumspect
here and say that Dickens clearly preaches moderation in all things, especially
in drinking, but even that bromide doesn't approach Stewart's honest but
(I think) extreme contention that "Dick drinks *too much*" (103, Stewart's
emphasis), which completely misses the point of Rabelaisian immoderation
in all things, especially drinking. And in the long-awaited wine-cellar temple

of the Holy Bottle, the questing Pantagruelists learn so much more than the simply too sententious Epicurean doctrine of *in vino veritas* or even more than that the Holy Bottle is a cornucopious Holy Grail.[54] Consequently, the penultimate four chapters of *Gargantua and Pantagruel* remain the most vivid testament to the value of Dick's living example that malt does more than Milton can and that growing high with the rosy personifies the real spirit of carnivalesque resurrection. Mrs. Jarley's "suspicious bottle" (26:196) is only suspicious in the unenlightened eyes of Little Nell, Little Bethel, and Miss Monflathers' unbecoming finishing school. The note accompanying Dick's gift of beer to the jailed Kit clearly announces the *real* value of the carnivalesque grail: "Drink this cup, you'll find there's a spell in its every drop 'gainst the ills of mortality. Talk of the cordial that sparkled for Helen! *Her* cup was a fiction, but this is reality (Barclay & Co.'s). If they ever send it in a flat state, complain to the Governor. Yours, R.S." (61:458). More simply if less eloquently, Dick's later pun suggests that "Richard on his bier" can be miraculously resuscitated by "a mug of beer" (65:487–88)—or at least by the vision of Mr. Abel drinking one.

In Rabelais' concluding episode, the oracular Bottle becomes, then, the ultimate cauldron of tripe or well of truth: "Bottle! whose mysterious Deep / Do's ten thousand Secrets keep" (415); and yet any serious attempt to allegorize its deep play is countered as much by Panurge reflexively urging a "merry Gloss" as it is by the single and "Panomphean Word" (415–16) TRINK or DRINK! which again implies that the answer to the mystery of life is simply to drink it all in and live it intensely like Dick Swiveller. As Joseph Campbell puts it in his Eastern version of the carnivalesque canon, *"The best discipline is to enjoy your friends. Enjoy your meals. Realize what play is. Participate in the play, in the play of life"* (214, Campbell's emphasis). At any rate, Bacbuc the Priestess stresses the self-reflexive nature of the Bottle's message when she advises the Pantagruelian reader to "drink" her book so "that you may be Clerk to your very Liver" (416), which significantly reminds us that *Liverer* suggests that part of the body particularly assaulted by drink, and yet Bacbuc's hair-of-the-dog philosophy hardly seems ironic against Swiveller's well-stocked *liver*. Rather it may recall what the *OED* describes as the "ancient notion that [the liver] was the seat of love and violent passion," and that for Rabelais this kind of intensely moving, gambling, devouring approach to *living* suggests the final meaning of *Liverer*-Deliverer. Mr. Liverer delivers the Marchioness, just as she later delivers him—in fact, a medieval meaning for *livery* is a gift of food or clothes to a servant. Dick momentously asks his "small servant," "Did you ever taste beer?" (57:427), before delivering her with the "transports" of purl, just as the Marchioness later momentously asks him, "Did you ever taste orange-peel and water?" (64:481), before delivering him with this "concoction." She then significantly imitates his healthy, imaginative alterations as she begs her mentor to "make believe it was wine": " 'If you make believe very much, it's quite nice,' said the small servant" (64:481).

No wonder that in *Gargantua and Pantagruel* "Drinking is the distinguishing Character of Man" and "Truth is in Wine" (417), as it is for the Swiveller. And no wonder that Panurge finally understands, "I shall be wedded" and "make a Dutchess of my Bride" (417), as Dick chooses to make a Marchioness of his. In fact, the Pantagruelians all climactically anticipate Dick by suffering "the fit [of] Rhiming," and all then *"rim'd with Poetick Fury"* (418). Under Bacchic inspiration, they even "Rhime in Crimson" (419), and Friar John's abusive praise poetically twits Panurge's decision to indulge in "a little Leap-frog play" (420) with his Duchess. Then Panurge and the Priestess both return to the carnivalesque myth of Proserpine, which again prefigures the "subterranean" Marchioness and her wine-cellar wooer playing in mockery of death. Panurge, repaying and replaying John's ribaldry, foretells the Friar's fate in hell by rhyming "Ev'n there, I know, thou'lt play some trick, / And Proserpine shan't ['scape] a prick" (429), while the demurring Priestess perhaps more subtly tells a fortune of similar unlawful games for the Queen of the Underground—and by extension for Dick's swivelling Marchioness—but unfortunately not for matronly Demeter or the underground servant's ironically lawful "Mother," Sally Brass: "certainly foreseeing that Proserpine would meet with more excellent Things, more desirable Enjoyments below, than she her Mother could be blest with above" (422). Whatever "bodily lower stratum" lurks in Rabelais' pun, though, the most excellent thing and desirable enjoyment that the Marchioness meets below is her swiveling, swilling, delivering, but most of all *living* embodiment of the carnivalesque grotesque, Mr. Richard Swiveller.

NOTES

1. For other relevant discussions of the *carnivalesque* besides Bakhtin's classic study of Rabelais, see Terry Castle's book and two essays, "The Carnivalization of Eighteenth-Century English Narrative" and "Eros and Liberty at the English Masquerade, 1710–90," Kinser's *Rabelais's Carnival*, and Barbara Babcock's "The Novel and the Carnival World: An Essay in Memory of Joe Doherty." See also Newman's development of the idea that *"The Old Curiosity Shop* is arguably

the greatest, as well as the first, proper nonsense literature" (65), which unintentionally suggests analogies with the carnivalesque and explicitly contends that the novel "is deeply connected to the central tradition of English folk art" (70). Finally see Winters' treatment of Nell's decidedly uncarnivalesque death scene. (180).

2. *Flow* or the "flow experience," a major topic in the behavioral sciences, has received special attention in ritualistic studies, and the interested reader should consult Turner's summary of this phenomenon *(From Ritual to Theatre* 55–58). For various discussions of feasting in Dickens, see Hardy *(The Moral Art of Dickens* 139–55), Thomas L. Watson, James E. Marlow's "Social Harmony and Dickens' Revolutionary Cookery," and Sarah Gilead's more general treatment of "Barmecide Feasts: Ritual, Narrative, and the Victorian Novel," which also discusses feasting in *Great Expectations*. Monroe Engle relevantly argues that "the landscape of *The Old Curiosity Shop* is at once unreal, recognizable, and coherent as the free play of the imagination is always necessarily coherent" (147).

3. We are using Urquhart's original English translation of Rabelais rather than a more fluent modern translation because, as we will see, Dickens himself was most familiar with this translation.

4. For two book-length treatments of the *grotesque* in Dickens, see Hill and Hollington, besides Dyson's essay "*The Old Curiosity Shop*: Innocence and the Grotesque."

5. The interested reader should consult Leach's entire discussion of the history and mythology of the Punch and Judy tradition.

6. For references to Dickens' love of Goldsmith, see Kaplan's biography (28, 316). In fact, Dickens even considered naming one of his sons Oliver Goldsmith before settling on Henry Fielding (Kaplan 241).

7. See Panofsky's relevant account of this motif, "*Et in Arcadia Ego*: Poussin and the Elegiac Tradition," especially its relationship to certain morbid curiosities or *les objets bizarres* (313) and to Pan pipes (317, note 38).

8. See Frye's treatment of the relation between primitive and popular forms in *The Secular Scripture* (29).

9. Carey briefly discusses limbs in Dickens (61–62, 92–93), and Arthur Washburn Brown almost predictably devotes an entire chapter of his *Sexual Analysis of Dickens's Props* to "The Erotic Meaning of Wooden Legs" (41–72). See also Turner's *The Forest of Symbols* (93–111) and *From Ritual to Theatre* (20–60).

10. Until reading Babcock's essay on the carnivalesque, I was unaware that the *just as* and *like* constructions which seem to dominate the above paragraph, if not the entire essay, are endemic to the syntax of the carnivalesque. Babcock, for instance, cites Julia Kristeva's commentary on Bakhtin: " 'The dialogism of the Menippean (and of carnival) which expresses a logic of relation and analogy rather than a logic of substance and inference is opposed to Aristotelian logic' " and then goes on to discuss this kind of "play with linguistic structures, logical forms, and literary genres" (919). The interested reader should also consult Rachel Bennett's relevant contrast of the roles of Punch and Bunyan's pilgrim Christian in the novel (423–34). But Leach's more general comparisons between Punch and other "archetypal tricksters" like Loki and Pan seem finally more provocative to me. For Leach, "Punch . . . needs to be comprehended as more than a puppet or a clown and more than the protagonist in a fantasy. He must be seen as a trickster, a character known in many mythologies as an ambiguous god on the fringe of normal society both in its mortal and immortal constructions" (174).

11. I have never been as confident as most readers seem to be that Codlin is really in league with Short to fleece Nell, and I believe this ambiguity is reflected in the fact that in the last chapter he is numbered among those who have been "kind" to Nell and her Grandfather (553). Again, then, he appears as a Trickster, an ambivalent, indeterminate force in the novel.

12. Whether or not the final rejection of "The Rabelais article" may have been the result of Bentley's veto power, which Dickens grew to resent bitterly, we do not know, though such a conclusion also seems plausible.

13. For a relevant account of Dickens' feelings about Mary's death, see Marcus (134–35).

14. See Schlicke's more historical approach to the carnivalesque context of The Old Curiosity Shop, particularly his discussion of the influence of Bartholomew Fair and its suppression (89–96). We should also note here that in many editions of Gargantua and Pantagruel, "dickens" is even spelled Dickens.

15. Given such remarkable correspondences, one can only wonder how much self-identification occurred during Dickens' reading of Banks's descriptions of Rabelais. For example, like Rabelais and like his creator, David Copperfield later also "had a greedy relish for volumes . . . of Voyages and Travels" (4:56).

16. See Bakhtin's pertinent discussion of philosophic feasting (168–71).

17. Nancy Hill makes the same comparison (104-05). See also Gabriel Pearson's discussion of the novel as a Quilpiad and a Nellyad (77).

18. Stanley Rosen's Plato's Symposium clearly articulates the dialectical or what we might now call the dialogic nature of Plato's thoughts on love.

19. In this light, it might also be interesting to compare Plato's attitudes toward homoeroticism with those at least implied in Dickens' characterizations of Sally Brass, Quilp, and the brotherhood of Nell's mourners.

20. See Bakhtin's discussion of the significance of the western voyage (397–400).

21. For different approaches to curiosity in the novel, see Jaffe's " 'Never be Safe but in Hiding': Omniscience and Curiosity in The Old Curiosity Shop," Greenstein's "Lenticular Curiosity and The Old Curiosity Shop," and Feinberg's "Reading Curiosity: Does Dick's Shop Deliver?"

22. It is a disjunctive example primarily because of Kit's ambiguous function in the novel as he at different times suggests both official and unofficial values, perhaps implying that Swiveller gradually assumes Kit's carnivalesque role.

23. S. J. Newman's spirited defense of the novel rests on the premise that "improvisation in The Old Curiosity Shop . . . ingests responsibility through a deeper [than that in the earlier fiction] comprehension of the play of the mind. Incoherence is no longer accidental and incidental but the principle of narrative energy" (63).

24. See also McMaster's relevant treatment of Ruskin's notion of the Gothic as related to the world of the novel (118–19).

25. If the emergent carnivalesque energy represents Renaissance Humanism gradually displacing Medieval Scholasticism even though, as Bakhtin suggests, that very Humanism was deeply rooted in the Middle Ages, then the Gothic spirit would also seem to signify a relevant phase of this enormous cultural upheaval.

26. In his introduction to The Dialogic Imagination, Michael Holquist argues that Bakhtin, the "supreme eccentric," was (like Dickens) a curiosity or "wonder" characterized by "intense strangeness" (xvi).

27. For other accounts linking Dickens with the uncanny, see Daleski's "Dickens and the Proleptic Uncanny," Sadoff's "Locus Suspectus: Narrative, Castration, and the Uncanny," and Ginsburg's "Dickens and the Uncanny: Repression and Displacement in Great Expectations."

28. See Gose on the relationship between *daimon* and *demon* (169–70). In "The Victorian Book of the Dead: *Dracula*" (344–45), I develop many of these same *uncanny* motifs.

29. Implicit in the play of Old Humphrey's ambivalent feelings about Nell, actually his grandniece, are the same Oedipal elements of sibling rivalry which occurred years earlier between himself and Grandfather over Nell's future grand-mother—whom the child uncannily resembles.

30. Consequently, Steven Marcus's concluding evaluation reflects the critical disad-vantage of being unfamiliar with the underground treasures of the carnivalesque tradition:

> But for all its charm of intelligence and sweetness, for all its seemliness and delicacy, the story of Dick and the Marchioness cannot counterbalance the dead weight of the novel's great theme. Its gratifying acrobatic resolution and the assurance it holds out for the future are simply too light and supple for a novel whose unremitting impulse is toward all that lies underground.
>
> (168)

In other words, Marcus sees the "underground" as the place only of Nell's death and not of her alter ego's rebirth.

31. Again, Quilp's daughter who "always remained somewhere in the bowels of the earth under Bevis Marks" also seems to play the carnivalesque game of *Nemo* with the reader and her fellow characters, for "Nobody ever came to see her, nobody spoke of her, nobody cared about" this "love child" (36:271). In fact, the Marchioness informs Quilp that her name is "Nothing" (51:380). The inter-ested reader should consult Bakhtin's discussion of "this play with negation" and "amusing game": "*Nemo* is the free carnivalesque play with official nega-tions and prohibitions" (412–15), which Dickens develops more sardonically with Esther's father *Nemo* in *Bleak House*.

32. Though Michael Hollington borrows this illustration to grace the cover of his *Dickens and the Grotesque*, it unaccountably receives short shrift in his following treatment (see 93, note 14). In her discussion of the grotesque, Nancy Hill relates the illustration to Quilp's "most extraordinary" example (103) of grotesqueness. See Kaplan (191) for the "Grimaldi reflex."

33. Pearson relevantly writes that "Quilp's very vitality savages Nell's pallid heroics. She is the puking heroine terrorized by that childhood arch-knock-about come-dian, Punch" (86). See also Westland on Nell and Quilp (69).

34. In his essay on "Dickens and the Dance of Death," Hollington relates Quilp to the "skeleton in Holbein's series" (73). See also Newman's discussion of Quilp's death scene (81) and Sander's development of the *as in life so in death* motif (1–36 *passim*) and then his reading of the motifs of death in the novel (64–93). Kucich also insightfully discusses the various meanings of death in the novel. Finally, the reader may wish to consult my treatment of Ambrosio's death scene in *The Monk* as almost a prototype of Gothic death ("*The Monk*'s Gothic Bosh and Bosch's Gothic Monks" 47–51), since his demise bears striking similarities to Quilp's, which again places the dwarf in the Gothic tradition.

35. See Bakhtin's relevant analysis of "the death series [which] . . . appears in Rabe-lais on a grotesque and clownish plane" (*The Dialogic Imagination* 194–206). The keynote here is "the generative power of death and of the fresh corpse (a wound is a womb) and the idea of healing the death of one by the death of another" (195).

36. Such ideas anticipate Quilp's role as Pan in the novel.
37. Again, Bakhtin's full development of his argument should be consulted since it so provocatively implies the curious connection between Quilp's carnivalesque death and Nell's Christian death: "Folk culture strove to defeat through laughter this extreme projection of gloomy seriousness and to transform it into a gay carnival monster" (395).
38. Again, Leach's discussion of the profound mythological functions of the Punch drama seems relevant here:

> Punch not only defies but actually seems to toy with and disdain the very idea of life and death, personified in the show by the devil, suggesting implicitly a wider frame of reference, perhaps pantheistic, or cosmic; and this, finally, is what *Punch and Judy* celebrates. Such a celebration is firmly pagan. It bears upon the mysteries of the individual's life and of all life, without recourse to theologies. Paganism is an affirmation of man, his appetites, his desires, and his indivisible unity with nature.   (175–77)

39. For treatments of the relationship between transvestitism, hermaphroditism, and the carnivalesque, see Bakhtin (411) and Castle's "Eros and Liberty" (170–71).
40. Leach sees both Quilp and Swiveller resembling Punch (68–69).
41. In *The Gaping Pig: Literature and Metamorphosis*, Massey makes much the same point (25).
42. The narrator even compares "a house on fire" to "a play" (62:461).
43. As suggested below, the motif of gambling or gaming also bears positive connotations in *The Old Curiosity Shop*.
44. Although Patten's belief that the novel is "an improvisation" (44) is at variance with our thesis regarding the influence of Rabelais, his conclusions (64) bear a curious resemblance to the motif of carnivalesque alterations. See also Horton's relevant discussion of the novel's "spirit of bricolage" (215).
45. See Leach's treatment of the art of improvisation in *Punch and Judy* dramas (151 ff.).
46. Dyson finds Dick to be "simply one of the most splendid creations in the world" (121) and suggestively a "partial self-portrait, an embodiment of that side of Dickens's manifold nature which loved to drink in convivial company, visit the theatre, play pranks, and sport in the light" (123). Horton even notes that the Swiveller is "a walking carnival of [the] theatrical" (200).
47. For the best treatment of the *pious fraud* motif in Dickens, see Eigner's chapter "The Benevolent Agent and Her Pious Fraud" in *The Dickens Pantomime* (especially 54–68).
48. Rogers relevantly argues that Dick and Nell are not antithetical but complementary: "In spite of the undeniable difference in tone of the Nell and Swiveller stories, Dick's growth is not the antithesis of Nell's death. Creation and destruction in *The Old Curiosity Shop* are complementary, inseparable processes, and Dick's development follows essentially the same pattern as that of the characters associated with Nell" (140–41).
49. For some of the most perceptive treatments of Dick Swiveller, see Daldry (63–67), Kincaid (99–104), Marcus (104–08), McMaster (110–12), Newman (83 ff.), Pearson (87–90), Schlicke (131–36), Feinberg, and Horton.
50. In the conclusion to her essay on the carnivalesque, Babcock quotes James A. Boon to suggest that while the official way is always linear, the unofficial carnivalesque way is invariably circular: " 'circularity is only an accusation if you

take linearity as logic's natural way' " (937). In this sense, Dick seems almost to personify Roger Caillois' notion of *ilinx* or "whirling rapidly," especially as it evolves from the childish play of *paidia* to the mature play of *ludus* (23–26). In a related sense, Dick does appear to develop from the purely ludic to a kind of paradoxically *lucid ludic* at the novel's conclusion.

51. In his *Sexual Analysis of Dickens's Props*, Arthur Washburn Brown devotes an entire interesting if misguided chapter (focusing on *The Old Curiosity Shop*) to answering the question, 'Why Cribbage Represents Sexual Intercourse" (13–40).

52. Cordery argues, for instance, that "the grandfather's card games lead to poverty, despair and eventual death, those of Dick and the Marchioness are a joyous affirmation of life" (43). See similar comparisons by Kincaid (102) and Pearson (90). Finally, Kucich finds Dick relevantly refusing "seriousness by transforming anxiety into the excessive, unreal world of play. . . . His gambling is a delight in risk as pure play" (67).

53. See Brice's and Fielding's account and reprinting of this article (1–19). See also Feinberg's comments on Dick's name (206, 211).

54. Marcus equates Dick's love of beer with "the magic chalice, the holy grail itself" (167). As its title may suggest, Wallace Fowlie's *The Clown's Grail: A Study of Love in its Literary Expression* offers several insights from the tradition of Christian mysticism which, like "Our Lady's Tumbler," reinforce some carnivalesque motifs and, like Pelton's (somewhat) Christian treatment of the Trickster, thereby clarify Dick's role in the novel. In *Our Mutual Friend*, of course, the (mock) quest is for "the secret of [the] Dutch bottle" (IV:14, 788) buried in the Mound, and there is an explicit reference to "a Gargantuan order for a dram" (IV:8, 719).

WORKS CITED

Arnold, Matthew. "The Function of Criticism at the Present Time." *Matthew Arnold's Essays in Criticism, First Series*. Ed. and introd. Thomas Marion Hoctor. Chicago: U of Chicago P, 1968. 8–30.

Awn, Peter J. "Path to the Center: The Whirling Dervishes in 'performance.' " *Parabola* 4 (Feb. 1979):94–96.

Bakhtin, Mikhail Mikhailovich. *The Dialogic Imagination: Four Essays*. Ed. Michael Holquist. Trans. Caryl Emerson and Michael Holquist. Austin: U of Texas P, 1981.

———. *Rabelais and His World*. Trans. Helene Iswolsky. Foreword by Krystyna Pomorska. Cambridge: MIT Press, 1968.

Banks, P. W. "Of Rabelais." *Fraser's Magazine*. 20 (Nov. 1839):513–29; 21 (Feb. 1840):212–27; 21 (July 1840):60–80.

Bennett, Rachel. "Punch versus Christian in *The Old Curiosity Shop*." *Review of English Studies* 22 (1971):423–34.

Bernheimer, Richard. *Wild Men in the Middle Ages: A Study in Art, Sentiment, and Demonology*. Cambridge: Harvard UP, 1952.

Billington, Sandra. " 'Suffer Fools Gladly': The Fool in Medieval England and the Play *Mankind.*" *The Fool and The Trickster: Studies in Honour of Enid Welsford*. Ed. Paul V. A. Williams. Ipswich, England: D. S. Brewer; Totowa, NJ: Rowman and Littlefield, 1979. 36–54.

Brice, Alec W., and K. J. Fielding. "A New Article by Dickens: 'Demoralization and Total Abstinence.' " *Dickens Studies Annual*. Vol. 9. Ed. Michael Timko, Fred Kaplan, and Edward Guiliano. New York: AMS, 1981. 1–19.

Brown, Arthur Washburn. *Sexual Analysis of Dickens's Props*. New York: Emerson, 1971.

Bunyan, John. *The Pilgrim's Progress*. Middlesex: Penguin, 1965.

Caillois, Roger. *Man, Play, and Games*. Trans. Meyer Barash. New York: Free Press of Glencoe, 1961.

Campbell, Joseph. *The Hero's Journey: Joseph Campbell on His Life and Work*. Ed. and introd. Phil Cousineau. *Foreword by Stuart L. Brown. San Francisco: Harper, 1990.*

Carey, John. Here Comes Dickens: The Imagination of a Novelist. New York: Schocken, 1974.

Carroll, Lewis. *The Annotated Alice: Alice's Adventures in Wonderland and Through the Looking Glass*. New York: Herder and Herder, 1972.

Castle, Terry. "The Carnivalization of Eighteenth-Century English Narrative." *PMLA* 99 (1984):903–16.

———. "Eros and Liberty and the English Masquerade, 1710–90." *Eighteenth-Century Studies* 17 (Winter 1983–84):156–76.

———. *Masquerade and Civilization: The Carnivalesque in Eighteenth-Century English Culture and Fiction*. Stanford: Stanford UP, 1986.

Chesterton, G. K. *Charles Dickens*. Introd. Steven Marcus. New York: Schocken, 1965.

Cordery, G. "The Gambling Grandfather in *The Old Curiosity Shop*." *Literature and Psychology*. 33 (1987):43–61.

Daldry, Graham. *Charles Dickens and the Form of the Novel*. Totowa, NJ: Barnes, 1987.

Daleski, H. M. "Dickens and the Proleptic Uncanny." *Dickens Studies Annual*. Vol. 13. Ed. Michael Timko, Fred Kaplan, and Edward Guiliano. New York: AMS, 1984. 193–206.

Dickens, Charles. *The Letters of Charles Dickens*. 6 vols. to date. Eds. Madeline House, Graham Storey, and Kathleen Tillotson. Oxford: Clarendon, 1965–.

———. *The Old Curiosity Shop*. Ed. Angus Easson. Introd. Malcolm Andrews. Middlesex: Penguin, 1972.

———. *The Oxford Illustrated Dickens*. 21 vols. London: Oxford UP, 1951–59.

Dooling, D. M. "Our Lady's Tumbler." *Parabola* 4 (Feb. 1979):34–37.

Dyson, A. E. "*The Old Curiosity Shop*: Innocence and the Grotesque." *Critical Quarterly* 8 (Spring 1966):111–30.

Eigner, Edwin M. *The Dickens Pantomime*. Berkeley: U of California P, 1989.

Engel, Monroe. " 'A Kind of Allegory': *The Old Curiosity Shop*." *The Interpretation of Narrative: Theory and Practice*. Ed. Morton W. Bloomfield. Cambridge: Harvard UP, 1970. 135–47.

Feinberg, Monica L. "Reading *Curiosity*: Does Dick's Shop Deliver?" *Dickens Quarterly* 7 (1990):200–11.

Forster, John. *The Life of Charles Dickens*. 2 vols. London: Chapman, n.d.

Fowlie, Wallace. *The Clown's Grail: A Study of Love in Its Literary Expression*. London: Dobson, 1947.

Freud, Sigmund. "The Uncanny." *On Creativity and the Unconscious: Papers on the Psychology of Art, Literature, Love, Religion*. Trans. Alix Strachey. Selected and introd. Benjamin Nelson. New York: Harpers, 1958. 122–61.

Frye, Northrop. *The Secular Scripture: A Study of the Structure of Romance*. Cambridge: Harvard UP, 1976.

Gilead, Sarah. "Barmecide Feasts: Ritual, Narrative, and the Victorian Novel." *Dickens Studies Annual*. Vol. 17. Ed. Michael Timko, Fred Kaplan, and Edward Guiliano. New York: AMS, 1988. 225–47.

Ginsburg, Michal Peled. "Dickens and the Uncanny: Repression and Displacement in *Great Expectations*." *Dickens Studies Annual* Vol. 13. Michael Timko, Fred Kaplan, and Edward Guiliano. New York: AMS, 1984. 115–24.

Goldsmith, Oliver. "The Deserted Village." *Collected Works of Oliver Goldsmith*. Vol. 4. Ed. Arthur Friedman. Oxford: Clarendon, 1966. 5 Vols. 287–304.

Gose, Elliott B., Jr. *Imagination Indulged: The Irrational in the Nineteenth-Century Novel*. Montreal: McGill-Queen's UP, 1972.

Greenstein, Michael. "Lenticular Curiosity and *The Old Curiosity Shop*." *Dickens Quarterly* 4 (1987):187–94.

Hardy, Barbara. *The Moral Art of Dickens*. London: Athlone, 1970.

Hennelly, Mark M., Jr. "Dickens's Praise of Folly: Play in *The Pickwick Papers*." *Dickens Quarterly* 3 (1986):27–45.

————. "*The Monk*'s Gothic Bosh and Bosch's Gothic Monks." *Comparative Literature Studies* 24 (1987):36–54.

————. "The Victorian Book of the Dead: *Dracula.*" *Journal of Evolutionary Psychology* 12 (1991):338–49.

Hill, Nancy K. *A Reformer's Art: Dickens' Picturesque and Grotesque Imagery.* Athens: Ohio UP, 1981.

Hillman, James. "An Essay on Pan." *Pan and the Nightmare.* By Wilhelm Heinrich Roscher and James Hillman. Dallas: Spring, 1972. 3–65.

Hollington, Michael. "Dickens and the Dance of Death." *Dickensian* 54 (1978):67–75.

————. *Dickens and the Grotesque.* London: Croom Helm; Totowa, NJ: Barnes, 1984.

Holquist, Michael. Introduction. *The Dialogic Imagination: Four Essays.* By Mikhail Mikhailovich Bakhtin. Austin: U of Texas P, 1981. xv–xxxiv.

Horton, Susan R. "Swivellers and Snivellers: Competing Epistemologies in *The Old Curiosity Shop.*" *Dickens Quarterly* 7 (1990):212–17.

Hyland, Drew A. *The Question of Play.* Lanham, MD: UP of America, 1984.

Jaffe, Audrey. " 'Never be Safe but in Hiding': Omniscience and Curiosity in *The Old Curiosity Shop.*" *Novel* 19 (1986):118–34.

Kaplan, Fred. *Dickens: A Biography.* New York: Morrow, 1988.

Kerényi, Karl. "The Trickster in Relation to Greek Mythology." Trans. R. F. C. Hull. *The Trickster: A Study in American Indian Mythology.* By Paul Radin. With Commentaries by Karl Kerényi and C. G. Jung. New York: Greenwood, 1956. 173–91.

Kincaid, James R. *Dickens and the Rhetoric of Laughter.* Oxford: Clarendon, 1971.

Kinser, Samuel. *Rabelais's Carnival: Text, Context, Metatext.* Berkeley: U of California P, 1990.

Kucich, John. "Death Worship among the Victorians: *The Old Curiosity Shop.*" *PMLA* 95 (1980):58–72.

Leach, Robert. *The Punch and Judy Show: History, Tradition and Meaning.* London: Batsford, 1985.

Marcus, Steven. *Dickens: From Pickwick to Dombey.* New York: Clarion, 1968.

Marlow, James E. "Social Harmony and Dickens' Revolutionary Cookery." *Dickens Studies Annual.* Vol. 17. Ed. Michael Timko, Fred Kaplan, and Edward Guiliano. New York: AMS, 1988. 145–78.

Massey, Irving. *The Gaping Pig: Literature and Metamorphosis*. Berkeley: U of California P, 1976.

McMaster, Juliet. *Dickens the Designer*. Totowa, NJ: Barnes, 1987.

Newman, S. J. *Dickens at Play*. New York: St. Martin's, 1981.

Panofsky, Erwin. *"Et In Arcadia Ego*: Poussin and the Elegiac Tradition." *Meaning in the Visual Arts: Papers in and on Art History*. Garden City: Doubleday-Anchor, 1955. 295–320.

Patten, Robert L. " 'The Story-Weaver at his Loom': Dickens and the Beginning of *The Old Curiosity Shop." Dickens the Craftsman: Strategies of Presentation*. Ed. Robert B. Partlow, Jr. Carbondale: Southern Illinois UP; London: Feffer, 1970. 44–64.

Pearson, Gabriel. *"The Old Curiosity Shop." Dickens and the Twentieth Century*. Ed. John Gross and Gabriel Pearson. London: Routledge, 1962. 77–90.

Pelton, Robert D. *The Trickster in West Africa: A Study in Mythic Irony and Sacred Delight*. Berkeley: U of California P, 1980.

Plato. *The Symposium*. Trans. Walter Hamilton. Middlesex: Penguin, 1951.

Rabelais, François. *The Works of Mr. Francis Rabelais Doctor in Physick, Containing Five Books of the Lives, Heroick Deeds and Sayings of Gargantua and His Sonne Pantagruel*. 1653. [Trans. Thomas Urquhart]. Illus. W. Heath Robinson. 2 vols. London: Navarre Society, n.d.

Rogers, Philip. "The Dynamics of Time in *The Old Curiosity Shop." Nineteenth-Century Fiction* 28 (1973):127–44.

Rosen, Stanley. *Plato's* Symposium. New Haven: Yale UP, 1968.

Ruskin, John. "The Nature of Gothic." *The Stones of Venice. The Complete Works of John Ruskin, L.L.D*. Vol. 2. Philadelphia: Reuwee, n.d. 152–230. 26 vols.

Sadoff, Dianne F. *"Locus Suspectus*: Narrative, Castration, and the Uncanny." *Dickens Studies Annual*. Vol. 13. Ed. Michael Timko, Fred Kaplan, and Edward Guiliano. New York: AMS, 1984. 207–30.

Sanders, Andrew. *Charles Dickens: Resurrectionist*. New York: St. Martin's, 1982.

Schlicke, Paul. *Dickens and Popular Entertainment*. London: Allen, 1985.

Stewart, Garrett. *Dickens and the Trials of Imagination*. Cambridge: Harvard UP, 1974.

Stoker, Bram. *Dracula*. New York: Modern Library, 1897.

Stonehouse, J. H. *Catalogue of the Library of Charles Dickens from Gadshill, Catalogue of His Pictures and Objects of Art, Catalogue of the Library of W. M. Thackeray, and Relics from His Library*. London: Piccadilly Fountain, 1935.

Strutt, Joseph. *The Sports and Pastimes of the People of England: From the Earliest Period, Including the Rural and Domestic Recreations, May Games, Mummeries, Pageants, Processions and Pompous Spectacles, Illustrated by Reproductions, from Ancient Paintings in Which are Represented Most of the Popular Diversions.* 1801. Rpt. 1903. Detroit: Singing Tree, 1968.

Tennyson, Alfred. *In Memoriam. The Poems of Tennyson.* Ed. Christopher Ricks. Vol 2. Berkeley: U of California P, 1987. 304–459. 3 vols.

Turner, Victor. "Betwixt and Between: The Liminal Period in *Rites de Passage.*" *The Forest of Symbols: Aspects of Ndembu Ritual.* Ithaca: Cornell UP, 1967. 93–111.

————. "Liminal to Liminoid, in Play, Flow, Ritual: An Essay in Comparative Symbology." *From Ritual to Theatre: The Human Seriousness of Play.* New York: Performing Arts Journal Publications, 1982. 20–60.

Watson, Thomas L. "The Ethics of Feasting: Dickens' Dramatic Use of *Agape.*" *Essays in Honor of Esmond Linworth Marilla.* Ed. Thomas Austin Kirby and William John Olive. Baton Rouge: Louisiana State UP, 1970. 243–52.

Westland, Ella. "Little Nell and The Marchioness: Some Functions of Fairy Tale in *The Old Curiosity Shop.*" *Dickens Quarterly* 8 (1991):68–75.

Wind, Edgar. *Pagan Mysteries in the Renaissance.* New Haven: Yale UP, 1958.

Winters, Warrington. "*The Old Curiosity Shop*: A Consummation Devoutly to Be Wished." *Dickensian* 63 (1967):176–80.

Construing the Inimitable's Silence: Pecksniff's Grammar School and International Copyright

Gerhard Joseph

> There is no binary division to be made between what one says and what one does not say; we must try to determine the different ways of not saying . . . things, how those who can and those who cannot speak of them are distributed, which type of discourse is authorized, or which form of discretion is required in either case. There is not one but many silences, and they are an integral part of the strategies that underlie and permeate discourse.
>
> Michel Foucault, *The History of Sexuality*, vol. 1

> Some architects are clever at making foundations, and some are clever at building on 'em when they're made.
>
> Mark Tapley in *Martin Chuzzlewit*

After finishing *Barnaby Rudge* in 1841, Charles Dickens set off with his wife for the United States, full of enthusiasm for the young country, but he returned, so the well-known story goes, thoroughly disillusioned. The texts that evince the grounds of that disillusionment are of course the *American Notes* of 1842 and the novel *Martin Chuzzlewit* of 1843–44: the braggart insularity, the vulgarity of manner, the rapaciousness of real estate speculation, the political corruption, the ugliness of the landscape both urban and rural—all such reasons emerge clearly enough in the critical comments within both texts, if in the American section of *Martin Chuzzlewit* most virulently.

But even during his lifetime the argument circulated that perhaps the primary, because most personal cause of Dickens' bitterness concerned his disappointments surrounding the issue of copyright law. One of the reasons Dickens had gone to America, though he subsequently denied that motivation, was to work for the acceptance of International Copyright so that his books, among those of others to be sure, would no longer be pirated by unscrupulous American publishers.[1] It was a mission in which he entirely, humiliatingly failed, and a copyright agreement between England and the United States was not concluded until 1891.

But one has little direct sense of the authorial impact of that failure in reading either the *American Notes* or *Martin Chuzzlewit*. So, at any rate, James Spedding argued in an anonymous 1843 review of *American Notes* in the *Edinburgh Review*:

> [Dickens] went out there, if we are rightly informed, as a kind of missionary in the cause of International Copyright; with the design of persuading the American public (for it was the public to which he seems to have addressed himself) to abandon their present privilege, of enjoying the produce of the literary industry of Great Britain without paying for it;—an excellent recommendation, the adoption of which would, no doubt, in the end prove a vast national benefit . . . In this arduous, if not hopeless enterprise Mr. Dickens, having once engaged himself must be presumed, during the short period of his visit, to have chiefly occupied his thoughts; therefore the gathering of materials for a book about America must be regarded as a subordinate and incidental task—the produce of such hours as he could spare from his main employment. Nor must it be forgotten that in this, the primary object of his visit, he decidedly failed; a circumstance (not unimportant when we are considering his position and opportunities as an observer of manners in a strange country) to which we draw attention, the rather because Mr. Dickens makes no allusion to it himself. A man may read the volumes through without knowing that the question of International Copyright has ever been raised on either side of the Atlantic.[2]

As Alexander Walsh comments in his study of Dickens and Copyright, there is a hidden, all but prosecutorial assumption in Spedding's argument not unlike that of the psychoanalyst who argues doublebindingly that an analysand's reticence on a matter *must* be the sign of repression: Dickens' silence on the Copyright issue in *American Notes* (and I would add in *Martin Chuzzlewit*) thus seems to Spedding, who did not know Dickens personally, to be an admission of some kind, most "decidedly" an admission of failure. But of course if Dickens failed, he must have intended to succeed in what Spedding insists was the "main employment" of his visit. And as Welsh comments upon such attribution of intention, "the positive argument from circumstances, that since Dickens spoke on behalf of copyright he probably intended to speak, is a strong one. Much weaker is the argument, from his silence [in *American Notes* and *Martin Chuzzlewit*], about his state of mind," though Welsh also adds that Dickens' subsequent change from silence to fierce denial that he went to America to work for International Copyright serves "to etch [Spedding's] argument deeper."[3]

It is within such a context of the positive of Dickens' speech and negative of his silence that I would like to consider an incident in *Martin Chuzzlewit* which may or may not provide evidence of Dickens' novelistic voicing of a concern with copyright. I say "may or may not" since it is up to the reader to accept or reject the argument. That is another way of saying that what follows is an example of the positive of speech and the negative of silence, but now displaced onto the listener who "hears" or "does not hear" the voicing of what this reader takes to be the novelist's concern.

In chapter 35 of *Martin Chuzzlewit* Martin and his servant Mark Tapley, having just disembarked in Liverpool from their American trip, seek out a cheap tavern in order to formulate plans for their immediate future. Their lodging is

> one of those unaccountable little rooms which are never seen anywhere but in a tavern, and are supposed to have gotten into taverns by reason of the facilities afforded to the architect for getting drunk while engaged in their construction. It had more corners in it than the brain of an obstinate man; was full of mad closets, into which nothing could be put that was not specifically invented for that purpose; had mysterious shelvings and bulk-heads, and indications of staircases in the ceiling; and was elaborately provided with a bell that rung in the room itself, about two feet from the handle, and that had no connection whatever with any other part of the establishment.[4]

The passage throws off a striking architectural metaphor and conceptual phrase for the structure of *Martin Chuzzlewit* as a whole: that novel too feels as if it were put together by a drunken architect—has more angles to it than the brain of an obstinate man; is replete with mad closets, mysterious shelvings, and useless bells; is full of odd, discrete units (notably the disproportionately long American section) that seem to have questionable connection with anything else in the novel. The greatness of *Martin Chuzzlewit*, that is (and it is a great novel, arguably Dickens' funniest), arises from a disjunctive fecundity of character and scene rather than from the tight coherence of its comic, melodramatic, and romantic plots. For better and worse, it lacks what Coleridge valorized as a unity of feeling; the qualities we admire are rather its energy and variety, its sharp discontinuities—the newspaper virtues of Dickens' early years. The novelist, that is, harks back to—as he never will entirely disavow or escape—the tendencies of the sketch-collector as he piles up memorable portrait after portrait, self-contained scene after scene to generate the impression of a drunken architect's variegated but rather disorderly urban structure.

Of course, the question of what does and what does not constitute aesthetic order, of how much *discordia* Coleridge's *concors* will allow, is always debatable once we get text-specific. As linguistically-inspired structuralists have taught us, all works of art (i.e., buildings and novels for the sake of the present argument) may be read like sentences, if ones with varying degrees of coherence. The certainty that even the most apparently seamless of works are marked by disruptions and redundancies, what Michael Riffaterre has called "ungrammaticalities," is the operative assumption of semiotic theory.[5] In some cases such ruptures seem momentarily healed when the work's grammar is construed from a wider focus; in others, however, the effort to transcend ungrammaticalities of structure results in a specious papering-over of a work's heterogeneity, in the falsification of parataxis into syntax, of mere contiguity into analogy, of metonymy into metaphor. The appeal of some works—of some novels and some buildings—is that they seem programmatically ungrammatical; they stubbornly refuse to satisfy first the writer and then the reader's profound psychological yearning for a stable integration of part and whole. The arts—indeed, the human sciences as a whole—may thus be seen collectively as a kind of "grammar school" through which we readers and viewers move as children, construing as best we can, accustoming ourselves to various sorts of texts, learning "to cipher and to sing," as Yeats puts it so memorably in "Among School Children."

Consequently, chapter 35 of *Martin Chuzzlewit*, which concerns itself with the disputed origin and hence the intellectual ownership of a grammar school, may be taken as yet another "allegory of reading," in Paul de Man's sense. For that chapter offers us a comic version of the structuralist's paradigm, the grammar of part for whole. To begin with, the "drunken architect's" room in which Martin and Mark plot their future seems a perfect architectural correlative for the idea of the "ungrammatical" in Riffaterre's sense. As I have said, the parts of the novel do not seem to cohere very well; they seem merely contiguous; no part of *this* structure leads very efficiently or directly to another, whatever the straightforward desires of its characters. As Mark and Martin are sitting in their tavern room, they are intent upon "losing no time," of "travelling straight" to the Dragon Inn where they hope to link up with the novel's other major characters, Tom Pinch and Mary Graham, in a meeting that will forward Dickens' plot. But in this leisurely, tangent-seeking, drunken idler of a novel, there are few straight lines: as Mark and Martin look out the window, their gaze is arrested by a figure that "slowly, very slowly" (and paratactically) passes:

Mr. Pecksniff. Placid, calm but proud. Honestly proud. Dressed with peculiar
care, smiling with even more than usual blandness, pondering on the beauties
of his art with a mild abstraction from all sordid thoughts, and gently travelling
across the disc, as if he were a figure in a magic lantern.

In their astonishment Mark and Martin make inquiries of the tavern's landlord
and discover that they have indeed seen Pecksniff—that they have returned
to England just in time for a momentous architectural event, the laying of the
first stone of a new grammar school by the local Member of Parliament under
the supervision of "the great Mr. Pecksniff, the celebrated architect" (as the
landlord describes him), whose design for the school has carried off first prize
in a competition. As an interested onlooker to the subsequent ceremony
Martin, catching sight of the plans, realizes that Pecksniff had stolen *his*
plans, ones that Martin had undertaken as an exercise during his architectural
apprenticeship to Pecksniff. "My grammar-school. I invented it. I did it all,"
Martin exclaims at his discovery. "He has only put four windows in, the
villain, and spoilt it all" (554; fig. 1).

The scene has the appearance of merely a redundant flourish that does
nothing to advance the plot, just one of many instances of the hypocrisies of
"the great Mr. Pecksniff." While possessed of a certain local charm, it is
structurally as functionless as one of the tavern architect's mad closets. But
that very redundancy is emblematic of the *idea* of redundancy, of superfluous
comic energy, of a profound carelessness that is part of Dickens' appeal and
for the taming of which he will pay a price in his mature work. (There will
always be those who prefer the virtues of the early to those of the late Dickens,
the exuberant looseness of *Pickwick Papers* to the more studied intricacy of
Bleak House or *Our Mutual Friend*.)

If grammatical part and whole are randomly related in the drunken architect's house of fiction, then there is a sense in which *any* chapter can be
shown to have a synecdochic force; if we can never be certain which part
most essentially stands for the whole, are we not then "drunkenly" free to
choose any part as doing so, depending on the critical point we want to make?
While J. Hillis Miller has shown that synecdoche is Dickens' major figural
strategy for achieving the impression of all-inclusiveness, he has also said
that when we concentrate upon any given "linguistic moment" or even a
combination of such moments we are necessarily dealing with *suggested*
contiguity or contingency.[6] Miller thus finds all literary study based upon a
highly problematic *assumption* of valid synecdoche, for there is something
arbitrarily perspectivist in the particular linguistic moment (or book chapter)
that the critic chooses to illuminate the whole.[7] *Miller's* "grammar school"

Martin is much gratified by an imposing ceremony.

Figure 1.

thus bears certain resemblances to Pecksniff's school back in Wiltshire, where in chapter 5 beginning students are encouraged to draw sketches of Salisbury Cathedral from every conceivable angle. Not that I mean to denigrate Miller's perspectivism, since my own critical practice exemplifies his thesis with some precision: while for the sake of an earlier essay on *Martin Chuzzlewit* entitled "The Labyrinth and the Library: A View from the Temple in *Martin Chuzzlewit*" I isolated the combined synecdochic force of chapters 9 and 39, in the light of my present architectural emphasis chapter 35 (and, as we shall see below, chapter 6) seem the isolatable shards which have the most relevant microcosmic significance.[8]

The significance I have in mind expresses itself as a confluence of writerly and architectural concerns. As an architectural plan presents a written forecast of built architecture (a "world to word fit"), so a novel working with realistic conventions strives to imitate the world (a "word to world fit")—the useful distinction is John Searle's; as the "first stone" of the building that the Member of Parliament lays is the part that gives us a ceremonial promise of the completed structure, so a single scene like the one in chapter 35 can operate as a synecdoche for an entire novel like *Martin Chuzzlewit*, which has the false building of the House of Chuzzlewit as its central theme.[9]

While that architectural theme has all sorts of local manifestations, it is most importantly built into the novel's earliest design. As John Forster observed, the novel's precarious sense of structure arose from the difficulty Dickens had in modifying portions of his original scheme as that scheme was implied by his lengthy original "architectural" title: *The Life and Adventures of Martin Chuzzlewit—his Relatives, Friends, and Enemies. Comprising All his Wills and Ways: With an Historical Record of What he Did and What he Didn't: Showing, Moreover, Who Inherited the Family Plate, Who Came in for the Silver Spoons, and Who for the Wooden Ladles. The Whole Forming a Complete Key to the House of Chuzzlewit.* That dynastic theme, the Fall of the House of Chuzzlewit, accounts for the opening chapter's genealogical frame (one of the earliest of the Chuzzlewits may have been Guy Fawkes, the unsuccessful underminer of the Houses of Parliament), as well as for the mythic resonances of Old Martin Chuzzlewit's climactic verdict upon the entire race of Chuzzlewits: "The curse of our house . . . has been the love of self; has ever been the love of self" (800). That English corruption has its American equivalent during Martin's and Mark's disastrous cross-Atlantic journey in Mr. Scadder's description of the factitious Eden (Cairo, Illinois, in Dickens' actual American odyssey in 1842) to which he sends the gullible pair as a flourishing "architectural city," a thriving community of "banks, churches, cathedrals, market-places, factories, hotels, stores, mansions, wharves" and other public and private edifices (353). The naive Martin discovers the reality beneath the verbal façade, the "paper city" of Phiz's illustration (fig. 2), soon enough in the fetid wilderness that is all but the death of him; and of course his cocky certainty that he will make his fortune in America through the application of "ornamental architecture" to "domestic American purposes" is shown to be a ludicrous pipedream when exposed to the enterprising scams of America's real estate swindlers.

But it is in Pecksniff's professional deceit that the novel launches its initial, most blatant, and most comic attack upon the "natural right" of property, for his appropriation of his students' architectural plans shows him to be the first and paradigmatic of the novels' believers that one can "own" a building—and by extension a House in the dynastic sense. I have asserted above that, as an example of the novel's "ungrammaticality," the laying of the grammar school's first stone in chapter 35 seems like a discrete, redundantly incremental instance of Pecksniff's villainy only loosely related to the larger plot. But that scene is at least prepared for by an earlier one in chapter 6, where Pecksniff defines his aesthetic principles while offhandedly assigning Martin the exercise of designing a grammar school, precisely the design which Martin and Mark stumble on in chapter 35:

> "Stay," said [Mr. Pecksniff]. "Come! as you're ambitious, and are a very neat draughtsman, you shall—ha ha!—you shall try your hand on these proposals for a grammar-school: regulating your plan, of course, by these printed particulars. Upon my word, now," said Mr. Pecksniff, merrily, "I shall be very curious to see what you make of the grammar-school. Who knows but a young man of your taste might hit upon something, impracticable and unlikely in itself, but which I could put into shape? For it really is, my dear Martin, it really is in the finishing touches alone, that great experience and long study in these matters tell." (87–88)

Such a master-apprentice procedure was typical enough for Pecksniff: to the preliminary sketch of his pupils he habitually added a "few finishing touches from the hand of a master"—"an additional back window, or a kitchen door, or a half-a-dozen steps, or even a water spout"—and then claimed the design as his own work. "Such," says the Dickensian narrator, "such is the magic of genius, which changes all it handles into gold" (88). And as a matter of fact Pecksniff, hypocritical parasite that he is, is endowed with alchemical powers, if not quite of the sort that he believes he has. Rather his genius is that of a subversive absurdity capable of estranging both the conventional moral and asthetic orders of the novel's surface—specifically, in the present

The thriving City of Eden, as it appeared on paper.

Figure 2.

emphasis, throwing into question nineteenth-century assumptions about the ownership of intellectual property. For no matter how powerful the attacks upon him, Pecksniff's confidence in the virtue of his procedures throughout the novel is absolutely unshakable: he is sincerely, unaffectedly, naturally pompous—the quintessential expression of an impregnable narcissism. For the rest of us self-deception can never be complete because the reality principle will probably not allow it, but Pecksniff's self-deception is totally sincere and therefore mock-heroic, a comic exemplification of Romantic egoism.[10]

Pecksniff's invulnerable egoism carries over quite naturally from his ethics to his aesthetics. When in the speech quoted above from chapter 6 he avers that he habitually adds the "finishing touches" of the master to the apprentice efforts of his pupils, he is merely defining a time-tested guild ethos whose successful results we see celebrated in the stone-laying ceremony of chapter 35. We must assume that he sees nothing dishonest in that method, that were Martin to accuse him of plagiarism to his face, he would answer quite sincerely in the tones of martyred innocence with which he outfaces Old Martin in the novel's closing confrontation scene. And indeed we (or at least I) believe him and am tempted to come to his defense, if only because his "theft" of Martin's design raises—again, in a comic register, to be sure—questions of serious import to intellectual property rights in general and to the authorship of architectural and literary texts in particular. As Peter Jaszi has pointed out to me in correspondence, a strictly legal analysis of the competing claims to the architectural work in question between master and apprentice would in the nineteenth century have supported Pecksniff's claim to ownership: he is arguably the intellectual "owner" of the grammar school twice over, by virtue of his status as Martin's master *and* by the addition of those marginal windows which by contemporary standards would have absolved him from any charge of plagiarism, a charge which has always been more common in a literary than in an architectural craft anyway. Indeed, it was not until 1990 that changes in American copyright law for the first time embraced architectural designs (as distinct from plans and drawings) as copyrightable subject matter.[11]

Furthermore, while it is easy enough to laugh at the broad absurdity of Pecksniff's appropriation of his pupils' work in an extralegal, moral context, what seems less obvious is that Martin's pride of invention ("*My* grammar-school. *I* invented it. I did it *all*.") is morally suspect in its turn. Indeed, the combined activity of master and pupil highlights the controversial status of originality, both architectural and—by extension—literary, in the nineteenth century.

As the career of Coleridge among others makes clear, authorial plagiarism became a significant moral and aesthetic issue in the nineteenth century precisely because of the high premium put upon the ideals of "originality" and "invention" at the expense of classical "imitation." (Hence, Dickens' half-joking characterization of himself as the Inimitable—and the public acceptance of the tag.) It is certainly not true, as one sometimes hears, that writers before the nineteenth century were not concerned with originality: they were concerned, but not so deeply and urgently as the Romantics. The key document in the transvaluation of imitation and originality was of course Edward Young's *Conjectures on Original Composition* in 1759. But as Thomas McFarland has recently shown, originality and imitation have never existed in isolation but have always been two terms of a ratio, two sides of a "paradox."[12] As originality is defined against its counter-ideal of imitation (and always involves a certain amount of it), so imitation is never merely slavish but always inclines toward its opposite, originality or invention.

All this sounds high-minded enough until we get to the dangerous ground of plagiarism, which is after all a dark variant of imitation and influence. (And Harold Bloom's "anxiety of influence" is arguably a disguised form of apprehension about plagiarism, the later writer's anxiety about his appropriation of an earlier one's intellectual property, so much so that McFarland suggests that plagiarism might well be added as an "ugly duckling" seventh to the six "revisionary ratios" Bloom summons forth as influence's tributaries).[13] Because it brings the bourgeois conception of coherent individual identity into conflict with itself, plagiarism tends to be easily dismissed from our cultural consciousness and has occasioned relatively little theoretical discussion, considering the number of writers who have been guilty or at least accused of it. At any rate, precisely because the honorific status accorded the concept of originality by Romantic writers came into conflict with their universal indebtedness, the accusation of plagiarism is one of the central embarrassments for many writers in the nineteenth century—as the careers of Coleridge, Poe, and Wilde in a serious register and Pecksniff in a comic one demonstrate.

For Pecksniff's architectural plagiarism may within such a context be seen as a mock commentary upon the imitation-originality paradox that McFarland describes. That is, we are no doubt meant to side with Martin in his outrage at Pecksniff's theft, but that theft also serves a critical function, putting into question the egoism and pride of ownership out of which such outrage arises. If *Martin Chuzzlewit* as a whole is meant to condemn the "love of self" that built the House of Chuzzlewit, that selfishness had been given an aura of theoretical respectability by the heroic egoism of post-Renaissance thought generally and the "egotistical sublime" of Romanticism in particular. Martin's insistence upon his originality does of course indict Pecksniff's knavery, his stealing of the sign of another's personality (not to mention whatever monetary theft is involved), which is what plagiarism attempts. But Pecksniff's theft serves in turn to question the pride of personality and ownership in Martin—and by extension in the entire graspingly individualistic House of Chuzzlewit.

Such an ambivalence swirls about the structure of a grammar school whose lessons are instructively hard to construe. Affirming the psychic dangers of plagiarism for *both* the plagiarizer and his accuser, that ambivalence captures the boundary anxiety concerning the structure of a fragile, coherent self which is relatively muted in plagiarism's more respectable cousins, imitation and influence.[14] Perhaps Mark Tapley's generous estimate of the combined work of Pecksniff and Martin is the most forgiving way to defuse the anxiety implicit in both sides of the originality paradox: "some architects are clever at making foundations, and some architects are clever at building on 'em when they're made. But it'll all come right in the end, sir; it'll all come right" (555). Wise servant that he is, Mark and his words may thus be said both to embody an ancient Christian charity and to anticipate a major thrust of postmodernist theory—the insistence upon the "intertextuality" and therefore the inter- or transpersonal nature of all intellectual enterprises.

On the grounds of such an argument it is now time to turn back to the subject with which we began, the silence of Dickens on the subject of International Copyright law in *American Notes* and *Martin Chuzzlewit*. And I trust the reader can anticipate what I am now going to say: the American piracy of Dickens' novels (as well as those of other English writers), arguably the primary reason for his American journey, gets displaced in *Martin Chuzzlewit* onto a meditation on Pecksniff's theft of Martin's grammar-school plans. On the face of it, such a connection may sound a bit bizarre; the differences between the two situations may at first glance seem more striking than the similarities, if only because the relationship between an architect and his apprentice in a comic fiction seems so very different from that between a master novelist and the publishers of his work in that more naturalized fiction, our construction of an author's life. And yet it is surely true that the dispute about authorial rights to an intellectual property within a fiercely individualist humanist-capitalist ethos is what is at issue for both Martin the apprentice and Dickens the author. To be sure, there is no money involved for Martin (at least the text mentions no prize money for the grammar-school design) as there was for Dickens over copyright, but that just makes the psychic connection tighter because less exclusively mercenary: the very fact that intellectual rather than monetary rights are in dispute for Martin would seem to argue, in the displacement I posit, that for Dickens the money seemed (or so he told himself and others) less important than the principle of a creator's "natural rights" to his words subject to whatever contractual arrangements he might wish to make.[15] (Marxist critics like Pierre Machery have of course long held that the theory of writer as an independent "creator" belongs to a historically specific humanist and capitalist ideology, to what Foucault would call an aspect of the "author function" within a modern, postclassical *épisteme*.)[16] The high ground of intellectual more than financial rights was, at any rate, the position Dickens tried publicly (and Pecksniffianly?) to occupy during his American journey—to the studied and deeply humiliating derision of a few American newspaper commentators.

The Inimitable Dickens no doubt felt he was entirely in the right in matters literary and financial—but why then the fierce denials once he returned from his American journey that International Copyright was a significant reason for the trip and why the silence about the matter in both *American Notes* and *Chuzzlewit*? Perhaps an oblique answer may be gained from the foregoing reading of the grammar-school episode: Dickens' text surely asks us to side with Martin's indignation at Pecksniff's highhandedness, and that authorial advocacy seems clear enough. But that text also, I would suggest, asks us to recognize the House of Chuzzlewit's "love of self" that taints, however slightly, Martin's self-affirming "My grammar school. I invented it. I did it all." The reason that Dickens was so perceptive about the corrupting egoism of the House of Chuzzlewit (and the way in which it frequently expressed itself through mercenary calculation) was that he was hardly a stranger to Pecksniffian hypocrisy, rampant egoism, and mercenary calculation himself. That was arguably the case in his reasons for the American journey, wherein he tended to mask a self-serving advocacy of International Copyright behind the less strictly commercial, more high-minded motives of gathering materials for a book. Pecksniff's theft of the grammar-school plans and Martin's response to it thus half reveal and half conceal Dickens' complicated, retrospective feelings about his reasons for the American journey.

NOTES

1. K. J. Fielding, "*American Notes* and Some English Reviewers," *Modern Language Review* 59 (1964):527–37, counters generally accepted opinion by accepting Dickens' word that he did not go to America "to engage in the copyright

controversy'' (534); and Sidney P. Moss, *Charles Dickens' Quarrel with America* (Troy: Whitson, 1984), believes that Dickens did not undertake the American tour as an advocate for copyright but only adopted the cause once here (65). For a detailed survey of the issue, see Alexander Welsh, ''Hypocrisy and Copyright,'' *From Copyright to Copperfield* (Cambridge: Harvard UP, 1987), 29–42.

2. *Edinburgh Review* 76 (1843):500–01; quoted in Welsh 36–37.

3. Welsh 37.

4. Charles Dickens, *Martin Chuzzlewit*, ed. Margaret Cardwell (Oxford: Clarendon, 1982), 846. Further references to the novel, its illustrations by Halbot K. Brown (''Phiz''), and its prefatory materials are to this edition and will be cited parenthetically within the body of the text.

5. *Semiotics of Poetry* (Bloomington: Indiana UP, 1978), 1–22.

6. See Miller's ''Optic and the Semiotic of *Middlemarch*,'' *The Worlds of Victorian Fiction*, ed. Jerome Buckley (Cambridge: Harvard UP, 1975), 126, for such a characterization of Dickens' ''strategy of compression.''

7. J. Hillis Miller, ''Nature and the Linguistic Moment,'' *Nature and the Victorian Imagination*, ed. U. C. Knoepflmacher and G. B. Tennyson (Berkeley: U of California P), 92–104.

8. *Dickens Studies Annual* 15 (1986):1–22.

9. ''I have never touched a character precisely from life,'' says Dickens, insisting upon the verisimilitude of Pecksniff and his characters more generally, ''but some counterpart of that character has incredulously asked me: 'Now realy, did I ever really, see one like it?' '' Preface to the Charles Dickens Edition, the Clarendon *Chuzzlewit*, 846n.

10. See Gerhard Joseph, ''Pecksniff and Romantic Satanism,'' *Dickens World* 2 (1986):1–2.

11. ''Architectural Works Copyright Protection Act,'' sponsored by Representative Robert Kastenmeier, an amendment to H.R. 536, the Judicial Improvement Act of 1990.

12. Thomas McFarland, ''The Originality Paradox,'' *Originality and Imagination* (Baltimore: Johns Hopkins UP, 1985), 1–30.

13. McFarland 22.

14. For a discussion of the ''scapegoating'' of the plagiarist by his accuser in the ''grammar school'' of academia relevant to the novel's continuing scapegoating of Pecksniff (posited in my ''The Labyrinth and the Library: A View from the Temple in *Martin Chuzzlewit*''), see Neil Hertz, ''Two Extravagant Teachings,'' *The End of the Line: Essays on Psychoanalysis and the Sublime* (New York: Columbia UP, 1985), 144–59.

15. As he told an audience in Hartford, Connecticut, in February 1842, ''I use [the words ''International Copyright''] in no sordid sense, believe me, and those who know me best know that. For myself, I would rather that my children coming after me, trudged in the mud, and knew by the general feeling of society that their father was beloved, and had been of some use, than I would have them ride in their carriages, and know by their banker's books that he was rich. But I do not see, I confess, why one should be obliged to make the choice. . . .'' From *The Speeches of Charles Dickens*, ed. K. J. Fielding (Oxford: Clarendon, 1960), 24–25; quoted in Welsh 32.

16. See Pierre Machery, *A Theory of Literary Production* (London: Routledge, 1978), 66; and Michel Foucault, ''What is an Author?'' *Language, Counter-Memory, Practice: Selected Essays and Interviews*, ed. Donald F. Bouchard (Ithaca: Cornell UP, 1977), 113–38.

WORKS CITED

"Architectural Works Copyright Protection Act," sponsored by Representative Robert Kastenmeir, an amendment to H.R. 536, the Judicial Improvement Act of 1990.

Dickens, Charles. *Martin Chuzzlewit*, ed. Margaret Cardwell. Oxford: Clarendon, 1982.

Foucault, Michel. "What Is an Author?" *Language, Counter-memory, Practice: Selected Essays and Interviews*, ed. Donald F. Bouchard. Ithaca: Cornell UP, 1977.

Hertz, Neil. "Two Extravagant Teachings." *The End of the Line: Essays on Psychoanalysis and the Sublime*. New York: Columbia UP, 1985.

Joseph, Gerhard. "Pecksniff and Romantic Satanism." *Dickens World* 2 (1986):1–2.

———. "The Labyrinth and the Library: A View from the Temple in *Martin Chuzzlewit*." *Dickens Studies Annual* 16. New York: AMS, 1987.

Machery, Pierre. *A Theory of Literary Production*. London: Routledge, 1978.

McFarland, Thomas. *Originality and Imagination*. Baltimore: Johns Hopkins UP, 1985.

Riffaterre, Michael. *Semiotics of Poetry*. Bloomington: Indiana UP, 1978.

Spedding, James. "Dickens's *American Notes*." *Edinburgh Review* 76 (1843):500–01.

Welsh, Alexander. *From Copyright to Copperfield: The Identity of Dickens*. Cambridge: Harvard UP, 1987.

The Cricket in the Study

Scott Moncrieff

The Cricket on the Hearth, though in immediate sales "the most popular of all Dickens's *Christmas Books*" (*Christmas Books* 2:11), has received little critical attention. George Ford felt he was speaking for a consensus of later readers in ranking it, along with *The Battle of Life* and *Pictures from Italy*, as "the worst ever written by Dickens" (53). In the Dickensian revolution of the thirty-five years since Ford's statement, *The Cricket* has remained a bystander, stuck at the hearth while the big novels were making their reputation in the study.

Those few who have commented on it have generally been unenthusiastic. Michael Slater seems to consider it an innocuous puppet show whose chief merit is a "general charm," bolstered by an "incomparably fine portrait" of a dog, and an amusing minor character in the nurse (Introd. to *Christmas Books* xviii). Harry Stone also likes the dog and the nurse, but feels that Dickens' "deepest energies" are "rarely" involved in the story (130). Deborah Thomas complains about the book's "lack of a clear focus," and its "labored emphasis on childishness" (45). And Edgar Johnson calls *The Cricket* "a weak book" (577–80). Perhaps the high point of critical opinion of *The Cricket* through 1980 comes in a footnote to Q. D. Leavis' *"David Copperfield"* chapter in *Dickens the Novelist*, where she asserts that the Peerybingles' unequal marriage gets "better treatment" from Dickens than that of the Strongs (67).

Andrew Sanders' brief 1981 introduction to the facsimile edition of *The Cricket* makes the most partial modern case for the work's merit. Sanders compares *The Cricket* and Shakespeare's late comedies on the rather broad basis that both allow "hope to transform despair and life to master death" (11). Furthermore, he forecasts, "it is possible that *The Cricket on the Hearth* will be seen both as a significant indication of the tastes of the 1840s and of

Dickens himself and re-emerge as vital to our proper understanding of both''
(15).

I hope to show that *The Cricket* is vital to our understanding of Dickens.
When an author has such a large oeuvre, it may be convenient and even
justifiable to pigeonhole certain works as insignificant. *The Cricket*, however,
deserves better. Dickens' energies, as I hope to show, are deeply engaged
with the story. Far from lacking a clear focus, the story is one of the most
cleverly structured of Dickens's short works. Through doubles—"glaring
instance[s]'' as Barbara Hardy calls them (52)—Dickens creates an impressive
range of possibility, yet with compression. Slater's appreciation of general
charm obscures the serious problems the story deals with, including the most
extensive treatment of an important recurring configuration in Dickens, the
January-May relationship. This examination of January-May stands out as
Dickens' most mature study of male-female relationships in the work before
1850. Finally, Dickens balances the superficially comic conclusion against
doubt of its validity. Without denying its juvenile moments, I would argue
that *The Cricket* is a complex, disturbing story deserving renewed attention.

I

Chaucer's "Merchant's Tale" and numerous Restoration comedies provide
literary models for the January-May tradition. Looking at the "Merchant's
Tale" as an example, we immediately notice that January-May is always a
triangular relationship, not a simple dichotomy. The term suppresses the
inevitable Young Man, just as January and-or May are apt to do. January's
motivation has traditionally been sexual. He wants a young wife to satisfy
his lust, and perhaps to give him an heir as well. May sells herself for the
wealth and social position January offers. But after marriage, disgusted by
lascivious January, she is romantically and sexually attracted by the Young
Man (Damyan), while the Young Man justifies his illicit attempt at May by
imagining himself to be rescuing her from January. Chaucer treats the situation as a joke on January, and minimizes the emotional and psychological
sides of the characters accordingly, just as he does in "The Miller's Tale."

Dickens treats the configuration quite differently. As a Victorian not only
bound by sexual reticence but supportive of it, Dickens emphasizes psychological and emotional, rather than physical aspects of January-May, especially
as his writing matures. In *The Cricket* he goes well beyond the grotesque
advances of Arthur Gride on Madeline Bray, and Quilp's more insidious

pursuit of Little Nell. Indeed, Dickens emphasizes the difference in his new January, John Peerybingle, by juxtaposing him with Tackleton, a throwback to the Gride stereotype.

John Peerybingle becomes the first of a Dickensian series of problematically good and sympathetic Januaries, followed by Doctor Strong (*David Copperfield*) and John Jarndyce (*Bleak House*), and, to a lesser extent, Arthur Clennam (*Little Dorrit*) and Joe Gargery (*Great Expectations*). The reason for the good January's appearance at the time of *The Cricket* may be biographical, as Sylvia Manning suggests (68–69). She cites Dickens' romantic interest in Christiana Weller, whom he finally helped his friend T. J. Thompson to marry, as a concurrent biographical occurrence of January-May in the author's life. Dickens, though only in his early thirties, appears to have felt like a premature January throughout the episode. Be that as it may, in *The Cricket* we have for the first time a sympathetically portrayed older man in love with, and indeed married to, a young woman.

Dickens enters new ground with this serious treatment of a romantic relationship. Love stories are neither the focus nor the high point of the early novels. The courtships and marriages of Mr. Winkle, Mr. Snodgrass, and Sam Weller in *Pickwick* are peripheral, mere finishing touches to the comic pattern. Almost the same could be said for the romance of Harry and Rose Maylie in *Oliver Twist*, the young Nicklebys and their respective partners, as well as Martin Chuzzlewit and Mary Graham, John Westlock and Ruth Pinch, even Walter Gay and Florence Dombey. Dick Swiveller and the Marchioness (*The Old Curiosity Shop*) are an exception, eccentric, not ideal, but comic, not serious. Not until *David Copperfield* does Dickens really probe the problems of a potentially good marriage; that is, unless we consider *The Cricket*, in which Dickens recognizes a positive January-May relationship as problematical, atypical, imperfect, yet a relationship which he wishes to defend.

The potential problems of creating a positive January-May relationship are numerous. Dickens must create sympathy for January, the traditional butt of the joke. The whole psychology and motivation of the relationship must be realigned. While January may be able to envision himself as a husband, May may not. This is especially true if January has been marking time as a benevolent guardian, like Doctor Strong or Mr. Jarndyce, waiting for May to grow up. May's motive, if she marries in this case, may be gratitude rather than love, and sooner or later she will have to come to terms with romantic love and/or sexual passion, finding it in a renewed vision of January—if the relationship is to hold up—and meanwhile resisting it in the person of the Young Man. Annie Strong resists Jack Maldon, and grows into an adult love for Doctor Strong. Esther Summerson, though willing to bury her love for Alan Woodcourt to submit to Mr. Jarndyce's proposal, rejoices when she finds that it is not necessary.

January's sexuality creates a particular dilemma. He can be made impotent, in order to make him a less offensive suitor—the Strongs are childless, and Mr. Jarndyce makes it quite clear to Esther that nothing will change in their relationship if they are married—but this asexuality leaves May unfulfilled, and thus prone to temptation from the Young Man.

Chaucer uses the encounter with the Young Man not to test the marriage, but rather to expose it. He allows no ambivalence toward January; that would undermine his comic intention. But Dickens, working with different purposes, recognizes that a credible test from the Young Man will decide the success of his new treatment of January-May.

In *The Cricket*, Dickens uses three January-May couples in a simple, yet ingenious interrelationship, which allows them to comment on each other. The central couple, John and Dot Peerybingle, have been married just long enough to have had a baby. Dot's friend May Fielding, the stereotypical "May" of this story, is about to be married to Tackleton, a sort of preconversion Scrooge. The third January-May couple is formed by Tackleton's employee, Caleb Plummer, and his daughter Bertha. Thus Dickens presents a married, an affianced, and a filial representation of January-May. Finally, we have the disguised Edward Plummer, a protean character who mysteriously acts as the Young Man for each of the three couples, and also happens to be Caleb's long-lost son, presumed dead. This limited cast creates multiple potential by its mutual reflection.

Dickens' central couple is particularly complex. John Peerybingle, unlike Mr. Jarndyce and Dr. Strong, is not impotent: the Peerybingles already have a baby at the story's beginning; nor is he an educated gentleman. John is a good-hearted, strong and slow-witted middle-aged man, along the lines of a Joe Gargery or a Mr. Peggotty. His psychological experience and vision, broadened by extension with Tackleton and Caleb, form the climax of the story.

But despite John's importance, Dot is at the center of the action. We do not enter her thoughts directly, as we do John's, but Dickens gives us numerous clues to her psychology through "objective correlatives," characters and objects that reflect her unspoken and sometimes unconscious thoughts. Even though the foregrounded psychological experience is John's, his thoughts center around Dot.

Much, and sometimes too much, has been made of Dickens' facility in naming characters. But if ever a name were cleverly conceived, it is Dot's. It functions as an expressive symbol of a role imposed by a world of male dominance. John names her thus to reflect his "playful" sense of her littleness. By naming her, he casts her in a role, much as David Copperfield's friends and relatives cast him in different roles by calling him separate names. The dot's place in our orthographic system resonates a patriarchal view of femininity, the circle which gives meaning to the upthrust stroke of the "i." This image is not inappropriate to Dot's role in John's mind. She is in a certain sense above him, yet insignificant, subservient, in place only at his extremity, given meaning only in reference to him, he the foundation, she the decoration. Dickens brilliantly actualizes this image in the text by the geographical placement of bodies at the Peerybingle hearthside: Dot sits on a little round stool at the end of John's extended feet. But through the course of the story Dot does much more than meet the "i." She escapes, at least temporarily, into a fantasy that eludes her orthographic and domestic prison.

It is possible to miss this rebellion at first, because in several ways Dot seems to be just another of Dickens' hearth angels, maybe even the paradigmatic one. One early reader went so far as to call her "the sweetest little woman that ever lived and moved inside a book" (Fitzgerald). Through the Cricket and the Kettle, she sings the domestic note; like Ruth Pinch, she bustles around the kitchen to the narrator's facetious delight; like Dora Spenlow, she makes a show out of little services for the husband, such as cleaning his pipe, and like Dora, she is consistently self-deprecatory and pleading; like Agnes Wickfield she is seen as a spiritual mediatrix between her man and the divine, with the hearth as the home's altar.

But the role of hearth angel is not to be taken for granted. Dickens complicates Dot's situation through her doubles. Dot expresses her dissatisfaction with John at a "safe" distance, through May. Although May is Dot's double, as indicated in part by John's sentiment, endorsed by the narrator, that "they ought to have been born sisters" (70), there is an important difference: Dot is irrevocably married while May is only on the verge of marriage. Dot sees a younger version of herself in May—not in years, but in potential. Bertha also calls Dot "My Sister!" (103); she doubles Dot in a different sense, to be explored later. But with May, she provides one of Dickens' more interesting sisterhoods, a trio of seemingly cardboard female characters, covertly sending out distress signals.

II

"Chirp the First" 's strident opening on the Kettle and the Cricket ends with Dot welcoming John home from work. After they talk for a while alone, John, a carrier, recalls that he has left a stranger, an old man, outside in his cart. The old man is called the Stranger throughout, a name which signifies his archetypal extension. The name would have carried an additional specific connotation to Victorian readers: *The Stranger* was the English title of A. A. F. von Kotzebue's play *Menschenhess und Reue*, a story of adultery, which was very popular in mid-Victorian England—David Copperfield goes to see it (*DC* 26. 446). Even though the Stranger in the play was the victim of adultery, rather than the perpetrator this Stranger appears to be, the very name would have conjured up the situation of adultery in the reader's mind, a crucial insinuation for *The Cricket.* In Dickens' story, the Stranger is really the Young Man in disguise, the Young Man to test the January-May marriages. That he is also Edward Plummer, Caleb's long-lost son returning from South America, reveals Dickens' love for coincidence (particularly in family relations), but should not diminish the Stranger's psychological and symbolic importance.

The Stranger's mythic significance is alluded to, even as he enters, through the inarticulate eloquence of Tilly Slowboy's thoughts. Tilly acts as a sort of audible unconscious or Victorian Chrous. She never seems alert, but her mumblings, which others ignore at their peril, are always to the point. When the Stranger enters, neither Dot nor John notices anything unusual about him. John refers to him as "the old gentleman," a harmless appellation, until the narrator lets us inside the mind of Tilly, who,

> conscious of some mysterious reference to The Old Gentleman, and connecting in her mystified imagination certain associations of a religious nature with the phrase, was so disturbed, that . . . she instinctively made a charge or butt at him with the only offensive instrument within her reach [the baby].   (36)

Tilly subconsciously ties Edward to the Devil, a threat to the home of her employers. The baby makes an appropriate weapon, as a symbol that this January-May marriage is not barren. The Peerybingles' fear of the Young Man still lies in the subconscious, as represented by Tilly's mumblings, but the reader, if not John and Dot, has been warned.

The Stranger's entrance begins in earnest the test of the Peerybingles' marriage. Ironically, John greatly enjoys playing host to the stranger at first, because in his apparent antiquity—signified by deafness, white hair, and slow responses—the Stranger makes John look young. John attempts to exploit this contrast but soon finds the tables turning. The Stranger, who (as Edward Plummer) knows very well the relationship between John and Dot, "innocently" asks John if Dot is his daughter. "Wife," answers John. "Niece?" asks the Stranger, pointedly exasperating John by emphasizing his seniority to Dot. "Wife," roars John. The Stranger does not even let him off here: " 'Indeed?' observed the Stranger. 'Very Young!' " (37). The stranger's conscious attempt to embarrass John recalls Mrs. Lupin's similar line of question to Mary Graham in *Martin Chuzzlewit*. But Dickens uses the interchange to much better purpose than idle titillation here. The question exposes and exacerbates John's insecurity in his relationship with Dot. Hoping to use the Stranger to show Dot his own youthfulness, John instead must suffer the Stranger's repeated allusions to his age.

Dickens also gives the reader clues as to the Stranger's imminent transformation into the Young Man. We are told that his features are "singularly bold and well defined for an old man" (37). The Stranger prefigures his transformative ability with his walking stick: "In his hand he held a great brown club or walking stick; and striking this upon the floor, it fell asunder, and became a chair" (37). When we remember Moses and the tradition of magical walking sticks, coming down to more recent figures like Tolkien's Gandalf, or, in Dickens' time, Harlequin and his magic bat, we realize that the Stranger is part of the magic fabric of the story, a magic tester with psychological importance that goes beyond the mere triangulation of a marriage.

But this opening scene gives only a foretaste of the Stranger's later transformations. Not only does he oppress John with a sense of his agedness; he himself can become young. He can actualize the fantasy that motivates a January. John/January marries a young wife, and repeatedly draws attention to her youth—by emphasizing her childlikeness, cuteness, innocence—because he denies his own age through her youth. Since he cannot make himself young, he marries a young woman. The Stranger, however, surpasses John. He can take off his white wig, change his slow mannerisms, drop the deaf act, become the young man John can only wish he were, and appear to steal Dot's affections. It is no surprise that John's reaction, upon "witnessing" Dot's later infidelity, is an uncontrollable desire to murder the Stranger.

The Stranger's effect is no less noticeable on Dot than on John. Their interaction around the house shows us that their relationship has produced fixed roles. John teases her about her name, while she snuggles up to him in a "half-natural, half-affected" way (28); she calls him "stupid fellow" and "old man" (though without the stigma the Stranger brings to the name). The narrator sees her as "a child at play keeping house" (30). Their relationship seems almost like a game, children playing at being adults.

But even in playing the game, Dot realizes that all is not well. She cannot handle her surge of emotions when she hints her greatest fear to John:

> I used to fear—I did fear once, John; I was very young you know—that ours might be an ill-assorted marriage: I being such a child, and you more like my guardian than my husband: and that you might not, however hard you tried, be able to learn to love me, as you hoped and prayed you might.	(33)

Dot clearly displaces her fear, as she later admits (112), that she cannot love John, at least as a wife should love a husband, into a more expressible fear that he would not be able to love her. She senses her failing the more sharply when John emphatically affirms his love for her: "She laid her hand, an instant, on his arm, and looked up at him with an agitated face, as if she would have told him something" (34). Dot hides her fear by immediately going back to the routine that keeps the marriage intact: "Next moment she was down upon her knees before the basket; speaking in a sprightly voice, and busy with the parcels" (34). This gesture, like Esther Summerson's frequent shaking of her keys, postpones rather than resolves the conflict.

Throughout the story we see Dot's inability to express herself to John, and a consequent displacement of her thoughts into the objects and people that surround her. As Dot discovers the wedding cake for Tackleton and May, which John has in his charge, she sits in a daze of "dumb and pitying amazement; screwing up her lips the while . . . and looking the good Carrier through and through, in her abstraction" (35). Her staring through John, while pondering the impending marriage of Tackleton and May, emphasizes Dot's unconscious connection of the two couples. Dot reproaches Tackleton as an unfit partner for May because—and her answer reflects her unwitting train of thought—"he's as old! As unlike her!—Why, how many years older than you, is Gruff and Tackleton, John?" (35). The little scene which follows takes on an ominous tone, with John's knife foreshadowing the coming storm:

> Absorbed in thought, she stood there, heedless alike of the tea and John (although he called to her, and rapped the table with his knife to startle her), until he rose and touched her on the arm; when she looked at him for a moment, and hurried to her place behind the teaboard, laughing at her negligence. But not as she had laughed before. The manner, and the music, were quite changed. The Cricket, too, has stopped. Somehow the room was not so cheerful as it had been. Nothing like it.	(35–36)

Any glitter of charm which Slater and others attribute to the story has disappeared. This is the point then, at which the Stranger enters. Dickens has taken considerable time setting up the scene, and preparing the attentive reader to expect tragedy to happen to John and Dot.

After his conversation with John, the Stranger soon becomes silent in the corner as Caleb Plummer comes and goes and as Tackleton, the bridegroom-to-be, arrives. Tackleton buttonholes John, and forces on him the kind of comparisons about the two couples Dot has already been making subconsciously: "Odd! You're just such another couple. Just! . . . We're in the same boat, you know . . . We're exactly alike, in reality, I see" (43–45). But although Dot has been thinking the same thing, as shown above, she cannot stand to take this comparison from another: "The indignation of Dot at this presumptuous assertion is not to be described. What next? . . . The man was mad" (43). Her attribution of madness to Tackleton is her only way to deny what she fears is true.

Dot has reached a point of fragile emotional imbalance, lacking only a final blow to fracture her remaining semblance of self control and cause her to fall into the madness she displaces on Tackleton. The blow is not long in coming. The narrator follows the conversation between Tackleton and John in one corner of the room, leaving Dot in a corner with the Stranger, but the men's conversation is interrupted by "a loud cry from the Carrier's wife: a loud, sharp, sudden cry, that made the room ring, like a glass vessel. She had risen from her seat, and stood like one transfixed by terror and surprise" (45). When her husband asks what has happened,

> She only answered by beating her hands together, and falling into a wild fit of laughter. Then, sinking from his grasp upon the ground, she covered her face with her apron, and wept bitterly. And then, she laughed again; and then, she cried again; and then she said how cold it was, and suffered him to lead her to the fire, where she sat down as before. (46)

We do not see inside Dot's mind—indeed, implication rather than clarity is necessary to the surprise ending of the story—but through Dot's physical gyrations Dickens goes out of his way to indicate a serious problem. In a few minutes Dot gains her composure and tries to pass off her attack as "[o]nly a fancy, John dear—a kind of shock—a something coming suddenly before my eyes—I don't know what it was. It's quite gone; quite gone" (46). But "visual" evidence belies Dot's verbal gesture.

On the last page of "Chirp the First," two conflicting interpretations of reality face John and the reader. The Cricket presents John with his first vision of Dot as hearth angel, emphasizing the traits which gratify a January's ego:

> Dots of all ages, and sizes, filled the chamber. Dots who were merry children, running on before him gathering flowers in fields; coy Dots, half shrinking from, half yielding to, the pleading of his own rough image; newly married Dots, alighting at the door, and taking wondering possession of the household keys; motherly little Dots . . . bearing babies to be christened.   (50)

Dot as child makes January young; Dot as coy object of desire inflames the passions; Dot as domestic caretaker ensures that the home will be properly tended as January's retreat from the world; Dot's fertility ensures John's immortality. The envisioned Dots go on through the stages of life, looking after John and finally burying him. If we connect the Dots, an interesting picture emerges. All the Dots serve to gratify John's/January's traditional male wishes. And this self-serving image seems to be enough to quiet John's fears at this stage: "as the Cricket showed him all these things . . . the Carrier's heart grew light and happy, and he thanked his Household Gods with all his might, and cared no more for Gruff and Tackleton than you do" (50).

But this self-serving image may be stolen by the Young Man, as the narrator emphasizes in the contrasting picture which closes the chapter:

> But what was that young figure of a man, which the same Fairy Cricket set so near Her stool, and which remained there, singly and alone? Why did it linger still, so near her, with its arm upon the chimney-piece, ever repeating "Married! and not to me!"
>
>   O Dot! Oh failing Dot! There is no place for it in all your husband's visions; why has its shadow fallen on his hearth!   (50)

The narrator balances suspicions regarding the Stranger against John's false security in his self-serving image of Dot. Present ego gratification is pitted against potential ego destruction. But this is only the first stage of John's treatment. The range of possibilities John can comprehend needs to be expanded.

III

The standard pattern of the *Christmas Books* is to thrust the protagonist into a perilous position, and then extricate him or her from it through a magically produced change of heart. In the three-part books, *The Battle of Life*, *The Haunted Man*, and *The Cricket*, the pattern is identical: Part the First, intimation of tragedy; Part the Second, the tragedy seemingly occurs; Part the Third, restoration of character and community. Therefore, we might expect the Narrator to intimate suspicion and doubt early on, to set up later demystification.

The purpose of "Chirp the Second" is to bring the suspicions against Dot to a climax, notwithstanding periodic hints that she is innocent, hints that will be reduced to "facts" in "Chirp the Third." Whereas "Chirp the First" primarily casts suspicion, leading to a reasonable conclusion that Dot is guilty of at least disliking her marriage, "Chirp the Second" at first alternates suspicion with approbation, leaving the reader to choose what to believe. But in the central scene, a little party at the Plummers' house, the Narrator and Tackleton join forces against Dot, and lead the reader and John to see her guilt "confirmed."

John gets caught up in a cribbage game, becoming oblivious of all around him until Tackleton taps him on the shoulder and ignites suspicion with a series of innuendoes: "I am sorry for this. I am indeed. I have been afraid of it. I have suspected it from the first" (83). Tackleton is a reader surrogate here; he speaks for the logical reader's conclusion, based on evidence in the narrative, that something illicit is going on between Dot and the Stranger. We have also felt, no doubt, that John ought to know what is going on, so Tackleton acts for us both in expressing our conclusion and telling it to John. Tackleton prepares John to look at a tableau through his counting-house window—an exquisite frame, fitting like the point of view of "The Merchant's Tale"—with some inflammatory instructions which recall Fagin's "charitable" concern for Nancy just before Sikes goes off to murder her: " 'Don't commit any violence. It's of no use. It's dangerous too. You're a strong-made man; and you might do Murder before you know it' " (83). As John steps to the window, to see Dot and the undisguised Stranger in playful conversation, the Narrator confirms our interpretation of the situation: "Oh Shadow on the Hearth! Oh Truthful Cricket! Oh perfidious Wife!" (83).

Dickens closes this crucial vision with an ingenious gesture from John: "He clenched his strong right hand at first, as if it would have beaten down a lion. But opening it immediately again, he spread it out before the eyes of Tackleton . . . and so, as they passed out, fell down upon a desk, and was as weak as any infant" (84). The raging impulse to kill that which threatens the ego overpowers momentarily, but the gesture gives way to a blocking of Tackleton's vision. This is more than preventing one's neighbor from seeing one's humiliation. It is through Tackleton's suspicions, his "counting-house" mode of vision, that the perception of Dot as an adulteress is possible. But the cost of squelching the natural impulse, the Tackletonian impulse, is great;

the energy exhausted by the warring selves leaves John collapsed and "as weak as any infant." As a little child, he now has the proper frame of mind to enter the Dickensian kingdom, after the appropriate visionary experience. His confidence at the end of "Chirp the First" has given way to rage, then numbing despair.

The postlude to "Chirp the Seond," in contrast to the doubt-enhancing movement of the preceding scene, revives the possibility that Dot is innocent. The toys, dolls, and animals lying around Caleb's shop "might have been imagined to be stricken motionless with fantastic wonder, at Dot being false" (85). Empirical evidence seems to confirm her guilt, but inanimate objects, which seem to represent some spiritual or second level consciousness, still support Dot.

IV

"Chirp the Third" is Dickens' attempt at problem solving, mainly in saving John's and Dot's marriage, but also in helping May to escape Tackleton and Caleb to undeceive Bertha. He cleverly does so, but as we will see in the final sentence of the story, Dickens recognizes the psychological fragility of his solution.

John, in order to be saved, must be sharply differentiated from Tackleton. When Tackleton formerly claimed to be just the same as John—his double—John could not deny the similarity. Tackleton's insinuation that John's attitude toward Dot is self-serving is demonstrated by John's egocentric vision of her charms. John begins rejecting the Tackletonian vision by covering Tackleton's eyes during the "discovery" scene. But at the beginning of "Chirp the Third," he reverts to the brooding sense of injury which so naturally suggests itself to Tackleton. Rising up, and on the point of murdering the Stranger, John is recalled by the Cricket, and prepared for the vision that will change his perceptions permanently.

In an introductory homily, the Cricket praises Dot as the spiritual priestess of the home, implying a spiritual deficiency in John if he doubts her. Then, in what nearly seems a pagan ritual, a troop of fairies bustles around and under an image of Dot on the hearth, doing honor to her as the goddess of the home. From this point on, the vision highlights a nonreligious domesticity. Dot is seen in various set pieces: sewing, rejecting other partners at a dance for John, rocking the baby, gossiping with other women, and so on. There is nothing striking about these visions, and nothing particularly different from John's earlier visions—except the all-important periodic intrusion of the shadow of the Stranger, "always distinct, and big, and thoroughly defined," although it "never fell so darkly as at first" (93).

The vision seems to call John back to an idealized and egocentric past, except that the past is punctuated by the intrusions of the Stranger. It presents the simplistic alternatives the reader sees for John at the end of "Chirp the First": grasping an idealized Dot or losing her to the Stranger's stronger attraction. But John chooses a third alternative: letting go. He awakes from the vision ready to give up all claim on Dot, yet without resentment toward her. Like Doctor Strong and Mr. Jarndyce, he reaches his moment of epiphany when he lets go.

Ibsen's *A Doll's House*, which seems to take *The Cricket* as a partial model, illuminates John's decision by contrast. Nora endures an unsatisfactory relationship with Torvald because she expects that if a tragedy strikes he will support her, and if need be sacrifice himself for her. This self-sacrifice is "the wonderful" that she anticipates throughout the play, and Torvald's gross selfishness, which appears when "the wonderful" was expected, kills her remnant of love for him. John, however, produces "the wonderful" and saves his marriage. His willingness to give up the doll in his doll's house lays the foundation for a new relationship.

Tackleton, conversely, proves himself to be a traditional January, and like Arthur Gride he has his bride snatched away at the last moment by the now undisguised Edward Plummer, who, having fulfilled his psychological testing of John and Dot, reverts to the melodramatic role of foiling January. If the reader has had any qualms about Dot's and John's January-May relationship, these qualms are diverted through the traditional resolution of the Tackleton and May relationship, in which Edward saves May from Tackleton's clutches.

Dot's role in "Chirp the Third," apart from her image's appearance in John's visions, is that of a Prospero who provides a final test for John, and then unravels all the mysteries she has created, like a magician. One might argue that the demystification scene is the least satisfying in the story, because the narrator's high hilarity, leading up to the dancing affirmation of community at the end, oversimplifies the early issues of the story; the potential tragedy, which gives the first two-thirds of the story significance, is too easily patched and declared as good as new. On the other hand, Dot's psychological imbalance does not need to be understood as a trick Dickens foists on the reader. I believe Dickens can have his cake and eat it too by having Dot operate on conscious and unconscious levels.

In that sense, Dot really is tempted on an unconscious or subconscious level. Her fits, screams, and moanings are real expressions of maladjustment to her marriage, not just instances of Dickens annoyingly misleading the reader. On the conscious level, however, Dot refuses to admit her dissatisfactions to herself, and, after seeing John's self-sacrificing response to her suspicious behavior, her vision of him ameliorates to a legitimate happy ending. To use an analogy from Gilbert and Gubar, Dot plays both Bertha Mason and Jane Eyre.[1]

V

The narrator's postscript reaffirms that Dickens, in this story, believes in no easy answers. The high hilarity associated with drinking, dancing, and community gives way to the narrator's wistful nostalgia; he is "left alone" by his characters, as "A Cricket sings upon the Hearth; a broken child's-toy lies upon the ground; and nothing else remains" (120). This final line has neither the thesis-mongering tone of its counterpart in *The Haunted Man*, nor the infantile personification of *The Battle of Life*, nor the unqualified affirmation of *A Christmas Carol* and *The Chimes*. It is beautifully enigmatic, but clearly creates an abrupt change in tone from the end of the story proper. It suggests something about the artist's relation to his creation, and carries some of the wistful regret at leaving it that Dickens first wrote of in his postscript to *The Pickwick Papers*. The broken toy suggests a counterpoint to any unqualified celebration.

This final ambivalence is prefigured in the analogy of author and audience represented by Caleb and Bertha Plummer. Although David Paroissen has noticed this relationship, no one has explored it in detail. Shortly after Bertha is born, Caleb, sadly thinking about his "motherless Blind Child," was inspired by the Cricket to change Bertha's "great deprivation" "almost" into a blessing by lying to her about everything potentially unpleasant. Thus, he tells her their house is beautiful and cozy, not the broken-down heap the narrator describes; he himself dresses well, is young-looking and in the pink of health, rather than shabbily dressed, greying, balding, and stiff-jointed; and Tackleton is a kind employer with an eccentric taste for irony, rather than a cruel taskmaster (52–53).

Caleb's "good" motives seem dubious on inspection: he has created a mind which thinks he is loved by his boss, lives in a nice house, wears fine clothes, is treated respectfully by the working class, and is young and vigorous, not old and decrepit. In short, Caleb has created a fantasy wish-fulfillment of himself in Bertha's mind, an image to which he can escape on demand. Manning writes that "Caleb and Bertha represent the proper, natural, or normal relationship of an older man and a younger woman," apparently referring to their father-daughter status (67). But we can see this is far from true, even without remembering the abusive tendency which characterizes the father-daughter relationship in Dickens. Caleb is actually the worst January of all. He has created his own "wife" by corrupting the family relationship, negating paternal responsibility to use Bertha to compensate for his own deficient life.

But Bertha, to some degree, recognizes Caleb's treatment of her as a game to play along with. Caleb's poor inventive powers have produced a limited repertoire of descriptions, which he and his daughter repeat to each other, almost like a pathetic vaudeville team:

> "I see you father," she said, clasping her hands, "as plainly, as if I had the eyes I never want when you are with me. A blue coat—"
> "Bright blue," said Caleb.
> "Yes, yes! Bright blue!" exclaimed the girl, turning up her radiant face; "the color I can just remember in the blessed sky! You told me it was blue before. A bright blue coat—"
> "Made loose to the figure," suggested Caleb.
> "Yes! loose to the figure," cried the Blind Girl, laughing heartily; "and in it you, dear father, with your merry eye, your smiling face, your free step, and your dark hair: looking so young and handsome!"
> "Halloa! Halloa!" said Caleb. "I shall be vain presently!" (57)

Caleb and Bertha show a sickening collusion here, a mirror of potential author-reader complicity in a sentimental story: the author creates a self-serving unrealistic vision of happiness which the reader uncritically supports.

But Dickens makes it clear that this mutual self-deceit debilitates both partners. Caleb, habituated to deceiving his daughter, cannot engage straightforwardly with others. At the Peerybingles' house, he is described as "having a wandering and thoughtful eye which seemed to be always projecting itself into some other time and place, no matter what he said" (39). Dickens liked to escape from the material world into the realm of ogres, godmothers, and fairies, but it was crucial for him to relate this world to the realistic world of his novels. When he failed to do so, as in *Master Humphrey's Clock*, he failed as an artist. A crucial pattern of his work is the juxtaposition of the fanciful with the realistic and ordinary, "the romantic side of familiar things.'' Caleb remains trapped in the land of the fanciful, as is shown by his aside when Bertha tells him about Tackleton's prospective marriage: '' 'I don't believe it. It's one of my lies, I've no doubt' '' (60). For her part, Bertha's debility appears when Caleb realizes she has fallen in love with Tackleton, thanks to her father's warped portrayal of that "domestic Ogre" (41). Her anguish, upon finding out she knows nothing real, is poignant: '' 'What and whom do I know! I who have no leader! I, so miserably blind' '' (104).

The Cricket itself could and has been seen like one of Caleb's little fictions, sentimental, childish, and immature. But such readings recognize neither the profound issues raised in the first two sections of the story, nor Dickens' undercutting of the happy ending. The story also marks a major development of the theme of self-sacrifice as the key to felicitous human relationships—a theme so pathetically carried out in The Battle of Life the following year, but central and powerful in David Copperfield, Bleak House, A Tale of Two Cities, and other major works of Dickens. The clever use of doubling makes The Cricket an artistic structure of note. The Cricket demonstrates considerable skill in depicting male and female psychology in a troubled love relationship, a skill rarely attributed to Dickens, and certainly not before Copperfield. Finally, The Cricket is Dickens' most specific examination of the January-May relationship, an important feature of several of his novels. Perhaps students of Dickens need to retain a vision of the dancing Jeddler sisters from The Battle of Life to remember just how badly Dickens could write. But the Stranger, Dot, and her circle deserve our attention for another reason: their merit.

NOTES

1. The doubling between Jane Eyre and Bertha Mason is discussed in the chapter "A Dialogue of Self and Soul: Jane Eyre" in The Madwoman in the Attic. See particularly pages 359–60.

WORKS CITED

Bandelin, Carl. "David Copperfield: A Third Interesting Penitent." Studies in English Literature 16 (1976):601–11.

Dickens, Charles. David Copperfield. New York: Penguin, 1986.

Dickens, Charles. "The Cricket on the Hearth." *The Christmas Books*. New York: Penguin, 1971. Vol. 2. 21–120.

[Fitzgerald, Percy]. "Dickens's Dogs; or the Landseer of Fiction." Quoted in Ruth F. Glancy's *Dickens's Christmas Books, Christmas Stories, and other Short Fiction: An Annotated Bibliography*. New York: Garland, 1985.

Ford, George. *Dickens and His Readers: Aspects of Novel Criticism since 1836*. Princeton: Princeton UP, 1955.

Gilbert, Sandra M., and Susan Gubar. *The Madwoman in the Attic: The Woman Writer and the Nineteenth-Century Imagination*. New Haven: Yale UP, 1979.

Hardy, Barbara. *The Moral Art of Dickens*. London: Athlone, 1970.

Johnson, Edgar. *Charles Dickens: His Tragedy and Triumph*. 2 vols. Boston: Little, 1952.

Leavis, F. R., and Q. D. Leavis. *Dickens the Novelist*. London: Chatto, 1970.

Manning, Sylvia. "Dickens, January, and May." *Dickensian* 71 (1975):67–75.

Paroissien, David. "Literature's 'Eternal Duties' '': Dickens's Professional Creed." *The Changing World of Charles Dickens*. Ed. Robert Giddings. New York: Barnes, 1983. 42–45.

Sanders, Andrew. Introd. *The Cricket on the Hearth: A Fairy Tale of Home*. Guilford, England: Genesis, 1981. 11–17.

Slater, Michael. Introd. *The Christmas Books*. By Charles Dickens. New York: Penguin, 1971. Vol. 1. vii–xxiv.

Slater, Michael. "Introduction to *The Cricket on the Hearth*." *The Christmas Books*. By Charles Dickens. New York: Penguin, 1971. Vol. 2. 9–12.

Stone, Harry. *Dickens and the Invisible World: Fairy Tales, Fantasy, and Novel-Making*. Bloomington: Indiana UP, 1979.

Thomas, Deborah. *Dickens and the Short Story*. Philadelphia: U of Pennsylvania P, 1982.

Dora and Doady

Margaret Flanders Darby

It is time to take Dora Spenlow seriously enough to perceive the self she reveals beyond her narrator's understanding. To do so requires that we set aside both David's interpretation of her and the critical tradition that has taken David's word for truth. Many critics now recognize David's bias as the narrator of his own story, and recognize that his storyteller's gift creates fictions that are also lies, but are so powerful that they seduce their readers and even, perhaps, their creator into belief. Further, critics increasingly see how far David falls short of the heroic status that his "pages," as he warns us at the outset, "must show."[1] Yet virtually no one has seen Dora for what she is throughout *David Copperfield*: clearheaded; wise and realistic; stunningly honest about herself, her husband, and her marriage; and, above all, always true to a self that David will not, finally, allow.[2] Following David's example, Dickens' readers have patronized Dora far too long, and the price they pay for continuing to stereotype her is a failure to understand either Dickens' complex depictions of David's blindness, or his complex sensitivity to the plight of child-wives in his novel and in his society.

David evades acknowledgment of the less heroic aspects of his character through storytelling, through the novelist's art. The text of *David Copperfield*, in paradoxical contrast to David's narrative, exposes the protagonist's story-telling as deeply self-evasive. Since David the novelist is himself the creation of a novelist in a novel widely recognized from Dickens onward to be complexly autobiographical, the juxtaposition of David's interpretation with the facts his account reveals suggests in tantalizing ways that Dickens himself may be engaged in still deeper evasions.

David learns how to manipulate the power of storytelling early in life; his carefully edited memories of his mother enable his attempt to camouflage the betrayal of her second marriage. From that point onward throughout the novel David creates interpretations that present him in the best possible light, "making up" his story through concealment and revelation as he goes along. His readiness to condone brutality and selfishness in his story of Steerforth enables his vicarious participation in Emily's seduction. His condescension of Traddles, whose integrity and worth he overlooks, supports his precarious, even essentially false, claim to superiority of social class. Above all, his grossly exaggerated story of revulsion toward Uriah Heep permits his evasion of his deepest fears concerning his own right to the status of gentleman. Eventually, his storytelling gift not only safely hides his shameful self, but makes him famous and prosperous. His self-indulgent interpretations would seem to be quite acceptable.

Yet Dickens' text successfully undermines David's pose of moral earnestness. The eerie shadows of Dickens himself in Mr. Dick's struggles to write remind us that "King Charles" always intrudes to expose a writer's effort to hide the darker truths. Aunt Betsey insists that King Charles the First—the metaphor for Mr. Dick's "great disturbance and agitation"—not be allowed in his autobiographical Memorial. Since Mr. Dick cannot keep Charles out, his storytelling cannot progress under her supervision, and is forever caught between a "businesslike"—or worldly—"way of speaking" and the truth (14:175).[3] When disturbing metaphors for truth cannot be either excluded or concealed, publication may be limited to a text made indecipherable by the length of a kite's string. With Dr. Strong and even the lunatic peering from David's room at Blunderstone Rookery, Mr. Dick is there to make clear that the price for the storytelling gift can be, at best, a pathetic ineffectuality, and at worst, insanity. Like Scheherazade, to whom the young David is compared in the first flush of his thralldom to Steerforth, David tells stories, night after night, day after day, for life itself.

Storytelling becomes particularly problematic in David's relations with the women characters, because the cultural codes of Victorian femininity give him wide scope for stereotyped interpretations of the women's words and actions, stereotypes that support his fiction of his own steadily more disciplined heart. This is particularly true of Dora; David shapes a radically warped Dora that the novel successfully undermines through her resistance and his eventual failure to make her over according to his desires. Within the constraints of the Victorian code of the ringletted heroine, Dora is an agent for subversion. A gendered reading of Dora, one informed by a fully conscious feminist resistance to those cultural codes, reveals a very different woman from David's condescending image.

In her award-winning essay "Toward a Feminist Theory of Reading," Patrocinio Schweickart offers a strategy for a feminist reading of a male-authored text, no matter how misogynist. But a gendered reading of Dickens reveals not so much his misogyny, as his capacity for a doubled vision that challenges and supports the feminist reader's own. Certainly, a feminist reader cannot avoid the androcentrism of a canonical text like *David Copperfield*. Because she is trained to read like a man, for her the act of reading this novel will necessarily involve the double bind of identifying as she resists; she will read with what Jane Miller calls a "learned androgyny" (4).[4] Her doubled reading will occur wherever the masculine is presented as generic, which is everywhere in Dickens, because she will always be aware of the difference between reading like a man and reading as a woman reading like a man. In short, she will always be aware of the failure of the generic masculine to be really generic. This doubled reading is by now well known in feminist criticism, but it has too often been used as a way to dismiss male-authored texts as having images of Woman so misogynist, even harmful to women readers, that feminist critical effort seems better spent elsewhere, especially on recently explored and justly celebrated writing by nineteenth-century women.

Nonetheless, I am not ready to give up on Dickens. I want to know why the power of his androcentric, canonical texts survives the exposure of their androcentrism, a possibility that Schweickart allows for some masculinist texts but does not fully explore. I would like to suggest that in *David Copperfield*, at least, this power lies not in the text alone, but in a dialectical relationship between the doubled vision of the reader and the ambivalence of the text. The outsider's vision inherent in a gendered reading grants us the great power of reading slant as well as straight. It enables us to uncover the space between reading with the text, according to its overt purposes and values, its androcentrism—even misogyny—and against the text, according to our gendered capacity. This tension between the two reading strategies exposes not only the androcentrism of the text, but also the limits of that androcentrism. Its particularities emerge in sharp relief against its claim to universality, and so a doubled reading paradoxically enables us to revivify the text for new generations of readers by more carefully delineating its cultural boundaries. In the case of *David Copperfield*, a gendered reading enables us to extend the exposure of David's hypocrisy that third-world male critics like Badri Raina have begun so well, and further understand Dickens' complex distance from and identification with his protagonist. By reading more complexly the ironic space enclosed within the three poles of what David claims to be, what Dickens suspects him to be, and what Dickens excuses him for being, we identify not with character or author but with the frustration and pain of the struggle with and within patriarchy that we share with Dickens. Schweickart reserves a fully dialogic feminist reading for female-authored texts, but a deeply ambivalent text like *David Copperfield*, the obvious antifeminism of its author notwithstanding, will illuminate by means of a gendered reading our strong empathy with Dickens' culture, a patriarchy that is, after all, only slightly younger than our own. I think such a reading enriches the Victorian canon as well, by posing new questions of texts that are themselves profoundly self-questioning. In Dora Spenlow's voice and circumstances, in Dora Copperfield's marriage, Dickens' rich ambivalence toward David and all he stands for comes clear.

Dora is the most intractably unknowable woman in *David Copperfield*; in her, David confronts a resilient otherness he never controls. Unable to fulfill his intentions, she becomes a counterforce to David's self-deceptions. Before her death, David struggles to muffle her by assigning her a conventionally feminine role in his comic dialogue of love; after her death, he abandons himself to self-pity and to Agnes, who manages him more in accordance with his marital expectations. As soon as it is clear she will die, David can manage Dora as he did his mother: escape painful realities—especially his own moral and social evasions—by telling his "story," by remembering only what he chooses to remember, and enshrining that selective memory in mourning. Just as his storytelling memory is one of David's favorite means of controlling others in order to escape self-knowledge, the warping of that memory is one of Dickens' favorite means of distancing himself from his first-person narrator.

To claim for either Dora or Dickens a modern feminism would be to dissipate the tension that so richly suffuses this text. On the contrary, Dora never speaks from outside a conventionally feminine role. In her analysis of narrative voice in Dickens, Kate Flint asserts that by virtue of the first-person narration, Dora is denied a space from which to speak (119). But it seems to me that Dickens sees to it that Dora speaks clearly from within the conventional codes; the problem has been that readers have colluded with David's refusal to listen. Dora is as innocent, young, and girlish when she meets David, and as severely crippled by baby-girl codes of behavior, as readers have always claimed. Yet however childlike at the beginning, she is never as childish as her "lackadaisical young spooney," as the older David indulgently calls himself. Critics have consistently failed to see her unyielding integrity, the strength of her weakness, and especially the persistence of her attempts to escape David's confining rhetoric, as well as his refusal to examine his assumptions about love and marriage.

Our initial sense of her is of someone barricaded. This inaccessibility begins as a social fact, but remains throughout as a deeper psychological reality: she will always be unavailable to David in the deepest sense. She suggests the powerful constraints that threaten her selfhood from her first words, which are as characteristic of her voice throughout *David Copperfield* as they are uncharacteristic of her image among critics: she is self-insightful and humorous.

> I had not been walking long, when I turned a corner, and met her. I tingle again from head to foot as my recollection turns that corner, and my pen shakes in my hand.
> "You—are—out early, Miss Spenlow," said I.
> "It's so stupid at home," she replied, "and Miss Murdstone is so absurd! She talks such nonsense about its being necessary for the day to be aired, before I come out. Aired! (She laughed, here, in the most melodious manner.) "On a Sunday morning, when I don't practise, I must do something. So I told Papa last night I *must* come out. Besides, it's the brightest time of the whole day. Don't you think so?"
> I hazarded a bold flight, and said (not without stammering) that it was very bright to me then, though it had been very dark to me a minute before.
> "Do you mean a compliment?" said Dora, "or that the weather has really changed?" (26:337)

This exchange not only begins the account of a courtship that will bury Dora in David's clichés, but demonstrates the relationship between his memory, which still has the power to make him tremble, and her voice, which expresses a restlessness his memory has never had the power to hear. Although the young David thinks he is in love with Dora, he is really in love with love, and the older, narrator-David is in love with his own youthful silliness, and more interested in his own linguistic excesses than in either Dora's response to them or the implications of the confinement of a sheltered young woman. We have no way of knowing what Dora feels, because neither of these Davids is concerned to discover and represent her emotions (33:404). The complete self-absorption of David's love song would be wonderfully comic if it did not portend so clearly his complete failure to resist his cultural license to invent his own Dora instead of seeking the real one. Everyone's failure to look—Julia Mills is as self-absorbed as Dora's father, chaperone, or lover—helps to account for the truncated image finally inscribed. Even the invitation to her birthday party, from her own hand on her own lace-edged note paper, is written in terms of her father's wishes, not hers: "Favoured by Papa . . . To remind" (33:410).

Every word Julia Mills utters as a go-between is an ironic, almost bitter, commentary on David's lovemaking. It is not enough to observe, with most critics, that Dickens satirizes her because the real Julia in his love affair with Maria Beadnell betrayed him. Her "remote irrevocable past," her "slumbering echoes in the caverns of Memory," her reiterated "desert of Sahara" make her language a telling parody of his storytelling memory. Their shared, empty rhetoric resembles a duet in a trivial, popular love song, so exactly do they harmonize. Julia's absurdly inflated clichés are the soprano line to the tenor of David's rhapsodies; Dora has no voice in this duet. Her few actions at her birthday party do suggest she is encouraging David, but the emphasis of his memory is not on what Dora does so much as what Julia makes possible—the first "reconciliation," the first kiss, arrangement for future meetings. Dora expresses herself by absence—evasion, self-removal. Her few words make her father a barrier between herself and David: "Dora stipulated that we were never to be married without her papa's consent" (33:417).

David's suppression of Dora's individuality in his narrative is especially evident in his triumphant account of his proposal, an event from which she is entirely absent:

> I don't know how I did it. I did it in a moment. I intercepted Jip. I had Dora in my arms. I was full of eloquence. I never stopped for a word. I told her how I loved her. I told her I should die without her. I told her that I idolized and worshipped her. Jip barked madly all the time.

We note how clichéd and self-absorbed this language is, how insistent its repetitions, how unintentionally revealing its "I never stopped for a word."

> When Dora hung her head and cried, and trembled, my eloquence increased so much the more. If she would like me to die for her, she had but to say the word, and I was ready. Life without Dora's love was not a thing to have on any terms. I couldn't bear it, and I wouldn't. I had loved her every minute, day and night, since I first saw her. I loved her at that minute to distraction. I should always love her, every minute, to distraction. Lovers had loved before, and lovers would love again, but no lover had ever loved, might, could, would, or should ever love, as I loved Dora. The more I raved, the more Jip barked. Each of us, in his own way, got more mad every moment.

David raves and Jip barks, but Dora says nothing; she has been subdued by emotional violence. "Well, well! Dora and I were sitting on the sofa by-and-by, quiet enough, and Jip was lying in her lap, winking peacefully at me. It was off my mind. I was in a state of perfect rapture. Dora and I were engaged"

(33:417). We learn nothing from this passage that we would like to know. Is Jip's barking the refusal Dora might speak if she could, or an excitement she might express if allowed? David has not stopped to find out. He has asked no questions, made no observation of her. Written so completely from David's point of view, the language of this passage crescendos to a climax and decrescendos quickly to a post-coital quiescence. Its rhythms are entirely David's. If it is a linguistic orgasm for him, for her it is only a deflowering. He neither cares nor knows the difference.

Once they are engaged we gradually learn, in spite of David's blindness, more about Dora. As soon as David introduces a problem, his new poverty, Dora's response shows that she is not going to submit; she will withdraw.

> "How can you ask me anything so foolish?" pouted Dora.
> "Love a beggar!"
> "Dora, my own dearest!" said I. "I am a beggar!"
> "How can you be such a silly thing," replied Dora, slapping my hand, "as to sit there, telling such stories? I'll make Jip bite you!"
> Her childish way was the most delicious way in the world to me, but it was necessary to be explicit, and I solemnly repeated: "Dora, my own life, I am your ruined David!" (37:460)

By refusing to join him in his melodramatic exaggeration, Dora also refuses to share his evasion of class realities by seeming to overstate them. She is quite right, of course, that he is not a beggar and that for her to marry one would be unthinkable. She correctly identifies this as his "story." Her direct grasp of social reality contrasts vividly with David's earnest pieties; for the rest of her life her words will cut across David's fulsome self-justifications with poignant truth:

> "Perseverance and strength of character will enable us to bear much worse things."
> "But I haven't got any strength at all," said Dora, shaking her curls. "Have I, Jip?" (37:461)

David's indulgence of his youthful enthusiasm for Love masks his embarrassment over the difference in social class between them, a difference he will not only never really face, but which he expects Dora to adapt to. His social class is significantly lower than her father's pretensions. It is only because of Aunt Betsey that David can even think of marrying Dora, a fact which her father does not fail to bring home to him. Dickens' willingness to kill Papa at the crucial moment excuses David's belief that he is a suitable match for her, but the truth is that he is not, for he cannot support her expectations of leisure. Like Traddles, David must expect to work very hard to consolidate his social and financial position, especially after Aunt Betsey must reduce her financial support. Dora, on the other hand, has every reason to expect to remain the gentlewoman she has been raised to be, decorating china and singing songs.

Once she realizes he is truly worried about poverty, Dora is sympathetic and directly practical—she offers him her money (37:463)—but, strikingly, she does not offer to join her "ruined David." Julia Mills is the one who "hears" him, who reacts the way David wants Dora to react, with clichés indistinguishable from his own:

> I told Miss Mills that she was evermore my friend, and that my heart must cease to vibrate ere I could forget her sympathy. I then expounded to Miss Mills what I had endeavoured, so very unsuccessfully, to expound to Dora. Miss Mills replied, on general principles, that the Cottage of content was better than the Palace of cold splendor, and that where love was, all was. (37:463)

The palace of cards, their flimsy love song, has been created by David and Julia, not by David and Dora. In contrast, Dora makes it very clear that getting up at five o'clock to work has nothing to do with her. To read a cookery book and study housekeeping would be to submit to a lowering of social status, a concession Dora never pretends to be willing to make. Throughout their courtship after his better expectations are dashed, David claims to be asking her to be consequential, sober, and practical, and finding only delightful but alarming silliness. But the language he uses to claim devotion to the work ethic is melodramatic and exaggerated—in a word, silly—and the realistic, sober, and practical terms he avoids are his social insecurity and mortification over how fine a line he actually walks between impoverished social nonentity and respectable prosperity. When he abandons his rhetorical flights and says something plain and simple—that he is getting up at five to meet his new obligations—even David can see that Dora understands perfectly well: "it made a great impression on her, and she neither played nor sang any more" (37:464). Dora refuses both the hidden request of shoulder-to-shoulder help and the linguistic hypocrisy of his appeals to the nobility of self-sacrifice.

When David begins to notice that Dora is not studying to become his housekeeper, she controls his scolding by her characteristic honesty, which directly exposes his hypocrisy: "if I didn't like her, why had I ever wanted so much to be engaged to her? And why didn't I go away now, if I couldn't bear her?" (41:516) He had wanted his mother's beauty, and, having secured it, now he wants Peggotty's competence, but he cannot afford both a good servant and a wife whose habits and accomplishments are suitable to the station in life to which he aspires. He does not acknowledge that from her viewpoint to hope for both in one is impossible, that a gentlewoman is by definition not a servant. That would be to descend to Traddles' and Sophy's level, and while David wants the comforts of Sophy's cossetting, he will not give up the glamour of Dora's style or position; indeed, he cannot even admit to the parallel with the Traddles' marriage. Dora responds to his selfish fantasy by training Jip to stand on the cookery book with the pencil case in his mouth. So much for David's definition of feminine earnestness: someone who will see to it he is comfortable.

When Dora asks her lover some penetrating questions on meeting Agnes, David evades their clear implication by dismissing them as nonsense:

> "Don't you think, if I had had her for a friend a long time ago, Doady," said Dora, her bright eyes shining very brightly and her little right hand idly busying itself with one of the buttons on my coat, "I might have been more clever perhaps?"
> "My love!" said I, "what nonsense!"
> "Do you think it is nonsense?" returned Dora, without looking at me. "Are you sure it is?"
> "Of course I am!"
> "I have forgotten," said Dora, still turning the button round and round, "what relation Agnes is to you, you dear bad boy."
> "No blood-relation," I replied, "but we were brought up together, like brother and sister."
> "I wonder why you ever fell in love with me?" said Dora, beginning on another button of my coat.
> "Perhaps because I couldn't see you, and not love you, Dora!"
> "Suppose you had never seen me at all," said Dora, going to another button.
> "Suppose we had never been born!" said I gaily.
> I wondered what she was thinking about, as I glanced in admiring silence. . . .
> (42:522)

David has no habits of conversation with Dora that would lead him to take her questions seriously. He is intensely aware of her physical presence, button by button, but has no access to her as a person.

Dora ends their engagement by asking, "And are you sure you like me very much?" (43:538). She begins their "fairy marriage," having held Agnes' hand throughout the ceremony, by asking, "Are you happy now, you foolish boy, and sure you don't repent?" (43:541). David will have much to say about his disappointment, but Dora has broken no promises. The housekeeping is chaotic; the servants are unmanageable, but servants have been taking advantage of David since he was eight years old—why is it suddenly Dora's fault? Dickens' contemporary readers would have known that many women of her upbringing managed their servants no more assertively than she. This problem is not really one of her youth and incapacity as David would have us believe, but rather its roots are David's incompatible expectations. The sense of humiliation over the tension with servants, which he projects onto her as blame, in fact comes from David. He is willing to share the blame, but he is not willing either to see her refusal of it or to face its real source: the conflict between his desire to meet their shared expectations of a gentlewoman's leisure, and his need for help in climbing the social ladder. In fact, he has run aground in the typical Victorian paradox of the trained incapacities of the upper class wife. Although Dickens clearly sees the tragedy inherent in the paradox, he forgives David's steady refusal to acknowledge it by giving him Agnes.[5]

When David "reasons with" her because dinner is late, Dora exclaims, "I didn't marry to be reasoned with. If you meant to reason with such a poor little thing as I am, you ought to have told me so, you cruel boy! . . . No, I am not your darling. Because you *must* be sorry that you married me, or else you wouldn't reason with me!" David feels "injured by the inconsequential nature of this charge," but we understand that it is very consequential indeed. At stake here is not only a marriage, or even the fragility of Little Blossom, but David's persistent deflection of her clarity of vision into the euphemisms of condescending affection that mask his insistence on his conjugal privileges: "My sweet, I am only going to reason . . . my own Dora, you are very childish, and are talking nonsense" (44:543). When David asks his aunt to intervene, she immediately refuses, reminding him explicitly of Murdstone's treatment of his mother.

When David finally articulates his disappointment, Dora demonstrates her usual grasp of essentials and her ability to name things accurately—her "Doady" is as tellingly precise as Steerforth's "Daisy"—by asking him to call her his 'child-wife.' In offering him this term for her identity, she captures the paradox in her oxymoron and speaks accurately, as always, about the impossibilities of their situation while at the same time, with far greater maturity than his, she reaches for a possible reconciliation:

"I don't mean, you silly fellow, that you should use the name instead of Dora. I only mean that you should think of me that way. When you are going to be angry with me, say to yourself, 'it's only my child-wife!' When I am very disappointing, say, 'I knew a long time ago, that she would make but a child-wife!' When you miss what I should like to be, and I think I can never be, say,

'still my foolish child-wife loves me!' For indeed I do.'' I had not been serious
with her, having no idea, until now, that she was serious herself.   (44:550)

But why should he have no idea? She has been serious all along. He has
allowed himself to be misled by the light, high-pitched intonation which we,
too, hear in our mind's ear, and which our culture, as his, stereotypes as
inconsequential. The critical tradition of Dickensian scholarship has accepted
David's Dora as the truth because of its own codes for diminutive blue-eyed
charmers. His next words, claiming to have listened to her carefully and
lovingly, are really the special pleading, with its complacent yet wistful tone
of self-justification, that he reserves for his own creations, as his image of
her so obviously is:

> This appeal of Dora's made a strong impression on me. I look back on the time
> I write of, I invoke the innocent figure that I dearly loved, to come out from
> the mists and shadows of the past, and turn its gentle head towards me once
> again, and I can still declare that this one little speech was constantly in my
> memory. I may not have used it to the best account, I was young and inexperi-
> enced, but I never turned a deaf ear to its artless pleading.   (44:550)

His ear is deafened, not by indifference, but by the power of his stereotyping
memory, in which her speech is always ''little.''
    The conflict between David and Dora culminates in David's trying to
''form'' Dora's mind intellectually, apparently because she is ''unreason-
able,'' that is, she speaks to the real issues between them:

> She sat sobbing and murmuring behind [her handkerchief] that, if I was uneasy,
> why had I ever been married? Why hadn't I said, even the day before we went
> to church, that I knew I should be uneasy, and I would rather not? If I couldn't
> bear her, why didn't I send her away to her aunts at Putney, or to Julia Mills
> in India?   (48:592)

Finally, it ''began to occur to me that perhaps Dora's mind was already
formed'' (48:593). When he claims ''to love her dearly as she is,'' Dora
intelligently asks, ''Without a story—really?'' (48:594). At last David admits
defeat in adapting his wife to his purposes, yet all the while taking enormous
credit for wisdom and resignation. He acknowledges that he cannot control
her, that she is herself. With her individuality finally manifest, Dora begins
to die; this close juxtaposition completes inescapably the symbolic identification of David with Murdstone. David kills Dora just as surely as Murdstone
killed Clara; the resemblance between the two women, and of both deaths

through a bullying rhetoric, through "forming," is stressed in this chapter. "Child-wives," in all their sexy littleness, are murdered by marriage.

As she dies, only Dora speaks honestly and directly about her death; only Dora analyzes openly the mistake of their marriage; only Dora acknowledges aloud what is wrong with her:

> I am afraid, dear, I was too young. I don't mean in years only, but in experience, and thoughts, and everything. I was such a silly little creature! I am afraid it would have been better if we had only loved each other as a boy and girl, and forgotten it. I have begun to think I was not fit to be a wife.   (53:657)

When David adds, "as fit as I to be a husband," Dora replies, "I don't know . . . Perhaps!" She goes on to explain that he would eventually have "wearied" of her, a choice of words that should remind him of Steerforth's treatment of Emily. But David never fully admits to his selfish manipulativeness; he only goes on to find another wife, one who will pamper him endlessly with perfect housekeeping, and, like an angel, grant him absolution without genuine confession, forgiveness without honest repentance. In giving him Agnes, Dickens relents, giving in to the fiction that David's self-indulgent heart is the disciplined one he tells us he has achieved. Dickens has managed David's failings as David manages Steerforth's, muffling the blame they know is just, but Dickens has also seen to it that we know better. Dora's intransigent integrity forces us to realize the stark Victorian tragedy of marriage between child-wives and childish young doadies.

In David's relationship with Dora the power of the novelist's imagination gradually acquires the capacity to crush this autonomous being. His storytelling becomes so ominous that when Dora asks to hold David's pens, we sense a poignant crippling in his insistence that for her, pen and paper must mean only the humiliation of her struggles with numbers in the account-book, "her own little right-hand middle finger . . . steeped to the very bone in ink" (44:550). Her pleasure and fuss in being allowed to copy his words, and to sign her copy with her name, become a powerful metaphor for her defeat at his hands, or rather his rhetoric. She will be confined, until she is forced to leave the text altogether, to the mechanics of writing, to its trivia and outward forms, while the spirit of art and imagination, the capacity to be "full of silent fancies" and to convey them safely to paper, is reserved for David. She may stay up to watch the miracle of composition because her eyes are so pretty to him, but they must remain mute. Although the experience of marriage has taught her to speak, David will not, or cannot, listen, and having listened, remember. Just as Mr. Dick must struggle to keep what disturbs him out of his writing, Mr. Dickens, David's collaborator, wrestles with Dora's autonomy. From the often-cited letter to John Forster we know how much her early death made him struggle: "Still undecided about Dora, but MUST decide to-day" (*Letters* 6:94). And so he banished her, even further away than to Julia Mills in India, in order that his storytelling might be released into print.

There is more at stake here than a modish reading of Dora, or even than a correction of sexist critical imbalance. David's very integrity is at stake, and to the extent of his special pleading for David's, Dickens'. When we begin to get David right and to understand his self-evasions and excuses, Dickens' readiness to smooth his ascent of the ladder of success, his willingness to silence with Dora's death an important source of potential reproach and clear-sighted judgement, becomes a grave and morally suspect act, for her death aids and abets an unworthy man.

A gendered reading of Dora intensifies the bad light shed on David in the increasing number of critical analyses of his covert identification with Steerforth, with Traddles, with Heep, analyses which preclude acceptance of David's complacency and willful blindness. His struggles with Dora's integrity illuminate the underside of the Victorian work ethic of self-help and unbridled individualism, making clear the extent to which such ideals depend on bettering oneself at the expense of those dispossessed by class or sex.

Dickens gives Dora the privilege of naming the least honorable parts of David's character; "Doady" reminds us of "toady," a fraught word for Dickens. "Doady" exposes David's identification with Uriah Heep, the most vivid sycophant in the canon. In *Great Expectations*, Dickens will come closer to acknowledging as his the deep fear of toadyism in Pip's uneasy relationship with the other toadies around Miss Havisham's dinner table. "Toady" is said to be derived from "toad-eater," the quack doctor's assistant who pretended to eat poisonous toads for the crowd in order to demonstrate the pretended efficacy of the worthless medicine. Like Miss Mowcher, the toad-eater was in the business of false appearances, willing to be seen swallowing anything for the sake of a fraudulent claim, in order to gain favor, in order to rise in the world.

Steerforth names David "Daisy"; Aunt Betsey names him "Trotwood." They name him after their desires, a power the storyteller can understand. David listens to them and suffers little loss of dignity in doing so. But "Doady" cuts deeper, to a level too embarrassing for Aunt Betsey's wisdom. Dickens gives the power of naming him Doady to Dora, and then excuses him from listening to her. But Dickens also knows that we are listening; it is up to us to hear what she is saying.

NOTES

1. See especially Jordan; Raina 77–101; and Rogers.
2. At least as recently as 1986, Dora has been dismissed in the traditional ways: for example, as a "doll-woman" who "fails tragically to be an adult" in Leavis 173; or as "entirely girlish—"one would hardly wish to make any great claims for her personality"—in Crawford 49. Most critics have been content to discuss Dora primarily as a stereotype. See, for example, Calder, Lane, Manheim, Stedman, and Welsh. Occasionally, critics are surprised by what they see as partial or late flashes of insight in Dora. See, for example, Lucas and, most notably, Slater's discussion of Dora in *Dickens and Women* 248–50. My point, in contrast, is that Dora is intelligent and practical, as well as possessed of great integrity, throughout the novel.
3. All references to *David Copperfield* are to the Clarendon edition, by chapter and page number.
4. My use of the feminine pronoun does not preclude a man's feminist reading of any text, but a man's feminist reading cannot be doubled in the same way as a woman's. The idea of "learned androgyny" applies to women.
5. See Poovey 115 for a discussion of the importance of a wife's perfect housekeeping in helping the middle-class male to evade class consciousness.

WORKS CITED

Calder, Jenni. *Women and Marriage in Victorian Fiction.* New York: Oxford UP, 1976.

Crawford, Iain. "Sex and Seriousness in *David Copperfield.*" *Journal of Narrative Technique* 16 (1986):41–54.

Dickens, Charles. *David Copperfield.* Ed. Nina Burgis. Oxford: Clarendon, 1981.

———. *The Letters of Charles Dickens.* Pilgrim ed. Ed. Madeleine House and Graham Storey. Oxford: Clarendon, 1965—.

Flint, Kate. *Dickens.* Brighton, Sussex: Harvester, 1986.

Jordan, John O. "The Social Sub-text of *David Copperfield.*" *Dickens Studies Annual* 14 (1985):61–92.

Lane, Margaret. "Dickens on the Hearth." *Dickens 1970.* Ed. Michael Slater. New York: Stein, 1970. 153–71.

Leavis, F. R. "David Copperfield and Jane Eyre." *English Studies* 67 (1986):167–73.

Lucas, John. "Dickens and Shaw: Women and Marriage in *David Copperfield* and *Candida.*" *Shaw Review* 22 (1979):13–22.

Manheim, Leonard F. "Floras and Doras: The Women in Dickens' Novels." *Texas Studies in Literature and Language* 7 (1965):181–200.

Miller, Jane. *Women Writing about Men.* New York: Pantheon, 1986.

Poovey, Mary. *Uneven Developments: The Ideological Work of Gender in Mid-Victorian England.* Chicago: U of Chicago P, 1988.

Raina, Badri. *Dickens and the Dialectic of Growth.* Madison: U of Wisconsin P, 1986.

Rogers, Philip. "A Tolstoyan Reading of *David Copperfield.*" *Comparative Literature* 42 (1990):1–28.

Schweickart, Patrocinio P. "Toward a Feminist Theory of Reading." *Gender and Reading: Essays on Readers, Texts, and Contexts.* Ed. Elizabeth A. Flynn and Patrocinio P. Schweickart. Baltimore: Johns Hopkins UP, 1986. 31–62.

Slater, Michael. *Dickens and Women.* London: Dent, 1983.

Stedman, Jane. "Child-Wives of Dickens." *Dickensian* 59 (1963):112–18.

Welsh, Alexander. *The City of Dickens.* Oxford: Clarendon, 1971.

What's Troubling About Esther? Narrating, Policing and Resisting Arrest in *Bleak House*

Jasmine Yong Hall

NO EXIT FROM BLEAK HOUSE?

William Axton was the first of many critics to characterize Esther Summerson's "trouble." Axton located the source of Esther's trouble in the ambiguity created by the clash between her inherited sense of worthlessness, her illegitimacy, and her inherent moral insight. Valerie Kennedy followed up on Axton's characterization by finding "More Trouble with Esther," but in contrast to Axton defined that trouble from a more political—particularly a more feminist—point of view. Kennedy was responding to other feminist critics like Kate Millett who see Esther as one of the " 'insipid goodies' " of Victorian fiction; instead, Kennedy pointed out, the ambiguity of Esther's position exposes the Victorian sexual stereotype to criticism. That critique is accomplished by showing "the repressive effect [the Angel in the House stereotype] has on [Esther's] speech and actions in the novel" (332).

Reflecting on all the trouble surrounding Esther, it is not surprising that she should recently have been placed under house arrest. D. A. Miller's "Discipline in Different Voices: Bureaucracy, Police, Family and *Bleak House*" makes Esther's trouble into a source of disciplinary power in the novel: her ambiguous position as both "the doubt-ridden, self-effacing orphan," and the " 'methodical' housekeeper 'with a fine administrative capacity' " (92) serves to turn the family into "its own house of correction" (103). Esther's illegitimacy makes her the novel's moral housekeeper, policing the family which is her protection from the social dangers posed by illegitimacy.

At the same time, Esther's illegitimacy always threatens the family's ability to provide protection, so that Esther must be ever vigilant in those duties.

Miller's analysis is arresting in two senses of the word. It is a powerful and compelling reading which demonstrates the way in which seeming critiques of disciplinary forces in the novel (Chancery, the police) only mask the source of discipline in the family. Using Foucault's definition of discipline, Miller shows that this apparent critique allows the individual to imagine a space free from discipline in the family, when discipline actually constitutes both the individual subject and the family. But Miller's reading is also arresting in the sense that it does not allow for any actual critique of discipline in the novel; a subversion of discipline always becomes a version of discipline. When Dominick LaCapra suggests, for example, that the "carnivalesque" (122) in *Bleak House* may serve to deconstruct bureaucratic institutions like Chancery, Miller counters by showing that the carnivalesque is actually a source of power for these institutions. In Miller's reply to La Capra, "Under Capricorn," he shows that the festive and chaotic atmosphere at the end of the trial does not deconstruct institutions like Chancery "but rather recharges them with the energy to keep going" (128).

LaCapra's deconstructive approach is anticipated in a footnote to Miller's original article. In this footnote, Miller criticizes the type of Althusserian reading which privileges the literary form as the means by which ideology can be subverted. Like Miller, I am wary of this attempt to counter ideology by revealing its built-in self-destruction (or self-deconstruction). However, in closing down any critiques of discipline in the novel, Miller ignores an important precept of Foucault's analysis: "Where there is power there is resistance" (95). Contradictions within a novel do not yield a revolutionary overthrow of the powers that be, rather contradictions are "interstices that exist because all power formations are incomplete" (Wolin 181). They allow one to locate a possible site of resistance which is "never in a position of exteriority in relation to power" (Foucault 95). Esther's "trouble" is, I suggest, just such a site of resistance.

The notion of "trouble," in and of itself, demonstrates the way in which domination and resistance lie within the same mechanism of power. As Judith Butler points out in discussing the title of her book *Gender Trouble*, "To make trouble" is "something one should never do precisely because that would get one in trouble. The rebellion and its reprimand seem[ed] to be caught in the same terms" (ix). Esther's very existence makes trouble in this way—because her mother was "in trouble" with Esther, Esther must strive to keep herself and the family out of trouble. As is clear in the above description, though, Esther's trouble bears a particular relation to gender, one that is never dealt with in Miller's reading. Hers is a "female trouble, that historical configuration which thinly veiled the notion that being female is a natural indisposition" (Butler x). Approaching Esther's trouble from a perspective that is both Foucauldian and femnist, I would not look to counter patriarchal ideology by asserting, as Kennedy does, Esther's "inherent emotional and sexual energies" (333), but I would emphasize the importance of considering the novel's construction of a trouble which originates in female sexuality. It is this gendered aspect of Esther's trouble which is, in fact, the most useful source of contradiction in the text.

Initially, the text's construction of trouble presents a simplistic relation between those who exert power, and those who are the objects of power: if trouble is the natural disposition of the female of the species, those who police that trouble are male. Tulkinghorn's oppressive surveillance of Lady Dedlock is a model of this relationship, while Jarndyce's relation to Esther, I would argue, is only a seemingly more benevolent version of this oppression. Two important objections can be made against this representation, however. The first is that the most effective "moral policeman" in the novel is Esther Summerson. In fact, Esther is a better "policeman" than the other characters because of a characteristic that seems to be a sign of her oppression—her "silent way of noticing7' (17). Esther's silent notice is both an effective means of surveillance, and is the means by which the other characters are presented to the reader: she is one of the narrators. The power which Esther can exert as a narrator is another important omission in Miller's article. That Miller overlooks Esther's narrative control is apparent in an analogy in which he likens the reader's subservient relation to Dickens to Esther's relation to Jarndyce. As Esther relies on Jarndyce for the outcome of the marriage plot, the reader must "rely on the full revelation of [Dickens'] design" (92). Miller sees Jarndyce as the director of a discourse in which Esther must play the part he assigns her. But while Jarndyce does play an authorial role in the construction of the Esther-Woodcourt marriage plot, it is Esther who represents Jarndyce playing that role. The reader relies on *her* for "the full revelation of his design."[1] Thus, it also becomes clear that the troubled position is not inherently female—men, too, can become the objects of surveillance. Again, to borrow from Butler's preface, "trouble [becomes] a scandal with the sudden intrusion, the unanticipated agency, of a female object who inexplicable returns the glance, reverses the gaze, and contests the place and authority of the masculine position" (ix).[2]

Esther's "female trouble," her illegitimacy, defines her as nonexistent, as the child who should never have been born. But by making her the narrator of half the novel, Dickens contradicts this definition, giving her an "I," a subject position.[3] This contradiction does not result in the simple overthrow of the dominant which is usually imagined as the result of giving the marginal a voice (in this sense, there is *No Exit* from *Bleak House*), but rather in a set of competing identities: [4] a policeman who is more successful at tracking down "female trouble" than Tulkinghorn, Bucket, or any of the other, more theatrically displayed representatives of masculine authority, but also a troublemaker who uses the same means of surveillance to resist and expose that authority.

POLICING FEMALE TROUBLE

Though it opens with a description of the interminable case of Jarndyce and Jarndyce, the novel does not follow the proceedings of that case (if, indeed, it were possible to undertake such a task). Most of those involved in the legal machinery, Tulkinghorn, Snagsby, Guppy, and Jobling, are not concerned with investigating the civil suit, but in investigating the sexual mystery, Lady Dedlock's secret. Lady Dedlock is "hotly pursued" not only by the "fashionable intelligence" (14), but by both narratives, culminating in the "Pursuit" which begins in the third person narrative and crosses over into Esther's.

Without that secret there would be no plot to follow in the third-person narrative. As Miller points out the problem with the civil suit is that it does not generate a story:

> If the Chancery system includes everything but settles nothing, then one way in which it differs from the detective story is that the latter is, precisely, a story: sufficiently selective to allow for the emergence of a narrative and properly committed, once one has emerged, to bringing it to completion.   (69)

Miller finds the solution to the text's seeming immobility in the detective plot, but readers would have to suspend the erotics of narrative for quite some time if they had to await the emergence of the whodunit. The novel makes itself desirable long before the murder mystery and the object of that desire is Lady Dedlock's sexuality.

This construction of woman as secret accords with a Foucauldian feminist analysis of the genealogy of "woman":

> If women have been marginal in the constitution of meaning and power in Western culture, the question of woman has been central, crucial to the discourse of man, situated as she is within the literary text, the critical text, the psychoanalytic situation, and social texts of all kinds as the riddle, the problem to be solved, the question to be answered.   (Martin 13–14)

The function of "female trouble" is therefore to generate text, or in Foucault's terminology to incite a discourse.

Within this discourse, woman as "problem" justifies the intervention and control of various fields of expertise. The hysterical woman is subject to the gaze of the doctor or psychoanalyst who must regulate her behavior. In *Bleak House*, the most obvious gaze directed at Lady Dedlock comes from Tulkinghron. Her own description of his domination of her makes it clear that that domination rests on the construction of her as spectacle, an object of his power-knowledge-pleasure:

> "I am to drag my present life on, holding its pains at your pleasure . . . I am to remain on this gaudy platform, on which my miserable deception has been so long acted, and it is to fall beneath me when you give the signal?"
> "Not without notice, Lady Dedlock . . . "   (512)

Tulkinghorn's answer is ironic, for it is just this notice which Lady Dedlock tried, and failed to avoid.

Her daughter, too, is introduced in this troubled position of being noticed. In Esther's portrait of her childhood, she seems always under the judgmental eye of her godmother, whose "knitted brow and pointed finger" define Esther as another source of female trouble. When Esther's godmother points to her illegitimacy—Esther's nonexistence within patriarchal culture—notice is explicitly connected with nothingness, with lack of identity. To be the object of knowledge for women implies annihilation of the self—either in a denial of existence, Esther's illegitimacy, or in execution, Lady Dedlock's metaphoric description of her position on the hangman's "gaudy platform."[5]

Esther's denial that "this narrative were the narrative of *my* life!7' (27) is, then, a strategy of survival; it takes her out of the dangerous position of being noticed, and puts her in the more powerful position of silent noticer. Paradoxically, self-denial is the means by which she establishes a self. Esther avoids drawing attention to her own notice not only in her self-deprecatory style, but also by highlighting the notice of others, so that in the representation of her godmother's censuring gaze one forgets that it is Esther's reciprocal gaze, her narration, which creates this picture of her godmother's oppression. Through her role as narrator, Esther turns her godmother's portrait of her as the child of sin to a representation of a child more sinned against than sinning. In this section of Esther's text, her godmother is condemned for her Old Testament condemnation of Esther. The attack which causes her death follows Esther's narration (here, in the sense of reading aloud) of the New Testament story of the adulterous woman: "So when they continued asking him, he lifted up himself and said unto them, He that is without sin among you, let him cast a stone at her" (John 8:7, quoted in Dickens 21). This story, which leaves judgment with God, judges and executes Miss Barbary for her harsh treatment of Esther.

That she is narrating God's words to her godmother removes any sense of Esther's own motivation in reading this particular story. Similarly, Esther's claim that she is writing someone else's story keeps the reader from noticing her position as the medium through which Miss Barbary's actions are viewed. But one must remember that the "Saviour . . . writing with his finger in the dust" (20) is being represented by another writing finger. Esther's writing finger replaces her godmother's pointing finger; it condemns her godmother as the woman who holds herself above sin—as the woman who, casting the first stone, must herself be struck down. Here is the first indication that the surveillance which disciplines female trouble can be reversed, turned against the authority figure such that discipline, itself, becomes the spectacle which is critiqued and condemned.

However, Esther's condemnation of her godmother relies on the same patriarchal Christian discourse by which her godmother (and society in general) would condemn Esther. To be a noticer, a narrator, Esther allies herself with the Savior. God becomes the father which Esther must have in order to gain legitimacy. The paternalism which Dickens frequently relies on to save his marginal characters is here shown to be double-edged. Because patriarchy bases identity on connection to the father, Esther must find a father-substitute, here God, but through most of the text John Jarndyce. So patriarchy first denies the female a self, and then provides one through paternalism. The initial paradox described above—self-denial leading to construction of the self—is shown to have a particular resonance for women. Esther's situation is very much like that enunciated by feminist critics today: how does a woman construct a self in a discourse which defines the "I" as male? In using that discourse, how does she avoid recapitulating the values that that discourse upholds?

In Esther's use of the story of the adulterous woman, she affirms a place for the excluded within a patriarchal Christian discourse. And in so doing, she exposes the contradictions of that discourse: it can be used to condemn those who sin, and to condemn those who condemn sin. But Esther also allies herself with this discourse, and risks reenacting its values—becoming an even more effective judge than her godmother.

Esther's capitulation to the patriarchal discourse is most fully illustrated by her relation to her mother. While the absence of the father can be compensated for through paternalistic substitutes, it is the mother's presence which poses the real danger, for it is her connection to her mother's sexuality which makes Esther "nobody"—the dead child. Thus, after Lady Dedlock confesses her secret to Esther, Esther feels that "it was right, and had been intended, that I should die in my birth; and that it was wrong, and not intended that I should be then alive" (453). Lady Dedlock's sin, Esther's illegitimacy, signals a disruption in the female function of "bearing" the male name. Having failed in this exchange of the patronymic from one generation to the next, both mother and daughter are threatened with annihilation. However, this failure does lead to another identification, the identification of both women with sexual transgression. In both cases, the woman is marked by her sex—"quali-fied and disqualified" by her relation to reproduction (Foucault 104). Esther's fear of having no identity, of having no right to exist, is also a fear of having an identity, an identity of sexuality connected with her mother. To divorce herself from this connection, Esther must make use of a discourse which defines both her mother and herself as "female trouble." To notice, rather than be noticed, Esther must inhabit the male authority position as noticer of the female. As Helena Michie points out, Esther assumes the male gaze in her erotic descriptions of Ada, and in her repeated reference to Ada as "my darling" (" 'Who is this in Pain' " 203). Even more central to Esther's text is the disciplinary gaze which she directs at her mother. Esther's narrative objectifies her mother as the source of sexuality in the novel. In this objectifi-cation, which ends with her mother as a lifeless object, Esther attempts to separate herself from the stigma of her mother's sin. She takes up God's patriarchal discourse to judge her godmother, and she will take up Bucket's detective discourse to pursue Lady Dedlock.

Throughout the section of the novel in which she accompanies Bucket in pursuit of her mother, Esther continually denies her central position of notice, her position as the narrator through whose eyes the reader witnesses the end of Lady Dedlock's story. Instead, she presents herself as powerless and ignorant, unable to comprehend what transpired, both at the moment that the events took place, and in the present moment of narration: "where we drove, I neither knew then, nor have ever known since; but we appeared to seek out the narrowest and worst streets in London" (704). She emphasizes that she is a completely passive agent in the hands of Mr. Bucket, who has a "plan" though Esther does "not feel clear enough to understand it" (675). But while Esther as character has no plan, her narrative does, which is to hide her own ability to note what is going on around her. This portrayal performs two functions: first, Bucket is used to draw attention away from Esther. He and Lady Dedlock play the central roles of pursuer and pursued; if "somebody" is to be blamed for hounding Lady Dedlock's final steps, if "somebody" is made to look like the male authority figure, that somebody is Bucket, not Esther Summerson. Second, maintaining her ignorance allows Esther's narrative to create suspense around the moment of Esther's recognition of her mother's dead body. That suspense, and Esther's confusion of Lady Dedlock's body with "Jenny, the mother of the dead child" (713), emphasize Lady Dedlock's illicit sexuality at the moment that her dead body is prominently displayed. Thus, "female trouble" and the annihilation which it threatens seem to be safely recontained within Lady Dedlock's dead body, and not within her living child.

While Esther states that she was incapable of taking "note of any particular objects" in her "perturbed state of mind" (675), the objects noted by her narrative lead to a feeling both of horror and of desire toward her mother's body. At the very beginning of the pursuit, Esther describes a nightmare scene which foreshadows Lady Dedlock's death:

> I could discern the words, "FOUND DROWNED;" and this, and an inscription about Drags, possessed me with the awful suspicion shadowed forth in our visit to that place . . . still it was like the horror of a dream. A man yet dank and muddy, in long swollen sodden boots and a hat like them, was called out of a boat, and whispered with Mr. Bucket, who went away with him down some slippery steps—as if to look at something secret that he had to show. They came back wiping their hands on their coats, after turning over something wet; but thank God it was not what I feared!   (676)

Esther's narrative temptingly holds out the possibility that a secret will be shown, but then postpones that revelation. The nature of the secret connects a forbidden primal scene with a horrible revelation of the mother's body as a corpse. The phallically identified man dressed in "long swollen" clothing, a man dressed in the sailor's uniform of Esther's father, threatens to display "something wet"   the mother's body "swollen" and "sodden" with death. Esther's description closely ties sex to death; it establishes that connection and then postpones its consummation. In that postponement, the reader too becomes caught up in the pursuit of Lady Dedlock. We desire the end of the narrative, the uncovering of the mother's fate, and we realize that that fate must fulfill Esther's narrative foreshadowing which links sexual sin to death.

Though Esther's narrative pursues Lady Dedlock, Esther's character is denied even the knowledge that the woman they are chasing is her mother. At the moment that Lady Dedlock's body is found, Esther believes that the body is Jenny's:

> On the step at the gate, drenched in the fearful wet of such a place, which oozed and splashed down everywhere, I saw with a cry of pity and horror, a woman lying—Jenny, the mother of the dead child.   (713)

On this second set of "slippery steps" the "something wet" is finally displayed. But the moment of narrative suspense is prolonged by Esther's failure to recognize what this something is. The real end of the pursuit must come with Esther's removal of Lady Dedlock's mask of hair to uncover "my mother, cold and dead" (714). Esther's confusion juxtaposes the image of the mother of the dead child with the image of the dead mother. This confusion produces in Esther's narrative a metamorphosis of Lady Dedlock from the live mother whose child should be dead to the dead mother whose child may begin to live.

Esther's mother tries to become unnoticeable by running away, by disguising herself, by doubling back on her own tracks. In her final letter to Esther she says that all that remains to her is "to be lost. I shall be soon forgotten so, . . . I have nothing about me by which I can be recognized" (710). But Esther's narrative will not allow her mother to go unrecognized. As she dies of exposure in Esther's narrative, she also dies exposed by that narrative.

GENDER TROUBLE

The introduction of the detective police in *Bleak House*, as Miller demonstrates, provides the novel with "a simplified representative of order and power" (73) which compensates for both the excesses and the weaknesses of Chancery. Miller connects the murder plot to this transfer of power from Chancery to the police:

> Of all mysteries that will crop up in *Bleak House*, not the least instructive concerns the formal torsion whereby a novel dealing with a civil suit becomes a murder mystery, and whereby the themes of power and social control are passed accordingly from the abyssal filiation of the law into the capable hands

of the detective police. (66)

As Miller points out, the question of whether power actually lies in the capable hands of the detective police is problematic. However, the first "mystery" that I would like to address in Miller's description is the mystery of whether the plot is even initially about the civil suit.

As I have demonstrated, the plot that emerges long before the introduction of a murder mystery is the plot generated by "female trouble." I would rephrase Miller's question, then, to ask why a novel which has centered on a sexual secret becomes, with Tulkinghorn's murder, one which centers on a criminal secret. Why must the sexual mystery of Lady Dedlock be confused with a criminal mystery at this point in the novel, when what has generated narrative suspense through most of the novel has been that sexual mystery? The answer does seem to lie with the "excesses and weaknesses" of Chancery's legal machinery, but not in the pursuit of the civil case, but in the pursuit of Lady Dedlock. In their involvement with "female trouble," the male characters reveal that this identification of sexuality with women alone is an ideological construction. Men also can be placed in this troubled position.

This gender reversal is interestingly played out in the relation between Guppy and Esther. Guppy's attentions to Esther, and his intuitive grasp of her connection to Lady Dedlock, again show how Lady Dedlock's secret threatens to turn Esther into an object of sexual notice. Guppy's notice of Esther is rendered less threatening than other forms of surveillance in the novel, however, because of Esther's satiric descriptions of that notice. Esther also makes use of her favorite strategy, emphasizing Guppy's notice rather than her own: "I never looked at him, but I found him looking at me, in the same scrutinizing and curious way" (112). Even Guppy's frequent oath—"My eye, miss"—apparently indicates that the gaze rests with him, though it is Esther who, while "never looking at him," has taken note of all his less than flattering characteristics.

Esther becomes most fully aware of Guppy's notice when they both happen to attend a play: "I felt all through the performance that he never looked at the actors, but constantly looked at me, and always with a carefully prepared expression of the deepest misery and the profoundest dejection" (155). Guppy's observation of her instead of the actors threatens to turn Esther into the performance. But in Esther's description of Guppy's "prepared expression" he becomes the actor; a rather foolish, tragic clown, whose antics are spotlighted by Esther's narrative.

The staging of this power struggle of watcher and watched is replayed in Esther's observation of her mother watching her at the theater later in the novel. Again, Esther is able to turn notice away from herself and focus it on the other. But the connection between these two scenes again highlights the problem with the secret of sexuality. In the two theater scenes, Guppy and Lady Dedlock are initially presented as the watchers, but upon reflection it is clear that they occupy the parallel positions of object of the gaze (Esther's gaze). If to become the object of the gaze is to become the sexual object, then sexuality is not essentially connected to one gender. Men, too, can fall under surveillance.

Thus, the rather impotent Mr. Snagsby is figured as the possessor of a secret which makes him suffer under his wife's more potent gaze:

> To know that he is always keeping a secret from her; that he has, under all circumstances, to conceal and hold fast a tender double tooth, which her sharpness is ever ready to twist out of his hand; gives Mr. Snagsby, in her dentistical presence, much of the air of a dog who has a reservation from his master. . . .
>
> (316)

Not only does Snagsby's position as the concealed keeper of the secret make him a dog to his wife's master, it also puts him in danger of a physical attack which threatens to extract that secret from within him.

Those who are watched in *Bleak House*, like Mr. Snagsby, enter a metaphorically female position, represented as always open to penetration from those who observe them. Vholes's observation of Richard, for example, is rendered as a penetrating vampire bite. This penetration reaches its climax (in both the narrative and sexual senses) with Richard's blood filling his mouth—an interesting connection to Snagsby' situation since a bloodied mouth is also the culmination of tooth extraction. In the female object position, the body is not inviolate; it is always subject to rape—a rape which not only breaks through the physical barrier of the self but exposes the inner self, the blood, to view.

It is the mobility of "trouble," of the secret of sexuality, which poses the greatest threat in the novel. Not only will that secret not remain reassuringly attached to Lady Dedlock, it will not remain attached to the female gender. Tulkinghorn's death represents the greatest crisis in this mobility of sexuality. The man who is composed of "impenetrabilities" (514) is penetrated by a woman's gun. By taking over Lady Dedlock's secret, Tulkinghorn also takes over her position as the penetrated object of notice. The blood stain which is the sign of this penetration calls forth a masculine power which will correctly realign the gender positions—the man whose "fat forefinger seems to rise to the dignity of a familiar demon" (626)—Mr. Bucket.

The realignment of gender positions begins with Bucket's arrest of Hortense. That arrest, as Michael Steig and F. A. C. Wilson show, is represented as a courtship ending with Bucket leading away Hortense "as if he were a homely Jupiter, and she the object of his affections" (653). Just as a suitor would show his "right of property in Mademoiselle" (651) by placing a ring on her finger, Bucket encircles Hortense's hand with a handcuff. Hortense's male penetrating energy is not only arrested, it is rendered as correct female passivity.

Esther makes use of this detective plot to distance herself from her mother's sexuality as she makes use of Bucket to distance herself from the role of pursuer. The original likeness which threatens to connect Esther to her mother is shared by Lady Dedlock, Esther, and her godmother. This likeness is refigured in the detective plot as a connection between Lady Dedlock, Esther, and Hortense. Esther takes part in this refiguring of the original connection by drawing attention to Trooper George's comment that he has seen a woman who looks like Esther leaving the scene of the crime:

> I cannot separate and define the feelings that arose in me after this: it is enough that the vague duty and obligation I had felt upon me from the first of following the investigation, was, without my distinctly daring to ask myself any question, increased; and that I was indignantly sure of there being no possibility of a reason for my being afraid.   (624)

While Esther avoids an explicit statement of the question "Is my mother the murderer?" her very denial works to bring that possibility to the reader's attention. Here again Esther draws attention away from herself—she is not the detective, pursuing her mother the suspect—and yet her narrative still throws suspicion on her mother.

The original likeness is one which presents problems of differentiation, for even as they are separated into mother, child, and aunt, the likeness of the women shows that they are connected through a biological-sexual link. The detective plot transfers this link from a sexual to a criminal discourse. Esther's likeness to her mother becomes a clue in a criminal investigation, not an association with her mother's sexuality. They are connected, and can be differentiated, along lines of guilt and innocence. Esther attempts to take up this differentiation of guilt and innocence which ends the traditional detective story to prosecute her mother's sexuality.

But Esther's narrative also reconfigures the triad of three women once more, and, at the same time, draws attention to the artifice of the detective story's resolution of guilt and innocence. In the pursuit of her mother, Esther highlights Bucket as the planner of that pursuit. His trick of allowing Esther to believe that they are following Jenny is akin to the confusion and suspension of identity in detective plots, the kind of novelistic trick which allows for teleological resolution—an ending which seemingly brings order to the world. But in Esther's depiction the trick seems an unnecessary artifice; there is no reason for Bucket to create this confusion. Esther's narrative thus not only exposes her mother, and her mother's sexuality, it also exposes the detective discourse which seeks to recontain "female trouble" by ending the story of Lady Dedlock's sexual secret as if it were the story of a criminal secret. And yet, Esther's narrative relies on the same trick to establish a chiasmus between Jenny and her mother, a chiasmus which will allow Esther to emerge as the live child of the dead mother.

Though Esther's narrative is successful in establishing this chiasmus, and in separating her from its artifice, it is not ultimately successful in establishing her separation from her mother's sexuality. In reconfiguring the detective triad of Lady Dedlock, Esther, and Hortense into the triad of Lady Dedlock, Esther, and Jenny, Esther again emphasizes the biological connection which the detective story conceals. In exposing her mother's sexuality, Esther exposes her own sexual origins, her birth in the illicit sexual act of her mother.

As in Richard's ejaculation of blood, the exposure of the inner self—of the sexual secret of Lady Dedlock—is accompanied by the bursting forth of liquid from inside to outside. Esther exposes her mother as "the something wet" but is unable to remain untouched by these liquid metaphors which stand for both the sexual act and birth. Bucket remarks on Esther's drenched condition as they near the end of the pursuit "Why, my dear! . . . How wet you are !" (703). And Esther, herself, feels as if she is the source of the "wet house tops, the clogged and bursting gutters and water-spouts" which surround the end of the pursuit, for it is as if "great water-gates seemed to be opening and closing"(712) inside her. Esther's rebirth as the live child is accompanied by the breaking open of gates, and the release of waters which would have accompanied her actual birth. Though Esther's narrative at one level adopts the male gaze which separates her from her mother and attempts to recontain her mother's sexuality, at another level it highlights the physical-sexual process of birth which connects her to her mother—a sexuality which is uncontained, which in fact "oozed and splashed down everywhere."

RAINING DAUGHTERS AND SUMMER'S SONS

> There is no question that the appearance in nineteenth-century psychiatry, juris-
> prudence, and literature of a whole series of discourses on the species and
> subspecies of homosexuality, inversion, pederasty, and "psychic hermaphrod-
> ism" made possible a strong advance of social controls into this area of "perver-
> sity"; but it also made possible the formation of a "reverse" discourse: homo-
> sexuality began to speak in its own behalf, to demand that its legitimacy or
> "naturality" be acknowledged. . . .   (Foucault 101)

In Foucault's conceptualization of power, power is not localized—contained in any one institution. Power is "the name one attributes to a complex
strategical situation in a particular society" (95)—a "mobile field of force
relations, wherein far-reaching, but never completely stable effects of domination are produced" (102). By creating a character who is at one and the same
time a narrator who can direct the disciplinary gaze, and a character who is
herself deeply in the kind of female trouble which makes one subject to that
gaze, Dickens creates just such a complex strategical situation. As a narrator,
Esther directs the gaze at her mother in order to separate herself from female
trouble. She is also able to direct that gaze at male characters like Guppy and
Bucket, and in so doing acts not just to enforce discipline, but to create
resistance to the "never completely stable effects of domination."

If men can also get into female trouble, then disciplinary forces must be
increased, more "moral policeman" deployed. However, revealing that female trouble is actually a more general "gender trouble" also creates resistance to an ideology which maintains that sexuality is intrinsically female.
Esther's narrative exposes the way in which constructing any one group as
the source of sexual pathology justifies the deployment of mechanisms of
power.

Finally, that narrative works as a force of resistance by making use of
" 'reverse' discourse"—a discourse written from within female trouble,
speaking "in its own behalf, to demand that is legitimacy . . . be acknowledged." That acknowledgment is most strongly recorded in Esther's descriptions of crying.[6] In these descriptions, Esther's connection with her mother
and her mother's sexuality is reaffirmed, while the erotic motivations of
paternalism are most fully revealed.

Lady Dedlock cries only twice in the novel, though the suppression of her
grief is acknowledged by the rain which pours down on Chesney Wold. Lady
Dedlock's first cry is uttered upon the discovery that Esther did not die at

birth. It is an outburst of grief which the Dedlock town house cannot quite keep locked up:

> Words, sobs, and cries, are but air; and air is so shut in and shut out throughout the house in town, that sounds need be uttered trumpet-tongued indeed by my Lady in her chamber to carry any faint vibration to Sir Leicester's ears; and yet this cry is in the house, going upward from a wild figure on its knees.   (364)

Lady Dedlock cries a second time at the meeting in which she confesses her identity to Esther. This second cry is, however, not an uncontrolled outpouring of "words, sobs, and cries," but "a suppressed cry of despair" which accompanies the statement that her secret must remain a secret: "I must keep this secret, if by any means it can be kept, not wholly for myself. I have a husband, wretched and dishonoring creature that I am!" (450). The second cry, unlike the cry uttered by "a wild figure on its knees," is the cry of suppression. Like her sexuality, Lady Dedlock's physical expression of grief must be contained in order to protect the male position. If she admits her grief for a child she should not have, she becomes the "dishonoring creature" of her husband. Esther's narrative releases the suppression of her mother's tears into the text in her description of the dripping, sodden atmosphere in which her mother's body is found.

John Jarndyce resists the intrusion of any such rainy atmosphere into Bleak House. His fear of the East Wind is a fear that any negative expression of feelings like tears may be given free rein (reign, rain) in his presence; his most direct commands to Esther are commands to suppress those tears. Interestingly, though, Esther's tears seem to be what first attract Jayndyce to Esther. His "old dream" of marrying her originates in having seen her when she was "very young" (751), and when Jarndyce sees the very young Esther she is crying:

> "What the de-vil are you crying for?"
> I was so frightened that I lost my voice, and could only answer in a whisper. "Me sir?" For of course I knew it must have been the gentleman in the quantity of wrappings, though he was still looking out of his window.
> "Yes, you," he said, turning around.
> "I didn't know I was crying, sir," I faltered.
> "But you are!" said the gentleman. "Look here!" He came quite opposite to me from the other corner of the coach, brushed one of his large furry cuffs across my eyes . . . and showed me that it was wet.
> "There! Now you know you are," he said. . . . "Don't you want to go there?" . . .
> "I am very glad to go there, sir," I answered.

"Well then! Look glad!"   (24)

As a character, Esther is once again represented as under the gaze of male
authority—an authority who not only draws attention to her physical reactions, but makes her name those reactions. This is a classic illustration of
discipline. On her way to "Reading," Esther is taught to read her own body
in order to make that body self-regulating.

However, stepping back from this scene to consider how it is being represented and by whom, one realizes that it is Jarndyce's body and physical
reactions that are the object of Esther's critical narrative gaze. Esther's mother
is first presented by the third-person narrator as a body wrapped in jeweler's
cotton—another means by which the female body is rendered as the secret to
be uncovered through the striptease of reading. Esther's portrait of Jarndyce,
"wrapped up to the chin" (24), duplicates this strategy: she presents Jarndyce's body as a mystery which becomes a center of narrative interest—a
body which "looked very large" to Esther, and looms very large for the
reader, just because it is so intensely concealed.

In general, Esther emphasizes Jarndyce's sexuality through her portrayal
of its repression as Barbara Gottfried points out in "Fathers and Suitors in
Bleak House." For example, in Esther's description of Jarndyce's room, with
its "cold bath" and "open window," the very starkness of the description
subtly suggests the necessity for the cold bath:

> Ostensibly, Esther means to suggest that Jarndyce does not indulge in luxuries,
> nor lavish on himself what others cannot afford. But her "monkish" description
> points to willful renunciation, the repression of sexuality. Of course, in order
> to renounce, one must first have desired . . .   (Gottfried 173)

What Jarndyce desires is more openly considered in Esther's description of
their first meeting. Here, Jarndyce comes surprisingly close to the stereotypical image of the child molester—a stranger offering candy to a child in order
to win her trust:

> "In this paper," which was nicely folded, "is a piece of the best plum-cake
> that can be got for money—sugar on the outside an inch thick, like fat on
> mutton chops. Here's a little pie (a gem this is, both for size and quality), made
> in France, And what do you suppose it's made of? Livers of fat geese. There's
> a pie! Now let's see you eat 'em."
>   "Thank you sir," I replied, "thank you very much indeed, but I hope you
> won't be offended; they are too rich for me."   (25)

The strongly sensual terms in which the food is described highlight the seductiveness of Jarndyce's offer. In addition, the food's richness, and its connection to large physical proportions ("sugar an inch thick," "fat on mutton chops," and "Livers of fat geese") connect the food to the large man also richly covered. Jarndyce makes an offer of himself which Esther, somehow aware of the threat these rich sensations pose, is able to refuse. Later, when Esther is aware of her dependence on Jarndyce's generosity, she can no longer refuse, but in her representation of Jarndyce's initial offerings she makes clear that paternalism offers more than charitable help to the illegitimate child. Male sexual interest is served by having women in female trouble, a trouble that not only requires male policing, but male rescue in the form of sugar plums for little girls, or offers of marriage to older ones.

In Esther's description of this meeting, and in her later reminder that Jarndyce first thought of her as a potential wife at this moment, the reader is made aware of an erotic motivation underlying the generosity of paternalism. When Esther cries here it is because she has been thinking of her dead godmother, and the excluded social position that her godmother names as belonging both to Esther and to her mother. Jarndyce is attracted to the crying child because her tears signal her isolation and dependency, an isolation which puts Jarndyce in the role of rescuing prince. Her tears allow him to exercise paternalistic power and control (his demand that she "look glad"). But as tears also signify the disgrace that Esther and her mother share as women, that is their sexuality, Jarndyce's interest in the crying child is also shown to be sexual.

Once Esther is more directly subject to Jarndyce's generosity, her tears must be more severely restrained. To continue to cry would be to show that Jarndyce's charity has not successfully contained and controlled female trouble. The discipline that Esther maintains over herself—her attempt always to "look glad"—is the price she pays as the object of paternalism. In Jarndyce's presence, she begins to hold back those tears, "choking" (90) on them. As Jarndyce's dependent she finds that it is better "to keep . . . to the bright side of the picture" (89).

Like Mrs. Pardiggle's children, Esther lives under a restraint which is "choking," but her narrative refuses to let her tears remain hidden. They are mentioned more and more frequently after Jarndyce's proposal:

> To devote my life to his happiness was to thank him poorly, and what had I wished for only the other night but some new means of thinking him? Still I cried very much . . . as if something for which there was no name or distinct

idea were indefinitely lost to me. I was very happy, very thankful, very hopeful; but I cried very much.   (538)

Esther's dependence on Jarndyce requires that she return his generosity. He holds the social power which protects her from the consequences of her illegitimate status. But she must also suffer the consequences of that illegitimacy by marrying him, by connecting herself to that power. In so doing she gives up something unnameable—her sexual desires for Woodcourt—but her text continues to name those desires in her tears.

Esther once again records those desires when Woodcourt confesses his love for her. Esther's "first wild thought" upon hearing Woodcourt's proposal is that it has come too late. Like her mother's grief, Esther equates her sexuality with the unrestrained—the "wild." Crying over this "first wild thought" once again connects Esther to her mother as her description reinvokes the scene of her mother's death: "the street was blotted out by rushing tears" (733). Esther's narrative attempts to control the expression of these desires by insisting that "they were not tears of regret and sorrow" (733). But she finds that she must still hide these feelings from Jarndyce, afraid that her "tears might a litte reproach" her. The reproach that Esther is actually signaling is the reproach she fears from Jarndyce by displaying her desires for Woodcourt.

In taking back his proposal and giving it to Woodcourt, Jarndyce remains in control of Esther's desires. But Esther also escapes that control in another outburst of tears: "I sobbed and wept afresh. . . . 'Hush, little woman! Don't cry; this is to be a day of joy' " (752). Jarndyce wants his acts of generosity to be acknowledged as the cause of joy. But like the "Infant Bond of Joy" Esther refuses to acquiesce completely in this acknowledgment. Jarndyce's acts of generosity are never represented by Esther as wholly joyful and innocent. In recording her own cries, she shows the disciplinary control of that generosity—a generosity which seeks to silence her, and commands her not to cry. Jarndyce, in fact, asks Esther to erase the history of the proposal and the pain that it has caused her: "I know that my mistake has caused you some distress. Forgive your old guardian, in restoring him to his old place in your affections; and blot it out of your memory" (753). But Esther's narrative enshrines his mistake and her distress in the memory of her narrative; by refusing to "blot . . . out" her tears, she exposes the darker side of the man on whose head "the sun's rays descended" (752).

In order to become John Jarndyce's heir, the summer's son, Esther must keep to the bright side of things. By successfully disciplining her own female

trouble, Esther is given her own Bleak House. She overcomes the disgrace
of her mother's position and the threat of personal destruction which that
position entails, instead taking her place as a character in the father's house
and as the narrator in the father's discourse. But her narrative also records
the times that "It rained Esther" (61), when female trouble escapes the
discipline of paternalism, and tears are not "shut in and shut out throughout
the house" but threaten to flood the streets.

"—EVEN SUPPOSING—" (770)

"Don't tell stories, Miss Summerson."

                                                   (Caddy Jellyby 44)
" . . . take the past for granted."
                                   (Jarndyce's note to Ada, Richard, and Esther 58)

"Forget your Mother."   (Miss Barbary 19)

When Caddy Jellyby asks Esther not to tell stories, the paradoxical nature
of Esther's silent notice is made clear. Esther's silence about the way in which
the Jellyby household is run angers Caddy, who then tells her not to lie ("tell
stories") about not having noticed the maid's drinking, and the "disgraceful"
(44) state of the children and Mr. Jellyby. Esther has noticed all of these
things, and recorded them as a narrator, but her silence to Caddy works to
draw out a confession of Caddy's anger after which Esther can remonstrate
with her about her "duty as a child" (46). Here, Esther's silent notice works
to discipline the family, but that notice does not serve the interests of discipline alone. For example, though Esther directs Caddy and Prince to seek the
blessings of their parents before marrying, her narrative completely undermines any sense of "duty as a child" owed to Mr. Turveydrop or Mrs.
Jellyby. When Turveydrop speaks about his own generosity to Caddy and
Prince, Esther interjects translations of these statements of his beneficence:
" 'My son and daughter, your happiness shall be my care. I will watch over
you. You shall always live with me'; meaning of course, I will always live
with you" (294). In Turveydrop, Esther directly criticizes paternalism—exposing its own dependence on what it labels "dependents." As one
of Jarndyce's "dependents," Esther cannot make such openly critical statements. Interestingly, however, immediately after the scene in which Turveydrop's seeming generosity is derided, Esther shows the reader an example of
Jarndyce's generosity which has even darker implications. Having come home

from Caddy's wedding, Esther is given "a little present" (299) from Jarndyce—her maid Charley. Just as Esther is given to Ada by Jarndyce, Charley is given to Esther. Esther here reveals the network of human beings owned by Jarndyce—this exchange of people as gifts lies behind his paternalism.

Esther's narrative does not, as Jarndyce directs, "take the past for granted." Rather it tells the story of her past, and of the connection to her mother which is a part of that history. In telling that story she records both Jarndyce's generosity and the paternalistic power exerted through generosity; she supports her godmother's censure of her mother by objectifying her mother as the source of sexuality in the text, and at the same time gives sexuality an authorized place in the text. She does not maintain sexuality as *the secret*;[7] instead she shows how this definition of female trouble as the censured disgrace is in the interests of the paternalistic power: it allows that power to both rescue and police the illegitimate girl-child.

The ambiguity of Esther's position is maintained in her final words "—even supposing—." In these final pages of the novel, Esther reiterates the connection of her tears with Jarndyce: "when I write of him my tears will have their way" (769). Although Esther's tears signify the repression of female trouble, they also give expression to that trouble; and here they are not repressed for Jarndyce's sake, but in fact "have their way." Caddy's deaf and dumb child, Esther's namesake, might also be taken as a sign of Esther's repression—her inability to directly confront the dominant discourse. However, Caddy is learning sign language—even silence can be given a discourse of its own, its own way of noticing. Finally, Esther is shown talking to her husband about her "old looks" (770). She is still thinking about those looks and what they stand for—her own and her mother's sexuality. Her husband directs her away from this remembrance of the past, just as Jarndyce and her godmother have, telling her that she is "prettier than she ever was" (770), but Esther refuses to "know that" (770). She directs attention away from herself and onto the beauty of Ada, the handsomeness of her husband, and the benevolence of her guardian. Such a redirection highlights the danger of Esther's being noticed, of once again becoming defined as "female trouble" in her husband's statement that she is prettier than ever. But the dashes which take the place of any direct statement of Esther's beauty also draw one's notice. What the reader is to suppose is represented by another silence at the end of the text, but a silence which is given representation by the dashes which take the place of words. Like Caddy's baby, Esther is given a way to bring silence into discourse, to render her "old looks," her sexuality, and her "old looks," her surveillance of the patriarchal power and its investment in reifying that sexuality.

Esther's narrative might also be described as a way of "even supposing," for its "supposing" balances between supporting and exposing discipline. It works to completely destabilize the binary division between the positions of a male regulatory control and a female trouble which seems to call for that control. In fact, one thing that *Bleak House* asks of its readers is to "even suppose" that its narrator is a woman, Esther Summerson, and not the man, Charles Dickens. In so doing, Dickens does not ventriloquize Esther, for he gives to Esther the power to expose the very ideology of paternalism which lies at the heart of so many of his novels. By placing one half of this novel in the hands of a female narrator, Dickens makes use of sexual difference; he shows that a female narrator can be given disciplinary power, and also be made subject to that power; she can be under the surveillance of paternalism and turn surveillance back on paternalism, exposing its reliance on its "dependents." And finally, an ideology of male control and regulation is undercut, for Dickens shows that discipline can put one in a position of power, and make one subject to power, no matter what one's gender. Like Esther, Dickesn supports paternalism, is subject to paternalism, and exposes paternalism. He is a participant in a field of power relations in which one can even suppose that the divisions of discipline and trouble, of male and female, begin to break down.

NOTES

1. Esther's powers as a narrator have been noted by other critics, though. In " 'The Mere Truth Won't Do' ": Esther as Narrator in *Bleak House*," Joseph Sawicki shows that Esther's narrative works to undermine the theme of interconnectedness which Jarndyce's marriage plot tries to bring about. Helena Michie's discussion of *Bleak House* in " 'Who is this in Pain' " is similar to my own in examining the relation between Esther's narrative and the problematic concept of female subjectivity, though Michie is more focused on Esther's use of her own body and that body's pain: Esther turns her "ailments into specifically narrative power" (200). And Barbara Gottfried's recent analysis of Esther's treatment of "Fathers and Suitors" in *Dickens Studies Annual* 19 demonstrates Esther's narrative ability to satirize Guppy, compete with Richard, and criticize Jarndyce. See also "I'll Follow the Other: Tracing the (M)Other in *Bleak House*" by Marcia Renee Goodman in the same volume.

2. Beth Newman describes this same unanticipated female agency in the uncanny gaze of the Medusa: "Medusa defies the male gaze as Western culture has constructed it: as the privilege of a male subject, a means of relegating women (or "Woman")

to the status of object (of representation, discourse, desire, etc.). Such defiance is surely unsettling, disturbing the pleasure the male subject takes in gazing and the hierarchical relations by which he asserts his dominance.'' Newman goes on to make use of this concept of the female gaze in an analysis of Catherine Linton (as character) and Nelly (as character and narrator) in *Wuthering Heights*.

3. Diana Fuss, in a discussion of the tension between essentialist and social constructionist approaches to feminism, suggests that the ''I'' be considered not as the representation of inherent subjectivity, but as a subject position (one reads ''like a feminist'' not ''like a woman''). The feminist ''I'' does not have to replicate the essentialism which defines and disciplines the subject; rather, ''when put into practice by the dispossessed themselves, essentialism can be powerfully displacing and disruptive . . . in the hands of a hegemonic group, essentialism can be employed as a powerful tool of ideological domination; in the hands of the subaltern, the use of humanism to mime (in the Irigarayan sense of 'to undo by overdoing') can represent a powerful, displacing repetition'' (85–86). Placing a woman in the ''I'' position gives her the potential both to act as a force for ideological domination, and a force disruptive of that domination. Frances Bartowski has also discussed the importance of establishing a subject position for those marginalized people, who, in Foucault's *History of Sexuality*, are defined as having to speak the ''truth'' of confession. Bartowski is critical of Foucault's construction of the subject position because he does not emphasize the difference between the one who speaks and the one who hears the confession: ''The receptive locus of power once again speaks of and for itself about that which is given no voice—resistance. By overlooking the mouth (who has spoken?) that produces the 'truth' of confession, we get yet another patriarchal history of sexuality, which may know itself as such but gives no voice to its 'other half' '' (45). It is important to note, however, that Bartowski's critique of Foucault focuses primarily on *The History of Sexuality*, vol. 1. In bringing attention to works like *The Memoirs of Herculine Barbin*, Foucault also gave a voice to sexuality's ''other half.''

4. Jana Sawicki's ''Feminism and the Power of Foucauldian Discourse'' shows how Foucault's idea of conflicting or competing identities intersects with many recent feminist concepts of self: ''In Foucault's relational view of identity, identity is fragmented and shifting. Black, lesbian, feminist, mother, and poet, Audre Lorde captures the conflict within the individual when she remarks: 'I find myself and present this as the meaningful whole, eclipsing other parts of self.' Eschewing the notion of a core identity, the genealogist attempts to mobilize the many sources of resistance made possible by the many ways in which individuals are constituted'' (175).

5. The definition of the female subject within a patriarchal discourse has been , perhaps, the central concern of feminist thought in this century from De Beauvoir's concept of woman as ''Other'' to Irigaray's notion that ''woman'' is only man in the disguise of the other. Perhaps the most important concept that a Foucauldian reading of sexual difference can offer in this consideration of the female subject is to shift the focus from a discussion of women's being—the possibility of subjectivity—to a focus on subject positions. ''Being'' a woman is then to be examined as ''*an effect*, an object of a genealogical investigation that maps out the political parameters of its construction in the mode of ontology'' (Butler 32).

6. For a further analysis of Esther's construction of an identity out of her own pain, see '' 'Who is this in Pain?' '' by Helena Michie.

7. "Is it not with the aim of inciting people to speak of sex that it is made to mirror, at the outer limit of every actual discourse, something akin to a secret whose discovery is imperative . . . '' (Foucault 35).

WORKS CITED

Axton, William. "The Trouble with Esther." *MLQ* 26 (1965):545–7.

Bartowski, Frances. "Epistemic Drift in Foucault." *Feminism and Foucault: Reflections on Resistance*. Ed. Irene Diamond and Lee Quimby. Boston: Northeastern UP, 1988. 43–58.

Butler, Judith. *Gender Trouble*. New York: Routledge, 1990.

Dickens, Charles. *Bleak House*. Ed. George Ford and Sylvère Monod. New York: Norton, 1977.

Foucault, Michel. *The History of Sexuality*. Trans. Robert Huxley. New York: Pantheon, 1978.

Fuss, Diane. "Reading Like a Feminist." *Differences* 1.2 (1989):77–92.

Gottfried, Barbara. "Fathers and Suitors in *Bleak House*." *Dickens Studies Annual* 19 (1990):169–204.

Kennedy, Valerie. "*Bleak House*: More Trouble with Esther." *Journal of Women's Studies in Literature* 1.4 (1979):330–47.

LaCapra, Dominick. "Ideology and Critique in Dickens' *Bleak House*." *Representations* 6 (1984):116–23.

Martin, Biddy. "Feminism, Criticism, and Foucault." *Feminism and Foucalut: Reflections on Resistance*. Ed. Irene Diamond and Lee Quimby. Boston: Northeastern UP, 1988. 3–19.

Michie, Helena. " 'Who is this in Pain?': Scarring, Disfigurement, and Female Identity in *Bleak House* and *Our Mutual Friend*." Novel 22.2 (1989):199–218.

Miller, D. A. "Discipline in Different Voices: Bureaucracy, Police, Family and *Bleak House*." *The Novel and the Police*. Berkeley: U of California P, 1988. 58–106.

——— "Under Capricorn." *Representations* 6 (1984):124–30.

Sawicki, Jana. "Feminism and the Power of Foucauldian Discourse." *After Foucault*. Ed. Jonathan Arac. New Brunswick: Rutgers UP, 1988. 161–78.

Sawicki, Joseph. " 'The Mere Truth Won't Do': Esther as Narrator in *Bleak House*." *Journal of Narrative Technique* 17 (1987):209–24.

Steig, Michael, and F. A. C. Wilson. "Hortense vs. Bucket: The Ambiguity of Order in *Bleak House*." *MLQ* 33 (1972):289–98.

Wolin, Sheldon. "On the Theory and Practice of Power." *After Foucault*. Ed. Jonathan Arac. New Brunswick: Rutgers UP, 1988. 179–201.

Acts of Enclosure: The Moral Landscape of Dickens' *Hard Times*

Efraim Sicher

I.

In 1948 F. R. Leavis lamented the lack of recognition given to *Hard Times*, which was owing, he believed, to the unpopularity of the moral fable. It was precisely the moral vision of the novel which Leavis singled out for praise and for which he was attacked by David M. Hirsch in 1964. John Holloway, writing in 1962 and in a 1989 modification of his views, likewise resented the "forced rhetoric" of the novel and the attempt by Leavis to read into it a "single vision." A healthy corrective to a polemic with the dead is the more recent realization that Victorian fiction presents not a universe, but what Jerome Meckier has termed "multiverses" in his aptly titled *Hidden Rivalries in Victorian Fiction: Dickens, Realism, and Revaluation* (1987). It is surely axiomatic that mid-century writing responded to the Condition of England debate, since the principles of utilitarianism and the supposed national prosperity questioned the poetics of the text, its orientation, ideology, and language. Even Jane Austen is no longer considered anachronistically "inconvenient" as A. C. Bradley once saw her. Ignoring the crisis, or, to co-opt a fashionable term, "resisting" it, was itself a response. The polyphony of the discourse embraced all fields of life, notably education, labor relations, and art, and intersected the essay, the novel, poetry, drama, public speeches, and journalism. When Macauley blasts Southey in his review of the *Colloquies* we cannot ignore the head-on clash of ideologies and poetics. Macauley ridicules the poet's critique of industrialization by negating his pastoral representation of the landscape. What Southey fancies he can see does not exist in fact for Macauley. Rival representations of the landscape essentially negate

195

the language of the competing ideologies by deconstructing their conventions and attempting to perpetuate an alternate poetics.

I use the word "deconstruct" advisedly, since Steven Connor, in his contribution to Terry Eagleton's *Rereading Literature* series, *Charles Dickens* (1985), has proposed *Hard Times* as a test case for a deconstructive reading, "a reading," he writes, citing Barbara Johnson, "that analyses the specificity of a text's critical difference from itself" (Connor 90). Dickens' later novels offer themselves for deconstructionist criticism, he continues, and even deconstruct themselves from within: "as the novels project increasingly complex and contradictory fictional worlds, the desire to enclose and control those worlds grows in proportion to the intensity of the internal arguments that the novels conduct with themselves" (Connor 90–91). Maire J. Kurrik has included Lewis Carroll and Charles Dickens in a study of Literature and Negation. Jay Clayton has found it difficult to overcome the temptation of which John Carey spoke, "to make Dickens look more modern than he is" (Carey 174), and has claimed that Dickens' deconstructive awareness of language anticipates postmodernism. The issue, however, is the cultural context of negativity when the definition and proprietorship of culture were in question and the Levites of culture felt themselves on the defensive. There was no greater debunker of convention than Dickens, and his novel *Hard Times* is a conscious deconstruction (though hardly a lone example) of utilitarian positions which makes a statement about its own existence as a negation of those positions. Paradoxically, deconstructive awareness of language leads Dickens to a new morality, however uncertain its ideology, and it will be apparent that Dickens holds a notion of discourse more characteristic of Bakhtinian polyphony as applied to the modern novel than contemporary deconstructionism: " . . . the dialogical approach can be applied to any meaningful part of an utterance, even to an individual word, if that word is perceived not as an impersonal word of language, but as the sign of another's semantic position . . . " (Bakhtin 152). I stress this because Dickens has been accused of inconsistency in *Hard Times*, as well as weak-headedness and incoherence, whereas the dialogizing of opposing discourses does not necessarily assume that all or any of the represented views are the author's own.

What I aim to do is to show how Dickens brings into binary relationship competing models of social reality and competing models of representation. These juxtaposed models are in binary opposition of *open* to *closed* systems and the oppositions operate dynamically to generate alternatively false and true representations of social space. Dickens' comic satire at the same time

exploits and parodies social as well as literary conventions, which may obscure any authorial position, though the concerns of the real-life Dickens are
never far away. In particular the boundaries of constriction or enclosure
have biographical and social relevance.[1] *Hard Times* offers the most obvious
example of visualization of spatial metaphor as a sustained structuring device
and it will be necessary to do some close reading to demonstrate the function
of spatial metaphor in the ideational thrust of the novel at all levels.[2] Since
Hard Times has been so controversial an example of fictional representation
of social discourse I shall conclude with a brief response that suggests a
need for a multidisciplinary and open-minded approach to the novel which
preserves the sense of what Barbara Hardy called Dickens' "moral art."

II.

Elsewhere I have argued that the strategies of spatial representation in nineteenth-century fiction reveal the homologies applied by Greimas to literary
texts, which manipulate imagery in the structuring of a visualized fictional
actuality (Sicher 211–24). Steven Connor demonstrates a juxtaposition in
Dickens' novels between *stasis* and *motion, openness* and *enclosure* that
relies on precisely such homologies of difference.[3] The territorial ordering of
perceptions of differentiation in human society, explored by Lévi-Strauss in
Structural Anthropology, may be found in Dickens' fictional landscape,
whose territorial boundaries are marked by similar oppositions of openness
to enclosure.

To get an idea of Dickens' set of oppositions, let us take an example from
Oliver Twist. Oliver is fleeing the supposed benevolence of the Poor Law,
but his first encounter with London anticipates the moral danger that awaits
him in the hands of Fagin.

> A dirtier or more wretched place he had never seen. The street was very narrow
> and muddy, and the air was impregnated with filthy odours. . . . Covered ways
> and yards, which here and there diverged from the main street, disclosed little
> knots of houses, where drunken men and women were positively wallowing in
> filth; and from several of the door-ways, great ill-looking fellows were cau-
> tiously emerging, bound, to all appearance, on no very well-disposed or harm-
> less errands. (103)[4]

The city environment—no less tainted and filthy than Oliver's native parish—matches the pollution of the reptile Jew as he slinks through the labyrinth

of London's underworld, except that Fagin's imprisonment of Oliver is moral, not merely physical as in the children's farm or workhouse, a structural opposition which has not escaped perceptive critics such as J. Hillis Miller who writes, "The main axis of the nuclear structure of *Oliver Twist* is a fear of exclusion which alternates with a fear of enclosure" (*Charles Dickens* 68).

In *Oliver Twist* there is an escape route from the Hogarth-like scenes of ginshops and wretched poverty, through the kindness of Mr. Brownlow and the Maylies. Redemption is achieved through a portrait (a visual sign and a framing structure parallel to that of the novel), which leads Oliver to his true inheritance, his secular salvation, as Steven Marcus has called it, and his identification as a gentleman both by virtue of class and by virtue of virtue. In *Great Expections* salvation has to be achieved from within, through a moral rereading of the landscape and a symbolic return to the goodness and virtue to be found in Joe's environs (Marcus 87–88).[5]

The consistent opposition of open to closed space works analogically to the opposition of open to closed systems of ethics and language and it may be further clarified by a scheme we can find in *Hard Times*. This has been for many years one of Dickens' less popular novels, partly because of its tendency to schematicism and caricature. The dissenting view, of course, is that of F. R. Leavis, who acclaimed the novel's moral intention in *The Great Tradition*. The past few years have fortunately seen a greater appreciation of *Hard Times*, but commentators have been slow to recognize one of the clearest examples of Dickens' deconstructive awareness of language. Ian Ousby, for example, has demonstrated how the novel's moral intention is invested in rich metaphorical play and grows out of its figurative use of language which opposes connotative to denotative signs (103–09). We will see that Dickens' sophisticated play of signification and identity satirizes a sign system that insists on the strict one-to-one literalness of the relationship between *signifier* and *referent* and that denies any value but a utilitarian one to the text. Dickens' language of representation uses the openness of metonymy in order to invalidate the enclosure of space and of mind in the Gradgrind system and in the industrial landscape of Coketown for which it is responsible. In a regrettably brief discussion of *Hard Times* Steven Connor shows metaphor and metonymy, or language as presence and language as difference, to be elaborate ploys in the signification of Fact and Fancy, Gradgrindery and the Circus (89–106).[6]

What greater affront could there be to Gradgrindery, which denies the legitimacy of fairy tales and figurative speech as means of representation, than to represent it in imagery borrowed from fairy tales and in flights of fancy? What could more efficiently debunk its official rhetoric than to ironically describe factories as Fairy Palaces? In the performance of the text, Dickens is borrowing the language of the popular theater, as David Lodge has shown, and exploiting the mixed-media form of the pantomine (Lodge 42–43).[7] By doing so he is, moreover, making a point and defending the legitimacy of his own aesthetics. Terence Cave has remarked in a critique of Lodge's structuralist analysis that the true analogy is the one that can be drawn between the soft-hearted circus-master Sleary and the producer of popular novels (Cave 411).

The novel opens in "a plain, bare, monotonous vault of a schoolroom," a scene packed with metaphors that reinforce the characterization of the facts taught there as useless merchandise destined for futile storage. The lines in this realm of facts are uniform, regular, and square. Gradgrind's forefinger, coat, legs, shoulders, his mind, all belie the inhuman inflexibility of his system, rendered ludicrous by the similes of the "plantation of firs" and the "plum pie." Storage is emblematic of an enclosure that is both physical and spiritual. The vault houses both death and material valuables. The square boundaries, suggesting closure of mind, are a recurrent motif, blatant in the description of Coketown, which is undermined by the very same fanciful imagery that it negates.

The realm of Facts is an arid desert of utility into which no human warmth is allowed, no irrational inspiration, no spark of the imagination just as there was no Fancy at Chesney Wold in *Bleak House,* another site of dead spirit and false representation. The fantasy which Louisa dreams into the embers of the fire is a punishable heresy and juxtaposes two conflicting ideological areas of fictional space, much as Lizzie Hexam's fireside dreaming in *Our Mutual Friend* suggests a similar will to good in terms of a spatial and structural break from evil.

The schoolchildren are treated as numbers from an early age, just as the workers are abstracted to the degree of disembodied statistics, "Hands," useful only in as much as they produce and meet planned ends. Anything connected with private life, anything that is at all individual, unaccounted for in the norms of Political Economy, is dismissed into nonexistence. Sissy Jupe's circus life has no place here, nor do representations of horses on wallpaper or flowers on carpets belong here, because they are not functionally useful in the manufacturers' world of production and profits. Closure of mind is the more terrifying because in its own terms it is total, absolute, unquestionable, and infallible. Dickens is prescient of the technological or totalitarian dystopia of the twentieth century and Meckier compares *Brave*

New World in this respect (50–51), for it is a dictatorship that seeks to control both knowledge and representation of the real world.

Knowledge is classified into little cabinets for the Gradgrind children. There can be no unknowns or maybes in an arithmetical "calculated" Stone Lodge where all must conform to $2 + 2 = 4$. Like the schoolroom, the spiritually vacuous mind of Mr. Gradgrind is "cavernous" and bounded by walls. But just as the universal system of rule and scientific logic is enclosed and finite, there exists another world of infinite possibilities. The first glimpse we have of this world is through a loophole—a legalistic and spatial metaphor—into Mr. Sleary's Horse-Riding establishment.

The loophole suggests a fundamental flaw in the perfect design of Gradgrind's ideological architecture, and Dickens builds up an amusing set of oppositions between the two structures. The very sounds issuing from the *wooden* structure of the circus clash with the mechanical harmony in Gradgrind's heartless, *stony* residence. Sleary's Horse-Riding establishment has encamped on "neutral ground upon the outskirts of the town, which was neither town nor country, and yet was either spoiled" (55). Its alien bohemian presence threatens, encroaches upon urban territory. Tyrolean Flower-acts, tricks by a performing dog, and astounding feats by the Emperor of Japan contradict the teaching of the schoolroom that a horse is a purely functional object and not a creature to pamper the Fancy. The wooden pavilion is itself an enclosure: a temporary tabernacle in the wilderness, the god enshrined "in an ecclesiastical niche of early Gothic architecture" is money, and the self-made man is its priest. However, Gradgrind, who seeks to raise his offspring as models of eminent Practicality, which accepts its due and knows no god except Fact, must be disappointed, for here are his own Louisa and Tom peeping in on Art and Nature, a rebellious Adam and Eve tasting from the Tree of Fancy in the utilitarian utopia. This is an illicit transgression of the boundary which marks off the circus rabble from the "civilized" urban society which would, if it could, confine them to the House of Correction. What divides the "neutral ground" of the Circus from the Town is a "space of stunted grass and dry rubbish" (56), emphasizing the sexual, spiritual and ideological aridity of Coketown. Louisa's imagination is starved, "a fire with nothing to burn," her will is subdued, but what she has seen beyond the wooden partition opens her eyes before she is forcibly led back to the castrating, claustrophobic, cold, damp, dark existence of Gradgrindery in Stone Lodge. Even the name of Josiah Bounderby recalls the confining *bounds* of the stifling imprisonment in which Louisa must grow up (but also suggests he might be a bounder).[8] Other names are also spatiallly significant: Harthouse is a man whose philosophy differs only in kind from Gradgrind's. Blackpool, a *natural* resort on the northern coast, suggests both the black chasm which threatens to divide men and masters, and the black abyss into which he eventually falls.

The modern industrial city is characterized as an immoral and inhuman space not just in the unsympathetic "keynote" descriptions of Coketown, the archetypal factory town, but also in the usurping of the entire landscape by its system. If Bounderby has taken a country retreat in a rustic spot, it is linked to the City "by a railway striding on many arches over a wild country, undermined by deserted coal-shafts, and spotted at night by fires and black shapes of stationary engines at pits' mouths" (196). On several occasions in his works Dickens does not hide his admiration for the magnificent railway "striding on many arches," yet he reserves his criticism for what the railway exposes as it mercilessly and indiscriminately cuts through town and country. Nature is spoiled, the City is civilizing the "wild country," organizing it into pits of hell-fire and monsters. Bounderby brings his non-natural City identity to his country retreat, "bullying" the very pictures, which he contemptuously devalues. Horsekeeping is not for him, though he bids Harthouse welcome to bring down horses, for he sees no value in having more than one horse (in keeping with the teaching of the model school). Moreover, the idea insults his self-image of a maggot grown large (197).

Coketown is an "unnatural" town of red-brick, blackened by smoke "like the painted face of a savage" (65), a simile that echoes Carlyle's criticism in *Past and Present* of laissez-faire economics with its jungle law of savagery, as well as exposing "civilized" man's true face. This is a conventional negation of the employers' deceitful idealization of factory conditions by making an analogy between the treatment of colonial slaves and English workers. Worst of all is the mind-deadening monotony of the streets and the daily routine. All buildings are the same, except the Bank and Bounderby's, which are the same only bigger. The canal is black and polluted by purple dye. The alienation of workers from the products of their labor, the "comforts of life which found their way all over the world," is also an alienation from environment. Following Carlyle's attack on worship of Mammon and in the spirit of the novel's dedication, or rather *inscription*, to the author of *Past and Present*, each of the different denominational chapels in the "ugly citadel" is made "a pious warehouse," so different from Sleary's equestrian temple, and the parody of the Doxology provides a sacrilegious representation of the new mercantile faith.

It can be legitimately inferred from the negation of the Gradgrind representation of things that the problem of the laborers is not reducible to such simple causes as alcoholism or narcotics. Their problem stems from the enforced urban condition in their "close rooms," from which they can only escape through death. Indeed, it is with difficulty that a coffin can be got through the window of the narrow houses. In the significantly titled chapter "No Way Out," Dickens again strikes the "key-note" for his description of the City.

> The Fairy palaces burst into illumination, before pale morning showed the monstrous serpents of smoke trailing themselves over Coketown. A clattering of clogs upon the pavement; a rapid ringing of bells; and all the melancholy-mad elephants, polished and oiled up for the day's monotony, were at their heavy exercise again.   (107)

The City of Man mocks Nature and consigns the work of God to oblivion next to that of man. The "fairy palaces" are really monstrous infernos and the "forest" of looms are scaffolds, not picnic-sites. The natural elements themselves engender death, not life, because of the high levels of environmental pollution, for "so does the eye of Heaven itself become an evil eye, when incapable or sordid hands are interposed between it and the things it looks upon to bless" (147). The heat is unnatural, confining, and asphyxiating. It is unpleasantly hot among the "smoke-serpents." In summer the heat is "stifling" and in autumn it is just as unpleasantly damp and cold on the streets.

In order to hammer home the opposition of the machine-world mentality of Gradgrindery and a more humane truthful outlook, Dickens sets up juxtapositions of class and of humanity versus inhumanity in accordance with the Key-note plan of Coketown's ideological territory. Stephen Blackpool walks along the streets of Coketown, chewing a little bread, on his way to see Bounderby, comfortably at lunch on chop and sherry. Stephen's desperate plight cannot touch the great man, who can only see simple causes and self-interest. There is a law for the rich and another for the poor. Stephen cannot afford a divorce, therefore he can have no redress for his personal troubles. His conclusion that " 'tis a muddle" (113) only provokes Bounderby's warning to mind his piece-work, for the institutions of England, the institutions of representation, are none of his piece-work. If Hands complain, reasons Bounderby, they must be looking for a golden spoon and turtle soup. In his blue chamber, surrounded by Blue Books, Gradgrind—the parliamentary representative—also fails to perceive the "muddle" which Stephen sees and which Carlyle in *Past and Present* saw as an unilluminated chaos. This example of false visual and political representation underscores the moral blindness of Bounderby and Gradgrind that is satirized by visual oppositions, which, though at times almost crude, fit in with the general symbolic patterning of what Leavis called Dickens' "moral fable" and create a "comprehensive vision" in the sense of both sight and prophecy.

Coketown remains ever ephemeral, abstract, and shrouded in haze, and, however much the Gradgrinds and Bounderbys claim to dispel the mysteries of life, it is the secrets to which they are blind which must inevitably undo them. These unscientific mysteries are penetrated by those who perceive an existence beyond the reality of the city, such as the members of the Circus who perform their art on the border of, yet beyond, the City.

The choice, however, is not between Town and Country, but between Good and Evil. Tom takes the money and goes to the Bad, implicating Stephen in his sinister machinations. Louisa, drawing on her sympathy of imagination, wants to put money to the good: she offers money to Stephen who has resolved to quit town. The key to social change is individual moral regeneration. Stephen, tied to a drunken woman by an unfair law, overcomes temptation. He fulfills his role as martyr by keeping his oath and suffering for it.[9] Later, he frees himself from the City with its poisonous chimneys that clutter up the sky and becomes a fugitive among birds, sun, trees (194), but feels compelled to return to clear his name. Louisa falls for the opportunist Mr. James Harthouse and goes down, down, lower and lower, her symbolic descent observed by Mrs. Sparsit on her fanciful Giant's Staircase, mindful of her own social descent, or her phony representation of it, as well as alluding to political fall on the grand staircase of the Ducal Palace in Venice in Byron's *Marino Faliero* (Ford and Monod 153 n 5). Yet Louisa is freed at last from her mental and moral servitude to the empire of Bounderby. In the three-dimensional model of the City, descent implies eventual spiritual ascent.

Louisa Gradgrind is in a sense, and in a very Christian sense, reborn and must adjust her spatial relationship to the City. She must reread the signs around her and recognize that strange fire which sometimes bursts out.[10] She must reread Stephen's behavior which she had earlier misinterpreted because she was indoctrinated by the Gradgrind representation of things. Louisa's "shipwreck" rocks the foundations upon which Gradgrind's principles are built. Moved by Sissy's compassion, even James Harthouse declares himself a Great Pyramid of Failure and sets off for the Nile to go in for camels (257).

The search for truth is a mythic journey which incorporates the chase scene and suspense element of the crime thriller, but the truth is not to be found in an escape to the country. If, with good luck and chance, one could escape the abuses of the parochial system in *Oliver Twist*, there is here "no way out." Indeed, when Sissy and Rachael go for a walk in the country, "midway between the town and Mr Bounderby's retreat," they discover that the "green landscape" is "blotted" by the urban industrial wasteland and the Sunday peace is broken only by nonconformist larks (283). It is here that they find Stephen Blackpool lying injured in a disused pit called, significantly, the Old Hell Shaft (286). Stephen is rescued from his descent into Hell, which had ensnared him on his path to truth, and his innocence is established, largely through the instrument of Louisa and her reformed father. He is then carried in the direction of the star that seemed to him to be the guide to the Saviour's house and he finds eternal salvation "through humility, sorrow, and forgiveness" (291–92). Again, descent to Hell leads to spiritual ascent to heaven and a shift in moral valuation. It will be observed that in *Our Mutual Friend*, too, Betty Higden escapes the cruel degradation of the Poor Laws by posthumous salvation, dying in the arms of Lizzie Hexam, a clear counterpart to Louisa in *Hard Times*. The Christological conclusion is emphasized by the book titles "Sowing," "Reaping," and "Garnering," which are also self-referential in the structuring of plot, as well as the New Testament references in the chapter headings "The One Thing Needful" and "Murdering the Innocents."

The moral is indeed serious and visionary. Sissy, alone untainted by Coketown morality, is rewarded with happy children, and Louisa does penance by

> thinking no innocent and pretty fancy ever to be despised; trying hard to know her humbler fellow-creatures, and to beautify their lives of machinery and reality with those imaginative graces and delights, without which the heart of infancy will wither up, the sturdiest physical manhood will be morally stark death, and the plainest national prosperity figures can show, will be the Writing on the Wall,—she holding this course as part of no fantastic vow, or bond, or brotherhood, or sisterhood, or pledge, or covenant, or fancy dress, or fancy fair; but simply as duty to be done,—did Louisa see these things of herself? These things were to be.   (313)

The City, with its mills and schools, can be put to the Good—just as the mill and the school in *Our Mutual Friend* are not inherently evil. Enclosure is opposed to a responsive and responsible relationship with environment, in contrast to the Marxist dictum. By substituting national for natural growth, by enforcing regulated, closed forms, the City is actually shown to be closer to an inferno than to Eden. Stephen Blackpool's negation of the supposed rational organization of the City as "aw a muddle" shows up the inhumanity of the Commissioners of Inquiry and Captains of Industry, whose attitude to

Charity is that the Good Samaritan was a bad Economist. Dickens clearly had no faith in Parliament, the nation's "dust-heap," as an effective instrument for reform. Nor is much faith shown in the ability of the Trade Unions to safeguard the individual interests of their members. Stephen's oath, which is not given a clear explanation, might be reflective of a belief (close to Dickens' own) that strike action would be counterproductive and that violence was reprehensible.

The City's *integrity* of purpose is spatially and metaphysically impervious to *multiplicity* and *individuality* of will. Yet Dickens' position on liberty and on the working classes is fairly conservative. His editorial and publicistic position in *Household Words*—where both *Hard Times* and *North and South* appeared—shows his awareness of the need for change (though Dickens as a social reformer is too often seen through the prism of the Dickens myth as the converter of Scrooge). He is indeed aware of the appalling conditions of the laborers. The factory accidents are alluded to by Stephen's mention of Rachael's sister and by the footnote reference in chapters 7–8 of the serialized publication to Henry Morley's piece "Ground in the Mill" in the same issue of *Household Words* (deleted in the book edition).[11] Dickens shows that established forms of religion are not of practical appeal to the laborers, who, not surprisingly, do not attend the various denominational churches, though some members of Parliament would have them conform by force. And of course he shows that they do not conform to the purely statistical representation of reality projected by Political Economists and would-be Reformers who follow the theories of Malthus and Adam Smith, for whom the younger Gradgrinds are named. But Dickens describes the laborers hazily, as an outsider, with far less sympathy, however sentimental, for their actual conditions than Mrs. Gaskell in *North and South*. Dickens holds far less committed a view, and in the long run a far less utopian one, than Mrs. Gaskell's when compared with the interclass cooperation and affirmative action which Margaret brings about through her ethical self-reformation and moral influence.

In his piece on the Preston lock-out "On Strike" (*Household Words* 11 Feb. 1854) Dickens pleaded for mutual forbearance and consideration, words not to be found in Mr. McCulloch's dictionary, because the greatest obstacle on both sides is dogmatism. To the manufacturer he met on the train he "retorted . . . that Political Economy was a great and useful science in its own way and its own place; but that I did not transplant my definition of it from the Common Prayer Book, and make it a great king above all gods." What Dickens objected to was not Gradgrindery as such but the making of it

into an absolutist system applied with coercion. Dickens wrote of Mr. Gradgrind that "there is reason and good intention in much that he does—in fact,
in all that he does—but that he over-does it" (letter to Henry Cole 17 June
1854). What Dickens was attacking was not the principles of Political Economy, but blind subservience to them, as he wrote to Charles Knight (30 Jan.
1855), by "those who see figures and averages, and nothing else." Dickens
was as much out of sympathy with the employers' monstrous claims as he
was with the workers' discontent.

Nicholas Coles has pointed out internal contradictions in the attack on
Gradgrindery in the novel as well as contradictions with some of the positions
presented in *Household Words*, where the novel first appeared (Coles
145–79).[12] However, such attempts to resolve the very real problematics of
the status of *Hard Times* on the borders of fiction and life underestimate the
difference between the mode and the aims of representation of art and journalism. The very notion of Fancy in *Hard Times* should tell us that our expectations of the meaning of the novel should be reconstructed in order to understand by imaginative effort what is "really" wrong with conventional
representation of society. It is a faulty vision which Dickens criticizes and
readers who test the historical accuracy or verisimilitude of Dickens' picture
of the industrial landscape miss that fundamental aim. As David Lodge noted,

> The reason is not that criteria of empirical truthfulness are wholly irrelevant
> (they are not); but that in referring from fiction to fact and back again, the
> critics are ignoring a vitally important stage in the creative process by which
> narratives are composed, viz. the transformation of the deep structure of the
> text into its surface structure. . . . It is in this process that the particular literary
> identity of a novel, and therefore the range of reader-responses apppropriate to
> it, are determined.   (38)[13]

Fancy is both aim and mode of representation. It is through the aesthetics of
Hard Times that Dickens preached the urgent necessity of communication
between employers and employees, of finding a language of representation
that would somehow bring them closer to mutual understanding.

At the end of the "key-note" description of Coketown in book I, chapter
5, in the transition to the introduction of the circus people, the narrator
wonders whether there was not in the employers' stereotype of the ungrateful
laborers and the Political Economists' statistical tables one thing that had
been

> deliberately set at nought? That there was any Fancy in them demanding to be
> brought into healthy existence instead of struggling on in convulsions? That

exactly in the ratio as they worked long and monotonously, the craving grew within them for some physical relief—some relaxation, encouraging good humour and good spirits, and giving them a vent—some recognized holiday, though it were but for an honest dance to a stirring band of music—some occasional light pie in which even M'Choakumchild had no finger—which craving must and would be satisfied aright, or must and would inevitably go wrong, until the laws of Creation were repealed?   (67–68)

Immediately following this plea, Gradgrind and Bounderby repair to the Pegasus's Arms, a pub which is appropriate "home" to Sleary's horseriders, since it was Pegasus's kick which brought out of the mountain the soul-inspiring waters of Hippocrene that came to be associated with poetic inspiration:

> Then who so will with virtuous deeds assay
> To mount to heaven, on Pegasus must ride,
> And with sweete Poets verse be glorified.
>   (Spenser *Ruins of Time*)

Of course the winged horse behind the bar displays a low form of entertainment, but Dickens writes sarcastically and punningly, in the introduction to the chapter "Stephen Blackpool," in a way that has apparently nothing to do with the subject:

> I entertain a weak idea that the English people are as hard-worked as any people upon whom the sun shines. I acknowledge to this ridiculous idiosyncrasy, as a reason why I would give them a little more play.   (102)

As Sleary advises Gradgrind and Bounderby, people must be amused.

What Sleary says is in line with the thinking behind Dickens' 1853 Birmingham speech and it neatly connects the themes of art, education, and industrial relations in the novel. The story of Sissy Jupe and the dog Merrylegs shows "one, that there ith a love in the world, not all Thelf-intereth after all, but thomething very different; t'other, that it hath a way of calculating or not calculating, whith thomehow or another ith at leatht ath hard to give a name to, ath the wayth of the dogth ith!" (308). The circus is not a model society, but the circus people represent a childlike sincerity, honesty, and spontaneous compassion absent in the calculating language of Gradgrindery—the "one thing needful", as Dickens knew from *Sartor Resartus*, in the hedonistic calculus of pleasure of the Motive-Grinders in the Mill of Logic. Dickens is not merely advocating the merits of popular culture but pleading for the necessity within the industrial city of art as recreation (in the sense of both leisure and creativity) and for the necessity of a nonutilitarian art which does not substitute model for reality and which recognizes the efficiency of symbolic representation: "People mutht be amuthed. They can't alwayth be a learning, nor yet they can't be alwayth a working, they an't made for it. You *mutht* have uth, Thquire" (308). The preaching of this moral imperative in the mouth of a man like Sleary sounds so uncharacteristic that he is surprised at being such a "Cackler." It is in *action* that the circus people must show compassion in order to refute Gradgrindery which allows for it neither in its arithmetic nor in its speech. The circus art is, moreover, a narrative art (Lodge 27), and its rhetoric (not to mention livelihood, like Jupe's) depends on art in the sense of skill as well as stratagem, like the deft sleight of hand Dickens learned when juggling bottles in the blacking warehouse. It is also, incidentally, art as craft in addition to art as imagination ("Fancy"), in opposition to the mechanization of production and of the spirit in the factory.

Fact and Fancy, the two competing metasystems of signification and designification which motivate character and plot in the ideational and spatial spheres of each oppositional model of representation, represent a theory of art and language. Sissy is taught that the sign "horse" represents a sum total of facts and figures, not a creature for amusement, as in her father's profession. Flowers cannot be represented on a carpet, according to the government officer inspecting Gradgrind's model school, because *such a thing does not exist in reality*. This absurdly reductionist argument is crushed by a plot which depends on the discovery of truth and humanity through the workings of fanciful imagination. When Gradgrind is unable to save Louisa in her Fall down the Giant's Staircase, in parodic negation of the conventional melodramatic tableau of the fallen woman, he is forced to admit the failure of the System lying insensible at his feet—the arrogance of the very word *system!*—because it is a lie and as false a representation as Bounderby's self-image is shown to be. When Tom learns the amoral lesson of self-interest only too well and implicates Stephen in his crime, it is the circus people and—supreme irony—a performing horse who save Gradgrind from shame and from another product of the Gradgrind school, Bitzer.

Dickens has been criticized for misunderstanding the utilitarian standpoint on art, just as he got several other points wrong in the novel, but the schoolroom scene was after all a private joke on Dickens' part aimed at his friend Cole, though it effectively attacked the tastelessness of Victorian design and in particular the barrenness of the industrial town (Fielding 270–77). In any case, as Collins points out, such a discussion would have been out of place in the model school (Collins 156–59). Moreover, the school was intended for the lower classes, who were not generally considered worthy of such refinements as art. Gradgrind's own children would not have been tutored there. Another joke might be that J. M. M'Culloch, the object of parody in the teacher M'Choakumchild, was a headmaster of a school in *Circus Place*, Edinburgh (Ford and Monod 303n). But, as we have seen, the novel is not "about" these things and that is no doubt why Mrs. Gaskell's work on *North and South* was both annoying and irrelevant for Dickens in his writing of the serial parts of *Hard Times*.

The present discussion does not intend to exhaust the surprisingly rich imagery of *Hard Times*, and one cannot ignore the agricultural patterns which highlight the spatial metaphor of Coketown as the City of Hell, its serpents symbolic of the Fall, the ultimate corrupted Garden which reaps an unnatural harvest (Bornstein 158–70). The analogous oppositions of Jerusalem and Babylon and the reference to the New Testament parable of the seed fallen on barren ground recall the search for a City of the Spirit found elsewhere in Dickens (Welsh). The twin images of Coketown as Babel and Babylon, like Rouhcewell's factory in *Bleak House,* exposes the lie of a unified sign system that conceals confusion in a city of immorality. The opposing discourse of Fancy functions as a dynamic negation of System by designifying its metalanguage. As Connor observes, citing one of Sissy's happy mistakes, statistics are exposed as "stutterings" (103).

Michael Goldberg has described Carlyle's 1829 essay "Signs of the Times" as "almost an ideological prospectus to *Hard Times*" (79–80), although it should be pointed out that Carlyle took his title from the New Testament verse which criticized those who lacked faith and needed Signs of the Times. However, Carlyle's diagnosis of mechanization as the *sign* of the times was surely in Dickens' mind both in his choice of title and in his choice of metacritical metaphor. Not only does the far-reaching notion of machinery or mechanism serve as the Sign of the Times in a semiotics of the Condition of England debate in both works, but both see the reigning utilitarian philosophy of Political Economy as blind to spiritual and visionary truth and to Fancy. They see it driving out the ability to "wonder" as "the sign of uncultivation": "It is the Age of Machinery, in every outward and inward sense of that word; the age which, with its whole undivided might, forwards, teaches and practices the great art of adapting means to ends. Nothing is now done directly, or by hand; all is by rule and calculated contrivance" (Carlyle 59). Carlyle, writing in the *Edinburgh Review* the year before Macauley's review of Southey's book in the same journal, might despair of his contemporaries *seeing* the dangers that confronted them. For Carlyle the times were "sick and out of joint." Dickens, twenty-five years and two European revolutions later, may well have been in sympathy with Carlyle's conclusion that in a world of physical force mankind's ultimate destiny depended on the slow process of moral reformation which was begun and perfected in *individuals* and was not furthered by the machinery of legislation or social reform (Carlyle 82).

III.

The importance of both political and fictional representation has been realized by Catherine Gallagher in her study of English society in the mid-nineteenth-century novel, *The Industrial Reformation of English Fiction* (1985). The representation of facts and the representation of values, she contends, were in a relationship of tension which made the form of the polemical novel itself an object of inquiry and of conflicting claims. The constraint on metaphorical analogies such as that of worker and slave or family and social institutions required a new practice of realism that would resolve the questions of environmental determinism and individual liberty.[14] Gallagher's reading of *Hard Times* as metaphorically discursive, together with Mrs. Gaskell's *North and South*, on the tensions between public and private realms and her insistence on the family-society analogy as the *primary* organizing principle of the metaphors in this novel suggest that, while important, social discourse provides no more than a partial reading of the text.[15] Gallagher asserts that in both *Hard Times* and *North and South* the authors "attempted to describe industrial society and present solutions to the problems of class antagonism"; both "ostensibly propose that social cohesion can be achieved by changing the relationship between family and society, by introducing cooperative behavior, presumably preserved in private life, into the public realm." Both, however, realize "contradictions latent in social paternalism and domestic ideology" and "ultimately propose the isolation of families from the larger society" (147–48; cf. Fabrizio).

It is a moot question, which discourse or discourses are referential to public debate on political issues and which determine the shape and form of the novel, not to mention the problem of determining to precisely what extent the artistic text is, accurately speaking, functional in public discourse and on what level. It should be remembered that *Hard Times* was derisively dismissed in its own day. The novel is certainly relevant to an understanding of the industrial city when read with Engels' description of Manchester or Charles Kingsley's *Alton Locke*. The latter is contextual like *Hard Times* with the writings of Carlyle, although Carlyle's candidacy of the Captains of Industry as social and managerial leaders might be contrasted with the false Bounderby type who, Ivan Melada thinks, results from a change of heart in Dickens after the example of Cheeryble in *Nicholas Nickleby* fell on deaf ears, and who is largely an instrument for the negation of two "popular fictions" (misrepresentations): the self-made man and the unjust claims of some mill-owners in hearings before parliamentary commissions (110–15).

Yet that imagination serves as both mode and metaphor for the vision of the novel speaks for the novelist's role as entertainer as well as a moralistic and didactic public figure. We can surely not take too seriously any proposal that the circus could be a real instrument in social change, though Paul Schlicke's extensive researches on the historical background in this arena are illuminating (137–89). Rather the circus—in the nineteenth century a form of adult entertainment—is illustrative of an argument against extreme utilitarian positions on art, as well as being morally instructive of the lessons of laissez-faire and education for self-interest. Its language—circus slang—is, like Mr. Sleary's lisp or Stephen's regional and class dialect, impermeable to the mind of Gradgrind or Bounderby, but it is the supposedly privileged discourse of Gradgrindery which proves defective and ultimately illegible. The argument assumes maintenance of the status quo in employer-worker relations but urges more humane treatment of the laborers through education and art. The light or flame of imagination must resist the choking of the human spirit by a totally utilitarian discourse, just as among the library readers of Coketown Defoe resists Euclid, Goldsmith resists Cocker. Alain Bony and Ian Ousby have pointed to the relevance of Dickens' editorial statement on the first page of the first issue of *Household Words* (30 March 1850):

> No mere utilitarian spirit, no iron binding of the mind to grim realities, will give a harsh tone to our Household Words. In the bosoms of the young and old, of the well-to-do and of the poor, we would tenderly cherish that light of Fancy which is inherent in the human breast: which, according to its nurture, burns with an inspiring flame, or sinks into a sullen glare, but which (or woe betide that day!) can never be extinguished.

We recall that it was fanciful instead of statistical representation that prompted Macauley to conclude that poets like Southey added grist to the mill of utilitarians who argued against literature in education and society.

The title of *Hard Times* sounds anachronistic for the prosperous mid-century when it appeared, even if the liberty of death in Stockport cellars was still maintained. The subtitle "For These Times" is too frequently ignored. Rather the hardness is a moral indifference that renders Dickens' plea the more urgent. His text negates the usual complacency of mid-century euphoria. Yet its deconstruction of the Gradgrind system of representation replaces it nevertheless with a moral vision. Our preoccupation with modernist or postmodernist attitudes may occasionally sunblind us to the fact that the "Victorian art of fiction is essentially a moral art. It questions the nature and purpose of moral action, and, at its best, shows the difficulty and complexity of giving, loving, and growing out from self in an unjust, commercialized, and denaturing society" (Hardy 3). What distinguishes Dickens' moral art "is his combination of social despair and personal faith, his capacity to distrust both society and social reform while retaining and perhaps deepening a faith in the power of human love" (Hardy 3).[16]

The representation of a moral space, as Eric Auerbach has pointed out in his discussion of the Binding of Isaac in *Mimesis*, is a scriptural device, and Dickens is in many ways a Christian artist. This may explain the lack of so-called "realistic" detail and the inaccuracy of the picture of factory life for which Dickens has been criticized. The physical landscape is subordinate to the larger, more fanciful abstractions of the mental landscape.

The fact that Dickens started *Pickwick Papers* by writing the text for sporting plates and that he worked closely with illustrators such as George Cruickshank, who later claimed credit for much of *Oliver Twist*, may explain the painterly approach to the organization of space. But I think that we have here some fundamental narrative strategies which go beyond the usual analogies between the sister arts and which question the shared aims and conventions of the eighteenth-century novel, drama, and painting (for example *The Beggar's Opera, Jonathan Wild*, and Hogarth's London scenes). This is not just analogy, not just Dickens' love of melodrama, or his often parodic reworking of romantic and Gothic plots or motifs. The visualization of space in competing representational models negates not by insisting on the indeterminacy of meaning but by mimicking the discourse with which it is dialogizing (as in the Bakhtinian principle of polyphony in the modern novel). Dickens' language represents—in an Aristotelian definition of the word in the *Poetics*—by imitation of voice; it is a "speaking picture," in Sir Philip Sidney's metaphor, "With this end—to teach and delight." Art is not just play; as J. Hillis Miller says of George Eliot, "the one thing needful" is a

mimesis that by representing the distorting mirror in the author's mind strives
for truth (*Ethics of Reading* 61–80).

NOTES

1. See my discussion of Dickens' reading of the landscape "Bleak Homes and
   Symbolic Houses: Athomeness and Homelessness in Dickens," in *Homes and
   Homelessness in Dickens and the Victorian Imagination*, ed. M. Baumgarten and
   H.M. Daleski (New York: AMS, at press).
2. The visual aspect of representation in the Victorian novel has been noted before
   in Michael Irwin, *Picturing: Description and Illusion in the Nineteenth-Century
   Novel* (London: Allen, 1979). Unfortunately, Irwin jettisoned a projected chapter
   on landscape and the broader context of the visual arts and theory of representation
   have not been developed. The recent work of Murray Krieger, Stephen Greenblatt,
   and Wolfgang Iser attempts to penetrate what might be described as "aw a
   muddle" in the theory of representation: see especially Robert Weimann, "History, Appropriation, and the Uses of Representation in Modern Narrative," *The
   Aims of Representation*, ed. Murray Krieger (New York: Columbia UP, 1987),
   175–215. Also relevant to the theoretical issue of visual representation are W. J.
   T. Mitchell, *Iconology: Image, Text, Ideology* (Chicago: U of Chicago P, 1986;
   and *Allegory and Representation*, ed. S. J. Greenblatt (Baltimore: Johns Hopkins
   UP, 1986).
3. Frederic Jameson also applies the four-term homology of Greimas to the binary
   oppositions in *Hard Times (The Prison-House of Language*, Princeton: Princeton
   UP, 1972, 166–68), but he is generally critical of the method behind Lévi-Strauss'
   mythological hermeneutics.
4. References to Dickens' novels are to the following editions: *Oliver Twist*, Harmondsworth: Penguin, 1966; *Hard Times*, Harmondsworth: Penguin, 1969.
5. On the problematics of a "straight" reading of the novel see Christopher D.
   Morris, "The Bad Faith of Pip's Bad Faith: Deconstructing *Great Expectations*,"
   English Literary History 54. 4 (1987):941–55.
6. Robert Caserio has compared Dickens' theory of the sign in *Hard Times* with that
   of Eco in *The Name of the Rose*, but this is surely too fanciful ("The Name of the
   Horse: *Hard Times*, Semiotics, and the Supernatural" *Novel* 20. 1 [1986]:5–23).
7. It was this melodramatic language to which John Ruskin objected in his assessment of the novel, and perhaps one reason for this frequent criticism is the way
   in which Dickens uses that kind of language to deconstruct the reader responses
   of his middle-class audience. Dickens' article "Fraud on the Fairies" (*Household
   Words*, 1 Oct. 1853) clearly indicates another mode of designification in the
   rhetoric and plot of the novel, the language of fairy tales. Regrettably, the notion
   of Fancy in *Hard Times* has rarely been given serious attention by critics, though
   see Philip Collins, "Queen Mab's Chariot among the Steam Engines: Dickens
   and 'Fancy,' " *English Studies*, 42 (1961):78–90; David Sonstroem, "Fettered
   Fancy in *Hard Times*", *PMLA* 84 (1969):520–29; and Robert Higbie, "*Hard
   Times* and Dickens' Concept of Imagination," *Dickens Studies Annual* 17
   (1988):91–110. The term "Fancy" was used too diversely and variously for us
   to seriously relate Dickens' use of it to Coleridge's distinction of "Fancy" and

"Imagination," but a similar opposition of Fancy and Fact can be found in
Discourse 5; vi and Discourse 7; ii of Cardinal Newman's anti-Utilitarian theory
of education *The Idea of a University*.

8. This is another example of the inversion of the specific and the universal, of sign
and referent, in parody of the kind of utilitarianistic positions on language satirized
by Humpty Dumpty in *Alice through the Looking-Glass*.

9. Stephen is named for a saint and almost incredibly shares with Oliver Twist a
"perfect integrity." He is also a Ministering Angel (to his drunken wife) like Joe
in *Great Expectations*, which makes him another archetypal Joseph with an
angelic countenance.

10. Compare Oliver's disorientation in the labyrinth of London when he reads the
signs of streets and shops. It is likewise a labyrinth of *signs* from which Stephen
emerges in I, 10 (102).

11. The deliberate omission of such documentation of the horrors of the factory
system seems to me to speak for Dickens' artistic purpose, not at all an attempt
to whitewash the employers or ignore abuses of the factory system. The question
which occupies so many critics, the bearing of the omission on Dickens' real-life
political position, can surely be relevant only if the literary text is put in a
polarized position of fictional *or* historical discourse. In comparing *Hard Times*
to Engels' *Condition of the Working-Class*, Stephen J. Spector has pointed to
Dickens' use of metonymy, but concludes that Dickens failed to represent the
working classes "truthfully" ("Masters of Metonymy: *Hard Times* and Knowing
the Working-Class," *English Literary History* 51 (1984):365–84). Patricia Johnson has responded that on the contrary Dickens portrayed the harsh reality of
working-class conditions by constructing the Factory as (in her interpretation) a
controlling metaphor and the controlling shape of the novel (128–37).

12. In his response to Coles, Grahame Smith has argued that Dickens as a fictional
author ("Dickens") is subversive of any serious intent in his representation of
both employers and laborers ("Comic Subversion and *Hard Times, Dickens
Studies Annual* 18 [1989]:145–60). The question of the factuality of the novel
and its implications (surely paradoxical in view of the satirical thrust of *Hard
Times*) has been much discussed in *inter alia* K. J. Fielding, "The Battle for
Preston," *Twentieth-Century Interpretations of Hard Times*, ed. Paul E. Gray
(Englewood Cliffs: Prentice, 1969), 16–21; K. J. Fielding and Anne Smith,
"*Hard Times* and the Factory Accident Controversy: Dickens versus Martineau,"
Dickens Centennial Essays, ed. Ada Nisbet and Blake Nevins (Berkeley: U of
California P, 1971), 22–45; and Phillip Collins, "Dickens and Industrialism,"
Studies in English Literature 20 (1980):651–73.

13. Lodge's argument has been reinforced by Roger Fowler, who treats *Hard Times*
in Bakhtinian terms as a polyphonic novel by applying M. A. K. Halliday's
terminology to a discourse analysis of the speech patterns in the text ("Polyphony
in *Hard Times*," in *Language, Discourse and Literature*, ed. Ronald Carter and
Paul Simpson [London: Unwin, 1989], 76–93). Jean-Jacques Weber has taken
Fowler's approach further and in a modal analysis shown the tensions between
the ideological discourses of the fictional worlds in the novel ("Dickens's Social
Semiotic: The Modal Analysis of Ideological Structure," Carter and Simpson
94–111). In Weber's view, the novel emerges as lacking any monological authorial or authoritative discourse because the issues it raises are left open; the covert
authorial voice, undiscerned by most critics, merely makes a humanitarian appeal
for reason and compassion in maintenance of the status quo.

14. Kate Flint demonstrates the complexity of Dickens' position on social change in her book *Charles Dickens* (Atlantic Highlands, NJ: Humanities, 1986), 85–111. The almost Stalinist term "ideological uncertainty" with which Flint sums up her assessment of Dickens' position on social change reminds us, however, of the politicization of readings of *Hard Times*, various examples of which are to be found in the evaluations of Macauley, Gissing, Ruskin, G. B. Shaw, Raymond Williams, and David Craig. "Ideological uncertainty," after all, is essential to the designification of Gradgrind's absolutist discourse.
15. On the problems of *Hard Times* for theories of reading see Nancy Armstrong, "Dickens between Two Disciplines: A Problem for Theories of Reading," *Semiotica* 58 (1982):243–75; and Valentine Cunningham, *In the Reading Gaol* (Oxford: Blackwell, 1989).
16. Hardy's analysis of *Little Dorritt, Hard Times, Great Expectations,* and *A Tale of Two Cities* gives credence to my view of Dickens' realism as being concerned with a broad view of society and social truths rather than with nitty-gritty details that can be held up to the test of verisimilitude. Hardy finds the psychological characterization of Louisa and Sissy no less serious for its being implied. Moreover, Hardy argues, the ending would not ring true if the central protagonists settled down to live happily ever after; the ending is a "sad and sober appraisal" which denies Louisa a bright new future but does look forward to rebirth.

WORKS CITED

Bakhtin, Mikhail. *Problems of Dostoevsky's Poetics*, trans. R. W. Rotsel. Ann Arbor: Ardis, 1973.

Bony, Alain. "Réalité et Imaginaire dans *Hard Times,*" *Etudes Anglaises* 23 (1970):168–82.

Bornstein, George. "Miscultivated Field and Corrupted Garden: Imagery in *Hard Times.*" *Nineteenth-Century Fiction* 26 (1971):158–70.

Carey, John. *The Violent Effigy: A Study of Dickens' Imagination*. London: Faber, 1973.

Carlyle, Thomas. *Critical and Miscellaneous Essays*. Vol. 5. London: Chapman, 1899.

Cave, Terence. *Recognitions: A Study in Poetics*. Oxford: Oxford UP, 1989.

Clayton, Jay. "Dickens and the Genealogy of Postmodernism." *Nineteenth-Century Literature* 46 (1991):181–95.

Coles, Nicholas. "The Politics of *Hard Times*: Dickens the Novelist versus Dickens the Reformer." *Dickens Studies Annual* 15 (1986):145–79.

Collins, Phillip. *Dickens and Education*. New York: St Martin's, 1963.

Connor, Steven. *Charles Dickens*. Oxford: Blackwell, 1985.

Fabrizio, Richard. "Wonderful No-Meaning: Language and the Psychopathology of the Family in Dickens' *Hard Times*," *Dickens Studies Annual* 16 (1987):61–94.

Fielding, K. J. "Charles Dickens and the Department of Practical Art." *Modern Language Review* 48 (1953):270–77.

Ford, George, and Sylvère Monod, eds. *Hard Times*. 2nd ed. New York: Norton, 1990.

Gallagher, Catherine. *The Industrial Reformation of English Fiction: Social Discourse and Narrative Form, 1832–1867*. Chicago: U of Chicago P, 1985.

Goldberg, Michael. *Dickens and Carlyle*. Athens: U of Georgia P, 1972.

Hardy, Barbara. *The Moral Art of Dickens*. London: Athlone, 1970.

Holloway, John. "Son and Father in *Hard Times*." *Art and Society in the Victorian Novel*. Ed. Colin Gibson. London: Macmillan, 1989, 29–42.

Johnson, Patricia E. "*Hard Times* and the Structure of Industrialism: The Novel as Factory." *Studies in the Novel* 21. 1–2 (1989):128–37.

Kurrick, Maire Jaanus. *Literature and Negation*. New York: Columbia UP, 1979.

Leavis, R. R. "*Hard Times*: An Analytic Note." *The Great Tradition*. London: Chatto, 1962. 227–48.

Lodge, David. *Working with Structuralism*. London: Routledge, 1981.

Marcus, Stephen. *Dickens from Pickwick to Dombey*. London: Chatto, 1965.

Meckier, Jerome. *Hidden Rivalries in Victorian Fiction: Dickens, Realism and Revaluation*. Lexington: UP of Kentucky, 1987.

Melada, Ivan. *The Captain of Industry in English Fiction, 1821–1871*. Albuquerque: U of New Mexico. 1970.

Miller, J. Hillis. *Charles Dickens: The World of His Novels*. Cambridge: Harvard UP, 1958.

Miller, J. Hillis. *The Ethics of Reading: Kant, de Man, Eliot, Trollope, James and Benjamin*. New York: Columbia UP, 1987.

Ousby, Ian. "Figurative Language in *Hard Times*." *Durham University Journal* ns 43 (1981):103–09.

Schlicke, Paul. *Dickens and Popular Entertainment*. London: Allen, 1985.

Sicher, Efraim. "Binary Oppositions and Spatial Representation: Towards an Applied Semiotics." *Semiotica* 60 (1986):211–24.

Welsh, Alexander. *The City of Dickens*. Oxford: Oxford UP, 1971.

Dogmatism and Puppyism: The Novelist, The Reviewer, and the Serious Subject: The Case of *Little Dorrit*

Edwin M. Eigner

When George Bernard Shaw called *Little Dorrit* a more subversive book than *Das Kapital*, he was not exaggerating the critical sentiments of his childhood. Even those reviewers of the 1850s and '60s who were aware of Marx would have regarded Dickens' novel as more dangerous, because, as a best selling work of popular fiction, it would of course reach a much wider audience and was therefore more likely to stir up discontent. They would also have regarded it as subversive because even the idea of a piece of "light literature" attempting to influence the minds of its readers on a subject of practical concern represented a serious revolution against the established order of public debate.

Dickens was by no means the only novelist whom critics of the time regarded as having invaded the sphere of political discourse. In 1858, one year after the completion of *Little Dorrit*, David Masson noted the recent spate of fiction either inculcating or arguing against positions of a political or ecclesiastical nature—novels of Chartism, socialism, Christian socialism, Anglo-Catholicism, Broad Church, Roman Catholicism, temperance, and woman's rights. "Hardly a question or doctrine of the last ten years can be pointed out that has not had a novel framed in its interest, positively or negatively. To a great extent tales and novels now serve the purpose of pamphlets" (264–65).

Masson was one of the few critics who did not feel threatened by this development, but the more typical Victorian attitude towards tendentious or polemical novels was very largely negative. Fiction, it was believed, should

217

perhaps seek to improve the minds and morals of its readers, or it should at least be careful not to pervert them, but most reviewers were strong in their conviction that novels should not touch on specific issues.

Often, the insistence that fiction and serious questions be kept apart was made with the avowed purpose not of protecting politics from literature, but of saving literature from the contaminating influence of politics. Here, for instance, is a review of an ecclesiastical novel published in 1857, the year in which *Little Dorrit* was completed. The review appeared in a weekly journal called *The Leader*, which claimed always to value "light literature,"[1] and which, as we shall see, was later on in the same year to be a champion of Dickens.

> Another novel with an earnest purpose. How long is our patience to be abused by these insults to our taste and understanding? . . . We protest against this desecration of light literature. Works of fiction are no longer a pleasing recreation after the toils and occupations of the day. . . . Every monomaniac who wishes to force his one idea upon his neighbors now writes a tale and thus under false pretenses induces the public to listen to his nonsense. Novels of this stamp are a literary swindle.   (Rev. of *The Mildmayes* 18)

In the previous decade another important weekly, *The Athenaeum*, had reviewed a factory novel, *The Young Milliner*, with a similar exasperation:

> The novelist has, of late, too largely become the abuse-monger. . . . We have had poor laws, Puseyism, and other vexed questions done into fiction; and now Mrs. Stone, following the lead of the Children's Employment Commission, and the indignant protest it has excited, puts forth her statement of the case in a rather maudlin story.

The reviewer tries to make it clear that he has no argument with the clearly benevolent motives behind the novelist's argument. "It cannot for an instant be supposed," he insists, "that we reject the humanity of any sincere intention to assist 'the desolate and oppressed.' " Nevertheless, he has a critic's obligation to protect the decorum of literature: "We no more like to see the grievance-trade intrude itself into the literature of leisure, than the rags and sores of the hospitals taken as subjects for pictures" (437).

Nor were such strictures applied only to minor writers. Indeed, the more major the offending novelist, the more strident was the outrage, for it was a matter then not only of reader betrayal, but of the betrayal of art itself. Thus, Victor Hugo was condemned in *The Edinburgh Review* "for having degraded his pen into a mere instrument for party warfare" when he wrote *Les Misérables* (Payronnet 212), and when *Quatre-vingt-treize* appeared, another reviewer lamented:

His works are no longer the outpourings of a splendid imagination, but the
vehicles of wild social and political theories, shrieks of eulogy, and howls of
denunciation; appeals to anarchy and bloodshed, votive offerings to sansculott-
ism, and frantic hatred against the rich and all that is.   (Baker 333)

"Why," asks a reviewer of *Tess of the D'Urbervilles*, "should a novelist
embroil himself in moral technicalities. . . . One half suspects Mr. Hardy of
a desire to argue out the justice of the comparative punishments meted to men
and women for sexual aberrations. To have fashioned a faultless piece of art
should have been sufficient" (50).

But polemical fiction was generally understood not only to spoil the art of
a novel; it was more frequently condemned as a blatantly unfair mode of
argument. Thus, *The Edinburgh Review* came down hard on the religious
novel *David Grieve*, because its author, Mrs. Humphry Ward, selected particular facts for presentation, a practice which "inevitably leads to the suppression of truth. . . . A religious novel . . . is written to persuade and to influence the judgment, and the omission of anything which can assist a man in
forming or attaining a true opinion is a perversion of truth" (Edmond 520).
Mrs. Ward's more popular and more controversial novel *Robert Elsmere* had
been attacked in the *Quarterly Review* on similar grounds:

It is easy to prove anything one pleases in such a composition. The author is
able at pleasure to give all the good qualities and all the good arguments to the
side which is favoured. . . . It is rare to meet a controversial novel in which
the beaten side makes any respectable fight, and this defect vitiates the whole
description. In "Robert Elsmere" this unfairness passes all tolerable bounds.
                                                                (Wace 276)

For similar reasons, James Stothert, writing in *The Rambler*, a Roman Catholic journal, "inclines" to "exclude" religious opinion "absolutely . . . from
the province of legitimate fiction. . . . General controversy is incongruous
and unsuitable . . . spoiling the story, as it is popularly expressed, without
any substantial gain to the cause of truth" ("Catholic Novelists" 252).

Political novels were even more suspect. Here is another *Rambler* article,
this one on *Uncle Tom's Cabin*, the immediate popularity of which presaged
its immense influence:

The unfitness of a work of fiction as an instrument of religious or political
propagandism was never more strikingly exemplified. The method of attack is
simply this. The authoress presents us with very lively sketches of a certain
number of slaves, slave dealers, slave-catchers, and slave holders; but unfortunately there is no voucher for the existence of the originals anywhere out of

her own imagination, and the same must be said of her incidents, anecdotes, sentiments, and conversations.   (Northcote 414)

Nor did the political issue need to be so dramatic as slavery for the reviewer to place it outside the province of the novelist. Harriet Martineau was said to have gone "a great deal too far when she made the inculcation of a doubtful (or at least a disputed) doctrine in political economy the main object of . . . [her stories], for in all such cases the question must be begged, and it is obviously just as easy to sketch a ploughman's family thrown out of employ through the abolition of the corn laws, as a weaver's or a cotton-spinner's reduced to the verge of starvation by the enactment of them. In fact, the mixture [of story and argument] spoils two good things, as Charles Lamb . . . used to say of brandy and water" (Hayward 53).

Charles Dickens had been subject to such strictures since the publication of *Oliver Twist* (1837), which was perceived as "directed against the poor-law and work-house system . . . with much unfairness" (Richard Ford 94), but the outcry against Dickens' social agenda became much more strident in the 1850s. His criticism of the Court of Chancery in *Bleak House* was particularly offensive to the conservative-minded barristers who staffed the *Saturday Review of Politics, Literature, Science, and Art* from its inception in 1855. They began a line of negative critical thought regarding Dickens which was used to damn him throughout the rest of his career and was to continue after his death as the chief set of arguments to be employed against those who were considered to be his followers. In the hands of Dickens and his imitators of the sensation school of fiction, it was argued, "polemical writing leads to grievously melodramatic excesses, heightened by every kind of exaggeration" which can be used to prove any point the author wishes to make. "The method is so far perfectly impartial that it may be applied with equal facility to the best things and the worst; but an argument that proves everything is of precisely the same value as an argument that proves nothing" (Mansel 488). Writing in *The Cornhill Magazine*, James Fitzjames Stephen, Dickens' greatest enemy among literary critics and a regular on the staff of *The Saturday Review*, concluded that writers of polemical fiction are more than merely misguided; they are "either weak, ignorant, or fraudulent":

A novel is, from the nature of the case, an appeal to the feelings, and to feelings for their own sake. A novelist never lays down a proposition properly limited and supported. . . . Novels can hardly ever be thrown into the form of propositions capable of being distinctly attacked or defended. They associate a strong feeling of disgust, or sympathy, or pity, with a particular class of facts; and they suggest to idle readers, or to any reader in an idle mood, conclusions which they do not really prove.

"A sentimental book," Stephen insisted, "is like a cooked account" (74–75).

There was, of course, another side to the argument, a pro-Dickens side, a pro-polemical side, and, more generally, a pro-didactic side. Some critics went so far as to state that it was possible for a book to fail as a novel and still succeed as a political or moral statement. Thus a novel might have "small value" as literature, and yet make "a brilliant noise on behalf of human progress" (Le Gallienne 1016). R. H. Hutton, one of the most important of Victorian reviewers, seemed sometimes to be saying that if a novel did not include a statement of social consequence, it could not properly be considered to have succeeded as a work of art. Thus he faulted Hawthorne for a failure to interest himself in political issues: "If he conceded less to his squeamish love of the beautiful, if he could cultivate a deeper sympathy with action and its responsibilities, he would not only begin to take some interest in the removal of wrongs . . . but might widen greatly the range of his artistic power" (481).

According to some critics, a great novelist had a sacred responsibility to improve society. An article by Alexander Allardyce and John Blackwood asserted that such a writer "has it even better in his power than a great preacher to justify to men the ways of the Almighty, [and he] . . . never for a moment loses sight of the responsibility which the exercise of his genius imposes upon him. He thinks it no shame to confess that his fictions are written with a purpose" (385). Like Hawthorne, Robert Louis Stevenson was sometimes criticized as a novelist who cared more about art than social consequences, and so he was reminded on one occasion by an otherwise sympathetic critic that "the masters of noble fiction have commonly judged that they were sent on a prophetic errand. Certain also of the greatest names—George Eliot, Thackeray, and, in his time, Balzac—are associated with a manner of teaching so consistent and precise, that did we separate the philosophy from the elements of the fiction, the romance would be carried away like the fine dust of the threshing-floor" (Barry 336). Nor, when he wrote criticism himself, did Stevenson disagree. "The moral significance" of Victor Hugo's romances," he writes, "is the organizing principle. If you could somehow despoil *Les Misérables* or *Les Travailleurs* of their distinctive lesson, you would find that the story had lost its interest and the book was dead. Having learned to subordinate his story to an idea, to make his art speak, [Hugo] . . . went on to teach it to say things heretofore unaccustomed" (192). Even Turgenev, whom we have come to see as the model for the aesthetics of Jamesian realism, was valued in his time because each of his novels contained "the statement and examination of some burning question of contemporary Russian life and politics" (471). Finally, Swinburne makes this same general argument central to his appreciation of Dickens, stating that

> Nothing can be more fatuous than to brand all didactic or missionary fiction as an illegitimate or inferior form of art: the highest works in that line fall short only of the highest ever achieved by man. Many of the truest and noblest triumphs achieved by the matchless genius of Charles Dickens were achieved in this field.   (598–99)

Some significant critics took a middle position. Bulwer-Lytton, arguing on the basis of Hegelian aesthetics, allowed that political science is indeed "within the competent range of imaginative fiction . . . but descend lower into the practical questions that divide the passions of the day, and you waste all the complicated machinery of fiction to do what you could do much better in a party pamphlet" (550). Richard Simpson, another important critic, acknowledged that "there is a very just prejudice against novels with a purpose. . . . Didactic novels are generally written by persons who cannot teach, and have no story to tell. But, on the other hand, no great work can be written without a purpose—religious, political, philosophical, or artistic" (227). And Walter Bagehot, who ruled that "the whole armory of pulpit eloquence" must be omitted from fiction, because "men who purchase a novel do not wish a stone or a sermon," felt nevertheless that "no delineation of human nature can be considered complete which omits to deal with man in relation to the questions which occupy him as a man" ("The Waverley Novels" 468).

Perhaps Leslie Stephen stated this middle position most powerfully:

> No poem or novel should be conspicuously branded with a well-worn aphorism. . . . And yet. . . . some central truth should be embodied in every work of fiction, which cannot be compressed into a definite formula, but which acts as the animating and informing principle, determining the main lines of the structure and affecting even its most trivial details. . . . Though the poem proves nothing, it will persuade you of much. It is not a demonstration, but an education.   (717)

Nor, to do him justice, would Leslie Stephen's less famous brother, James Fitzjames Stephen, have contradicted this position. For as much as he disliked Dickens and the polemical novel, he and his colleagues on *The Saturday Review* felt an almost equal distaste for any novel without intellectual content. But it was possible, both Stephen brothers felt, to make a clear distinction between the writer who seeks to improve the moral or mental character of the reader and the novelist who tries to direct the reader's political or religious thinking.

The specifically pro-Dickens and pro-polemic fiction, as well as some aspects of the anti-position which we have not yet considered, are perhaps best examined by looking at the debate over *Little Dorrit*, which appeared in the pages of *The Saturday Review* and its rival, the more radical weekly *The Leader*. The argument, as we shall see, was fueled on both sides by personal considerations, but it nevertheless developed seemingly diametrically opposed points of view on the subject of the propriety of tendentious fiction. As I shall ultimately argue, this opposition, as expressed by the two critics who defined it, may be more apparent than real; nevertheless, it established a dichotomy which shaped subsequent discussions of the question and which has remained powerful well into our own century.

The personal consideration which may have influenced *The Saturday Review*'s position on *Little Dorrit* was James Fitzjames Stephen's belief that his father, Sir James Stephen, was the original of Lord Decimus Tite Barnacle, whom Dickens satirized as the leading figure of the Circumlocution Office, the department of government which specializes in the quintessentially British art of how not to do it. But Stephen and the other writers for *The Saturday Review* had more than personal reasons for resenting Dickens' novel, for it seemed to attack everything they most valued in English life. As Merle Bevington, who has written the history of *The Saturday Review*, explains:

> The *Saturday* stood for the preservation of English institutions because they were bound up in their historical development with the growth of English liberty. It accepted as right the rule of England by governing classes made up of a well-born, intelligent, educated, and propertied minority. . . . It recognized frankly that the English system was a system of privilege which it argued was justified by the fact that it supported a civilized life for the greatest minority the world had ever known. . . . The fear of democracy as something likely to destroy the whole fabric of civilized society is the dominant note of the *Saturday*'s politics. (58–59)

The general tone of the journal is apparent in an article describing "Society in California." America figures frequently in the columns of the *Saturday*, almost always as a negative example of a radical culture without stabilizing institutions. Because of the "force of the orderly instincts which are never quite extinguished in the Anglo-Saxon race," there is some order and industry to be found among the Californians, but this is overbalanced by "so much outrage and anarchy, such a deal of trouble and confusion, as may teach us to put up patiently with some of the inconveniences of our [English] social system'' (410–11).

In *Little Dorrit*, of course, Stephen and his patriotic, pro-establishment associates immediately alerted to a subversive impatience with the ''inconveniences'' of the English social system, and they recognized the chapters on the Circumlocution Office as an expression of the Administrative Reform Association, to them dangerously radical, which Dickens had ardently supported. Thus the *Saturday*'s counter-attack began with the lead article of 22 November 1856, more than half a year before Dickens had completed his novel. The article is an unapologetic defense of red-tape bureaucracy, and the writer does not trouble even to avoid Dickens' term, circumlocution. Indeed, he uses it without quotation marks. The piece is called ''Circumlocution *versus* Circumvention,'' and the argument simply stated is that what Dickens calls circumlocution is the necessary and worthwhile price the English should be willing to pay for honest government.

In the succeeding months Stephen published a series of attacks on *Little Dorrit* in the *Saturday Review* and elsewhere. Again and again he characterized Dickens as a mere popular entertainer, with no talent, no background, no qualifications, and thus certainly no business to address the British public on any serious subject. ''We admit that Mr. Dickens has a mission,'' Stephen wrote in July 1857, when *Little Dorrit* was complete, ''but it is to make the world grin, not to recreate and rehabilitate society'' (''Little Dorrit'' 15). Earlier in the year he had dismissed Dickens as a social reformer on the grounds that ''He is utterly destitute of any kind of solid acquirements'' (''Mr. Dickens as a Politician'' 9). Dickens' lack of ''solid acquirements'' is an issue that will echo throughout our recapitulation of the debate over *Little Dorrit*. It means, essentially, that he had not been to university or benefited from a classical education.

The Leader entered the fray on June 27 with what is perhaps the most positive review of a Dickens novel, or at least of a political novel by Dickens, which had ever been published. Whereas the *Saturday* had begun its most recent attack on *Little Dorrit* with the words ''Mr. Dickens has just concluded his long libel on his own genius and on the institutions of his country'' (''Circumlocution'' 514), *The Leader* ended its glowing tribute with the sentence ''In *Little Dorrit*, Mr. Dickens has made another imperishable addition to the literature of his country'' (''Little Dorrit'' 617). Clearly, *The Leader* was reading the *Saturday*.

The Leader review has been attributed, on the basis of an entry in his *Journal*, to George Henry Lewes (Kaminsky 109).[2] And there is also strong internal evidence to suggest that Lewes was the author not only of this review but of the subsequent pieces arguing with the *Saturday* on the issue of *Little Dorrit*. For one thing, the writer of the review uses the same strategy to praise Dickens as Lewes later employed to establish the greatness of his favorite novelist, Jane Austen. He begins with a flattering comparison with Shakespeare and goes on to insist on the essentially dramatic nature of the novels he admires ("The Novels of Jane Austen" 102, 105). But an aspect of the review which points even more strongly to Lewes as the author of the Dickens review is the inclusion of a digressive aside aimed at the university graduates who wrote for the *Saturday*. The article asserts that Dickens "is never disputatiously theological or academically dogmatic," and then goes on to castigate "certain University bred reviewers, whose shriveled souls cannot understand the fresh, spontaneous efflorescence of genius" (617). This attitude was so important to Lewes' state of mind that it, too, was repeated and expanded in the Jane Austen article, where he noted that "the writing and thinking of accomplished men is excessively cheap, compared to the smallest amount of invention or creation, and it is cheap because more easy of production and less potent of effect."

> This is apparently by no means the opinion of some recent critics, who evidently consider their own *writing* of more merit than *humour* and *invention*, and who are annoyed at the notion of "mere serialists," without "solid acquirements" being regarded all over Europe as our most distinguished authors. . . . If it is a painful reflection that genius should be esteemed more highly than solid acquirements, it should be remembered that learning is only the diffused form of what was once invention. "Solid acquirements" is the genius of wits, which has become the wisdom of reviewers. (109)

The sentiment here expressed became so much an article of faith with Lewes that he later repeated it almost word for word in his book *The Principles of Success in Literature* (17–18).

The issue of solid acquirements was as personal with Lewes as the business of Tite Barnacle was to Stephen. Just two weeks before Lewes' laudatory review of *Little Dorrit* appeared, the *Saturday* had condescendingly noticed the new edition of his own *Biographical History of Philosophy*. The review was generally favorable, but it took the opportunity to remark that the first edition "certainly was superficial" and that it bore "many marks of hasty writing." Such criticism must have been galling to Lewes because he was himself an occasional contributor to *The Saturday Review*, and especially because, as he was well aware, his book had been widely used for the past ten years as a crib by Oxford and Cambridge undergraduates preparing for their examinations. No doubt Fitzjames Stephen, who was not a brilliant student, had had recourse to it. But as Lewes was also aware, he was just the sort of self-educated man, without solid acquirements, whom the Saturday Reviewers despised. As Rosemary Ashton, Lewes' best and most recent biographer, writes, he "always felt anxious about his credentials. It was the one sore spot in a man otherwise remarkable for his lack of sensitivity about his reputation" (147).

He may have felt the sting even more sharply on 27 June, the date of his Dickens article, for on that very day, a reviewer for *Saturday* denigrated the late Douglas Jerrold—he had died just the week before—as "utterly uninstructed" ("The Tory Press" 587). Jerrold was also self-taught. He was also, like Lewes, of a theatrical family and had made his living, again like Lewes, as a playwright, a minor novelist, and a radical journalist. It may very well have been himself he was thinking about when he wrote in his review of *Little Dorrit*, "the world will recognise its great ones whether or not they wear the uniform of cap and gown" (617).

In any event, Lewes struck back quickly and bitterly the Saturday following the offensive Jerrold obituary:

> Our amiable contemporary, the Peelite Review, has come forward with characteristic generosity. . . . The late Mr. Douglas Jerrold, we are informed with refined truthfulness, was "utterly uninstructed." . . . In their Quixotic zeal to put down all popular writers and popular literature, they tilt against a newly made grave as blindly as against the sturdiest living celebrity . . . . They have no patience with the praises lavished on such men as Dickens and Jerrold. . . . Jerrold himself, indeed, had happily characterized the spirit that animates our contemporary long before it took weekly form, in his celebrated definition of Dogmatism as "Puppyism come to maturity."
>
> ("Literature" 4 July 640)

But Fitzjames Stephen was by no means finished with his attacks on Dickens and other writers lacking in solid acquirements. On the day on which Lewes' puppyism piece was printed, Stephen published a further criticism of Dickens, claiming never to have met "the man or woman, boy or girl, who can honestly say that he or she has read *Little Dorrit* through" ("Little Dorrit" 15). And he went on condescendingly to allow, "Mr. Dickens can, we believe, recover himself—he has simply mistaken his calling and his powers" (16). The next week's issue contained a condemnation of *Madame Bovary*, which managed somehow to drag Dickens' name in, and it also featured an angry response to Lewes' most resent criticisms. Stephen defended the tactless slur on the dead Jerrold lamely but as best he could, and then he set his sights on Dickens once again. His strategy for defending English institutions should be familiar to us as we look back on the rhetoric of the Cold War:

> Esther Summerson might fret her heart out in vain about the Court of Chancery, and Mr. Doyce would have to stifle his virtuous indignation if a Russian circumlocutionist throught fit "not to do it." . . . The *Leader* favours us with a definition of Dogmatism. Will it accept from us a description of "Puppyism come to maturity?" When a mere lad discovers in himself great powers of fancy, great humour, great facility of language, and employs them against other things in melodramatic descriptions of the evils of a real abuse, or in harmlessly exaggerated caricatures of a court of law, we can admire his genius, and forgive or enjoy the liberties which he takes with our understanding. But when the clever youth, developing his powers by constant exercise, becomes beyond all comparison the most popular, and one of the most influential writers of the day, and when, intoxicated by success, he thinks it his duty to run a tilt at institutions of which he knows nothing, and to claim to be the regenerator, because he is the most distinguished buffoon, of society—when in this he is abetted by a crowd of writers like himself, who think that white paint and a cap and bells are the proper costume for legislators, and that, because a man can make silly women cry, he can dictate the principles of law and government to grown men—such a person and his followers appear to us to afford the strongest of all illustrations of that which Mr. Jerrold considered a synonym for dogmatism.
>
> ("Light Literature" 640)

Nor was even this the end of it: Lewes and Stephen continued to exchange volleys throughout July. Finally, it was Dickens who put a stop to it. This part of the story is well known, but worth repeating anyway. Stephen published an anonymous attack on Dickens and Charles Reade in *The Edinburgh Review* called "The Licence of Modern Novelists." Their license, which Stephen of course utterly denied, was to argue a real issue with wholly imaginary and highly selected evidence. He also criticized Dickens for the collapse of the Clennam house in the final number of *Little Dorrit*. The incident was included, so Stephen believed, simply because the issue was topical: a house had recently fallen down in Tottenham Court Road. Stephen then followed this up with another anonymous piece in *The Saturday Review*, craftily praising the "powerful" article in the *Edinburgh* which "abundantly proves" that Dickens and Reade are "deliberate perverters and falsifiers of facts." The only fault he has to find with the "eloquent" *Edinburgh* reviewer (himself, of course) is that he "deals more harshly, on the whole, with Mr. Reade than with Mr. Dickens. . . . Mr. Dickens," Stephen maintains, "has as clear a right to be heard upon politics as anybody else. But when the [Administrative Reform] Association to which he tried to lend assistance went out like a candle snuff, Mr. Dickens was not entitled to invent in his novel the *data* which his associates had failed to establish on the platform; nor are his friends [read George Henry Lewes] justified in asking for the romance-writer that immunity from deference to truth which it would have been impudence to demand from the spokesman of the Administrative Reformers'' (''The *Edinburgh Review* and Modern Novelists'' 57–58).

Dickens never bothered with the upstart *Saturday*, but one could respond with dignity to the *Edinburgh Review*, the most venerable of all nineteenth-century journals. In an emphatically signed article, ''Curious Misprint in the *Edinburgh Review*,'' he pointed out that even reviewers sometimes got things wrong and that their evidence was not always so factual as they would like us to believe. He showed first how a moderately careful reading of *Little Dorrit* would have revealed that the collapse of the house had been prepared for from the beginning of the novel, which was, of course, written long before the Tottenham Court Road incident. More significantly, he recounted in detail the frustratingly sad career of Rowland Hill, the inventor of the penny post, whom Stephen had instanced to argue that the Circumlocution Office could indeed recognize and amply reward the instigator of an idea when a really good one was put before it. This is the ''curious misprint,'' Dickens wrote, ''the name of Mr. Rowland Hill. Some other, and perfectly different name must have been sent to the printer'':

> Mr. Rowland Hill!! Why, if Mr. Rowland Hill were not, in toughness, a man of a hundred thousand; if he had not had in the struggles of his career a steadfastness of purpose overriding all sensitiveness, and steadily staring grim despair out of countenance, the Circumlocution Office would have made a dead man of him long and long ago.   (98)

And he goes on for three columns to detail Hill's much more than Doyce-like struggles with the bureaucracy. Obviously, there could be such a thing as license among modern reviewers as well as among novelists, and an essay written by a man of solid acquirements was as likely to be a ''cooked account'' as any work of sentimental fiction.

Lewes was ecstatic. He must have received an advance copy, for on the day in which Dickens' article was printed, the *Leader* published a four-column paraphrase, ''Mr. Charles Dickens and the 'Edinburgh Review,' '' and, ten pages later, Lewes provided a separate and triumphant analysis:

> The most amusing part of Mr. Dickens's article is his exposure of the critic's disgraceful ignorance in dealing even with recent facts. . . . Such stolid blundering . . . is also instructive. It shows that those who bluster moral condemnations against the alleged unveracity of others are not, therefore to be trusted

themselves. . . . And it enables us to estimate at their true worth the facts and assertions of writers who, because their knowledge of law may happen to be a little beyond "that of an attorney's clerk," assume the airs of jurists and philosophers, think themselves entitled to sit in judgment on poets and humorists of the highest genius, and to impose laws on literature and art.   (737)

Stephen did not reply. Indeed, his father, the alleged original of Lord Decimus Tite Barnacle, warned him in a letter to lay off Dickens. "He is a rather formidable enemy to deal with," the elder Stephen cautioned (Smith 20).

As we have seen, Dickens did not enter the debate when it was between the *Saturday* and the *Leader*, and if he had, it is by no means certain which side he would have taken. The *Leader* always spoke respectfully of him, even reverently at times, while Stephen treated him with constant contempt, as "the most distinguished buffoon of society." But Stephen at least always did him the justice of assuming that he was serious about his political agenda, however mistaken it might be and however unqualified Dickens was to pursue it. Lewes, on the other hand, believed that Dickens was only "pleasantly satirising some of the admitted shortcomings of Government Officials" ("Literature" 18 July 689). One of the most telling points he tried to score against Stephen and the *Saturday* was that they simply couldn't take "a joke. It is amusing to hear him censure Mr. Dickens' pleasant fiction of the Circumlocution Office in the most solemn tones, as if it were offered as a full and fair account of the whole science and art of government" ("Literature" 11 July 664).

"Pleasant fiction" indeed, one can almost hear Dickens grumbling. If Dickens had responded, it would have been the 1852 argument with Lewes about *Bleak House* all over again. In that case, Lewes did not begin arguing in earnest until it became clear to him that Dickens really believed in the possibility of a death by spontaneous combustion. Krooks' incineration was only mildly objectionable to him so long as it was intended merely as a symbol in a work of light literature; if, on the other hand, it was meant as a contribution to a truly serious subject like science, it had sternly to be corrected. The evidence from his unpublished journals indicates that in 1857, the year of the debate with the *Saturday*, although Lewes was strongly encouraging the woman he was living with to become a novelist, he was attempting to break his own ties with literature and was turning instead to an interest in marine biology.

Ironically, Stephen's principal difference from Lewes may have been only that he, Stephen, took fiction more seriously. Indeed, writers for *The Saturday Review* took everything seriously. As far as Dickens was concerned, the argument between the two reviewers was finally superficial, as Stephen's most recent biographer concludes when he writes that "as a critic of Dickens, Stephen's views and public stance bear a clear resemblance to those . . . G. H. Lewes" implied in his 1872 *Fortnightly* article, where Lewes expresses himself as shocked by the sight of Dickens' "bookshelves, on which were ranged nothing but three-volume novels and books of travel" (Smith22), a library bearing no evidence, as Stephen would say, of "solid acquirements."[3]

The fact is that neither Stephen nor Lewes felt comfortable with tendentious fiction. Here is a review by Lewes of Thackeray's *The Book of Snobs*:

> Perhaps no advocate of a cause should be more seriously watched than he who laughingly teaches. Against the dogmas of the politician, philosopher, or theologian we prepare ourselves . . . . His seriousness alarms us. We scrutinize his proofs, we combat his conclusions. Not so with a jester. He is privileged. He throws us off our guard, and storms conviction by enveloping us in laughter. A semblance of truth has more effect in a jest, because we do not look for it there, than a demonstration in a serious essay.   (3)

This was his position in 1848. When he wrote "Dickens in Relation to Criticism" almost a quarter of a century later, Lewes betrayed the seriousness of his problem with Dickens and with a great deal of Victorian fiction, a problem which amounted almost to a terror of the imagination. "He was 'imagination all compact,' " Lewes wrote of Dickens. "If the other higher faculties were singularly deficient in him, this faculty was imperial. . . . Psychologists will understand both the extent and the limitation of the remark, when I say that in no other sane mind (Blake, I believe, was not perfectly sane) have I observed vividness of imagination approaching so closely to hallucination" (144). Somewhat earlier he had written that "A too active imagination is apt to distract the attention and scatter the energy of the mind" (*Principles of Success* 32).

Lewes shared this fear and distrust of the imagination with many men of letters of all ages, including our own, but it was a characteristic especially common among the novel critics of his own century. Kenneth Graham notes how "The novel's innate appeal to the imagination can . . . arouse distrust and comdemnation," and he instances Ruskin's "latent fear of its effects" (2), his " 'dread . . . [of the] overwrought interest' " which an imaginative novel might spark (Ruskin 129). Another critic, a reviewer of *Adam Bede*, warns of "the aid which the play of the imagination lends to evil. . . . simply because the imagination is strong to stamp pictorial representations on the mind and weak to register the prudential or moral motives which serve to counteract them" (307).

Sometimes the language which the critic uses to warn his readers of the dangers of the polemical novelist seem to be taken from the melodrama of sexual seduction. Thus Diana Mulock, a successful novelist herself, paints an insidious picture of the novelist who "creeps innocently on our family-table in the shape of those three well-thumbed library volumes—sits for days after, invisibly at our fire-side, a provocative of incessant discussion: slowly but surely, either by admiration or adversion, his opinions, his ideas, feelings, impress themselves upon us" (442). And James Augustus Stothert writes of "the subtle poison [which] may flow into the mind from . . . [the novelist's] insidious periods, sapping the life of faith or morality":

> The novelist approaches his readers when they are least on guard; in their moments of ease, when they are little disposed to question too closely the gay provider for the gratification of a careless hour, when the higher powers of the mind are inactive, and to be pleased and amused is the only aim of life. The minds of many young readers are chiefly formed upon the thoughts and principles of the novelist: he has access and influence denied to graver or better informed men; his smiling address is welcome when the professed moralist might instruct in vain. So much more powerful is he for good or for evil. ("Duties and Responsibilities" 477)

This picture of the polemical novelist as a masculine seducer or sexual aggressor occurs frequently in Victorian criticism of the novel, and is perhaps echoed unconsciously by George Eliot when she praises Meredith's *The Shaving of Shagpat* with the words "there is no didactic thrusting forward of moral lessons" (16). But more frequently, the seductive polemical novelist is seen not as male but as female, and is thus a figure of much greater terror to the man of letters. Certainly this is the case with Fitzjames Stephen, who characterizes Dickens mind as "feminine, irritable, noisy . . . always clamouring and shrieking for protection and guidance" ("Mr. Dickens as a Politician" 9).

> There is sex in minds as well as in bodies, and Mr. Dickens's literary progeny seem to us to be for the most part of the feminine gender, and to betray it by . . . a very tiresome irritability of nerve.　　　　　　("Mr. Dickens" 475)

Elsewhere, in the review of a now forgotten pro-slavery novel, Stephen writes:

> We are all familiar with the religious novel as a weapon of controversy and with the abnormal logic peculiar to the fair disputants who select this mode of mingling in the fray. *Tant pis pour les faits*, said the Frenchman, when it was

> pointed out to him that the facts would not agree with his theory. But our feminine teachers are much more considerate towards the facts—they take effective precautions that the facts shall not be left in that undignified position, by the simple process of previously altering them, so as to meet the theory.

This mode of arguing the reviewer calls "the feminine syllogism" ("A Word for Slavery" 18).

A somewhat later reviewer, George Scott, who like Stephen dismissed Dickens as a social critic because he could "think of no writer of mark who shows a more uninstructed mind, or on whose judgment on any question involving mastery of facts, or breadth of view, or critical acumen, we should set less store," also followed Stephen in regarding such an intellect as essentially feminine.

> Mr. Dickens is no doubt entitled to the credit of making weak people, women, and children cry copiously, but [he] . . . is insensitive to . . . the aims and pursuits of intellectual men. . . . Not only has he no reverence for abstract speculation, or learning, or statesmanship, he does not seem to believe that there *are* such things. . . . He has . . . an almost feminine incapacity for grasping abstract notions."   (222)

And Walter Bagehot faulted Dickens for "his deficiency in those masculine faculties of . . . the reasoning understanding and firm far-seeing sagacity . . . which stiffen the mind, and give a consistency to the creed and a coherence to its effects" ("Charles Dickens" 465).

From the Victorian point of view, these "masculine faculties" were essential for anyone treating a serious subject. Even a lady Victorian, like Mrs. Oliphant, would agree. Writing in *Blackwood's*, which was in many ways the conservative grandfather of the *Saturday Review*, she described *Hard Times* as a "lamentable *non sequitur* . . . [because] fiction breaks down when it is . . . compelled to prove and substantiate a theory. This, which is the proper work of reason, is by no means the business of the poetic faculty, and Pegasus is too restive a steed to be bound to the plough" ("Charles Dickens" 453). The poetic faculty, the imagination, was strongest, according to widespread Victorian prejudice, among the inferior species (like the dog, whose dreams of running were obviously so vivid as to make his legs move), among the inferior races (like the Irish), and with the inferior sex. In the same essay, Mrs. Oliphant had nothing but praise for the feminine sensibility of Dickens's nonpolitical portrait of the artist, *David Copperfield* (451).

There were, of course, other positions expressed in the range of Victorian criticism of fiction, positions which tended to place the imagination on a level with the reason. The Bishop of Ripon is reported in a *Spectator* article of having stated that "the theory for a novel was the same as for a discourse or a sermon" (61). Some few critics tended even to valorize the imagination as an intellectual faculty. Thus, A. H. Japp argues that "An artist is a teacher, indeed, simply because he has more power than others of abandoning the individual [intellectual] sphere and of making his more memorable experiences pillars and pedestals on which his imagination may spring up into the region of the universal, enabling him by appeal to the emotions to exalt and purify others" (163). Japp, writing from a strong basis in Schiller, is arguing that *only* the imaginative faculty is appropriate to the writer who deals with a serious subject. David Masson, coming at the novel with an attitude toward literature and thought which equipped him to be one of the leading Miltonists of his century, denies the opposition-of-faculties argument altogether:

> The imagination is not a faculty working apart; it is the whole mind thrown into the act of imagining; and the value of any act of imagination, therefore, or of all the acts of imagination of any particular mind, will depend on the total strength and total furnishings of the mind, doctrinal contents and all, that is thrown into this form of exercise. Every artist is a thinker, whether he knows it or not; and ultimately no artist will be found greater as an artist than he is as a thinker. (299)

Nevertheless, the position taken by the *Saturday Review* on *Little Dorrit* and implicitly endorsed by its opponent in the debate had a powerful hold on the less elevated Victorian mind. Although Dickens ended Stephen's attacks on *Little Dorrit* with his own effective foray into criticism, his opponent was hardly quelled. Two years later Stephen's review of *A Tale of Two Cities* insisted that "the moral tone" is not "more wholesome than that of . . . [the novel's] predecessors, nor does it display any nearer approach to a solid knowledge of the subject-matter to which it refers" (742).

Indeed, some of Stephen's friends believed he had won the earlier argument with Dickens, and it is possible to see why they might think so: the very fact that Dickens was able to discredit Stephen's *Edinburgh* article by calling him on the specific facts could be seen to prove Stephen's more general point that essayists had a responsibility to be rational and factual, a responsibility from which imaginative novelists were exempt. Since there was no way to discredit the message of *Little Dorrit* with an appeal to facts, Stephen was arguing, there was also no way to credit it.

Of course, Dickens kept insisting that the novelist, in spite of his imaginative powers, had at least as much responsibility as the essayist to be both factual and rational, but his voice was drowned out even by those critics, like Lewes, who seemed to be his strongest supporters. Irrespective of their positions on the propriety of polemical fiction, most Victorian critics agreed that masculine reason and feminine imagination were at odds with one another and that when important public decisions had to be made on questions of a practical nature, only the masculine or rational faculties were to be relied on.

NOTES

1. In 1854 Lewes, writing for *The Leader*, carried on a debate with the *Times* on the subject of light literature, defending the cheap publication of novels meant only to amuse and the republication at cheap prices of novels by Bulwer-Lytton, Dickens, Gaskell, and others.
2. Other scholars, Philip Collins, for instance, venture no identification either of the review or of the subsequent *Leader* contributions to the debate, and I assume this caution is based on the knowledge that although Lewes had been in sole charge of the literature section in the early days of *The Leader*, he had been only an occasional contributor since the time of his elopement with George Eliot in 1854. Besides, on the basis of articles both he and George Eliot are known to have written, it is clear that they were hardly Bozolitors. Indeed, George Ford has properly termed an article Lewes wrote in 1872, "Dickens in Relation to Criticism," the most effective attack on Dickens ever written.
3. Curiously the two are even alike in the practice of quoting with obvious approval their own anonymous words from the *Edinburgh Review*. The motto of the literature section of the *Leader* from its inception by Lewes in 1850 ("Critics are not the legislators, but the judges and police of literature. They do not make laws—they interpret and try to enforce them.—*Edinburgh Review*") is taken from the article "Shakspeare's Critics," which Lewes published in the journal in 1849.

WORKS CITED

Allardyce, Alexander, and John Blackwood. "Samuel Warren." *Blackwood's Magazine* 122 (1877):381–90.

Ashton, Rosemary. *G. H. Lewes: A Life*. Oxford: Clarendon, 1991.

Bagehot, Walter. "Charles Dickens." *National Review* 7 (1858):458–86.

———. "The Waverley Novels." *National Review* 6 (1858):444–72.

Baker, Henry Barton. "Victor Hugo and Romanticism." *Temple Bar* 42 (1874):317–33.

Barry, William Francis. "Robert Louis Stevenson." *Quarterly Review* 180 (1894):324–53.

Bevington, Merle M. *The Saturday Review, 1855–1868: Representative Educated Opinion in Victorian England.* 1941. New York: AMS, 1966.

"The Bishop of Ripon on Novels." *Spectator* 61 (11 Aug. 1888):1091–92.

Bulwer Lytton, Sir Edward George, Lord Lytton. "Caxtoniana (Part XVI)." *Blackwood's Magazine* 93 (1863):545–60.

"Circumlocution *versus* Circumvention." *Saturday Review* Nov. 1856:649–50.

Collins, Philip, ed. *Dickens: The Critical Heritage.* London: Routledge, 1971.

Dickens, Charles. "Curious Misprint in the *Edinburgh Review.*" *Household Words* 1 Aug. 1857:97–100.

Edmond, Rowland, Baron Prothero. "*David Grieve.*" *Edinburgh Review* 175 (1892):518–40.

Eliot, George. Rev. of *The Shaving of Shagpat*, by George Meredith. *Leader* 5 Jan. 1856:15–17.

Ford, George. *Dickens and His Readers.* Princeton: Princeton UP, 1955.

Ford, Richard. "*Oliver Twist.*" *Quarterly Review* 64 (1839):83–102.

Graham, Kenneth. *English Criticism of the Novel 1865–1900.* Oxford: Clarendon, 1965.

Hayward, Abraham. "Thackeray's Writings." *Edinburgh Review* 87 (1848):46–67.

Hutton, Richard Holt. "Nathaniel Hawthorne." *National Review* 11 (1860):453–81.

Japp, A. H. "The Morality of Literary Art." *Contemporary Review* 5 (1867):161–89.

Kaminsky, Alice R. *George Henry Lewes as Literary Critic.* Syracuse: Syracuse UP, 1968.

Le Gallienne, Richard. "Grant Allen." *Fortnightly Review* os 72 (1899):1005–25.

Lewes, George Henry. "Dickens in Relation to Criticism." *Fortnightly Review* 17 (1872):141–54.

———. Journal X. 24 July 1856–31 March 1859. George Eliot Papers. Beinecke Library, Yale University, New Haven.

———. "Literature." *Leader* 4 July 1857:539–40.

———. "Literature," *Leader* 11 July 1857:664–65.

———. "Literature." *Leader* 18 July 1857:689–90.

———. "Literature." *Leader* 1 Aug. 1857:737–38.

———. Rev. of *Little Dorrit*, by Charles Dickens. *Leader* 27 June 1857:616–17.

————. "Mr. Charles Dickens and the 'Edinburgh Review.' " *Leader* 1 Aug. 1857:726–27.

————. "The Novels of Jane Austen." *Blackwood's Magazine* 86 (1859):99–113.

————. *The Principles of Success in Literature*. London: Walter Scott, n.d.

————. Rev. of *The Book of Snobs*, by W. M. Thackeray. *Morning Chronicle* 6 March 1848:3.

————. "Shakspeare's Critics: English and Foreign." *Edinburgh Review* 90 (1849):39–77.

"Lewes' Biographical History of Philosophy." *Saturday Review* 13 June 1857:552–53.

Mansel, Henry Longueville. "Sensation Novels." *Quarterly Review* 113 (1863): 481–514.

Masson, David. *British Novelists and Their Styles*. Cambridge: Macmillan, 1858.

Mulock, Diana. "To Novelists—and a Novelist." *Macmillan's Magazine* 3 (1861):441–48.

Northcote, James Spencer. Rev. of *Uncle Tom's Cabin*, by Harriet Beecher Stowe. *Rambler* 10 (1852):412–24.

Oliphant, Margaret. "Charles Dickens." *Blackwood's Magazine* 77 (1855):451–66.

Payronnet, La Baronne Caroline-Philipine-Elizabeth. "Victor Hugo's *Les Misérables*." *Edinburgh Review* 117 (1863):208–40.

Rev. of *Adam Bede*, by George Eliot. *London Quarterly Review* 16 (1861):301–07.

Rev. of *The Mildmayes: Or, The Clergyman's Secret: A Story of Twenty Year Age*. *Leader* 3 Jan. 1857:18.

Rev. of *Tess of the D'Urbervilles*, by Thomas Hardy. *Athenaeum* 9 Jan. 1892:49–50.

Rev. of *The Young Milliner*, by Mrs. Stone. *Athenaeum* 6 May 1843:437.

Ruskin, John. *Sesame and Lilies*. London: Allen, 1905. Vol. 18 of *The Works of John Ruskin*. Ed. E. T. Cook and Alexander Wedderburn.

Scott, George. "Charles Dickens." *Contemporary Review* 10 (1869):203–25.

Shaw, George Bernard. Foreword to *Great Expectations*, by Charles Dickens. Edinburgh: Limited Edition Club, 1937.

Simpson, Richard. "George Eliot's Novels." *Home and Foreign Review* 3 (1863):522–49. Rpt. in *George Eliot: The Critical Heritage*, ed. David Carrol. London: Barnes, 1971. 227.

Smith, K. J. M. *James Fitzjames Stephen: Portrait of a Victorian Rationalist.* Cambridge: Cambridge UP, 1988.

"Society in California." *Saturday Review* 6 Sept. 1856:410–11.

Stephen, James Fitzjames. "Curcumlocution." *Saturday Review* 6 June 1857:514–15.

———. "The Edinburgh Review and Modern Novelists." *Saturday Review* 18 July 1857:57–58.

———. "How to Do It." *Saturday Review* 27 June 1857:591–92.

———. "The Licence of Modern Novelists." *Edinburgh Review* 56 (1857):124–56.

———. "Light Literature and the *Saturday Review.*" *Saturday Review* 11 July 1857:34–35.

———. Rev. of *Little Dorrit,* by Charles Dickens. *Saturday Review* 4 July 1857:15–16.

———. Rev. of *Madame Bovary,* by Gustave Flaubert. *Saturday Review* 11 July 1857:40–41.

———. "Mr. Dickens." *Saturday Review* 8 May 1858:474–75.

———. "Mr. Dickens as a Politician." *Saturday Review* 3 Jan. 1857:8–9.

———. "Sentimentalism." *Cornhill Review* 10 (1864):65–75.

———. Rev. of *A Tale of Two Cities,* by Charles Dickens. *Saturday Review* 8 May 1859:741–43.

———. "A Word for Slavery." Rev. of *The Olive Branch: Or, White Oak Farm. Saturday Review* 4 July 1857:18–20.

Stephen, Leslie. "Hours in a Library (No. VII): Nathaniel Hawthorne." *Cornhill Magazine* 26 (1872):717–34.

Stevenson, Robert Louis. "Victor Hugo's Romances." *Cornhill Magazine* 30 (1874):179–94.

Stothert, James. "Catholic Novelists." *Rambler* 11 (1853):251–62.

———. "Duties and Responsibilities of Writers of Fiction." *Rambler* 9 (1852):477–83.

Swinburne, Algernon Charles. "Wilkie Collins." *Fortnightly Review* os 52 (1898):589–99.

"The Tory Press." *Saturday Review* 27 June 1857:586–87.

Turner, Charles Edward. "Tourgenieff's Novels as Interpreting the Political Movement in Russia." *Macmillan's Magazine* 45 (1882):471–86.

Wace, Horace. "*Robert Elsmere* and Christianity." *Quarterly Review* 167 (1888):273–302.

Inimitable Double Vision: Dickens, *Little Dorrit*, Photography, Film

Joss Lutz March

1: INTERPRETATION AND ADAPTATION

In 1987, working from a converted warehouse in London's run-down Docklands by the Dickensian name of Grice's Wharf, the little-known director Christine Edzard and Sands Films released an adaptation of Dickens's 1855–57 novel *Little Dorrit* that rivaled as few had thought film could do the convolutions and sheer length of its "un-cinematic" and sociocritical original. Her two-part film of *Little Dorrit* runs six hours—four times as long as a standard Hollywood movie. Part 1, *Nobody's Fault*, views the action from the point of view of diffident, middle-aged Arthur Clennam, just returned from twenty years' service to the family firm in China; part 2 is *Little Dorrit's Story*—the action retold from the perspective of the retiring seamstress he first glimpses in the shadows of his mother's crumbling house, the child of the Marshalsea debtors' prison.

Perhaps the first thing one needs to grasp about this gargantuan cinematic oddity is what Alec Guinness (who plays William Dorrit, her father and the "Father of the Marshalsea") calls the "ramshackle oddity" of the place the film was made (Malcolm 22), and the budget it was made on—only $9 million, about a tenth of the money Hollywood spent on *Robocop II* (1990). Sands Films' studio is almost as small as the budget, and it is unique. Cobbled together out of two warren-like warehouses, it houses a picture library, a model-shop for making miniature sets, a small pottery (which made all the pink Sèvres china that loads the speculator Mr. Merdle's dinner-table, too expensive to buy or rent), production offices (where a visitor finds herself sitting on Mrs. Merdle's chaise-longue—everything gets recycled here), two

239

sound stages, a canteen, a dressmaker's shop, and editing and projection suites. Everything, in fact, down to the only bricklayer employed full time by any studio in the world: Sands Films is a complete cottage industry. It is wholly owned by Edzard and her husband, Richard Goodwin, co-producer of *Little Dorrit*. They set up here fifteen years ago, and live over the shop: "Good films," says Goodwin, "are made because people are poor," and prepared to live "on the precipice of some dreadful financial abyss."[1]

Edzard was born in Paris in 1945 of a German painter father and a Polish-born painter mother. She studied economics in Paris, but gradually drifted toward theater. She served a kind of film apprenticeship as Franco Zeffirelli's assistant on *Romeo and Juliet* (1968), and created stage sets for the Hamburg and Welsh national operas before designing and co-scripting the ballet film *Tales of Beatrix Potter* (1971).

On one of my visits to Sands Films, in March 1990, I spent two hours watching Edzard shoot a one-minute breakfast-table scene for her latest film. She is a perfectionist, and the peculiar set-up of Sands Films allows her absolute artistic control over her films, as editor, designer, and sound person, and also director: it was easy to see why *Little Dorrit* took nine months to shoot (most films take two or three), let alone two and a half years for preproduction, and another nine months in the editing room. On that Monday morning, I saw her constructing a natural "opening" to her scene, placing a small girl so that for a second her shape would fall across the foreground, as she leaned forward, and then fall back to disclose the family at table. "Right—shall we?" she says quietly, to commence the next take. The dialogue is tightly timed, orchestrated. "Jonathan," she says to one actor, "I'm just wondering about your laugh at Derek's joke—perhaps too big?" "Well, I want to ingratiate myself," says Jonathan, "Does it sound false?" "Just titter a bit," she decides, "and leave the jam business until a little later." Derek Jacobi listens intently as she asks him to alter the inflection of his voice, or the precise moment at which to raise a morsel of congealing "prop" sausage to his mouth.

In Edzard's film of *Little Dorrit*, you will not find the moustachioed villain Rigaud-Blandois (whose sole act in the novel is to poison the dilettante artist Henry Gowan's dog, though he appears in no fewer than seven of the original illustrations, hovering vulture-like over the body of the story after his dramatic take-over of the opening chapter). Mrs. Clennam's twisted henchman, Flintwinch, not undeservedly, suffers his death-by-crushing instead; and his unwilling Italian sidekick Cavaletto, alias Mr. Baptist, remains trapped in the novel's pages. Nor will you find Flintwinch's twin brother. They have been swept away, like the melodramatic superstructure of which they were a part, and along with most of the overcrowded, "overdetermined" ending, with its multiple tentacles in the past (Dickens had to write it all down to help himself wrap up the novel). "I wanted to avoid the exaggerative, the melodramatic, and the sentimental," Edzard contends, "because they put a distance between the subject and the spectator." Thus the feeble flute-player Frederick Dorrit, too, fails to enjoy his moment center-stage, dying of grief by his brother William's deathbed: insignificant to the last in Edzard's film, he fades away offscreen, unseen. We don't see anybody meet anybody else in the Great St. Bernard Monastery or Marseilles, which provide Dickens with atmospheric settings for mid-action and opening tableaux; Gowan disappears with Minnie, the picture-perfect beauty whom Clennam imagines himself in love with for much of the novel, after their ill-starred marriage; the Dorrit family's peregrinations across Europe upon their sudden accession to wealth are cut down, lest we get lost among the multiple locations; Clennam first bumps into Meagles the businessman and Daniel Doyce the inventor in the hallway of the Circumlocution Office—reasonable chance, not narrative machinations, engenders friendship.

Edzard's film, then, seeks to clarify the main romantic storyline, throws more emphasis on the Marshalsea and its "Father" (who gets a much more impressive death scene), roots itself in the "roaring streets" of Dickens' London—at about the time Dickens was writing the novel, not at the time he sets it, a generation before—and embraces what has been called the stationary or plot-less quality of *Little Dorrit*: "plot" does not have for modern European filmmakers the overwhelming importance it once had for Classical Hollywood Cinema. The self-tormentor Miss Wade too has vanished, with her story-within-a-story, obliquely and analogically related to the novel's central story, and difficult to film; with her departs the Meagles' maid, Tattycoram, whose predisposition to passion she inflames. Innocuous Mrs. Meagles, Edzard's assistant Olivier Stockman told me, was killed off to throw a greater emphasis on the father-daughter relationship of Meagles and Minnie ("Pet"), which now more closely parallels that between Dorrit and his daughter. Minnie's dead twin sister suffered a second death in a general reaction against siblings and doublings. The varnishing services of Mrs. General, whose favors as a chaperone and social secretary Dorrit thinks himself lucky to overpay, are dispensed with. A somewhat brutal decision to kill Daniel Doyce, Clennam's partner, meanwhile, was taken, Olivier Stockman remarked, to make his sense of irretrievable betrayal more cruelly final.

Only a very few changes were made late in the day, after shooting. Edzard found the scene between Mrs. Clennam and Pancks, the big-hearted rent-collector whose persistence uncovers Dorrit's inheritance and unbars his prison, played like a "monosyllabic stand-off"—and cut it. Then, feeling there was "too much of the Circumlocution Office" in the second half of part 1, Edzard moved back Pancks's showdown with his proprietor, Mr. Casby, a wolf in philantropist's clothing (it would otherwise have occurred even earlier than it does).

Inevitably, these changes were not to every critic's taste, particularly the academic critic with a vested interest in the Dickens text: Gary Wills's review in the *New York Review of Books* is one long academic lament for murdered characters, Grahame Smith's article in *Yearbook of English Studies* an excellent hatchet job driven by the author's urge himself to (re)film the novel. But changes had, no less inevitably, to be made. To translate from one medium to another is not as simple as translating from English to French (and even that is far from "simple"). Doting fidelity to a novel or a play is an overvalued virtue: at worst it produces unfilmic and frigidly respectful films. Besides, what does "faithfulness" mean? Coppola's *Apocalypse Now* (1979) is perhaps a better "translation" of Joseph Conrad's *Heart of Darkness* even than Orson Welles's once-planned adaptation might have been.

Film must substitute for much of the indirect narration of the novel the direct narration of action and dialogue: Dickens' introduction of the newly imprisoned Dorrit as "a very amiable and very helpless middle-aged gentleman, who was going out again directly" (Dickens 98) must become a scene in which he demonstrates his limpness, and Bob the turnkey delivers the judgment "He'll never get out." And film must therefore somehow "settle," although Dickens tells us this "would be very hard to [do]," the question of "At what period in her early life the little creature began to perceive that it was not the habit of all the world to live locked up" (108). We cannot be told about an atmosphere: so, to express the distance that opens up between Little Dorrit and her father in their Italian days of riches, we must see her glide into his room and perch upon his bed, in Edzard's film, only to be told to move, because "someone might come in."

Film can be intolerant of ambiguity and disorder, and Edzard's film in particular often seems intent on smoothing out every fascinating deviance in Dickens' text, or turning the exultantly chaotic—at worst—into the tamed, the near complacent. This is one critical charge against her adaptatin that sticks. The letters "D.N.F."—engraved in Clennam's father's watch—mean only one thing in Edzard's *Little Dorrit*; Arthur becomes less of the father-replacement who magically materializes in the same old Marshalsea prison room, upon his own financial collapse, and Little Dorrit much less "little," much less "my child"—the disturbing confusion of sexual and familial affection in Dickens' text diminishes. More importantly, what Elaine Showalter has identified as the doubling of characters by dark "shadows" who voice and act out their thwarted desires—Rigaud-Blandois Clennam's urge to turn on his mother, Mr. F's Aunt (whose aggressive non sequiturs pepper the dialogue) fat Flora Finching's impulse to fight her rejection by her one-time suitor, Clennam—is lost in Edzard's film, partly because she strips the novel of its melodramatic superstructure, partly because her personal emphasis is on the subtly naturalistic revelation of character across the six hours of her film—a type of psychologizing fundamentally different in kind to Dickens' which works through twinnings and displacements. (Film, which in its early years thrived on the doppelgängers of *The Student of Prague* [1913, remade 1925] or *Dr. Jekyll and Mr. Hyde* [1886], the most-filmed novel in cinema history, has stumbled over Dickens' dark doublings: David Lean similarly cut Pip's murderous double Orlick out of his *Great Expectations* [1946].) Edzard's *Little Dorrit* is dark enough, but not so dark as Dickens'.

2: "MAGIC DEMOCRACY": THE DICKENS CHARACTER AND DICKENSIAN DIALOGUE

Yet much remains unaltered. Edzard's leisurely pacing and breadth of canvas were hailed by David Robinson in *The Times* as pioneering an "original" cinematic form that works through small incidents rather than suspense and surprise. But if Dickens is the most cinematic of novelists, Edzard is the most writerly of filmmakers. As Robinson himself added, her *Little Dorrit* has the "patient episodic flow of a novel" (Fuller 28). What is least changed in this film, as in any Dickens film, are the characters that seem to enjoy, like the gods and goblins of mythology, a life independent of their creator or the texts that contain them (they hang over the edges of the plots, you might say). One testimonial to the impact of Edzard's *Little Dorrit* on its first release was the Royal photographer Lord Snowdon's production of a series of twenty postcard-portraits of characters from the film: these in their turn testify to the existence of Dickens' creations in a manner curiously detached even from the newest film in which they have been incarnated—the captions at bottom of each card, we notice, give the characters' but not the actors' names ("Frederick Dorrit in *Little Dorrit*," and so on). His cards take their place in a long line. Every major Victorian illustrator at one time turned his hand to Dickens, and every one inflected each character anew: the *Punch* contributor Frederick Barnard infuses into his portrait of Little Dorrit the romanticism of late century, and draws liberally on the stylistic conventions that governed innumerable Victorian representations of the toiling, reflective seamstress (fig. 1). Leading late Victorian actors, in the first days of the postcard, liked to have themselves taken in costume as every conceivable Dickens character—with Fagin, and the opportunity he offered for hamming, perhaps the favorite. The great Beerbohm Tree had himself taken in the role, while the ambitious thespian Bransby Williams posed for his portrait in costume as both Fagin and Bill Sykes (fig. 2). Dickens' characteristic association of people with objects is a mode of characterization that translates smoothly into film, with its (necessary) reliance on the visual motif, the symbol that is also part of the physical reality of the film: in Edzard's adaptation, Little Dorrit's "tunnel-vision" bonnet, as one reviewer dubbed it (Winn 27); or the quill that inks bespectacled Arthur Clennam's fingers (fig. 3). Early films were often nothing but such character-vignettes as Dickens offered in abundance: one of the earliest preserved by the British National Film Library is R. W. Paul's *Mr. Pecksniff Fetches the Doctor* (1903). Dickens characters were addictive, like nicotine: smokers could collect a series of Dickens cigarette cards—Arthur Rowe, the reclusive hero of Graham Greene's *The Ministry of Fear*, has a "complete set" (Greene 14). They prominently featured precisely the characters a melodramatic and "stagey" adaptation would pull from the pack: *Little Dorrit*'s chosen representatives in a Player's card-series of 1912, for example, were the pompous grotesque Tite Barnacle and "Patriarch" Casby (fig. 4), together, inevitably, with the moustachioed villain Rigaud-Blandois.

But more, just as Edzard asks of her cinema audience the right of directorial interpretation that the director of the Royal Shakespeare Company's *Nicholas Nickleby* enjoyed, or that Verdi exploited when he turned *Othello* into opera, so each member of her cast prefers his right to "his" Dorrit, or "her" Flora Finching. The casting of every role in a film affects the inflection of that role, above all when the actor is a star. The inspired choice of W. C. Fields, in the splendid 1935 Hollywood production of *David Copperfield*, laid down a foundation of irony under Mr. Micawber's whimsical optimism. But the traditions and signifying properties of stage stars are a little different. The challenge for stage acting has always been to assume the role—to *become* Fagin, say, to *create* Bill Sykes. This was the challenge for Dickens himself, whether acting out a scene before the mirror, as he used to do while he was writing, or impersonating his own characters (above all, Fagin, Bill, and Nancy) on stage toward the end of his life (fig. 5). And it is out of these stage traditions that Christine Edzard and a great many of her cast come: the Shakespearean actor Derek Jacobi as Arthur Clennam, for example, or the chameleon Alec Guinness as William Dorrit (fig. 6), who followed his screen debut as Herbert Pocket in David Lean's *Great Expectations* (1946) with a controversial portrayal of Fagin in the same director's *Oliver Twist* two years later, and (courtesy of trick photography) undertook no fewer than eight roles in the British comedy classic of 1949, *Kind Hearts and Coronets.* "The characters in Dickens are not so much caricatures as distortions of reality," Edzard told a British interviewer, "real [human] life compressed" in journalistic shorthand (Fuller 30): she took pains in this film to avoid what has become almost a film and stage tradition of *over*-acting up to their larger-than-life quality. Her actors wear no makeup. They are not allowed to buttonhole the camera in close-up. Most drifted in to talk about being in the film with no particular parts in mind, and slipped into place. The children came from local East End schools (the little girl who plays Amy Dorrit as a small child, yearning to unlock the mysteries of print, really couldn't read or write).

What also is least touched by the translation from page to screen are the words in these characters' mouths. Dickens, said all the filmmakers I talked to, "is a gift to actors."[2] His dialogue loses its linguistic context—the financial grounding of Dorrit's euphemistic promise, in his riches, say, to "remember" everyone (the term is changed, to my regret, to "reward" in Edzard's film)—but it gains the resonance of performance: Pip Torrens as Henry Gowan calling himself, to his rival Arthur's face, at his wedding, a "disappointed man"; Joan Greenwood as Mrs. Clennam reciting the horrors of Biblical plagues in a voice in which one can almost hear a hungry mouth salivating. It would be worth sitting through six hours of positive tedium to hear Alec Guinness as Dorrit Frenchifying his genteel thanks as he pockets another handout—"much *obleeged*"—or delivering his verdict upon Old Nandy the workhouse pensioner—"Spirit broken and gone"—and turning back upon the threshold to enunciate with relish a revising afterthought—"pulverised."

3: FILMING TONE: THE "SLAPBAG RESTAURANT" SCENE

Toward the end of part 1 of Edzard's film occurs a two-and-a-half-minute scene between Clennam and Pancks, set in the "Slapbang" restaurant. It has several functions to serve. In it, Edzard must convey story information—that time has passed, that the Dorrits are still in Italy; she must provide a natural means of introducing the subject in Italy; she must provide a natural means of introducing the subject of Merdle and money-mania; she must forward the characterization of Pancks and Clennam, and keep before us the one's building obsession with Casby, his "Proprietor," and the other's much more unconscious concern with Little Dorrit; and she wants to realize a fragment of forgotten history and expose her audience to the experience of a Victorian chop-shop in all its steamy, bustling actuality. The marvelous economy of film, when all four of its dimensions—camerawork, *mise en scène*, editing, and sound—come together in a unified whole yet can each further a different end, allows her, I think, to do all of this at once. This is the scene as it is transcribed in Edzard's post-production Release Script:

ACTION	*DIALOGUE*
DOYCE AND CLENNAM OFFICE	*ARTHUR:*
ARTHUR puts on his coat	Come, come, Mr Pancks. Come and dine with me. My partner's working late tonight. We'll go to the slap-bang place round the corner, eh? Come on, Mr Pancks.
The two exit R	
INTERIOR RESTAURANT	
CLOSE-UP Plate of food being placed on table	*WAITRESS:* Two nice slices . . .
CLOSE-UP Plate of food being placed on table	*WAITRESS:* . . . from the joint . . .
MEDIUM CLOSE SHOT WAITRESS AND PANCKS	*WAITRESS:* . . . of beef and gravy.
MEDIUM SHOT PANCKS and ARTHUR seated opposite each other	*PANCKS:* He says to me . . . you must squeeze them, . . . squeeze them.
MEDIUM CLOSE SHOT over PANCKS favouring ARTHUR	*PANCKS:* Don't I squeeze them, says I? What else am I made for?
MEDIUM SHOT over ARTHUR favouring PANCKS	*PANCKS (imitating Casby):* You're made for nothing else, Mr Pancks, . . . you're paid to do your duty. You're paid to squeeze and you must squeeze to pay.

WIDE ANGLE across crowded
  restaurant. PANCKS and ARTHUR
  seated centre

MALE DINER:
And more portions of cabbage . . .

WAITRESS:
Yes, Mr Poppedou.

MEDIUM SHOT Two male diners

MAN # 1:
Yes, and just as he was about to mount
  the steps, the doorman greeted him,
  and shouted in his loudest voice:
  "Twopence, please!"

MEDIUM SHOT over ARTHUR
  favouring PANCKS

PANCKS:
How can I squeeze them, Mr Clennam,
  if they're dry? They haven't got any
  money!

MALE VOICE (out of shot):
Hey, more wine, Polly!

PANCKS:
They say to me they haven't got it.

MEDIUM CLOSE SHOT over PANCKS
  favouring ARTHUR

PANCKS:
They say to me, if we had it, we'd gladly
  pay. If they had it . . .

ARTHUR notices something

WIDE ANGLE across restaurant to
  kitchen area,
LITTLE GIRL at servery

PANCKS (out of shot):
If they were Merdle . . .

MEDIUM CLOSE SHOT
LITTLE GIRL at the servery. She places
  her change in her purse

PANCKS (out of shot):
. . . they's pay of course . . .

MUSIC

WIDE ANGLE across restaurant, past
  men at bar, to LITTLE GIRL taking
  dinner outside R

MUSIC continues and fades

MEDIUM CLOSE SHOT over PANCKS
  favouring ARTHUR

PANCKS:
They say to me . . .

MEDIUM SHOT over ARTHUR favouring PANCKS	PANCKS: . . . if *you* were Mr Merdle, it would be better still . . . for all parties. You wouldn't have to worry at all. You'd be easier in your mind. That's what they say. Maybe. *MALE DINER (out of shot):* Polly, more wine, please! PANCKS: I'm looking into it. I say, Mr. Clennam . . .
MEDIUM CLOSE SHOT over ARTHUR favouring PANCKS	PANCKS: . . . you aren't listening. ARTHUR: Oh, I . . . I do beg your pardon, Mr Pancks. I was . . . thinking about Little—about Miss Dorrit. PANCKS: Little Miss Dorrit? ARTHUR: I was wondering how she is in her new life. PANCKS: You know, I've heard . . . her sister's quite often . . .
MEDIUM CLOSE SHOT over ARTHUR favouring PANCKS	PANCKS: . . . to be seen with the great Merdle's stepson. Isn't it curious how this Merdle turns up everywhere?
WIDE ANGLE across restaurant—general activity	WOMAN'S VOICE OVER: I've heard it reported, Ma'am, that it was Mr Merdle that took it and it's not to be expected that he should lose by it, . . .
EXTERIOR GROCER'S SHOP WIDE ANGLE DOYCE and WOMEN outside shop	WOMAN'S VOICE OVER: . . . his ways being, as you might say, paved with gold. (Continues unintelligibly.) I was just saying to

Mrs Kidgerbury here that according to
what we was told . . .

BLEEDING HEART YARD MEDIUM
SHOT ARTHUR entering yard

Small actions are film's primary mode of creating character: the bit-player
Mr. Wobbler and his fellow clerk at the Circumlocution Office, for example,
who are summed up in the one's dribbling marmalade on to the documents
on his desk and the other's mindless poking of holes in a piece of paper
(inspired refinements on the "stage business" they're given in the text [fig.
7]). What most characterizes Pancks in this scene is what is not recorded in
the script's dry record—his eating habits: he stabs his food, jerks his knife
and fork with prickly precision. It is interesting to see how large his role
looms here, and in the film as a whole—as opposed, say, to Mrs. Clennam's
nervous old maid-servant Affery, once the *raison d'être* for her "dreams"
(acually not dreams at all), Flintwinch's twin, is gone. Pancks, however,
remains responsible for what now become the main actions of the film's plot:
the retrieval of Dorrit's fortunes (he hunts down the inheritance), and the
collapse of Arthur's (he gives him the fatal speculator's tip that leads to his
ruin during the Merdle crash). He is necessary to the plot, and so Edzard can
allow him to develop into still more of a friend to a lonely man than the
Pancks of the text. His roles in the Slapbang Restaurant scene are to supply
the necessary story information—which also locates us in time—and to trigger
the Merdle theme: money "grubber" that he is, he is the natural choice of
character to do it.

In terms of *mise en scène*, Edzard's restaurant is a feast of accurate period
detail (fig. 8)—sputtering gas-lighting, brown settles, hats on the hooks, dish
covers, clay pipes, steam in the atmosphere, and bulbous-bottomed wine
bottles (our Victorian ancestors regularly tossed off a bottle of claret with
dinner: they needed bottles that didn't fall over as easily as ours do).

But there is, of course, no "Slapbang Restaurant" in *Little Dorrit* as
Dickens wrote it, any more than there exists the dingy chop house in which
we meet Arthur in the first scene of Edzard's film (fig. 9). Nevertheless, it
exists in other Dickens novels, if not in name: there Mr. Guppy entertains
his friends (and Phiz depicts him doing so) in *Bleak House*, for example (fig.
10); and it is in the Slapbang Restaurant that "Boz" and Cruikshank picture
the thin man (in "Thoughts about People" in the *Sketches*) reading the communal newspaper over supper (balancing it against the water-bottle), as we
see the diner next to Pancks do in Edzard's scene (fig. 11). Her restaurant is

suggested, too, in the shop with steamed-up windows to which feeble Frederick Dorrit slopes off at dinner-time (283). The needs of Edzard's plot determine the need for this "inauthentic" scene, but the materials she quarries for
it are all authentic: not only does one suspect, watching this film, that every
bit player has read the novel, but that Edzard has read all of Dickens' novels.
From *Pickwick*, for example, she snaps up the name of "Dobson and Fogg,
Solicitors," and from *The Old Curiosity Shop* the law firm "Samson and
Samson," all members of which descend like vultures when Arthur goes
bust.

Which brings us back to characters. The Dickens world bursts with them.
It is, Vladimir Nabokov once said, a "magic democracy"—one fundamental
reason, some would argue, for the popularity of Dickens in a Western cinema
tradition that itself "extoll[s] the importance of individuals within a massive
society" (Caramagno 96). Every one you meet could at some point step
center-stage and do his "turn." This is evident in Phiz's illustration of the
Dorrit brothers in the Marshalsea Yard (fig. 12). We notice at once the seedy
types to the far left, the more upper-class "Collegian" in his "dressing
gown" (270), and the anxious lower-class family group on the right. It is
equally evident in this scene: as she hands Pancks and Clennam their "Two
nice slices from the joint" the face of the chirpy waitress (Polly) dominates
the frame; and the voice in which she delivers her one line rings with self-
assured relish. It is evident most of all in each of the faces we see in the
crowded restaurant, as we repeatedly survey it in wide-angle shot, or glimpse
bits of the bodies crammed in to the settles next to Pancks and Arthur Clennam. The faces of anonymous men and women at home in their own worlds
people the film, because Edzard took the unprecedented steps not merely of
persuading well-respected actors to undertake small roles for small fees in
the cause of Dickens and British cinema (there are 242 speaking parts in the
film—"such a nonchalant array of the cream of British actors as to verge on
the indecent" [Benson 1]), but also of personally casting every one of the
extras—the directorial equivalent of granting life, as Dickens does, to everyone from the spider-like doorman at the theater where Fanny works (278), to
the dancing master from whom she learned her trade. And Edzard
allows—even foregrounds—exactly the kind of flavorful Dickensian excess
that gets cut in films that run the prescribed ninety minutes of commercial
cinema. For the Dickens world is a world in which stories, as much as
characters, multiply and proliferate—"a crowded, many-voiced, anonymous
world," as Raymond Williams puts it, "of jokes, stories, rumours, songs,
shouts, banners, greetings, idioms, addresses" (15). Hence here the first

diner's story about the doorman and his "twopence, please!" which we half-hear in this scene, or the Circumlocution Office clerk's story of the "inestimable" dog.

But to appreciate fully the artistry of the Slapbang Restaurant scene, and the problematics of film adaptation, we should consider this question: How can you say in film—"he is thinking of Little Dorrit"? It is difficult. Film imagery works differently to the metaphor and simile of the novel because film itself is not a figurative but an actual language—if we can consider it a "language" at all. So it has been said that if novelists sometimes face the problem of making the significant somehow visible, filmmakers often find themselves trying to make the visible significant. Which is where the little girl in this scene comes in, collecting her father's dinner, and carefully drawing the strings of her purse. We do not have the Marseilles Gaoler's songbird daughter in Edzard's film (we cannot, since she has thrown out the first chapter and torn down the prison), but we do have this other child-woman, to bring Little Dorrit to mind, so that we do not even need Arthur to tell us, as he tells Pancks, "I'm thinking about Little Dorrit." And the intensity of his thoughts is signaled in the jump from long shot to medium close-up as he (and we) look at the child—camera distance is determined not by his distance from her (he does not move) but by the emotional attention with which he regards her.

What is passing in Clennam's mind is clear also from the subjective use of sound in this scene. We can hear Pancks getting more and more steamed up about Casby, as he rattles through his complaints, but—like Arthur—we don't really hear the words (and we don't need to, since Pancks is repeating himself); nor do we catch the punchline to the anonymous diner's story about the doorman—all we get is the laughter that follows it. As Arthur slips into reverie of Little Dorrit, the purely emotive strains of Verdi, entering from outside the world of the action, drown the sounds of the restaurant, creating a privacy of intimacy in his thoughts. Interiority in this scene is a function of sound as well as image.

In short, the Slapbang Restaurant scene demonstrates, I think, that what matters most in adaptation is the tone of the work: if that is lost, if the novelist's viewpoint has not been been absorbed into the emotional blood of the film, then the work is lost. In this scene that Dickens never wrote, Edzard finds visual and aural equivalents for words he did write and she had to cut: its apparent distance from Dickens' *Little Dorrit* actually conceals an extraordinary sensitivity to the text.

4: POINT OF VIEW AND THE TWO-PART FILM

The overwhelming question about Edzard's *Little Dorrit*, of course, is why she chose to make *two* three-hour feature films, and at what stage in the production process that decision was made. The *New York Times* declared the two-part format "maddening," burdensome, and "exhausting"—a modernist distortion of Dickens' novel (Canby 11). Another American reviewer, like many of his countrymen frazzled beyond endurance by the leisurely pacing of part 1 (the British, by contrast, preferred its long-drawn-out miseries and reflective gloom to the brisker storytelling of part 2), called it a "leaden" and "comatose" "behemoth" of a production (Edelstein 29). We need to consider point of view, and the sheer length of the film.

Edzard's *Little Dorrit* was conceived, from the start, for theatrical distribution, not for television: the unwary viewer does not find himself watching eight or thirteen episodes revamped into two gargantuan portions. In opting for treating that part of the novel that she films at comfortable length, she was gambling on a change in our tastes. TV mini-series and phenomena like the Royal Shakespeare Company's eight-hour *Nicholas Nickleby* have accustomed us to getting as near as damn it the whole novel, not condensed versions or slices (fig. 13). When *Little Dorrit* is the novel in question, that means a lot of novel—a veritable "Dickensathon." Yet in any adaptation, some things have to go. The director Ross Devenish grieved, he told me, over cutting Mrs. Jellaby from his *Bleak House* (1985) for the BBC, but his eight hours of television time were just not enough. Once the subplots and melodramatic superstructure of *Little Dorrit* were dropped, her six hours of film allow Edzard to retain instead Dickens' proliferating minor characters and their multiplying stories, and with them the flavor of his world: one can imagine her seconding George Orwell's verdict on Dickens—"rotten architecture, but wonderful gargoyles"—and scripting accordingly (Orwell 447). Whether her gamble works I think remains a matter of taste, and of our ability to override our Hollywood-bred predilictions for fast action and plot interest.

Edzard's *Little Dorrit* was also, most importantly, from the first conceived as a two-part film. (At one point she even considered a third part: it takes a reader with a strong sense of structure to guess that it would have adopted the point of view of Young John Chivery, but the guess once hazarded seems well justified.) What determined Edzard's decision was her feeling that the difference in point of view between Arthur Clennam and Amy Dorrit was sufficiently meaningful to demand such a structuring, that the material could tolerate it, and that it would allow for effects and explorations worth making both for the sake of the book and for the sake of film art: to those critics who charged that part 2 simply "retold" the story Edzard even retorts—"It's not the same story at all. It's two stories which cross each other at certain points." A very few films have experimented with the retelling of the action from another character's point of view—Hitchcock's *Vertigo* (1958) is one famous case, Alain Resnais' *Hiroshima, Mon Amour* (1959) and *Last Year at Marienbad* (1961) a moving second and a mysterious third—but none ever to this degree, and at this sustained length. (In 1991 Paramount Pictures attempted to cash in on the success of Edzard's two-part *Dorrit* with *He Said, She Said*—"the true story of love . . . both versions"—adding, as an extra novelty, two directors, a he and a she.)

Of course, these two perspectives, and many others, are there in the text; and only a few years before, in *Bleak House*, Dickens had experimented with interweaving two completely separate narratives. To talk about *Little Dorrit* and film is inevitably also to talk about point of view and structure in Dickens' work. Edzard's decision on a two-part film to some degree reflects his efforts, in a medium that was a long way from moving narrative forward upon the waves of stream-of-consciousness, at crucial moments to share the emotions and viewpoint of, say, Arthur Clennam (who is obliged instead to soliloquize), or Mrs. Clennam (who "expresses herself" at interminable length), Young John Chivery (the composer of epitaphs), Affery the dreamer, even Merdle's Physician, and—of course—Little Dorrit herself (whose curious letters to Arthur occupy two whole chapters of book 2). Miss Wade (who conveniently hands over her manuscript "History of a Self-Tormentor") is the vehicle of Dickens' exploration of the paranoid limits of subjective perception; Ferdinand, the "sprightly Barnacle" of the Circumlocution Office, is the unwitting spokesman of an officialdom adrift from reality: " 'Regard our place from the point of view that we only ask you to leave us alone,' " he tells Clennam, " 'and we are as capital a Department as you'll find anywhere' " (804).

But while Dickens was clearly much concerned with subjective experience and its limits, he kept some distance from the position that writers like Robert Browning took a decade later: in his great twelve-part poem *The Ring and the Book* nine characters tell and retell the same story of a love-death triangle. Point of view stops short of being the dominant structural principle in *Little Dorrit*, even though it interplays with what Dickens calls "the destined interweaving" of the parallel stories of Clennam and Little Dorrit (140)—a process which plays off, for example, treatment of Arthur's infatuation with Pet

Meagles against seriocomic handling of John Chivery's adoration of Little Dorrit, switching back and forth from one to the other, in time honored multiplot-novel fashion.

Rather, Dickens' chosen structuring device in *Little Dorrit* was determined by thematics. Late in the day he made the decision to "overwhelm the [Dorrit] family with wealth," and from this sprang his division of the novel into its two books, "Poverty" and "Riches."[3] But for Edzard the practical film-maker, there were problems with this thematic division: in terms of scenes, locations, and character, "the novel falls in half in the middle," she said. Dickens' structure would not work on film, any more than would, say, the whole chapters of *Little Dorrit* that are controlled by metaphors, like that in which Arthur catches Merdle-speculation disease. What Edzard wants to deliver is the interior Dickens ("Dickens as Chekhov," sniffed Richard Corliss in *Time* magazine [92]), and the romantic Dickens. Her part 1 poses questions, and leaves Arthur Clennam in the lurch: part 2 offers answers, above all to Arthur.

How does this work, in practical terms? Partly it is a question of angling and balancing the two parts: in Edzard's film, not only does Arthur Clennam's story become the detective investigation into Little Dorrit's story that Dickens suggests, but part 2 becomes also her journey into his life. It is a matter of distributing material: the Merdles are only mentioned in part 1, because Clennam has no direct contact with them; Mr. Meagles fades out of part 2, because Little Dorrit has hardly heard of him; the Pancks-Casby showdown and Arthur's bankruptcy are the climaxes of part 1; Dorrit's accession to fortune and his breakdown at the Merdles' dinner table the high spots of part 2. A few scenes occur in their entirety in both parts of the film: the tea party in Dorrit's Marshalsea room, for example.

The question of point of view is for another thing a matter of camera placement and angle: Clennam watches the Dorrit Processional departing from the Marshalsea from the Yard (fig. 14), for example, whereas Little Dorrit looks down upon it from her room above the lock, necessitating a high-angle shot (fig. 15). It is also a question of whether certain shots are taken at all: in part 2 of the film, we see Little Dorrit blench when Clennam tells her how he has loved Minnie Meagles; in part 1, so oblivious to her pain is unwary Arthur, that no reaction shot lets us see how she takes the news at all. But there are far more subtle and unusual techniques afoot in this film: Edzard's film moves far beyond the crudity of the unremitting subjective "camera eye" technique that turned the 1946 detective thriller *The Lady in the Lake* into a stillborn curiosity, for example, and only once has recourse to film's point-of-view technique of last resource, the voice-over, and that briefly, when Arthur "hears" a fragment of her letter to him read in Little Dorrit's voice (the same letter that we see her sitting down to write in part 2, when the opening formula, "Dear Mr Clennam," turns into a subdued litany of affection).

Most importantly, there is the almost subliminal effect of adjustments to the *mise en scène.* The Marshalsea room we see in *Little Dorrit's Story* is literally bigger and brighter than the room we saw in *Nobody's Fault*—it has contained more experience, it is viewed with affection: the walls of the set have been bodily moved out by several feet; the set has been repainted and redressed in slightly brighter colors; potted plants blossom (fig.16); Dorrit's bare chair grows a cover, and his dressing gown sprouts tendrils of embroidery; and when Little Dorrit stands up and moves around in it, the ceiling is not visible in the frame only six inches above her head (whereas it bears down upon Clennam as if about to crush him). The film animates and illustrates Dorrit's hopeful words of welcome to new inmates of the Marshalsea: " "The space is limited, . . . but you will find it apparently grow larger after a time" (708). The two points of view produce an image of a place and a time in 3-D depth—curiously like the Victorian stereoscope.

We can best see how Edzard's point-of-view structuring works by looking in a little more detail at one of the few scenes that occur in their entirety in both parts of the film. Let us take Little Dorrit's midnight visit to Clennam's lodgings, chapter 14 of book 1 in the novel, which Dickens prefaces with a sentence that testifies even in its slight awkwardness to the newness of what he is doing, and which Edzard uses to close part 1 and open part 2 of her film: "This history must sometimes see with Little Dorrit's eyes" (208).

Like all the scenes that occur twice in the two parts of the film, these two different versions of Little Dorrit's visit were shot on consecutive days, to help the actors. But no two shots are exactly the same between the two versions: part 2 dwells more, with Little Dorrit, on Arthur's face; part 1 seeks less intimacy. But it is the differences in script and *mise en scène* that strike one most. The next sentence of chapter 14 gives us our clue: "Little Dorrit looked . . . timidly . . . into a dim room, which seemed a spacious one to her, and grandly furnished" (208). So in Edzard's part 2 she perceives a huge room illuminated by comfortable firelight. But in her part 1, Clennam had poked, embarassed, at his feeble fire, in a smaller room, holding a newspaper over the fireplace to help it draw, in time-honored makeshift British fashion. The concern with the fire was a cloak for his concern that Little Dorrit should be out alone late on a cold night. She, meanwhile, in part 2 is wary not to make herself seem pitiful, and thereby throw on her father any suspicion of neglect: in her half of the film, she hastily draws in her feet to hide her shoes when Clennam remarks "And your shoes are so thin!"

Just before Little Dorrit arrived, in part 1, Clennam had been struggling clumsily to open a wine-bottle, and sprayed himself in the face; in part 2, Little Dorrit finds him not mopping his cheeks but reading in his chair, the picture of a gentleman at his ease. Each of these two shy people remembers different embarassments and inadequacies. For the Arthur of part 1 this scene is his first meeting with Maggy, Little Dorrit's oversized retarded friend: in part 1, he stands by disconcertedly as she stuffs her basket with every cake on the plate he holds out; Little Dorrit, who is accustomed to her, notices only that she accepts one slice of bread (not cake)—in part 2, we do not even cut to a shot of Maggy when Little Dorrit introduces her. And each recalls different moments of tenderness or pleasantness—Arthur, his wonder that Little Dorrit seems to appear at his uttering of her name (as she does in the novel, and as she will do at the very end of the film), as if summoned from the disturbed dream her knock interrupts; Little Dorrit his gentleness, and her own excitement at her first night away from "home." She recalls, too, in part 2, that she told him one of the truths of her existence—"I could never have been of any use, if I had not pretended a little" (211)—and told it, too, in a voice that is perceptibly louder and more merry than the voice Clennam heard in part 1. The two versions of the scene, then, contradict and comple- ment each other, each trading on the illusions of "presence" and veracity that film creates (and we shall discuss later): the allotting of different scraps of dialogue exclusively to one or the other makes not only for a sharpenng of point of view, and the minimalizing of repetition, but for a more dynamic interchange between the two parts of the film. Edzard's "twice-told tale," as one reviewer remarked, "becomes an open-ended investigation of ambiguity, the relative authority of memory and experience" (Winn 27), an exploration on its own filmic terms of the "ambiguous edge," as Edzard puts it, "to [Dickens'] own view of the people he invents."

5: DICKENS IN THE FOUR DIMENSIONS OF FILM

Of the dimensions of film that create the whole—*mise en scène*, cam- erawork, editing, sound—sound is perhaps the most critically neglected. It would be a great mistake to ignore it in the case of Edzard's *Little Dorrit*. On the soundtrack we hear multiple layers of noise—dialogue, birdsong, buzzing flies, distant dog barks, the hiss of steam machinery at the Doyce and Clennam works, the ticking of clocks, the sounding of bells, the over-loud chink-chink-chink of money, scuffling footsteps, the roar of traffic, street-vendors' cries, the rustle of leaves, the rustle of bedclothes, sounds of neighbors seeping through thin partition walls, the haunting restless noises that echo through the Marshalsea, the sound of a bottle smashing in the Yard as Clennam takes in the truth John Chivery tells him, that Little Dorrit has loved him all along. The film relies for much of its emotional impact on sound: our sense of finality after the wedding of Minnie Meagles to Gowan, for example, is signaled in the abrupt cutting off of a song; the emotional burden of Mrs. Clennam's fierce religion is captured in the sound of her monstrous dusty tome of a Bible thudding on her lap. Dickens' use of the folk song "Compagnon de la Majolaine" as a recurring aural motif helps pave the way for the expressive use of snatches of music in Edzard's film, or the repetition of key phrases, like Casby's *bon mot*, "you are paid to squeeze, and must squeeze to pay" (866).

Above all the film relies on music—Minnie Meagles playing the piano, Frederick Dorrit his doleful clarinet, a violin striking up in Bleeding Heart Yard, but above all the music of Giuseppe Verdi. The film theorist Christian Metz has said that the role of music in film is "to make more explicit, not a dramatic fact, but an audio-visual *rhythm*" (metz 55); as the great pre-talkies melodramas like Griffith's *Broken Blossoms* (1919) can still demonstrate, in the teeth of our "modern" resistance to the genre, accompanying music can have a visceral, emotional impact that meshes us into the film. Edzard's script sticks remarkably close to Dickens' dialogue. But one element is noticeably absent: coy beatings about the bush, proliferating sentimental tags like "my poor child," tearful prayers and thanks that to our ears smack of religiosity. Yet Edzard's *Little Dorrit* feels very much still like a romantic and emotional story. The reason why is that the sentiment has not evaporated: the cut words have been replaced in spirit by the music of Verdi—swelling, as it does in the Slapbang restaurant scene, with the swell of Clennam's emotion, as his attention is caught by the child who reminds him of Little Dorrit, or setting the rhythm of the bustling streets. Edzard's opera background suggested Verdi: his popularity, she remarks, had very similar roots to Dickens', and they were exact contemporaries.

Predictably, while many loved the music, some critics hated the unconventional visual rhetoric of Edzard's film. Static and theatrical, playing into a proscenium *mise en scène*, was the verdict. But a more complex camera-style might well have undermined the two-part structure of the film, cluttering up what is already complicated.

What you lose when you film Dickens is considerable. How could you film his asides, or his description of Arthur's bedstead at his mother's, with its four posts, "each terminating in a spike, . . . for the dismal accommodation of lodgers who might prefer to impale themselves" (77–78)? His *voice* and his narratorial presence cannot be filmed: yet for most of us the interest of a Dickens novel lies as much in the teller as in the tale. Some filmmakers have attempted, filming other novelists' works, to translate a particular verbal into a particular visual style: Tony Richardson's 1963 version of Fielding's picaresque *Tom Jones*, for example, unfolds at breakneck speed, replete with joke shots through keyholes and stylized old-fashioned wipes and dissolves.[4] Working closely with the veteran French cinematographer Bruno Keyser, Edzard decided, wisely in my view, not to try any visual tricks with Dickens. She is careful to avoid any sense of the camera knowing and intruding ("we didn't want another narrator," her assistant Olivier Stockman recalled). The camera never preempts a character's action, and only occasionally follows it, so that what little camera movement there is has considerable impact: most movingly, there is the painfully slow pan around the enormous Merdle table to catch the last of the outraged upper-crust guests abandoning Dorrit to the society of the new inmates he imagines he is welcoming to the Marshalsea, in part 2. Less usual camera angles are motivated by a character's point of view, literal or emotional: high angle shots in the Circumlocution Office scenes intensify their alienating and weirdly comic quality—as if the Monty Python team had turned its attention to Kafka. These are moments which make us aware of the agency of narration, and they are rare. More generally, Edzard and Keyser work primarily to capture the performances of the actors, as if indeed they were recording a theater performance: "she took the camera," Miriam Margoyles (Flora Finching) told me, "and shone it like a light at the actors' vulnerabilities as people." This partly accounts, I think, for the scarcity of long shots in the film—overviews of the streets, and the like: we are immersed instead, in medium shots and occasional close-ups, in the human comedy the camera witnesses.

The film excels in its lighting effects, often "naturalizing" its light sources by grouping characters near windows and in doorways, and never using spots to pick out principal characters, as classical Hollywood style once would have dictated, or filters to soften or glamorize. But Edzard chose not to reproduce the famous lighting effects of "Phiz" 's frontispiece to the novel (in which the light source, we notice, is inside the prison [fig. 17]): instead, she develops her visual imagery of frames and bars, which links her Marshalsea prison to the Clennam house (first seen through the bars of its wrought iron gate), and even the rustic haven of the Meagles (first seen through the white bars of its wooden garden gate). This confining imagery is associated most of all with Little Dorrit herself, particularly in part 2 of the film, in which Edzard's priority is to lay down the psychological foundation of her character. We see her again and again "framed" by the window in which she sits sewing (fig. 18), or by a doorway at which she hesitates, or by the bars of the Marshalsea Gate (fig. 19).

It is perhaps when we consider editing, and the manner of storytelling in each part of the film, that we come to understand more deeply how the interiority of Arthur Clennam and Little Dorrit that Dickens conveys through soliloquy, speech, imagery, and indirect narration is differently conveyed in the two different parts of Edzard's film. We come to understand Little Dorrit, in part 2, through a biographical format that recovers from the retrospective summary of Dickens' text the immediacy and the shaping impact of small Amy's experiences as the "Child of the Marshalsea." Edzard's film explanation of how Dorrit learned to find "testimonials" "acceptable" is succinctly interwoven with telling us how his daughter came to work for him: a visitor to the goal gives the child a sixpence, and she in her turn hands it to her father, who quietly pockets it. The growth from small child to girl and to woman is smoothed over by a simple continuity of costume (Little Dorrit is always in blue), and an economical trick cut that asserts continuity over a leap of time: in one shot, small Amy looks at her sewing and says, "This won't do, my dear" and in the next, the grown-up Little Dorrit, sitting in the same window in the same room, answers herself, with "no, that's better." We feel close to her because we see her grow.

Arthur, however, we encounter over a much shorter stretch of time. "Nobody"'s Story, as it is in the novel, is not a story of progression but a story about remembering—of return to a home where time has stood still, to a youthful sweetheart whom the years have ravaged, and to an obsessive injunction "not to forget."[5] (Early in preproduction, Edzard cut a sequence between young Arthur and young Flora that would have paralleled the childhood sequences of *Little Dorrit's Story*, partly to make the stylistic and experiential differences between the two parts of the film more sharp.) Near the very close of part 1, Arthur finally returns in memory to the first image his mind registered of Little Dorrit at his mother's house—an image skimmed over and suppressed in its proper chronological place, but finally remembered: one is tempted to call it the film's primal image, the visual equivalent of his final

realization in the novel that if Little Dorrit's "deep, timid earnestness" had
any "new meaning . . . , the change was in his perception, not in her" (826).
The editing style of part 1 is designedly different: its characteristic device is
montage, the quick editing together of disparate images to convey a sensation,
an emotion, a dream, a sense of time past and present jumbled together, and
it takes its cue from the quasi-flashback to the long childhood "train" of his
"miserable Sundays" triggered by the sound of bells in Dickens' novel (69).
Time and again, in Edzard's film—when Arthur is in his bed (at his mother's,
in the "snuggery" of the Marshalsea), or dozing in his chair at his lodgings—he dreams a dream, a montage of past and present images, accompanied
by fragmentary sentences and haunting sounds. So, for example, the night
after Affery reminds Arthur of his long-lost love, Flora, and again in the
instant before he sees her again, there flashes through his mind a sequence
that succinctly signifies young Flora—a china bowl of rose leaves; lace gloves;
silk slippers; a pile of chocolate bonbons; her quick step as she is glimpsed
across a passageway; and the sound of her laughter. *Little Dorrit's Story*, in
sharp contrast, is as linear and goal-oriented as *her life*.

Of the four dimensions of film *mise en scène* plays the largest role in
Edzard's *Little Dorrit*, as we might expect from a writer-director who started
her professional career as a theater and opera designer. Edzard built eighty-
nine separate sets for the film—an enormous number by any filmmaker's
standards—and started building while she was still working on the script,
since what she could build would affect what she would write. Her camera
was overloaded, too, with the front-projection equipment needed to merge
together in the frame painted backings of London skylines and miniature sets
of house tops and roofs with real-size sets of house fronts, and the characters.

Taking her cue perhaps from such brief passages as Dickens' description
of Mrs. General's cavernous room, a third the size of the whole Marshalsea
(524), Edzard took the crucial decision to reduce the quantity of furniture
Victorians actually stuffed into their rooms not only in all the Italian scenes,
but also in the opulent Merdle house, to increase our sense of the luxury of
space the rich enjoy, while the poor are crammed into their hovels and into
the very frame of the film (in one scene we see Mrs. Plornish reduced to
putting the baby in the chest of drawers). The endlessly repeating identical
doors of the Circumlocution Office, meanwhile, speak as loudly as the
"sprightly Barnacle"'s surreal nonsense monologue about how to apply for
a patent of the mindless circularity and frustration that awaits all those who
enter here.

Individual pieces of furniture tell us of the frigid emotional climate in which the rich of the novel and the film live: the alienating back-to-back sofa on which Frederick and William Dorrit sit, in an enormous empty Italian salon; the social gradations of chair styles, from the humble style of the secondhand cast-offs we see in the Marshalsea room, to the old-fashioned chairs with backs carved like funerary urns in the Clennam house, to the Regency chairs in Casby's substantial home, to the fake Louis Quinze gilt-and-red-velvet pieces of the Merdles; their enormous dinner table, enlarged still further by the angle at which it is shot, groaning under its load of grotesque fruit centerpieces and gilt dishes of food (all the courses were put on the table at once in this period [fig. 20]). The dressing of each set counts towards the total effect: there is a dead pot plant on the window-ledge in the Marshalsea room, when Arthur Clennam comes to inhabit it—a legacy from the days of Little Dorrit; posters on the wall outside the Marshalsea Gate where Frederick Dorrit first meets Arthur Clennam shriekingly advertise a popular Bulwer-Lytton drama called *MONEY!* (fig. 21). Even the mere placement of characters within the *mise-en-scène* can have an almost subliminal emotional and thematic impact: Little Dorrit's discomfort in her days of wealth, for example, is encapsulated by her placing *outside* the salon door during the musical evening in Italy. And these Italian settings literally "pale" by comparison with the London she yearns for: faded pastel colors are the cause.

6: THE FILM AND THE "PHIZ" ILLUSTRATIONS

One source for Edzard's expressive *mise en scène* was, of course, the original illustrations to the novel by Hablot K. Browne ("Phiz"), all minutely overseen by Dickens. From the first, filmmakers have invoked the aid of his illustrators in revisualizing Dickens—costumes for George Cukor's *Copperfield*, for example, were cut with Phiz's portrait of Micawber et al. as patterns, in the mistaken belief that this would also guarantee historical accuracy; more generally, Victorian illustrators influenced the visual style of many early films. (Advertisements for a sixteen-scene *Alice in Wonderland* by the pioneer English filmmaker Cecil Hepworth in 1903 proudly proclaimed that it "reproduced in animated form with remarkable fidelity" John Tenniel's original illustrations [Low and Manvell 1:83]). Furthermore, as Paul Davis has suggested, the picture narratives of Hogarth, *The Rake's Progress* for example, which were a powerful influence on Victorian book illustration (explicitly cited not only as ancestors of the visual style of Dickens and of his first illustrator, Cruikshank, but as guarantors of Dickens' moral intent in his preface to his "Parish Boy's Progress," *Oliver Twist*), "became the technical and philosophical bridge between the visual narratives of the graphic satire tradition and those of the cinema," and thus Dickens himself became the mediator and hinge between cartoon and screen (158).

Edzard's *Little Dorrit* draws most heavily on Phiz's illustrations in its creation of Dorrit's room in the Marshalsea, the Clennam house, and the Doyce-Clennam workshop. Indeed, it reproduces almost exactly Phiz's illustration of Dorrit's room, the central location (fig. 22). There are a few interesting differences, however: the door moves from the right to the left-hand corner in the film—making the room more photogenic; the table-cloth shrinks to cover only half the table.

The painterly "Rembrandt" effect of chiaroscuro that Dickens wanted was achieved by Phiz in the "dark plate" technique he first used when he was illustrating *Dombey and Son*, to complement Dickens' increasingly dark vision of his society. There are eight "dark plates" in *Little Dorrit*. Edzard moves toward some filmic realization of the same effects that Phiz achieves in, say, "The Room with the Portrait" (Arthur's father's study [fig. 23]) and "Damocles" (the exterior of the Clennam house, with Rigaud-Blandois perched smoking in the window, one of the best known and most reproduced of the *Dorrit* illustrations) through low-key lighting and a predominance of browns in the settings: the sober effect she achieves goes a long way toward deflecting these scenes' potential for B-movie ham. There is a striking resemblance between her shot of Flintwinch at Mrs. Clennam's shoulder and Phiz's illustration "Mr. Flintwich, mediates as a friend of the Family": the variety artist Wax Wall, a master of contorted "body language," brings the novel's Flintwinch to scuttling, crab-like larger than life.

For her rustic scenes, however, Edzard draws not on Phiz's very unusual "dark plate" "Floating Away" (fig. 24), in which Clennam watches the roses Pet gave him drift away upon the river, but on the favorite Victorian genre of the rustic vignette, exemplified, say, by Phiz's own *Pickwick Papers* illustration of a comic tryst: the joke-romantic scene, we notice, is artfully "framed" by foliage (fig. 25). This seems to me appropriate, on one level, given the quality of fakery in the pastoral and rustic scenes of *Little Dorrit*—Young John Chivery wandering among his mother's washing lines "as if it was groves," and so forth. A similar principle governs Edzard's visual handling of Bob the turnkey and Little Dorrit on their afternoon jaunt (fig. 26), and Clennam's and Pet Meagles' walk in the woods. But there is no question that it also lightens the look and mood of the film, as compared to the novel Dickens wrote, and whose illustrations he oversaw with extreme care. Edzard's vision is less dark, and her shadows less deep, and this is not merely a matter of a design decision on Edzard's part.

Another of Phiz's "dark plates" perhaps gives us a first clue to some of the reasons for this lightening. It also illustrates the ideal of interdependence between Dickens' text and Phiz's engravings. Dickens chose each of the scenes to be illustrated: one, of Flora and Mr. F's aunt's visit to the Doyce and Clennam workshop, gives us a far closer view than his text of the works and the machines (fig. 27), and the inspiration for Edzard's much-expanded work scenes (fig. 28). And it can serve to suggest to us Edzard's drive to ascertain who is at "fault" for at least some of the ills of the novel's world. Dickens sees no solutions to the questions he asks in *Little Dorrit*; Christine Edzard is driven to provide a few answers, and so to lighten the Dickensian darkness. She does so partly by importing from *Our Mutual Friend* a character Dickens calls Sloppy and she calls Smiles, a "wonderful reader of a newspaper" who "do the police in different voices" (the famous line T. S. Eliot chose as the original title of his multivocal, modernist *Wasteland*). His arm—picking up on a scene Dickens reluctantly canceled from *Hard Times*—gets caught in the bands that dominate almost every shot of her workshop.[6] Whereupon Daniel Doyce has a rather un-Dickensian outburst of faith in technological progress: "The belts are to be blamed," he says, "and I am to be blamed because I knew of it."

Some effects possible for Dickens and Phiz are not possible in film. The illustrations frequently underline the self-seeking theatricality of the Dorrit family by arranging groups left to right across the page, as if posed on a stage. Edzard's film is unable to "cheat" in the fashion that Phiz does, say, in his illustration "The Marshalsea becomes an Orphan"—melting away the prison walls in order to allow a "long shot," as it were, of the departing Processional (fig. 29). A film audience's sense of the continuity and reality of space is very finely tuned: had she similarly melted away the walls to allow such a shot, we would have felt disoriented. But the potential of film, unlike theater, for offering a multiplicity of points of view is considerable compensation.

7: THE "ROARING" STREETS OF LONDON

"*Little Dorrit* is unique," writes F. S. Schwarzbach in his *Dickens and the City*, "in its insistence upon London" (151). The Phiz illustrations were one first step toward creating the world of the film. Another was to visit what remains of the locations today: little more than the gates of the Marshalsea Prison, letting on to a cramped lozenge of land thinly carpeted with fish-and-chip wrappers. And a most important step was picture research, in the rich field of Victorian illustration. The mid-nineteenth century was the golden age of black-and-white boxwood book engravings, and saw both the rise of photography and the spread of illustrated papers using newly patented reproduction processes. Picture research starts to bring Little Dorrit's London to life: a later nineteenth-century etching uncovers the lost courtyard of the Marshalsea Prison (fig. 30); the uneven paving and disconsolate pump figure large in Edzard's reconstruction (fig. 31).

But central to Dickens' vision, to Edzard's film, and to any sense of London as it was then, are "the roaring streets" (136). The opening sequences of Cukor's *David Copperfield* and of David Lean's *Great Expectations* show the pages of Dickens' novel rustling open to begin the story: the very opening credits of Edzard's part 1 plunge us into "streets, streets, streets." At the very end of her film, during the marriage of Arthur and Amy, her camera circles back to those streets, "wandering and searching and marvelling" (Winn 27) at all it sees (figs. 32, 33, 34).[7] The film's final image is a freeze frame of Borough High Street that aims to give us the "feel" of its higgledy-piggledy architecture, evident in period photographs, or in the changing panorama meticulously recorded by the watercolorist and pencil artist George Scharf during the building of London Bridge railway station in 1843, Edzard's primary pictorial source for her street sets and models (fig. 35).[7] She heightens the sense of bustling commercial traffic and teeming London crowds by shooting, say, Arthur Clennam following Little Dorrit to the Marshalsea from behind passing carts and pedestrians, and in constricting medium shots.

Another source for the novel's swarming streets might be Phiz's illustration for *Martin Chuzzlewit* of that same scene filmed by the pioneer English filmmaker R. W. Paul as *Mr Pecksniff Fetches the Doctor* at the turn of the century (fig. 36), or Cruikshank's for *Sketches by Boz* (fig. 37). The upstairs offices of Sands Films, which incorporate a picture library, bulge with source-books. The Victorian photographic record (exemplified by a very early sepia photograph of tottering sixteenth- and seventeenth-century houses in Cloth Fair Slum [fig. 38]) reminds us that early-to-mid Victorian London was an assortment of buildings of all periods, the older the slummier: the skyline on which Clennam looks out from his mother's house in Edzard's film captures this effect of historical layering, as does the maze-like appearance of close, "crooked and descending" London streets (70) seen in almost every photographic cityscape of the 1850s and '60s.

Besides Scharf, one invaluable pictorial source was certainly the French artist Gustave Doré's 1872 *London: A Pilgrimage.* This represents not only the pinnacle of achievement for Victorian book illustration, but also (in the days before the mechanical mass reproduction of photographs became possible) a kind of Victorian "documentary." It has perhaps been the single most important influence on the design of all Dickens films: the bridge between warehouses he drew in the brewery area south of St. Paul's turns up both in David Lean's 1948 *Oliver Twist* and in the 1968 musical *Oliver!*, which thematizes its relationship to Victorian black-and-white illustration in an opening-credits sequence that ends with a picture of boys on a treadmill "coming alive," on film (fig. 39); Doré's full-page illustrations—of London Bridge swamped with traffic, or Fleet Street in rush hour, say, crammed with figures to the very borders of the page—audibly suggest the "roar" of Dickens' and Edzard's streets.

Their Borough High Street is thronged, too, with the characters Doré drew—the Apple Woman, the street-butcher and his poor customers (fig. 40), the ballad seller (fig. 41); and the street-people recorded by such early masters of the camera as the anonymous photographer employed by Charles Spurgeon, a Greenwich clergyman—the match-seller (fig. 42), the window-mender (fig. 43). Spurgeon had W. Thompson, "Champion Pie Maker" (fig. 44), photographed outside one of the many print shops that prospered in England from the turn of the century, retailing the first wave of products of the age of mechanical picture reproduction that would eventually spawn the photograph and the film. Appropriately, the print shop is a location with symbolic resonance in Edzard's *Little Dorrit* (fig. 45): she places one along her Gray's Inn Road, and we see Mr. Merdle going into it, customers window-shopping, and passers-by bumping into Arthur Clennam outside it ("Sorry!" and "My fault!" they say, underlining in passing the theme and title of part 1). Fanny Dorrit's lodgings and Dorrit's Marshalsea room have cheap prints and playbills pinned on the walls, like patchy wallpaper.

London shopped, worked, lived on the streets. The Cheap Fish Stall holder photographed by John Thomson (fig. 46) for his pioneering documentary collection *Street Life in London* (1877) would keep his wares out without ice until well past midnight, the only time when poor folk could get out to market—hence the activity among the Borough High Street traders the night Little Dorrit and Maggy get locked out in Edzard's film. Their reek would add to the general stench of the streets, through which animals were driven to market, and horses toiled with carts and carriages of every description, as in George Scharf's lightning sketches of Covent Garden and its market folk (fig. 47).

London slept on the streets, too. When they cannot get into Maggy's lodging, she and Little Dorrit figuratively join the enormous numbers of homeless Londoners (fig. 48). Railway and bridge arches and doorways were favorite places to "doss down." Thomson titled his photograph of a downtrodden baby-minder, with her charge wrapped in her shawl like Mrs. Plornish's baby in Edzard's film, "The Crawlers": all day long they would "move on" from doorway to doorway, seeking shelter (fig. 49).

The old slums of London began to be demolished in the decades after *Little Dorrit* was written. Bleeding Heart Yard (figs. 50, 51) had ten thousand reeking relatives, where washing, chickens, dirt, and sewage shared the space with people whose rooms were too close and smelly for them to sit indoors (fig. 52). As Ross Devenish, director of BBC TV's *Bleak House* series told me, what is "normally lost" in adaptations of Dickens is "the fact that London at that period was like a third world city . . . [with] none of the modern support systems like drainage, sewerage, and so on." "People get befuddled," he added, "by the costumes and the Christmas card image"—which Dickens himself, ironically, also helped to create. The novelist had only to reach into his memories of childhood to remember what it felt like to be cooped up in houses hardly much more respectable, and Edzard needed only to refer to this photograph of the staircase of the house in Camden Town where Dickens' family lived before his father was imprisoned for debt in the Marshalsea to get a sense of just how cramped and dingy she should make the staircase up to Dorrit's room (fig. 53). All these sources, and many more like them, went to her reconstruction of the historical background of *Little Dorrit*: it remains to consider exactly what her film's relationship with history is.

8: FILMING HISTORY, FILMING TIME

The camera obscura and the camera lucida shaped early Victorian perception, ordering the eye's fluid experience of the world into series of views that the hand could trace on paper.[8] It was only a matter of time until (in Fox Talbot's phrase) these "fairy pictures, creatures of a moment" were chemically fixed, and photography was born (Gifford 23). Much of the visual imagery that has attracted commentators on *Little Dorrit* (most memorably,

Clennam's final realization of Little Dorrit as the perspectival "vanishing point" of his own story [801]) seems to me to demand a specifically photographic frame of reference if we are to appreciate it to the full. The novel's constant play on the imagery of sun and shade partly suggests the highlights and contrasts of black-and-white book illustration, but it suggests too the dual negative-positive quality of the daguerreotype or ambrotype, or such latticework of sunlight and shadow as one sees in the very first paper negative, made by Henry Fox Talbot at Lacock Abbey in 1835 (fig. 54).[9] Some early Victorian photographers called their images "sun pictures" or "heliographs" (the term "photography," after all, means "light-writing"): fixing the photographic image, meanwhile, in the terms of Fox Talbot's 1839 Report to the Royal Society, was "fixing the shadow" (quoted by Pollack 32). The words brings vividly to mind the "shadow" of her loved one that the tiny woman keeps in a cupboard, in Little Dorrit's story of the Princess (341).

Photography was, as Terry Castle puts it, "the ultimate ghost-producing technology of the nineteenth century" (64);[10] Dickens had very mixed feelings about his own photographic replication—"haunt[ing] mankind with my countenance," as he put it (quoted by Ackroyd 853), through the medium of the mass-produced portraits of the great turned out in the 1850s and '60s. More, in uncanny play with notions of presence and absence, the new technology profoundly queried the Victorians' sense of the one-way onward flow of time. It is an index of the speed with which Dickens absorbed its imaginative possibilities (as he did too those of the railway, for example), and of the depth of his engagement, from childhood, with one of the camera's primary ancestors, the magic lantern (fig. 55), that his imagery of "sun" and "shadow" pictures in *Little Dorrit* allowed a striking refocusing of his novel's anxiety about Time, (mis)representation, and that "marking time" which is mere animal existence. Oliver Wendell Holmes dubbed the daguerreotype "the mirror with a memory": it had turned moments into eerie eternities (quoted by Pollack 28).[11] Lengthy exposures—up to eight hours in the 1820s—meant that busy thoroughfares were imaged as empty streets in the City of the Dead, since figures moved too quickly to be registered. The very physical process by which the mind marked the passing of time—the movement of the sun—was obliterated in the first images, in which buildings were shaded by both morning and afternoon shadows. Thus, time and light converge in the image of feeble Frederick Dorrit " 'merely passing on, like the shadow over the sun-dial' " (120), and while sinister shadows "hover" on the wall of the her house "like shadows from a great magic lantern" (221), for Dickens' Mrs. Clennam, fifteen years a prisoner in one room, the natural progression of the seasons has been suspended, and (in most suggestive phrase) memories and imaginings of the world outside have become "controllable pictures" that deny "the rush of reality" (856).

Film went still further than photography, abolishing time. When D. W. Griffith's *The Birth of a Nation* premiered in 1915, Woodrow Wilson hailed its ability, as he put it, to "write history in lightning"(quoted by Carter 9). No other medium, save perhaps the three-dimensional holograph, has such a power of reconstructing history: the eternal present tense of film, as theorists have called it, denies the very pastness of the past. So it was that a reverent (if risible) review in the influential trade paper *The Bioscope* of a 1912 Eastertide release, piously entitled *From Manger to Cross*, celebrated cinema's ability to carry us "back through the countless ages to the time when Christ himself trod this earth," and restore to us even "the Divine presence" (quoted by Low 2:185). In exploiting her medium's capacities—indeed, its very nature—Edzard sensitively connects with the imagistic heritage and legacy of the novel itself. One need only think of the sudden flashback, during the scene between Clennam and his mother in part 1 of her film, which presents before us, "present" *now*, in a shot not visually distinguishable from those that precede it or come after it, and in all the sharpness of agonized memory, young Arthur as he was *then*, in his painful childhood days, a mute and pale-faced boy in a sailor suit. The double narrative of her *Little Dorrit*, too, intensifies our sense of film's suspension of time, rendering it as lived experience rather than historical progression or (to use William Dorrit's term for his self-pitying petitioning of the authorities) mere "memorialization."[12]

Not only in terms of their (re)registering of time did the two technologies of photography and moving pictures trace parallel parabolas of development. The early filmmakers, like the early photographers before them, first exploited film's apparent "guarantee" and "transcription" of reality: each responded in turn to the craving for total realism that clinched the success, in turn, of the magic lantern, the diorama, the stereoscope, the "dissolving views" of the popular melodrama, and then—at last, from 1895—the "Animated Photographs, the First and Finest in London"—prominently of the "Picture Palaces" of the twenties (fig. 56).[13] The attraction of the very first book of photographs ever published, Fox Talbot's *The Pencil of Nature* (1844–46), as its title indicates, was the same which drew audiences to the "actuality" and educational nature films made in Britain from as early as 1900 (so potent a draw was film's ultrarealism that a 1907 "kinematic" production of *The Pied Piper of Hamelin* proudly announced "absolute fidelity to detail—real rats").[14] Photographers and filmmakers after them turned next to providing "reliable records" of the historical events of the day.[15] Mathew B. Brady's photographic record of the Civil War finds its parallels and descendants in films of Queen Victoria's Diamond Jubilee of 1897, her funeral in 1901, the Boer War, Scott's Antarctic Expedition of 1912. Then came the day, not long after, when photographer and filmmaker each in turn realized the potentials of his medium for restaging—and even rewriting—history. Early admirers of photography lapped up Oscar G. Rejlander's composite "art" pictures (perhaps his most famous showed John the Baptist's head on the notorious platter), and film audiences were similarly untroubled by latter-day notions of historical authenticity. The English Precision Film Company openly advertised its film of the notorious Tottenham shooting affray, which dominated news headlines in 1909, as a "reproduction" (the term is intriguing) without its losing any of its attraction as a "documentary" item (see Low and Manvell 2:148). As the photographer Edward Steichen remarked in the first issue of *Camera Work*, in January 1903, all artists—and all photographers, and all cinematographers—"fake" and take liberties with reality. The angle of vision, the type of lens, the progression of images—all inflect the actual; even unmediated technological "objectivity" is an illusion; realism is a style (see Pollack 84). Griffith's revisionist epic of the Confederacy and what it stood for is a case in print. And Christine Edzard's version of Dickens' *Little Dorrit* is another. On the one hand her film reconstructs the lost world of early Victorian London with a concern for historical accuracy that is almost obsessive—"for this director there is no such thing as *background*, only detail at a distance," as one reviewer rightly remarked (Mars-Jones 16 [fig. 57]). "I wanted it to be as real . . . as . . . what you see on the London Underground," she added. But on the other hand, her film bends some of the facts about Victorian sex roles and society in the interests not only of accommodating a modern audience which might be alienated by them, but also of satisfying personal desires.

Nowhere is the concern for historical accuracy more apparent than in the film's costumes. Edzard and her team visited museums to learn exactly how clothes were made in the mid-nineteenth century. And they found, for example, that shirts were very wide and very long, because people did not wear underclothes, and that the fabrics were of a different quality, no longer produced in the West (so they shipped muslins and hand-woven cottons from India, instead). Modern dyes were not right either: cheap aniline dyes had just been invented when *Little Dorrit* was written, and when Edzard sets her film. So aniline dyes were used—hence the rather luridly bright costumes of the Bleeding Heart Yard folk. Every single shirt Dorrit wears till his accession to fortune in the novel is made by Little Dorrit, every shirt every earlier

Victorian wore was made by hand, and so was every single costume for
Edzard's film. It took twenty-five people two full years to cut and sew these
costumes, using only original patterns. ''The purpose,'' Edzard says, ''is to
re-create from inside the reality of Dickens's time'': people stand and walk
differently in authentic clothes. Once made, they were not chemically
''aged,'' but washed with soap and water, dozens of times, to break them in.
The straw bonnets were plaited by hand; the fabrics were hand-printed; collars
and waistcoats were hand-embroidered. Edzard was personally involved with
every step of the process: she cut many of the clothes herself, and gave cast
members their first fittings in person. She herself designed and made some
of the replicas of the accoutrements and heavy jewelry of the period that even
such minor characters as Mrs. Gowan and Mrs. Barnacle display in her film.
Each costume has thematic and psychological import as well: Fanny Dorrit's
relish of her accession to wealth, for example, is written in the six flounces
of the fashionable dress she parades in at Mrs. Merdle's; ''conspicuous con-
sumption'' was not just a modern-day American phenomenon. The ''presence'' in Edzard's film of a world past and gone had ramifications that might
make some historians reel: forty of the costumes had an afterlife as a ''hands-
on'' exhibit of ''historical'' artifacts at the Museum of London.

Edzard's passion for history took her from the filming of Dickens to the
adaptation for the screen of what seems virtually unadaptable, Henry
Mayhew's *London Labour and the London Poor*, another of her source-books
for *Little Dorrit* (*The Fool*, released in Europe 1991). But in the end, just as
Dickens wrote for his own time, so Edzard must film for hers, lest her *Dorrit*
end up crushed beneath the weight of the period cobblestones shipped in to
pave her ''roaring'' streets. What most astonishes about her historical passion
is that it does not dim her sense of narrative or soften her emotional focus on
her characters. Nothing is dwelt on with an eye to social history: everything
is simply, casually *there*, and it becomes easier, not more difficult, for a
modern audience to make the connections Edzard invites us to make between
one compartmentalized society driven by money-mania for Merdle's ''junk
bonds,'' and encumbered with parasites and hangers-on, and another—ours.

9: LITTLE DORRIT'S HERSTORY

Of the several adjustments of historical emphasis that Edzard makes, her
handling of Little Dorrit herself asks most attention.

She wanted a complete newcomer for Little Dorrit, someone "dry and unexpansive," she says, and after interviewing hundreds of girls under five feet tall, chose the twenty-year-old drama student Sarah Pickering (quoted by McAsh 18). If Pickering does finally reveal what one reviewer called a "gosling beauty" by the end of the film, it is in the teeth of Edzard's direction (Corliss 93). There is no concession in Edzard's portrait of Little Dorrit to modern ideals of female attractiveness, not much to Victorian (the tightly scraped-back hair gives her the look of a skinned rabbit), and little to conventional standards of film acting (fig. 58): Pickering is a "drip," moaned the film's American reviewers, "a humorless, brooding pill" (Vineberg 10). She wins through the film, in the end, on her own terms—Edzard's terms.

Dickens himself foregrounds—unusually for Victorian fiction—a man's emotional needs and dependencies in the person of Arthur Clennam. And he paints a picture of a "strong" Little Dorrit. But she is strong in the Victorian ways of female strength, which to our eyes sometimes look more like "weakness." In Dickens's novel, tears—virtuous, sympathetic tears—well in her eyes at the drop of a hat—when she visits Clennam at his rooms, when Tip becomes a prison "regular," when the news of her father's fortune is broken to her, and so on. We see her on her knees to her father, uplifting her arms to heaven, preaching charity to Mrs. Clennam, kissing Clennam's hand in gratitude: the Victorian woman as humble Angel. In Edzard's film, she weeps only once—when her father tells her she has humiliated him by walking through the public streets arm in arm with Old Nandy, the pauper. The reasons for this change do not only lie in the fact that the film (unlike a TV soap, or a novel issued in monthly parts) cannot bear too many emotional climaxes, nor in Edzard's eschewing of sentimentality and in changes in public taste, nor in the need that her two-part structure creates for a strongly characterized and convincing Arthur and Amy ("it says something about the peculiar nature of Dickens's genius," wrote John Gross in the London *Sunday Times,* "that . . . their inadequacies don't prevent the book from being a major masterpiece" [Gross 22]).

No. This is a very personal film: it must be, to be a good film. It understands that film must interpret, not "adapt" Dickens; and that such interpretation is always a form of (literary) criticism. Christine Edzard is a painfully thin woman so extremely shy as at times to appear withdrawn, a woman director who has risen to prominence in a profession dominated by men, and a mother whose own daughter has carried cans of film around Grice's wharf since she was knee-high, like the "Child of the Studio." Her *Little Dorrit* is the first "woman's film" ever made of a Dickens novel. One reviewer may have dubbed Miriam Margoyles's fat widow "a human Miss Piggy" (Edelstein 29), but her Flora is also granted vulnerability and kindness (she caresses Arthur's hat); Minnie Meagles is shorn of her "Pet" name and most of her pettishness; Mrs. Tickit, the Meagles' housekeeper, gets promoted to full status as family friend; Affery remains Arthur's ally—but in the film gets his help making his bed; the balance of factors in Edzard's Mrs. Clennam between melodramatic villainy, perverted religiosity, and thwarted motherhood is shifted (it is she, not Doyce, who springs Arthur from the Marshalsea in the film): the women of this production more than hold their own. Edzard adds innumerable details to Dickens' portrait of Little Dorrit, "like her constantly busying herself about." In a sense, she solves the perennial problem of the vague, flat, and virtuous Dickensian child-heroine simply by *showing* her to us; the details of themselves grant her a kind of gritty life. "Dickens didn't go close enough," she says: "People weren't expected to take much notice of women in his day. He hardly knew what the women who looked after him were doing most of the time" (quoted by Malcolm 22). What drew her to this novel, of all the novels, she says, was partly its qualities of compilation and panorama ("cramming everything in," as she puts it), partly the directorial freedom it offered precisely *because* it is imperfect, but most of all the strength of the heroine: to prove that strength, her film goes beyond mere emphasis—like the frequent repetition of a line Little Dorrit speaks only once in the novel, "I have always been strong enough to do what I want to do" (333), or her dressing in a blue that stands out against her dingy background, or increasing Arthur's ineffectualness so that her capability looms larger. More, Edzard's film refashions Dickens' text and his times. When images and judgments delivered by the novel in indirect speech survive translation into film, it is often because Little Dorrit inherits them. She has an answer to the question that rattled around part 1—"Who's to blame?": not "nobody" but "everyone who was at Mr. Merdle's feasts was a sharer of the plunder," she says—a line of impersonal narration recontextualized and immeasurably strengthened (776). She turns Arthur's reflective murmur, "Do Not Forget," into only the first half of her own sentence, "I love you." And she takes from him the first gentle breaking of the great news to her father: "The wall . . . is down, melted away." Masculine ventriloquism, Arthur's services as mouthpiece, is no longer required, just as she no longer ascribes to her love for him (as she does in her curious letters from Italy) her ability to penetrate character or weigh judgments (608): those faculties are not borrowed from love, or from men, in Edzard's film.

This Little Dorrit's desire for Clennam is clear from the very beginning of her Story, when the camera lingers with her eyes on the oblivious Arthur passing her in the doorway of the Clennam house (in Arthur's half of the film, and in the novel, Little Dorrit doesn't even come into focus in the background). She arranges the first meeting on the Iron Bridge, which in the novel is accidental. She faints in the Marshalsea room, the day the family leave, because Clennam has asked her to look out for Minnie Gowan in Italy: two scenes from the novel are here fruitfully collapsed upon one another. And while she may lose consciousness at this climactic moment, for the Little Dorrit of the film loving Arthur Clennam certainly does not mean what it means in the novel—"los[ing] and forget[ting] herself" (648). The kiss with which in the film she answers the protestations of "honor" and "too late!" that threaten to abort the romance in the novel is a real woman's kiss. Such an awakening and consummating kiss may accord with the fairy-tale element in Dickens; it is also well-nigh impossible to imagine a Victorian woman bestowing it, even upon a despondent Clennam.

9: DICKENS, CINEMA, AND THE CULTURE OF THE COUNTRY

It is a cliché of cinema history that when the great Soviet silent filmmaker Sergei Eisenstein came to reach back into the history of narrative for the roots of his own experimental style, he reached back directly to Dickens, to proclaim him the conceptual "father" of the film. The "Inimitable" was, said Lillain Gish, the "idol" of D. W. Griffith, the ancestor (and respectable guarantor) of the technique of "parallel editing" that made his first feature films possible.[16] Dickens' concern for locating us in space and time might have made him as natural a film director as he was a theatrical producer (the same concern brings both novel and film time and again to the Iron Bridge). His visual sensibility "invents" the close-up and the motif. He anticipates Edzard in the use of subjective sound and what we might call sound "fade-ins" and "fade-outs": we hear only what Arthur can catch, for example, of Miss Wade's conversation with Rigaud (Dickens 587). It is a naive critic who would deliver the blanket statement that Dickens is "inherently cinematic" (though many have delivered it); and only the unwary theorist would trace an unbroken line and an unmediated link between the nineteenth-century novel and film (thought several have done so, "repressing," as Rick Altman persuasively writes, cinema's—and indeed Dickens'—disreputable inheritance from popular melodrama).[17] Yet while Victorian fiction is not film's sole parent, and Dickens is not cinema, it is clear that there are profound similarities between these two narrative media that (like dreams) engage their mass audiences on the most private and interior levels, and that Dickens' novels were seedbeds for cinema's techniques.

But to look at Dickens and film, particularly English film (curiously neglected by the commentators), is not only to engage crucial issues in film and narrative theory but also to understand better the culture of the country and Dickens' role in both—and even the very Englishness of England. The history of the perenially struggling English film industry has as much to teach as the well-known stories of Grifith, Eisenstein, and stars from Fields to Guinness. The filmmakers of earlier times quarried and paid homage to Dickens' novels for entirely different reasons from those that brought Christing Edzard to *Little Dorrit* in the 1980s, and English film production has been tied up, from the very first, with their adaptation.

The first multi-scene film of the English film innovator R. W. Paul in 1901, was, as we might have suspected, a thirteen-scene thriller somewhat confusingly called *Scrooge: Or, Marley's Ghost*—an artistic advance, at a time when Gaumont (France) were still offering up their "Novel in a Nutshell" series for the public's edification.[18] In these uncertain early days of the cinema, Dickens was English filmmakers' most bankable commodity. The first feature-length film by Cecil Hepworth, one of the originators of continuity editing (in his 1905 *Rescued by Rover*), who dominated English filmmaking for the first thirty years—and only the second feature-length film made in England (the first was Shakespeare's *Henry VIII*)—was, no less inevitably, an adaptation of a Dickens novel: his rousingly melodramatic *Oliver Twist* (fig. 59) was "rapturously" received in 1912 (it is listed in his catalogue as a "crime story" [Low 2:190]).[19] As films got longer and subjects more ambitious (though not, alas, more hard-hitting in their social criticism—Dickens, like others, was tamed) filmmakers across the world were drawn to the English Victorian novelists like wasps to a honey pot. And no novelist tasted sweeter than Dickens, and no filmmakers (or audiences) became so addicted, for good or ill, as the English, for whom by mid-1916, claimed the *Bioscope* trade magazine, adaptation counted for all but 5% of output.

Oliver Twist started Hepworth (and others) on a successful chain of adaptations.[20] In 1913 he delegated direction to Thomas Bentley—and a Dickensian character actor and well-known Dickens impersonator became one of the driving forces of English filmmaking. Bentley's ambitious *David Copperfield* (1913), over two hours long, primitively edited and dependent for story development on pretentious "literary" intertitles, nevertheless represented a major aesthetic advance and a brief renaissance for British cinema after the doldrums of 1906 and after: his eye for composition within the frame and innovative camera placement and movement make for a distinctive visual style (fig. 60). Above all, the film comes alive in its location scenes, praised for their Englishness (fig. 61). Hepworth's publicists claimed they were the actual places "immortalized by Dickens" (quoted by Low 2:293)—exactly the point sold hard in publicity for Disney's 1989 *Great Expectations*: across the twentieth century, and on both sides of the Atlantic, it is the Englishness of the "real" Dickens that sells.[21] Bentley's restraint drew plaudits, too: the "distorting mirror" of Dickensian characterization, wrote one overenthusiastic reviewer, had been eliminated by dignified acting (quoted by Low and Manvell 2:191).

Nevertheless, the early silent cinema, even in more decorous England, was a proletarian entertainment, addicted to sudden reversals, romantic sacrifices, violent action: what attracted early filmmakers was often precisely that melodrama that Edzard excises. Typical of his breed, like the great D. W. Griffith in America, the artistic Bentley also combined a taste for "blood and thunder" with a Victorian penchant for the sentimental, perhaps believing, with the *Kinematograph Monthly Film Record*, that the public "likes its melodrama mellowed by a little literary tradition" (quoted by Low and Manvell 3:204): his 1914 version of *The Old Curiosity Shop* was considered the best of his Dickens adaptations, better even than the historical spectacle he made of *Barnaby Rudge* later in the same year; he liked the novel so much that he filmed it again in 1921 (fig. 62), and yet again in 1935 (fig. 63).[22] Nell's story vies with *David Copperfield, Oliver Twist,* and *A Christmas Carol* for the greatest number of screen adaptations of a Dickens novel. These last two turn up in versions called *Nancy, Fagin,* and *Scrooge*, outnumbering even the thirty-plus adaptations of *David Copperfield*, and forcing our attention again to the independent extratextual existence of the Dickens character. (In sharp contrast, there have been only four films of *Little Dorrit*: a 1933 German talkie, and silent versions made in America, England—with the stately Lady Tree as Mrs. Clennam dominating the action—and Denmark, whose filmmakers, driven by the dictates of the text in an age and a climate less kind to location shooting and large sets, seem nevertheless to have shared Edzard's fascination with street scenes.)[23]

As early as 1906 the British film industry suffered from: foreign penetration of a home market smaller than America's (which in turn restricted profits and reinvestment); the lack of language barriers across the Atlantic; amateurish business methods and under-capitalization of production (the profits lay in distribution and exhibition, especially of American films, and no British companies were vertically integrated); questionable practices like block and blind-booking (which often left no space in screening schedules for home-grown products); institutional indifference to the idea of a national cinema; the dead-weight of tradition, and artistic and social snobbery; and plain bad weather, which made a mockery of shooting scedules in the open-air days before arc lights and covered stages (see Chanan 39–58).[24] By the mid-twenties, Hollywood had taken 95% of the British market. Some thought Dickens was the answer, and rushed to make no fewer than five adaptations in a single year, 1922; others thought high "art" held the key. Herbert Wilcox (with his splendid designer, Norman Arnold) tried both remedies at once, borrowing prestige from the stage for good measure, in his costly 1925 adaptation of Sir John Martin Harvey's much-revived theatrical version of *A Tale of Two Cities, The Only Way*, first staged in 1899 (figs. 64, 65). But foreign companies responded to Dickens with more Dickens. As early as 1913, for the American comedian John Bunny this meant making a four-part *Pickwick Papers* series for Vitagraph UK, which had tackled *Oliver Twist* three years before Hepworth; for the English wing of the French company Pathé it meant making *David Copperfield* the first in its "Britannia" series; for Americans at home in Hollywood it was progressively to mean "less-en[ing] sales resistance" in foreign markets, as a producer was to tell a class of Harvard business students in 1927, by "drawing on their literary talent, taking their choicest stories[,] . . . and sending them back into the countries where they are famous" (Chanan 56). And so (to think only of more benign cultural-imperialist implications) W. C. Fields came to play Micawber.

After the Second World War, in the "golden decade" of native film production, before Hollywood reestablished its grip, and while English people (after their close shave) still felt the need to celebrate their Englishness, it was again to Dickens that they turned, and one adaptation succeeded another to the screen. In them we can chart—almost scientifically, since Dickens provides the "control" in the experiment—the artistic fortunes of film in Britain. David Lean's 1946 *Great Expectations* (figs. 66, 67) and 1948 *Oliver Twist* (fig. 68) excelled in their evocation of atmosphere through the contrasts and highlights of black-and-white stock, and a suggestiveness of style that their director rarely again achieved (the murder of Nancy, for example, happens off-screen while Bill Sikes's dog scrabbles frantically at the door);[25] Caval-canti's 1947 *Nicholas Nickleby* had a lighter touch (fig. 69). The fifties, decade of the "angry young man" and the new realism, wanted a more gritty

Dickens, but plenty of production value: exteriors for the 1958 Rank film of *A Tale of Two Cities* were shot on location in France (fig. 70). The sixties returned to Dickens-as-play, and in turning his murderous melodrama into musical turned us back with gusto to the fabulous quality of his art (fig. 71): for the price of a massive semistylized street set for one of the production numbers in Lionel Bart's *Oliver!* (fig. 72), Christine Edzard could have built half her studio, not only made her film. And now there is her *Little Dorrit*: not, in my opinion, the "part Marxist, part deconstructionist" and all-"sterile" intellectual-academic's film that its most hostile critics dubbed it ("about as subtle as *Monarch's Notes*" jeered one [Sragow C3–7)), but perhaps the "first postmodern Dickens film" (Kroll 118), certainly a feminist's, and without question the most personal re-vision of Dickens ever to reach the screen. It is a most honorable addition to the family. There never can be a "perfect" Dickens film, or even a "whole" Dickens film: *Oliver Twist*'s peregrinations through cinema history, its transformations from 1912 "crime story" to authority-mocking sixties musical—with chameleon Fagin, that extraordinary focus of the novel's creative energy, casting off the demonic treacherous Jew for the role of benign Pied Piper—perhaps best exemplify how making a Dickens film means making a choice between the modes and genres that compete for dominance within each Dickens text. Edzard's *Little Dorrit*, for me, comes close to perfection—but so do films as different from it as chalk is from cheese, above all David Lean's taut, class-conscious *Great Expectations*: just as every stage director assumes the right to "his" or "her" *Macbeth* or *Lear*, so every film director has the right to his or her *Dorrit* or *Twist*. The Dickens who endorsed stage productions and reprocessed his novels as dramatic readings, the literary entrepreneur who invented Christmas (the *Carol* is surely the direct ancestor of every Yuletide movie release in America), the novelist bred on folk-tale, magic lantern shows, and popular art, would surely not have been surprised at his own cultural reproduction. "Dickens," as Mike Poole writes, "has always been a mass media phenomenon" with a "massive cultural profile" and "*extra*-literary" identity (148).[26] What delights always is the fertility of the Dickens who inspires, the abundance and textual excess that keeps the cameras (and the critical industry) turning.

NOTES

1. Sands Films press release. All unattributed quotations in this essay come either from press releases or from the author's interviews with the filmmakers in March and November 1990.

2. Miriam Margoyles (Flora Finching in *Little Dorrit*) and Ross Devenish (director of BBC TV's 1985 series *Bleak House*) interviewed by the author, June 1990.

3. Letter of 16 September 1855, quoted by Stone 267. Dickens reinforced the division into two books by numbering the chapters of each separately, and insisting upon it on the very title page of the first edition; it is reflected in such factors as the careful mirror-effect of the distant and designedly "objective" openings of each book—one in Marseilles, one at the Great St. Bernard.

4. Both editing devices associated with the Hollywood cinema. During a wipe, one shot progressively replaces another on the screen, sometimes from left to right, sometimes from one corner diagonally to another, and so on, with a sharp demarcating border always visible between shot A and shot B. The dissolve superimposes one shot over another for a varying amount of time (hence brisk and slow dissolves): in the "grammar" of classical Hollywood cinema, it came to signify the passage of time.

5. Little Dorrit's very first line in the film, by way of sharp contrast to the emphasis on memory in *Nobody's Fault*, is "I don't remember."

6. I am indebted for this observation to Professor George Ford, whose edition of *Hard Times* gives details of a "gruesome" *Household Words* article, "Ground in the Mill" (278), which stirred Dickens' indignation and inspired a scene, not finally included in the novel, in which Stephen Blackpool bitterly recalls "how Rachel's angelic little sister had suffered when her arm had been torn off by a factory-machine" (279).

7. For more on George Scharf, see Jackson, and Nadel and Schwarzbach.

8. For a full discussion of technology-assisted shifts in our mode of perceiving the world, see Gifford 17–47.

9. The daguerreotype process produced a single image, reversed, as in a mirror—a positive in certain lights, and a negative in others: "in direct rays of the sun it became a shiny sheet of metal" (Pollack 20). Not until Fox Talbot invented the negative-positive principle was modern photography made possible, with its potential for multiple reproduction, enlargement, and reduction. Ambrotypes (from the Greek for "imperishable") were cheaper, newer substitutes for the daguerreotype: "negative portraits on glass deliberately underexposed to make a faint image," and then "backed up with black paper or velvet or sometimes painted black" (Pollack 38).

10. Castle notes: "Wraithlike actors and actresses, reflected [by a series of mirrors] from below the stage, mingled with onstage counterparts in a phantasmagorical version of Dickens's 'The Haunted Man' on Christmas Eve, 1862" (39–40).

11. For a full discussion of this subject, see Thomas.

12. I have been encouraged to expand these notes on time, film, and the photographic imagery of *Little Dorrit* by conversation with Diane Elam of Bryn Mawr College. See her "Another Day Done and I'm Deeper in Debt: Dickens and the Debt of the Everyday," a paper given at the Dickens Project Summer Conference in Santa Cruz, California, 1990. Dickens, she argues, is most interested in *Little Dorrit* in "exploring the debt of the past within everyday life: exploring the condition and function of memory." For Elam, the novel makes a sharp distinction "between what time it is and what time *is*, the difference between 'time for what?' and 'what is time?' "

13. Magic-lantern slide shows first became popular at the end of the eighteenth century, and enjoyed a renaissance during Dickens' childhood. The diorama, invented in 1822 by the father of the daguerrotype, Louis Daguerre, offered

sweeping semi-animated prospects on history and the Orient. One of cinema's several ancestors, it used a series of paintings, some opaque, some transparent, seen from a distance through a series of movable screens and shutters, to create an illusion of perspective and movement. Miniature cardboard versions on the English market—of the great gallery of the Crystal Palace, for example—were known as "perspectives." The "left" and "right" "eye" images of the stereo-scope, viewed simultaneously, created an illusion of 3-D depth: few middle-class homes were without one by the time *Little Dorrit* was written.

14. See Low and Manvell; and Low 2:185.

15. The press's high term of praise for Brady's photographs (Pollack 59). As early as 1839, when François Arago reported his experiments and achievements to the Academy of Sciences, France signalized its recognition of the importance for the future and for the recording of history of Daguerre's invention by "adopting" it and awarding large state pensions to him and the heir of his co-inventor, Joseph Nicephore Niepce, who had taken the world's first photographic image, on pew-ter, in 1826 (Pollack 21).

16. For more on Griffith's debt to Dickens, see Zambrano 148–204. Zambrano exem-plifies the "repression" against which Altman argues, but is nevertheless a useful resource.

17. In their anxiety to establish film's credentials, Altman writes, both the filmmakers of the preclassic silent years, when the "movies" played cultural second fiddle to the respectable stage, and the classier critics of today (to their cost, and film theory's) have "repressed" early cinema's inheritance from its prime rival, popular melodrama (the disreputable stage), with its spectacle, larger-than life "mythic" characters, and episodic multifocus plots (utterly unlike the well-made play's). Sensational theatrical adaptations from Balzac, Zola, and (of course) Dickens very often "mediated" film's experience of the texts; but it was the novels and the novelists who were mentioned on the posters outside the picture-houses.

Indeed, Altman argues, it is the very fact that of all "highly respected nine-teenth-century novelists," the "most closely allied to popular sensibility and the melodrama is surely Charles Dickens," that both guaranteed his novels' cannibalization by the popular theater and ensured they would be more filmed in more countries than any other novelist's—a fact which in turn, as cinema studies have gained respectability and Dickens' postwar reputation has continued to rise, has given his works a "spuriously pivotal function" in "arguments about the relationship between novel and cinema." By investigating the "repressed" melo-dramatic mode and appeal of Dickens, Balzac, and other canonized "classical" novelists—always returned to center-stage by now equally "repressed" stage versions—Altman arrives at a suggestive reformulation of classical Hollywood narrative's "linear causality" and character motivation as (in Freudian terms) the "secondary elaboration" of filmic (dream) work: underneath, like bedrock, is the melodramatic content (329, 330, 348).

18. Not surprisingly, writes Rachel Low, the novels were "mercilessly con-densed"—mere illustrations (2:184).

19. Also see Denis Gifford, *The British Film Catalogue 1895–1970: A Reference Guide* (New York: McGraw-Hill, 1973), and Ivan Butler, *Cinema in Britain: An Illustrated Survey* (London: Tantivy, 1973).

20. "[Dickens'] works occupied a particularly important position in the British re-vival, for Hepworth, seeking to keep pace with the great world producers and at

the same time retain his reputation for a characteristically English atmosphere, found in the novels of Dickens and the services of . . . Bentley, the ideal channel for his desired development'' (Low 2:190).

21. Publicity releases for Disney's *Great Expectations* read: ''Many of the scenes were filmed in England at the locations described in the novel.''

22. Bentley left Hepworth in 1915 for Trans-Atlantic, the European representative of the Universal Film Company of America, which then opened its operations in style with his *Hard Times* (Low 3:80). This appears to have been one of the tamest of Dickens adaptations. As the *Kinematograph Monthly Film Record* for October 1915 put it: ''the sense of bitterness and indignation and biting satire left by the book has almost entirely disappeared'' (quoted by Low 3:196–97).

23. An incomplete copy of the Danish *Little Dorrit* is held by the British Film Institute.

24. In ''Black November,'' 1924, not a single foot of film was exposed in British studios (Chanan 52–53).

25. For a comparison of Dickens' 1868 dramatic-reading ''Sikes and Nancy'' to David Lean's version of the scene, see Manning 99–108.

26. Poole's is an excellent short survey of the subject; although sketchy on pre-war film history, it is particularly incisive on British television's involvement with Dickens (to its detriment as well as its benefit) and on Dickens as an easily packaged, if not pre-chewed, international media product. ''In [the] kind of climate,'' he concludes, ''where an economic drive towards globalizing the television product meets a socially-led boom in nostalgia generated by recession, it seems safe to predict that . . . future Dickens adaptations . . . will be heavily weighted towards the picturesque, the reassuring and the traditional'' (159).

WORKS CITED

Ackroyd, Peter. *Dickens*. New York: Harper, 1990.

Altman, Rick. ''Dickens, Griffith, and Film Theory Today.'' *South Atlantic Quarterly* 88 (1989):321–59.

Benson, Sheila. Review of *Little Dorrit*. *Los Angeles Times*, 16 Nov. 1988:6.

Canby, Vincent. Review of *Little Dorrit*. *New York Times*, 26 Mar. 1988:11.

Caramagno, Thomas Carmelo. ''The Dickens Revival at the Bijou: Critical Reassessment, Film Theory, and Popular Culture.'' *New Orleans Review* 15 (1988) 88–96.

Carter, Everett. ''Cultural History Written with Lightning: The Significance of *The Birth of a Nation* (1915).'' *Hollywood as Historian: American Film in a Cultural Context*. Ed. Peter C. Rollins. Lexington: UP of Kentucky, 1983:9–19.

Castle, Terry. ''Phantasmagoria: Spectral Technology and the Metaphorics of Modern Reverie.'' *Critical Inquiry* 15. 3 (1988):26–31.

Chanan, Michael. ''The Emergence of an Industry.'' *British Cinema History*, ed. James Curran and Vincent Porter. London: Weidenfeld, 1983.

Corliss, Richard. Review of *Little Dorrit. Time*, 28 Nov. 1988:92–93.

Davis, Paul. "Imaging *Oliver Twist*: Hogarth, Illustration, and the Part of Darkness." *Dickensian* 62. 3 (1986).

Dickens, Charles. *Little Dorrit.* Ed. John Holloway. Harmondsworth: Penguin, 1967.

Doré, Gustave, and Blanchard Jerrold. *London: A Pilgrimage.* London: Grant, 1872.

Eisenstein, Sergei. "Dickens, Griffith, and the Film Today." Collected in *Film Theory and Criticism*. Ed. Gerald Mast and Marshall Cohen. 3rd ed. New York: Oxford UP, 1985:370–80.

Edelstein, David. Review of *Little Dorrit. New York Times Weekend*, 21 Oct. 1988:29.

Ford, George, and Sylvere Monod, eds. *Hard Times.* New York: Norton, 1966.

Fuller, Graham. "Daring Dorrit." *Film Comment* September-October 1988:28–30.

Gifford, Don. *The Farther Shore: A Natural History of Perception, 1798–1984.* New York: Atlantic Monthly, 1990.

Greene, Graham. *The Ministry of Fear.* Harmondsworth: Penguin, 1978.

Gross, John. Review of *Little Dorrit. New York Times*, 30 Oct. 1988:22.

Jackson, Peter. *George Scharf's London: Sketches and Watercolours of a Changing City, 1820–50.* London: Murray, 1987.

Kroll, Jack. Review of *Little Dorrit. Newsweek*, 7 Nov. 1988:118.

Low, Rachael, and Roger Manvell. *The History of the British Film.* 3 vols. London: Bowker [vols. 1, 2] Allen [vol. 3], 1948–50.

Malcolm, Derek. "Double Dorrit." *Guardian* [London], 27 Nov. 1987:22.

Manning, Sylvia. "Murder in Three Media: Adaptations of *Oliver Twist*." *Dickens Quarterly* 4. 2 (1987):99–108.

Mars-Jones, Adam. "Victorian Principles." *Independent* [London], 10 Dec. 1987:16.

McAsh, Iain. "Dockland *Dorrit*." *Films and Filming*, Dec. 1987:18.

Metz, Christian. "Christian Metz on Jean Mitry's L'Esthétique et Psychologie du Cinéma, vol. II." *Screen* 14. 1–2 (1973):40–87.

Nadel, Ira Bruce, and F. S. Schwarzbach, eds. *Victorian Artists and the City: A Collection of Critical Essays.* Oxford: Pergamon, 1980.

Orwell, George. "Charles Dickens." *An Age Like This:1920–1940.* Vol. 1 of *The Collected Essays, Journalism and Letters of George Orwell.* Ed. Sonia Orwell and Ian Angus. New York: Harcourt, 1968. 413–60.

Pollack, Peter. *The Picture History of Photography: from the Earliest Beginnings to the Present Day*. London: Thames and Hudson, 1977.

Poole, Mike. "Dickens and Film:101 Uses of a Dead Author." *The Changing World of Charles Dickens*. Ed. Robert Giddings. Totowa, NJ: Barnes, 1983:148–62.

Schwarzbach, F. S. *Dickens and the City*. London: Athlone, 1979.

Showalter, Elaine. "Guilt, Authority, and the Shadows of *Little Dorrit*." *Nineteenth Century Literature* 34. 1 (1979):20–40.

Smith, Grahame. "Novel into Film: The Case of *Little Dorrit*." *Yearbook of English Studies* 20 (1990):33–47.

Sragow, Michael. Review of *Little Dorrit*. *San Francisco Examiner*, 16 Dec. 1988: C3+.

Stone, Harry, ed. *Dickens's Working Notes for His Novels*. Chicago: U of Chicago P, 1987.

Thomas, Alan. *Time in a Frame: Photography and the Nineteenth-Century Mind*. New York: Schocken, 1977.

Vineberg, Steve. Review of *Little Dorrit*. *Boston Phoenix*, 16 Sept. 1988, Sec. 3:10.

Williams, Raymond. Introd. to *Dombey and Son*, by Charles Dickens. Harmondsworth, England: Penguin, 1970.

Wills, Gary. "Dorrit without Politics." *New York Review of Books*, 2 Feb. 1989:16–18.

Winn, Steve. "Dickens Story Lives in Potent Adaptation." *San Francisco Examiner*, 25 Dec. 1988:27.

Zambrano, A. L. *Dickens and Film*. New York: Gordon, 1977.

Fig. 1. Frederick Barnard's late-century Little Dorrit.

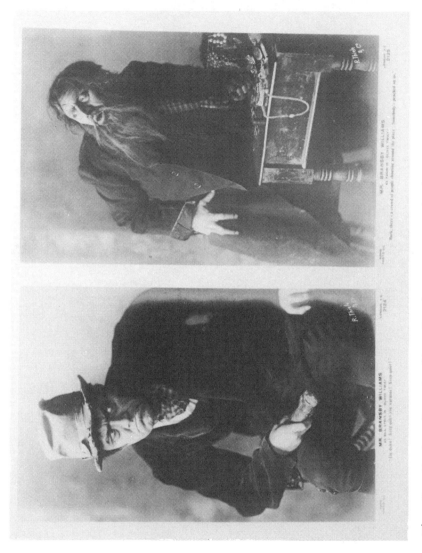

Fig. 2. Postcard-portraits of actor Bransby Williams as
Fagin and Bill Sikes (Dickens House Museum, London).

LD 4   DEREK JACOBI as Arthur Clennam.

CHARLES DICKENS'
Little Dorrit

JOHN BRABOURNE and RICHARD GOODWIN in association with THE CANNON GROUP, INC. Present a SANDS FILM Production, "LITTLE DORRIT," by Charles Dickens. DEREK JACOBI, ALEC GUINNESS, JOAN GREENWOOD, ROSHAN SETH, CYRIL CUSACK, Introducing SARAH PICKERING as "Little Dorrit." Produced by JOHN BRABOURNE and RICHARD GOODWIN. Adapted for the Screen and Directed by CHRISTINE EDZARD. © 1988 SANDS FILM (DORRIT) LTD.

Fig. 3. Characterization by object-association: Derek Jacobi as Arthur Clennam (courtesy of Sands Films).

4. Mr. Tite Barnacle usually coached or crammed the statesmen at the head of the Circumlocution Office.

10. An invitation to rest and be thankful, when there was no place to put up at, and nothing whatever to be thankful for.

32. If I could poison that dear old lady's rum and water, I'd die happy.

20. My father is a partaker of glory at present, Master Copperfield, but we have much to be thankful for.

3. There was an old principle within him, and a young surface without.

22. Step this way, Nickleby; my dear, will you follow me? Ha! ha! They all follow me, Nickleby; always, demmit, always.

Fig. 4. Players cigarette cards. Clockwise from top left: Tite Barnacle, "Patriarch" Christopher Casby, Daniel Quilp, Mr. Mantalini, Bailey Junior, Uriah Heep (Dickens House Museum, London). A characteristic line of dialogue or description accompanies each portrait.

Fig. 5. Artist's impression of Dickens "as" Nancy (Dickens House Museum, London).

Fig. 6. Chameleon Alec Guiness as William Dorrit: the quintessence of genteel self-pity (publicity portrait courtesy of Sands Films).

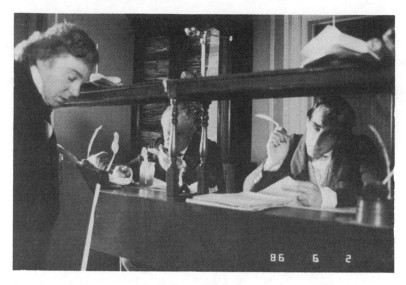

Fig. 7. Mr. Wobbler (Ken Morley) dribbles marmalade on documents, while the storytelling clerk (Michael Mears) pokes holes in them with a quill pen (continuity shot courtesy of Sands Films).

Fig. 8. Edzard's Slapbang Restaurant: every face asks our attention, every bit-player has a story to tell (courtesy of Sands Films).

Fig. 9. Arthur Clennam's solitary dinner in an anonymous chop shop commences the action of Edzard's <u>Little Dorrit</u> (continuity shot courtesy of Sands Films).

Fig. 10. Hablot K. Browne, "Mr. Guppy entertains his friends," from <u>Bleak House</u>.

Fig. 11. George Cruikshank, "Thoughts about People," from
Sketches by Boz:
 He hangs up his hat--he took it off the moment he sat
 down--and bespeaks the paper after the next gentleman.
 If he can get it while he is at dinner, he eats it with
 much greater zest; balancing it against the water-
 bottle, and eating a bit of beef, and reading a line or
 two, alternately.

Fig. 12. Hablot K. Browne's Marshalsea Yard. "Phiz" brings
the bit players to left and right to seedy life as vividly
as he creates the Dorrit brothers at center.

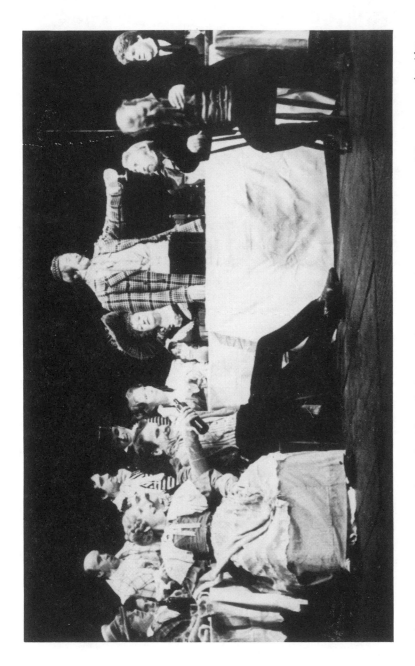

Fig. 13. As near as damn it the whole novel: one of numerous ensemble scenes in the Royal Shakespeare Company's Nicholas Nickleby (courtesy of the R.S.C.).

Fig. 14. The Dorrits leaving the Marshalsea, from Arthur's point-of-view (continuity shot courtesy of Sands Films).

Fig. 15. The Dorrit processional from Little Dorrit's point of view (production still courtesy of Sands Films).

Fig. 16. Under Little Dorrit's watchful eye, withered plants in the Marshalsea room break into leaf and bloom (production still courtesy of Sands Films).

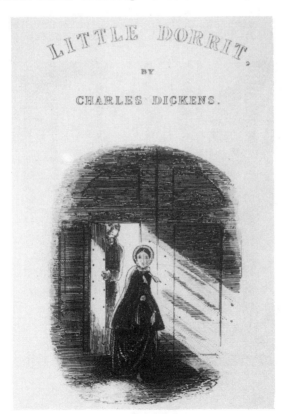

Fig. 17. Hablot K. Browne, frontispiece to <u>Little Dorrit</u>.

Fig. 18. The visual imagery of film: Alec Guiness as William Dorrit, with Susan Tanner as Little Dorrit, age eight, "framed" in the window behind him (courtesy of Sands Films).

Fig. 19. Sarah Pickering as Little Dorrit, seen through the bars of the Marshalsea Gate (courtesy of Sands Films).

Fig. 20. The groaning Merdle board looms still larger
thanks to a combination of camera lens, placement, and angle
(continuity shot courtesy of Sands Films).

Fig. 21. Arthur Clennam meets Frederick Dorrit (Cyril
Cusack) outside the Marshalsea: posters on the wall
advertise Bulwer Lytton's MONEY! (production still courtesy
of Sands Films).

Fig. 22. "Phiz"'s model for the Marshalsea room of Edzard's
<u>Little Dorrit</u>: the door at right moves to the left-hand
wall, to Fanny's right as she sits on the sofa, to allow the
camera in.

Fig. 23. Hablot K. Browne, "The Room with the Portrait."

Fig. 24. Hablot K. Browne, "Floating Away."

Fig. 25. Hablot K. Browne, "The Fat Boy Awake on this Occasion," from <u>The Pickwick Papers</u>.

Fig. 26. Bob the turnkey (Howard Goorney) takes Little Amy Dorrit (Susan Tanner) for a pastoral walk (continuity shot courtesy of Sands Films).

Fig. 27. Hablot K. Browne, "Visitors at the Works."

Fig. 28. Arthur in the Doyce and Clennam workshop (continuity shot courtesy of Sands Films).

Fig. 29.   Hablot K. Browne, "The Marshalsea Becomes an
Orphan."   "Phiz" the illustrator can melt away the
Marshalsea walls to allow this perspective on the departing
Dorrit processional; film, more rooted in actuality and
continuity of space, cannot so "cheat" the mind--compare
figs. 17 and 18.

Fig. 30.   Turn-of-the-century engraving of the Marshalsea
courtyard, produced for the Charles Dickens Edition of the
complete works.

Fig. 31. Edzard's reconstruction of the Marshalsea courtyard, the sense of imprisonment intensified by framing that cuts us out the sky (still courtesy of Sands Films).

Fig. 32. Setting up a shot of Edzard's "streets, streets, streets" on the sound stage at Grices Wharf: hanging miniatures photographed to fit exactly with the "skyline" of the flats and "rooms" of the set will supply the upper storeys in the finished process images (continuity shot courtesy of Sands Films).

Fig. 33. Through the street markets to Arthur's lodgings (continuity shot courtesy of Sands Films).

Fig. 34. Miniature London skyline and mock-up ship masts that sway on request: shot from the correct angle, they will create the prospect Arthur and Little Dorrit see from the Iron Bridge (continuity shot courtesy of Sands Films).

Fig. 35. George Scharf's sketch of London Bridge railway station under construction, 1843. Reproduced from George Scharf's London. Edzard captures this splendid display of individualism in shop-fronts and rooflines in her flat sets and hanging miniatures.

Fig. 37. George Cruikshank, "The Streets--Morning," from Sketches by Boz.

Fig. 36. Hablot K. Browne, "Mr. Pecksniff calls upon Mrs. Sairah Gamp," from Martin Chuzzlewit.

Fig. 39. Dore's bridge and tottering warehouses, background to the central location of Oliver! (1968), Fagin's den, and reproduced with photographic exactitude in David Lean's adaptation twenty years earlier.

Fig. 38. Backyard in Cloth Fair (Society for Photographing Relics of Old London; Museum of London).

Fig. 40. Doré, butcher's stall.

Fig. 41. Doré, ballad seller.

Fig. 42. Portrait commissioned by Charles Spurgeon of a Greenwich seller of "Vesuvians" (courtesy of Greenwich Public Library).

Fig. 43. In the days before telephones, street traders who could not afford donkeys or handcarts had to carry their wares and their tools on their backs, like Spurgeon's window-mender (courtesy of Greenwich Public Library).

Fig. 44. Spurgeon, "W. Thompson, Champion Pie Maker" (courtesy of Greenwich Public Library).

Fig. 45. Filming the bustle outside Edzard's print-shop (continuity shot courtesy of Sands Films).

Fig. 46. John Thomson, Fish Stall holder, from <u>Street Life</u> <u>in London</u> (1877).

Fig. 47. Scharf, Covent Garden.

Fig. 48. Dore's vignette of homeless Londoners.

Fig. 49. John Thomson, "The Crawlers," from <u>Street Life in London</u>.

Fig. 50. Pancks denounces "Patriarch" Casby (Bill Fraser) to the slum-dwellers of Bleeding Heart Yard (courtesy of Sands Films).

Fig. 51. Setting up a take on the Yard set (continuity shot courtesy of Sands Films).

Fig. 52. Edzard's Bleeding Heart Yard is based on such Doré engravings as this of Orange Court, round the back of Drury Lane Theater. The old slums of London, where pigs and geese shared space and central sewers with human inhabitants, began to be demolished in the decades after <u>Little Dorrit</u> was written.

Fig. 53. 16 Bayham Street, Camden Town, a four-room house with a basement and garret, into which were crammed the eight members of Dickens's family, their lodger, and a maid, in 1821.

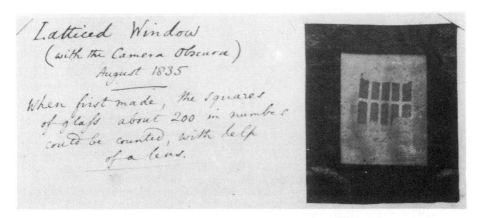

Fig. 54. Fox Talbot's first "sun picture" (Science Museum, London).

Fig. 55. The Victorian renaissance of the magic lantern, as visualized by the Boy's Own magazine (Museum of London).

Fig. 56. Design of this 1896 poster reflects both the public's fascination with the technology of moving pictures, and the kinds of subject matter that first took its imagination (Museum of London).

Fig. 57. "Detail at a distance": a continuity shot allows
us to see close up the plates hand-thrown by Sands Films'
own potter, the clay pipe that Pancks is about to light with
a long "fusee", the pewter tobacco tin, the broad-bottomed
and slightly irregularly blown bottle (courtesy of Sands
Films).

Fig. 58. No concession to Victorian or modern standards of
beauty and acting: unknown drama student Sarah Pickering as
Little Dorrit in her "tunnel-vision" bonnet (courtesy of
Sands Films).

Fig. 59. The climactic moment of the murder--the scene that got early stage versions banned by the Lord Chamberlain's Office--in Hepworth's 1912 <u>Oliver Twist</u> (courtesy of the British Film Institute).

Fig. 60. Steerforth elopes with Little Em'ly. A leap forward in composition within the film frame: Thomas Bentley's 1913 <u>David Copperfield</u> (courtesy of the British Film Institute).

Fig. 61. Dickens as England: David on the White Cliffs of Dover, in Bentley's <u>Copperfield</u> (courtesy of the British Film Institute).

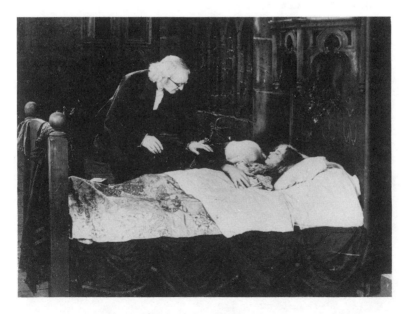

Fig. 62. Director Bentley's return in his 1921 remake to the central scene of <u>The Old Curiosity Shop</u> (courtesy of the British Film Institute).

Fig. 63. Death calls again, in Bentley's third and final telling of Little Nell's story, in 1935 (courtesy of the British Film Institute).

Fig. 64. Wilcox's 1922 <u>The Only Way</u> blends traces of its theatrical origins with a filmic sense of space and peripheral incident (courtesy of the British Film Institute).

Fig. 65. Art-still from <u>The Only Way</u> (courtesy of the British Film Institute).

Fig. 66. Young Pip promenades around the wedding-breakfast table with Miss Havisham in David Lean's atmospheric <u>Great Expectations</u> (1946). (Courtesy of the British Film Institute.)

Fig. 67. The soldiers capture the convict: a stunning
visual image from Lean's <u>Great Expectations</u> (courtesy of the
British Film Institute).

Fig. 68. David Lean setting up the pivotal Workhouse scene
in his <u>Oliver Twist</u> (1948). (Courtesy of the British Film
Institute.)

Fig. 69. Cavalcanti's nostalgic <u>Nickleby</u> (1947): all frills and froth (courtesy of the British Film Institute).

Fig. 70. A grittier Dickens: location shot from <u>A Tale of Two Cities</u> (1958). (Courtesy of the British Film Institute.)

Fig. 71. Sound stage shooting of the funeral sequence in
Oliver! (1968). (Courtesy of the British Film Institute.)

Fig. 72. Setting up a crane shot on the giant set for the
"Beautiful Morning" production number in *Oliver!* (courtesy
of the British Film Institute). The author's father is
right of camera.

Trevelyan, Treasury, and Circumlocution

Trey Philpotts

It is generally recognized that the Circumlocution Office in *Little Dorrit* reflects Dickens' dismay over bureaucratic bungling during the Crimean war. But little has been done, beyond this general proposition, to get at the specifics of Dickens' analysis. Consequently, much of the particular import of his satire has been lost. In this article I will resurrect the context in which *Little Dorrit* was begun and show how Dickens' use of the Civil Service and the Crimean War is far from vague and generalized, but reflects a specific analysis of particular events. We shall see that much more underlies Dickens' use of the Circumlocution Office than has been heretofore expected, much that has been lost to the modern reader.

First and foremost, Dickens' presentation of the Circumlocution Office is an attack on a specific government department for specific reasons. At the beginning of chapter 10, in which Dickens discusses "the Whole Science of Government," he takes pains to intimate to the contemporary reader exactly which department he is attacking. But because Dickens' description can be easily misread by a modern reader as merely metaphorical, the particular force of the description is lost. The Circumlocution Office, the narrator begins, was

> the most important Department under government. No public business of any kind could possibly be done at any time, without the acquiescence of the Circumlocution Office. Its finger was in the largest public pie, and in the smallest public tart. It was equally impossible to do the plainest right and to undo the plainest wrong, without the express authority of the Circumlocution Office. (100)

The narrator then explains that "the Circumlocution Office had risen to over-top all the public departments" (101). For a contemporary reader, these

283

allusions would have been unmistakable: Dickens would have been referring to the Treasury Office. The Treasury, one of its mid-Victorian leaders has written, was "the heart of our whole administrative system";[1] the *North British Review* in May 1855 referred to it as "the supreme and controlling department of the Executive" (78); a modern historian has called it "the department of departments" (Wright 1). It is surely no accident that in *The Three Clerks* Trollope has the Office of Weights and Measures, which "is exactly antipodistic of the Circumlocution Office," "so conspicuously confronting the Treasury Chambers" (1). Of the estimated 42,000 civil servants, 32,898 were employed in the Treasury and its subordinate departments in 1856 (Wright xxiv). Because it had the power of the purse strings, the Treasury was able to exert a de facto control over most other departments. It had control over expenditures such as salaries, pensions, and allowances. Before a department could add employees, it had to appeal to the Treasury for approval. The Treasury might also recommend that departments make reductions, though it lacked the power to enforce its recommendations. Dickens makes a subtle, but quite accurate, distinction when he writes that "No public business of any kind could possibly be done at any time, without the acquiescence of the Circumlocution Office." For the Treasury would, in the end, almost always "acquiesce" in the requests of the other departments, however grudgingly.

The Treasury's most effective means of control was through formal inquiries into the practices of other departments, the mere fact of inquiry often forcing compliance. Dickens alludes to this last power in his opening description of the Circumlocution Office:

> This glorious establishment had been early in the field, when the one sublime principle involving the difficult art of governing a country, was first distinctly revealed to statesmen. It had been foremost to study that bright revelation, and to carry its shining influence through the whole of the official proceedings.
>
> (100)

Behind this allusion lie the thousands of pages of blue books generated by the Treasury investigations, those *Parliamentary Papers* devoted to the examination of the government and its bureaucracy, which in Dickens' view were merely recipes for discovering the "bright revelation" of the perfectly obvious. Included in the Treasury's "shining influence" would have been the Assistant Secretary's most recent report which had come out the year before, the "Report on the Organization of the Permanent Civil Service" (usually referred to as the Northcote-Trevelyan report).

On the surface, this fact seems surprising. It has been standard practice in modern introductions of *Little Dorrit* to suggest that the Northcote-Trevelyan report represents current thought about Civil Service reform. This current thought, so the argument goes, helped form Dickens' own views on the subject, though critics are wary of saying he was "influenced" by the report itself, presumably because he never seems to mention it. While it is true that Dickens never refers to the Northcote-Trevelyan report by name, he alludes to it in "Cheap Patriotism," an article he wrote for *Household Words* and published in early June 1855, just as he was beginning his novel.

This article bears analysis, because the attitudes espoused in it are not those normally associated with Dickens. The article is presented from the point of view of a recently retired civil servant with over forty years experience, who received his position through family influence and admits to having been dilatory in his younger days. But he claims to have "shed some of my impertinences" over time and to be doing "what I had to do, reasonably well" (434). As becomes clear, he represents Dickens' generally approving view of a career civil servant, of someone who perhaps benefited from patronage, but who all in all has credibly performed his job—exactly the type of bureaucrat that Trollope (and later C. P. Snow) was so fond of. Early in the article, the civil servant refers to the Northcote-Trevelyan report when he attacks the concept of open exams:

> There is a considerable flourish just now, about examining candidates for clerkships, as if they wanted to take high degrees in learned professions. I don't myself think that Chief Justices and Lord Chancellors are to be got for twenty-two pound ten a quarter, with a final prospect of some five or six hundred a year in the ripe fullness of futurity—and even if they were, I doubt if their abilities could come out very strongly in the usual work of a government office.
>
> (434)

This is a considerably more sophisticated view of the civil service than has been allowed Dickens. For one thing, the passage suggests that he was familiar with the Northcote-Trevelyan report (or at least with detailed journalistic accounts), since it closely echoes opinions put forth by Sir James Stephen in one of a series of letters appended to the original report and published with it in 1855. In his letter Stephen, the Permanent Under-Secretary of the Colonial Office from 1835 to 1847, opposes many of the report's recommendations, doubting the likelihood of low pay being a sufficient inducement to draw "any men of eminent ability to whom any other path in life is open" ("Re-Organization" 75). He also explains that the successful candidate of

open competition would find his "gifts ill suited, and even inconvenient, to
one who is entombed for life as a clerk in a Public Office in Downing Street"
(76). Administrative reform and civil service reform were not, as Olive Anderson has pointed out, the same thing ("Janus Face" 234; "Administrative
Reform" 278). It is entirely consistent that Dickens could have supported the
one and rejected, at least in part, the other. Administrative reform meant
tossing the aristocratic rascals out of office and replacing them with experienced men of the world, those whom Dickens and other reformers equated
with the practical middle class. Civil service reform meant open exams requiring considerable formal education, which those of humbler birth—those, in
other words, like Dickens—would have lacked. In the end the exams might
well only strengthen the hold of the aristocrats on the bureaucracy, or so it
was feared. The Administrative Reform Association was itself, at least in its
early stages, quite skeptical of open competition, one Association pamphleteer
fearing that the examination board would be susceptible to the "secret influences of the Treasury" (qtd. in Anderson "Janus Face" 233).

If Dickens essentially agreed with Stephen's strictures on the Northcote-
Trevelyan report, then the question arises, what was his attitude toward the
great mid-century reformer himself, Sir Charles Trevelyan? Again, the answer
can be found in "Cheap Patriotism." For Dickens (in his guise of the knowledgeable civil servant) goes on to introduce Sir Jasper Janus, the ministerial
head of a representative department of the civil service, and an obvious
stand-in for Trevelyan. Janus, the clerk explains, "acquired in the House the
reputation of being a remarkable man of business, through the astonishing
confidence with which he explained details of which he was entirely ignorant,
to an audience who knew no more of them than he did."[2] Dickens is here
taking aim at the "cheap patriotism" of those like Janus who make a career
and a considerable reputation out of promulgating what were, for Dickens,
factitious reforms. Janus, Dickens makes clear, is really a two-faced bureaucrat, a cynical opportunist whose main concern is "to make out a case for
himself" (434). Among other supposed improvements, he wants to install
"an entirely new system of check, by double entry and countersign, on the
issue at the outports of fore-top-gallant-yards and snatch-blocks to the Royal
Navy" (435), an allusion to Trevelyan's involvement in the Crimean War (as
we shall see). Dickens pointedly has Janus intend to explain a proposed
consolidation of his staff to the "committee on Miscellaneous Estimates."
In fact, it was Sir Charles Trevelyan's testimony before the committee of
Miscellaneous Expenses in 1847–48 that served as the source for many of the
recommendations of his later report. And Dickens has Janus explain "details

of which he was entirely ignorant'' (434), much as Trevelyan had the temerity to write a book on the Irish famine, *The Irish Crisis* (1848), though he himself rarely visited the country and seemed ignorant of many of its entrenched problems (Hart 100). Trevelyan could be a hard, unsympathetic man, regarding the countless deaths during this catastrophe as a judgment of God and ''a discipline'' (Hart 99) and, in an attitude particularly anathema to Dickens, he was more interested in the poor's moral welfare than in their material well-being (Hart 109). He was also a bit of a hypocrite. Despite his censures against patronage, he was not above insuring that his own family and connections found jobs, pressing their claims even after they had come to disappoint him (Hart 97–98). Trevelyan's imperious, self-righteous, and tactless character was accurately limned by Trollope in *The Three Clerks*. Sir Gregory Hardlines, like Sir Janus, is willing to ride roughshod over others to further his own ambition.

To modern critics this interpretation of Dickens' views may seem surprising: Dickens agreeing with Stephen and lambasting Trevelyan, the great civil service reformer? Dickens and Trollope seeing eye to eye on such a matter? Nearly fifty years ago, Humphry House wrote that there was ''nothing stranger than Henry Reeve's assumption in the *Edinburgh* that in *Little Dorrit* Dickens was attacking the 'universal system of jobbing and favoritism which was introduced into the public service by Sir Charles Trevelyan and Sir Stafford Northcote'' (189). But, as we shall see, there was nothing strange in this assertion at all, for that is precisely what Dickens *was* doing—attacking Trevelyan.[3] For Trevelyan was more than a civil service reformer. From 1840 to 1859 he was the Assistant Secretary of the Treasury, its chief permanent (not Parliamentary as with Sir Janus) civil servant.

The question remains: Why *would* Dickens be so opposed to Trevelyan; after all, was not he the one who wanted to simplify matters, to eradicate all the red tape? Surely, Dickens' doubts about competitive exams would not justify such a vehemently ad hominem attack. Dickens clearly favors *some* reform of the civil service, even a cursory reading of *Little Dorrit* would attest to that, so why would he set out to denigrate one of the harshest critics of bureaucratic red tape, one who had, after all, made significant improvements in his own department, the Treasury?

In many ways, the Treasury was exactly the wrong department for Dickens to attack. Under the leadership of Trevelyan and Northcote, and with the imprimatur of Gladstone, the Treasure led the fight for administrative reform in 1854 and 1855, already practicing, though imperfectly, many of the recommendations made by the Northcote-Trevelyan report. Indeed, qualifying exams, though not the desired open competition, had been in effect in the

Treasury for several years. And by 1854, largely because of Treasury efforts, promotion by merit was becoming increasingly accepted by other departments, though, as Maurice Wright observes, it was far from evenly applied (285). But competition, even in the Treasury Office, was often in name only. Sometimes, for example, departments would nominate three candidates for one vacancy, knowing that two of the three could not hope to meet even minimal standards. In a famous and perhaps apocryphal story W. G. Hayter, the Patronage Secretary for the Treasury, supposedly reserved two young men, known as the "Treasury idiots," to compete against the favored candidate (Wright 68). Moreover, the very size of the Treasury and the influence it wielded made it a likely point of attack. With many departments under its sway, the Treasury possessed the largest share of patronage in the Civil Service. Because the patronage Secretary had "the distribution of the largest portion of the good things in Government," an anonymous pamphleteer explained in 1855, "a friend at the Treasury is better than a thousand good arguments" ("Red-Tapeism" 8, 15–16), which explains why Dickens refers to this Secretary as "Jobbiana" in "A Thousand and One Humbugs," his satire of April 1855 (290). And because the Treasury had responsibility to present items of civil expenditure to Parliament, it was often the focus of those who attacked sinecures (Pellew 4).

But while the Treasury's size and influence explains much, there is more at work here than is apparent on the surface. For Dickens' antipathy toward the Treasury Office goes back to at least 1850 and reflects a deep-seated antagonism against specific actions of the department. Once again we must resort to *Household Words*. The Treasury and the Assistant Secretary are attacked by name in "The Royal Rotten Row Commission," an article written for the magazine by William Taylor Haly and W. H. Wills and appearing on 15 June 1850. Haly and Wills depict a Treasury committed to bureaucratic formula, to complex schemes of oversight that do nothing to improve the "rotten rows," those terrible hovels within which the people slowly die. The writers particularly comment on "the delays which ["poor widows, orphans, and other troublesome and disagreeable complainants"] suppose they encounter in getting even the most reasonable claims attended to" (275).

Six months later, Dickens invoked the cholera epidemic of the preceding two years in "A December Vision," imagining the shadow of death to be descending on the land. "I saw that not one miserable wretch breathed out his poisoned life in the deepest cellar of the most neglected town," he wrote, "but, from the atmosphere, some particles of his infection were borne away, charged with heavy retribution on the general guilt." Against this "poisoned air,'' Dickens set those "attentive and alarmed persons" who were obstructed by "the noisy fools and greedy knaves, whose harvest was in such horrors" (266). Most notable among those "attentive and alarmed persons" was Edwin Chadwick, instrumental in the movement for sanitary reform and a lightning rod for its critics, and by 1847 a friend of Dickens. Dickens' allusion to "poisoned air" particularly refers to the (false) theory promulgated by Chadwick and the Board of Health that cholera was transmitted through the air and could be detected by smell. As Chadwick saw it, perhaps the biggest obstacle to sanitary reform was from the government itself, in particular the Treasury department.

To follow Chadwick's reasoning, we must first understand the role of one of Dickens' least favorite political figures, the butt of some of his bitterest invective: Lord Seymour, the 6th Earl of Somerset. Lord John Russell had appointed Lord Seymour to be Head of the Department of Woods and Forests at the end of March 1850, which meant that Seymour would replace the Earl of Carlisle, a supporter of reform and a friend of Chadwick, as ex-officio President of the General Board. Seymour was a proud and haughty man with little sympathy for social reform. "There must be poor," he informed Chadwick, explaining that "his rule in office was never to act until obliged and then to do as little as possible" (Finer 387). The Department of Woods and Forests was a subordinate department to the Treasury, and one of Lord Seymour's main purposes on the Board was to act as Treasury agent. Because the Treasury worried that Chadwick's plans to improve the peoples' health would be too expensive and that the General Board was assuming too many powers without adequately consulting the Treasury, Lord Seymour intervened to obstruct the board. With the bickering back and forth between the Treasury and the General Board, each trying to dominate the other, the pace of reform slowed considerably.[4] Ultimately, Treasury interference contributed to the demise of the General Board itself (at least as it included Chadwick, Shaftesbury, and other hard-core reformers). "For this," a modern historian writes,

Chadwick henceforth began to blame a sinister alliance of the Treasury and vested interests. He alleged that the Treasury was slow to act, instancing its delay in sanctioning the cholera inspectors and its delay in answering the Board's letters. He alleged that it had determined from the start to ruin the Interment Act and quoted Sir William Hayter, the Financial Secretary, as saying that 'Ashley and Chadwick were no better than a couple of socialists'. . . . He also charged that public officers had shares and interests in the works which the Board had a duty to condemn, and that these forewarned the vested interests of the Government's attitude to the Board. When they served compulsory purchase notices on two of the cemeteries, they discovered that the chairman of one was the father of one Under-Secretary of State, and the Chairman of the second was the uncle of another Under-Secretary.[5]   (405)

In Chadwick's furious allegations lies, I think, the seeds of Circumlocution. For Dickens, Chadwick's "most outspoken public champion," shared his anger (Finer 239). In "Red Tape" (15 February 1851) Dickens cites a pamphlet which was reprinted from the *Westminster Review*, and which has apparently fallen into his hands. The pamphlet describes an incident from 1844. In the spring of that year a deputation from the Master Carpenter's Society and the Metropolitan Improvement Society—including Dr. Southwood Smith, later on the Board of Health—visited the office of the Chancellor of the Exchequer, which Dickens calls "the Incarnation of Red Tape," to make a case for the repeal of the window tax. But the Chancellor, along with the Prime Minister the key Parliamentary figure on the Treasury Board, refused to make any concessions, his confused defense of the tax only complicating matters. In his summary, Dickens complains of "the miles of red tape" piled into barriers "against—a General Interment Bill, say, or a Law for the suppression of infectious and disgusting nuisances!" These are precisely the measures which the interference of Seymour and the Treasury Office blocked, Dickens here drawing a connection between an earlier instance of obstruction and a later. He then goes on to rail against "the interminable perspectives of Exchequers, Woods and Forests, and what not, all hung with Red Tape, up and down which ["the public functionary"] will languidly wander, to the weariness of all whose hard fate it is, to have to pursue him!" (183). Dickens further alludes to the obfuscation of the Treasury in his speech to the Metropolitan Sanitary Association on 10 May when he jokes bitterly about the "Woods—and Forests" being responsible for the delay in sanitary reform (Fielding 129). This association was also in Dickens' mind in late April 1855, as he was beginning *Little Dorrit*. In "The Thousand and One Humbugs" he describes "a great river of liquid filth which ornamented that agreeable country [England] and rendered it salubrious." This filthy river, Dickens writes, was "in the neighborhood of the Woods and Forests," a neighborhood "famous for casting prodigious quantities of dust into the eyes of the Faithful" (289).

As for Lord Seymour, Dickens had only disgust, some of which is evident in his article "It Is Not Generally Known," published in *Household Words* on 2 September 1854. With cholera striking England for the second time in five years and the powers of the Board of Health set to expire, Seymour felt it time to unleash a terrible joke on the floor of Parliament: "*The cholera is always coming when the powers of this Board are about to expire (A LAUGH).*" Dickens, assuming the voice of Seymour, wrote that

This well-timed joke of mine, so neatly made upon the greatest misery and direst calamity that human nature can endure, will be repeated to-morrow in the same newspaper which will carry to my honorable friends here, through electric telegraph, the tidings of a troop-ship [off to the Crimea] put back to Plymouth, with this very pestilence on board. What are such trifles to me? I wanted a laugh; I have got a laugh. Talk to *me* of the agony and death of men and brothers! Am I not a Lord and a Member!   (50)

On 7 October Dickens, apparently still irritated, repeated the allusion in "To Working Men," sardonically remarking that Seymour "exhibited his fitness for ever having been placed at the head of a great public department" by cutting jokes on the floor of Parliament (169). The return of cholera had given the association between Seymour, the Woods and Forests, and the Treasury Office new life.

In all of this, it should be remembered that *Little Dorrit* begins with a cholera quanrantine (incidentally, Chadwick firmly opposed quarantines as useless) and that Dickens' own daughter, Mary, became "very ill" with cholera while the Dickenses vacationed in Boulogne in September 1854. Critics have often seen *Dombey and Son* and *Bleak House* as satires on sanitary reform. Rarely, if ever, have they done so with *Little Dorrit*, though much of its original impetus derives from just that. When in the novel Dickens invokes the "ill-advised public servant" whose plans run afoul of the minutes of the Circumlocution Office and refers to the "projects for the general welfare" which get lost in the bureaucratic shuffle (101), he probably has in mind Edwin Chadwick and his measures for sewage disposal and the removal of burials to the suburbs of London. Indeed, Chadwick, who pushed the idea of small-bore, self-cleaning pipes for sewers as opposed to man-size brick tunnels, probably serves as one of the originals for the character of Daniel Doyce. It is no coincidence that Henry Austin, Dickens' brother-in-law, was the engineer for what was at the time a radical, and quite suspect, method of sewage removal.

By mid-1855 there was a more immediate reason that Dickens would attack the Treasury and see it as the source of the red tape that he felt had come to bury England. For among his many duties, the Assistant Secretary of the Treasury was responsible for the Commissariat, and it was the Commissariat which had come to be held accountable, more than any other department, for the miseries in the Crimea. Indeed, it must have seemed to Dickens as if what he most feared had become a terrible reality.

The Commissariat had tremendous responsibility. It was charged with paying the troops; feeding the men and their animals; furnishing clothing, light, and fuel; and insuring that land transport was provided. This last responsibility was particularly onerous, given that the Commissariat had to transport not merely the army's stores, but heavy guns, siege materials, ammunition, field equipment, forage, and clothing, as well as being responsible for removing the sick and wounded (Kinglake 7:36). A harsh winter, a small harbor at Balaclava, lack of sufficient stores, and sheer administrative ineptitude led to the needless deaths of thousands of English troops in the winter of 1854. By the spring of 1855, much of the blame had fallen on Commissary-General Filder for his slowness in meeting demand, lack of preparation, excessive paperwork, and failure to overcome difficulties. Testimony was given during the hearings of the Sebastopol Committee in April and May 1855, just as Dickens was beginning to plan his new novel, which seemed to confirm the public's worst suspicions. This testimony was reproduced in many places. *The Times* ran a regular column and most of the journals of the day carried long excerpts of the testimony. In addition, Dickens was close friends with a member of the committee, Austen Henry Layard, who met with him several times during the spring of 1855. The testimony rehearses, in quite specific ways, many of the motifs that would later show up in *Little Dorrit*. In May *Fraser's Magazine* carried the testimony of Sir George de Lacy Evans, who specifically arraigned the "higher authorities," those whom he equated with the Treasury Office:

> [On arriving at Malta] I was astonished to hear from the authorities that the commissary-general . . . had made no necessary purchases, or scarcely any, with regard to mules, and no purchases with regard to carts, or scarcely any, *of both of which there was a considerable quantity in the island.* . . . The whole commissariat department that was sent out from this country was practically completely inadequate to its duties in all its parts.
> . . . [In Scutari he finds] that there was a good deal of difficulty about the issue of rations, and I was rather surprised that the commissary-general did not come to know whether I had any directions to give him, *but he was living, it appears, at Constantinople.* [He goes on to blame] the very great inconveniences of those *Treasury regulations*, for frequently there were great delays owing to these misarrangements; large detachments of soldiers had to wait four or five hours very often for their rations, sometimes even being obliged to go away when the evening closed without receiving them. . . . I do not bring this as a complaint against the commissariat department so much as against, I think, the spirit of the Treasury authorities of the Cabinet.[6]   ("Sebastopol Committee" 593–94)

Thus we have it: the waiting, the being turned away, the failure of oversight. de Lacy Evans went on to complain of the incompetency of a large number of the clerks on hand: "They were very good *accountants*, and at the Treasury

I suppose they thought if a man kept his accounts very well he was a competent commissary; but *the greater number of them knew nothing whatsoever about field duty.*"[7] After further testimony, *Fraser's* sums up:

> The feeding of the army at Gallipoli was undertaken in the same dull spirit of routine, consulting nothing beyond the precedents, bound together with red tape, and deposited in the archives of the public offices, which unless some patriotic incendiary reduces them to ashes, will, we fear, continue to mislead us, and even future generations.　　　　　　　　　　　　　　　(595)

Again, we see the connections: red tape, routine, a reliance on precedents (William Barnacle's favorite means to reduce his parliamentary critics to silence), the hope for a "patriotic incendiary" (Pancks raises "the hand of the incendiary" against Mr. Casby). Employing a particularly telling expression, *Fraser's* goes on to condemn those who insisted that keeping the hospital in Scutari clean—it was a horrid mess—was "nobody's department, and therefore nobody would meddle with it" ("Sebastopol Committee" 601).

The report of the Sebastopol committee—issued in June 1855 but published in part throughout the spring—is a veritable treasure trove of likely source material for *Little Dorrit*. One of the most resonant pieces of testimony comes from a letter written by Lord Lucan to the quartermaster general and included in his testimony of 15 March. "Repeatedly," Lord Lucan said,

> I have . . . remonstrated with Commissary-general Filder, and entreated his attention to the wants of the cavalry, but to no purposes whatever. He insists upon leaving the Commissariat duties with youths altogether without experience, and who do not show any zeal or desire to make up for their personal deficiencies. Seeing them, as I do myself every day . . . I have still failed in getting them to exert themselves sufficiently to afford a hope that they will at all adequately discharge their duties. Unlike other divisions, Commissary-general Filder persists in leaving the Cavalry Division without any superintending Commissariat officer. It appears irrational that the cavalry, requiring more and larger supplies than the rest of the army, should be left in the hands of the most inexperienced and the most inefficient, and without a head to instruct or control them.　　　　　　　　　　　　　　　("Minutes of Evidence" Part 1:299)[8]

Fraser's carried a paraphrase of this testimony in May, particularly remarking on the Treasury Clerks, who it noted were "proverbially the most worthless class of public servants that the country is encumbered with" ("Sebastopol Committee" 600).

The excessive amounts of paperwork required by the Commissariat came in for particular attack. In an oft-repeated story, Major-General H. J. Bentinck described to the committee how the Commissariat was "apt to be very strict with regard to those papers being filled up, and duly signed.'' He elaborates on one instance when he had a voucher for forage returned to him because it was signed a half an inch too low. Meanwhile, the troops were kept waiting (''Minutes of Evidence'' 1:102). On 15 March *The Times* repeated this story and added another. The Duke of Cambridge testified, the paper reported, that the Commissariat had obstructed his request:

> [A]*lthough the men were in want of daily rations*, instead of sending those rations at once, the Commissariat sent a printed form to the officer for him to fill up. Hence there was considerable delay, and then, not satisfied with that, the officer was supposed to have put down one or two more horses than he was entitled to. Instead of sending the rations for the men and pointing out the inaccuracy in the return of horses, *they would send no rations at all, because the form was wrong.* (6)

Mid-Victorian readers of *Little Dorrit* would have had such anecdotes firmly in mind as they perused Dickens' satire, current events having supplied a new context and meaning to Dickens' long-standing conceits of delay and red tape.

Toward the end of April 1855, Sir Charles Trevelyan, as the Assistant Secretary of the Treasury and the administrative head of the Commissariat, testified before the Sebastopol Committee. This was only two weeks before Dickens began his new novel. Trevelyan's testimony, as a sort of capstone for the months of evidence that preceded it, directly contributes to the ''Nobody's Fault'' atmosphere of *Little Dorrit*.[9] For as his testimony proceeds, it becomes increasingly evident that the evasive Secretary will accept no blame. ''Sir Charles Trevelyan has told his story, and like all the actors in this tragedy of errors, he seems to succeed in shifting the blame from his own department,'' declares *The Times*. ''One thing only is clear,''ironically comments the paper two days later, ''the Commissariat cannot be very much in the wrong.'' The final report of the Committee makes the same point: ''Sir C. Trevelyan . . . desirous of relieving the department from responsibility, affirms their conduct throughout to have been irreproachable, and ascribes blame to other persons'' (''Fifth Report'':17). In May *Fraser's* refers to the ''mockery'' of Trevelyan's ''apologizing for the supineness of his department'' (''Sebastopol Committee'' 601). It should be noted that in *Little Dorrit*, Dickens leaves the reader with the clear impression that Tite Barnacle, who refuses ''to give a straightforward answer'' and directs Clennam elsewhere for help, is the immediate head of the Circumlocution Office. This position would correspond with that of the Assistant Secretary of the Treasury. We know, for example, that "at the period in question" Tite Barnacle usually "coached or crammed the statesman at the head of the Circumlocution Office" (102). As the nonpolitical officer most directly involved in the day-to-day business of the Treasury, it was the Assistant Secretary's responsibility to keep those political appointees like the First Lord and the Chancellor of the Exchequer—those "statesmen" who were removed from this day-to-day business—informed about current Treasury activities and precedents. While this association is revealing, Tite Barnacle does not "represent" Trevelyan in some direct way. Barnacle is too generalized a figure for that, lacking most of Trevelyan's (and Jasper's) characteristic traits.

Dickens' apparent antipathy toward the Commissariat enters *Little Dorrit* in another way as well. In the 1857 "Preface" he cites the Crimean War and "a Court of Enquiry at Chelsea" as evidence for the truthfulness of his supposedly exaggerated fiction. Critics have routinely identified this Court of Enquiry at Chelsea, also known as the Chelsea Board, with Roebuck's Sebastopol Committee which met in the spring of 1855.[10] In fact, the Chelsea Board, which did not meet until the spring of 1856, was altogether unrelated to the Sebastopol Committee. Their purposes were considerably different. If the Sebastopol Committee was expected to mete out criticism, the Chelsea Board was established to investigate the conclusions of two of the critics, Sir John McNeill and Colonel A. M. Tulloch. McNeill and Tulloch were sent to the Crimea in 1855 by the new Prime Minister, Lord Palmerston, "to inquire into the whole arrangement and management of the Commissariat Department." Their final report was issued in January 1856. In it they criticized the Commissariat, particularly Commissary-General Filder, for his lack of imagination in overcoming difficulties and the rigidity of his approach. They also blamed the Commander-in-Chief for not seeing that Filder satisfied the soldiers' needs. In early 1856 the Chelsea Board, a board of general officers appointed to examine McNeill's and Tulloch's report, effectively exonerated the military leaders, finding that no one was to blame, at least not overseas in the Crimea. It is this conclusion which Dickens implicitly criticizes in 1857 in his "Preface." This criticism springs directly from his recent reading of Colonel Tulloch's defense of his conclusions, *The Crimean Commission and the Chelsea Board* (1857). In this book, Tulloch closely examines the Chelsea Board's conclusions and rebuts them, one by one, citing a passage in *Household Words* as proof. Dickens refers to this book at some length in "Stores [a reference to the Commissariat] for the First of April," an article published in *Household Words* on 7 March 1857. "Colonel Tulloch's 'enclaircissements' . . . incontestably prove," Dickens wrote, "every conceivable detail

of murderous muddle and mismanagement, by English administrators of one
kind or another in the Crimea.'' He was particularly offended by the Chelsea
Board itself, that ''one-sided tribunal constantly wrestling the case out of the
truth, by stopping short when they see that damnatory pea in danger of rolling
out from among the thimbles'' (219). Thus, it should be noted, Dickens'
inclusion of this reference in his preface, written after he had finished *Little
Dorrit*, makes it unlikely that he would have dropped ''Nobody's Fault'' as
the title of his novel because he realized on some conscious level, so the
argument usually goes, that the intended irony was misplaced, that England's
problems were indeed ''nobody's fault.''[11] For Dickens such an argument
would have amounted to absolution for those in charge. He explicitly addresses this issue in ''Cheap Patriotism,'' significantly tying it to Trevelyan
and Civil Service reform. Once again, he assumes the voice of the experienced
civil servant:

> [reformers] will never get any good out of those virtuous changes that are
> severely virtuous upon the juniors. Such changes originate in the cheapest
> patriotism in the world, and the commonest. The official system is upside down,
> and the roots are at the top. Begin there, and the little branches will soon come
> right.   (435)

This worry about who was to blame was not, of course, unique to Dickens.
''Discussions are going on everywhere,'' writes *Fraser's* in June—the same
month Dickens writes ''Cheap Patriotism''—''on whether it is the men who
are to blame for the recent disasters and mismanagement which the country
has to deploy, or whether it is the 'system' only that is to blame'' (607). Two
pamphlets widely circulated in 1855 stood as representatives of either side of
the debate. In ''The One Thing Needful'' W. R. Greg argued that the ministers at home were guiltless, since they were ''neither ubiquitous, nor omniscient, nor despotic,'' but had found themselves ''*at the head of a vast and
cumbrous machine composed of human wheels, nine-tenths of whom they did
not put into it, nine-tenths of whom they cannot put out of it*'' (6). An
anonymous pamphleteer countered Greg's argument in ''Red-Tapeism: It's
[sic] Cause.'' This writer maintained that the Civil Service was not to blame,
but rather ''the political branch of the administration'' (3), lamenting that
''all the power is vested in the Political Chief'' (5). The journals of the day
tended to avoid taking sides by blaming both parties. Dickens, on the other
hand, takes an uncompromising stand: he unreservedly blames ''the roots at
the top,'' which, as with the anonymous pamphleteer, would ultimately mean
''the Political Chief.''

In mid-1855 the "Political Chief" was Lord Palmerston, the new Prime Minister. Hopes were high when he took office in February. With a tradition of vigorous foreign policy behind him, the new Prime Minister, "whose accession to power three months ago was greeted with acclaim by a considerable section of the public," was expected to make short work of the muddle at Balaclava. But "Palmerston, the favourite of February, is Palmerston the mistrusted of May" ("The Palmerston Administration" 726). It was generally believed that he had simply replaced Aberdeen's Cabinet, that "small junta or restricted clique of aristocratic families," with more aristocrats, and ones considerably less talented than their predecessors. Thus, Dickens' depiction of the Barnacles reflects not just some generalized animus against the upper class, but a particular antipathy to Palmerston and his unwillingness to make changes upon taking over, to break the "systematic monopoly of office, on the principle of exclusive family arrangement" ("The Palmerston Administration" 727) and open his ministry to the middle class.

Significantly, Palmerston was also First Lord of the Treasury, the politician with the most patronage at his disposal. But more than that, and perhaps most importantly for Dickens, he had the temerity to point out (and he was not alone in this) that the Commissariat was composed of middle-class clerks and to argue that, if blame were to be placed, it should be with the middle class and not their aristocratic superiors back home in England. Thus, we can understand the true meaning of the "men" versus "system" debate, if we realize that the "men" were commonly identified with the aristocrats and the "system" with the middle-class clerks. *Fraser's* plays on these associations in June 1855, employing a phrase close to Dickens' original title to *Little Dorrit*, while ironically voicing the sentiments of Palmerston and his ilk. " 'Oh,' but say the Lords, 'that is not our fault [that the "machine" of government has been brought to a halt]. It is the doctors, agents, and the lower people who break down. The incompetency is not with us, but with the middle classes" (719). *Fraser's* rebuts this charge by explaining that "It is more especially with reference to the heads of departments that the evil effects of monopoly are visible" (719). For Dickens to criticize the Northcote-Trevelyan report, which laid heavy emphasis on the incompetency of the lower-level clerk,[12] and to blame the "men" like Trevelyan and Palmerston, was to defend the middle class against aristocratic attacks. So, too, Dickens' insistent identification of the Circumlocution Office with "gentlemen"—though his comments in "Cheap Patriotism" suggest that he knew the truth was more complicated—bespeaks, in part, a defensive reaction.

Although Dickens might be willing to stretch his case to emphasize upper-class culpability, he was not ready to absolve the middle class altogether. William Dorrit, it must be remembered, had been a partner in a company that was to supply (as Ferdinand Barnacle carelessly puts it) "spirits, or buttons, or wine, or blacking, or oatmeal, or woolen, or pork, or hooks and eyes, or iron, or treacle, or shoes, or something or other that was wanted for troops, or seamen, or somebody," a clear if anachronistic reference to the Crimea (547). But "the house burst" and, the Circumlocution Office, one of its main creditors, lodged a detainer against Dorrit, who winds up in the Marshalsea. Thus, allusions converge: middle-class speculation cooperates with aristocratic neglect to insure that the country will end both morally and financially bankrupt, unable to take care of its children, whether those children suffer in the precincts of a debtors' prison, in the rookeries of Bleeding Heart Yard, or (the implication is) in the mud of Balaclava. In the broadest sense, Dickens condemns an aristocracy, the Barnacles writ large, which has relinquished its responsibility while maintaining its power. But he also condemns a financial elite, which speculates in the peoples' credulity, and a middle class, which worships the empty form and the glittering spectacle of authority, while failing in its own duties, both domestic and political. As the narrator says quite simply, referring to the Barnacles and Merdle: "They sat at his feasts, and he sat at theirs." Meanwhile, "the multitude [worships] on trust" (539). For Dickens "Circumlocution" was present at every level of society, though the "men" in charge—those aristocrats like Palmerston and gentlemen like Trevelyan—bore the largest share of the blame.

Thus it is that the Circumlocution Office achieves a meaning which transcends its origin. For Dickens only begins with the Treasury; he does not end there. As his satire extends beyond the immediate to embrace larger political concerns as well as private and psychological ones, so the Circumlocution Office gains in connotation. Meanings accrue to it. By explaining the particular associations behind the conceit, I have not sought to circumscribe it. Dickens chooses the Treasury Office precisely because of its comprehensiveness, because of its central position in the English bureaucratic system, because, as his narrator explains in *Little Dorrit*, it keeps "the all-sufficient wheel of statesmanship, How not to do it, in motion" (101). Treasury control reached from the Royal Exchange to the crowded burying-ground at St. Martin-in-the-Fields, from Whitehall to Balaclava. It joined troubles at home with those abroad, metropolitan interments with cholera in the Crimea, administrative "acquiescence" with the failure to provide for the troops. It also joined people: Trevelyan, Seymour, Filder, Palmerston, and the "gentlemen accountants'' overseas. It brought together the window tax and sewage treatment, patronage and poisoned air. In the end, the Treasury served as a net in which Dickens could catch a variety of distasteful fish.

NOTES

1. The leader is George Alexander Hamilton, the assistant secretary of the Treasury from 1859 to 70 (qtd. in Wright 1).
2. The ''remarkable man of business'' phrase recurs in *Little Dorrit*. ''Such a nursery of statesmen had the department become . . . that several solemn lords had attained the reputation of being quite unearthly prodigies of business, solely from having practised, How not to do it, at the head of the Circumlocution Office'' (89–90).
3. It is simply incorrect to assert, as Humphry House does, that ''It is obvious, in spite of Reeve, that [Dickens] was attacking the pre-Benthamite, pre-Chadwick, pre-Trevelyan offices'' (190).
4. The specifics of the Treasury's intervention are described in S. E. Finer's *The Life and Times of Edwin Chadwick* (397–406).
5. In a speech before the House of Lords on 31 July 1851, the Earl of Shaftesbury, Chadwick's colleague on the General Board, blames the Treasury by name for the delay of the Interments Act. He cites a long pattern of obfuscation that extends from 23 November 1850 to 18 July 1851, at which point the Board is refused a necessary loan and the act is effectively killed.
6. To preserve the flavor of the evidence as it would have reached the journal's readers, I have retained the emphasis added to the original testimony and the sometimes subtle changes made by the reporters.
7. de Lacy Evans' actual testimony (in my text, I have provided *Fraser's* version) is even more revealing:

gentlemen were sent to me as commissaries who were totally incompetent for their duty. I dare say they were very good clerks in the Treasury, but I found immediately that they knew nothing about their field duty, and that they did not care much about it; they were always employed in writing letters to the Treasury, and making out accounts in triplicate, and all those sort of things, which I did not think of the most importance.   (''Minutes of Evidence'' 1:24)

8. In its daily summary of testimony, ''State of the Army before Sebastopol,'' *The Times* does not include the actual letter, but summarizes instead:

The noble lord . . . repeatedly remonstrated with Mr. Filder upon the subject [of insufficient supplies of forage], but to no purpose. Mr. Commissary-General Filder continued to intrust the Commissariat duties to youths utterly inexperienced, and who, moreover, showed no great zeal or desire to make up by their exertions for their personal deficiencies.   (16 March 1855, 9)

9. The only exact use of the ''Nobody's Fault'' phrase I have found occurs in

Bentley's Miscellany in February 1855. *Bentley's* disparages those like the writer in the *Edinburgh Review* who see the mismanagement in the Crimea as "nobody's fault," also deriding "some few persons who consider that no one is to blame" ("State of the Army" 111). Perhaps significantly, Dickens had once been a member of *Bentley's* staff. Most likely, however, the phrase was the product of a general atmosphere of evasiveness—we have seen how *Fraser's* had used a similar expression in May—culminating in Trevelyan's testimony.

10. As in the Penguin and Oxford editions of *Little Dorrit*.

11. Whether the system materializes on some *un*conscious level in his fiction is, of course, another question. But this decision to change the title is usually viewed as a conscious recognition on Dickens' part that England's problems were "systemic," and not a matter of individual blame.

12. A pamphleteer on the Northcote-Trevelyan report wrote, "The City movement for administrative reform was mainly concerned with *ministers*, Sir Charles Trevelyan's with the civil service" (qtd. in Anderson, "Janus-Face" 234).

WORKS CITED

Anderson, Olive. "The Administrative Reform Association, 1855–1857." *Pressure from Without in Early Victorian England*. Ed. Patricia Hollis. New York: St. Martin's, 1974.

———. "The Janus Face of Mid-Nineteenth-Century English Radicalism: The Administrative Reform Association of 1855." *Victorian Studies* 8 (1965):231–42.

Dickens, Charles. "Cheap Patriotism." *Household Words* 9 June 1855:433–35.

———. "A December Vision." *Household Words* 14 Dec. 1850:265–67.

———. "It Is Not Generally Known." *Household Words* 2 Sept. 1854:49–52.

———. *Little Dorrit*. Ed. Harvey Peter Sucksmith. Oxford: Clarendon, 1979.

———. "Red Tape." *Household Words* 15 Feb. 1851:481–84.

———. *The Speeches of Charles Dickens*. Ed. K. J. Fielding. Hemel, Hempstead: Harvester, 1988.

———. "Stores for the First of April." *Household Words* 7 Mar. 1857:217–22.

———. "The Thousand and One Humbugs." *Household Words* 21 Apr. 1855:264–67; 28 Apr. 1855:289–92; 5 May 1855:313–16.

———. "To Working Men." *Household Words* 7 Oct. 1854:169–70.

Finer, S. E. *The Life and Times of Sir Edwin Chadwick*. New York: Barnes, 1952.

Greg, W. R. "The One Thing Needful." London: Ridgeway, 1855.

Haly, William Taylor, and W. H. Wills. "The Royal Rotten Row Commission." *Household Words* 15 June 1850:274–77.

Hart, Jenifer. "Sir Charles Trevelyan at the Treasury." *English Historical Review* 74 (Jan. 1960):92–110.

House, Humphry. *The Dickens World*. 2nd ed. Oxford: Oxford UP, 1942.

Kinglake, A. W. *The Invasion of the Crimea*. 9 vols. Cabinet ed. 1863.

"Minutes of Evidence Taken before the Select Committee on Army before Sebastopol." *Parliamentary Papers*. 1854–55. Vol. 9. Pts. 1–3.

"Fifth Report from the Select Committee on Army before Sebastopol." *Parliamentary Papers*. 1854–55. Vol. 9.

"The Palmerston Administration." *Blackwood's Edinburgh Magazine*. June 1855:724–39.

Pellew, Jill. *The Home Office 1848–1914: From Clerks to Bureaucrats*. Rutherford: Fairleigh Dickinson UP, 1982.

"The Political Crisis." *Fraser's Magazine*. June 1855:715–24.

"Red Tapeism: It's [sic] Cause." London: Ridgeway, 1855.

"Reform of the Civil Service." *North British Review*. May 1855:73–103.

"Reports Papers and a Treasury Minute Relating to the Re-Organization of the Permanent Civil Service 1854–55." *British Parliamentary Papers: Government Civil Service 2*. Shannon: Irish UP, 1969.

"The Sebastopol Committee." *Fraser's Magazine*. May 1855:593–606.

"State of the Army before Sebastopol—Mismanagement of the War." *Bentley's Miscellany* 37 (Feb. 1855):111–23.

Times [London]. 15 March 1855:6.

Times [London]. 19 April 1855:8.

Times [London]. 21 April 1855:8.

Trollope, Anthony. *The Three Clerks*. Oxford: Oxford UP, 1989.

Tulloch, Colonel A. M. *The Crimean Commission and the Chelsea Board*. London: Harrison, 1857.

Wright, Maurice. *Treasury Control of the Civil Service 1854–1874*. Oxford: Clarendon, 1969.

Reading Trollope: Whose Englishness Is It Anyway?

Julian Wolfreys

It should not be possible to read nineteenth-century literature
without remembering that . . . [it] was a crucial part of the
cultural representation of England to the English. The role
of literature in the production of cultural representation
should not be ignored.

Gayatri Chakravorty Spivak

Clearly a regard for "tradition," which is, above all, a
cultural construction, where what is "right" and "makes
sense" is preserved in historical memory and identified with
the fate of the community, with a social group or class, and
ultimately with the nation, has much to do with the formation of a native "common sense" and a historical cultural
bloc.

Iain Chambers

Ideological domination—the everyday acceptance of the
world and its existing relations of power and social relations—is not imposed from "above," but established across
the shifting fields of relations that constitute a shared "consensus." This consensus has to be continually constructed
and produced inside the different fields of public representation and social life; it involves not merely political but also
"intellectual and moral leadership." In other words, the
exercise of power becomes a decentred and profoundly cultural affair.

Iain Chambers

I

This essay is concerned with the question of Englishness and its problematized mapping in the Palliser novels of Anthony Trollope. The novels in question are heavily traced by crises of identity, rooted specifically in the local, the political, and the discourses of cultural *realpolitik* that inform the hegemonic situation of the English bourgeoisie in the 1870s. Both crisis and situation are inseparable; and both have a particular resonance for readers today, after the 1980s and the discourse of Thatcherism, especially with the Thatcherite call for a return to Victorian values.

This imperative on the part of Margaret Thatcher and her Tory-liberal disciples, which has led to the deep economic confusion of John Major's government resulting in subsequent systematic sacrifice and callous betrayal of the working class,[1] is an imperative founded on acts of highly selective, ideological memorialization. Involved in remembering the past is a capitalization on favored fictions, a narrative re-telling of events and a narrative retailing of those events through the currency of Tory-liberal discourse. Such retail has been effected in order that the past may be made to conform somehow to an idea of what the past is, in accordance with a particular, dominant ideology in the present. This project is something that we all participate in, either willingly or unwillingly, at one time or another. Narrative reformation is crucial to any project of national identity, but especially so for the New Right, in their dream of a post-empire England. That dream consists in an homogenization of past situation and present crisis. Trollope, on the other hand, can be read as comprehending such projects and questioning the ideal of unity as political strategy. Trollope's questioning is presented at times with a ferocious irony, as he dismisses supposedly eternal values and the narratives that support them.

The figure of Anthony Trollope imagined behind this essay is one who resists narrative and other forms of co-optation. This Trollope is "comprehensible, hence complex and fragmentary and not the solid referent of a traditional art discourse, a Hollywood film or a neat historical tale" (Chambers 1). Such a Trollope might seem an estranged figure, especially given his own often repeated political beliefs in Tory-liberalism (a discourse which, in another study, could be seen as differing greatly from the 1980s variety). But I insist on this estranged characterization because, if we are to move towards a consistently dissident series of readings that manoeuvre counter to the "[i]deological domination" of which Iain Chambers writes above, then it is important that our reading should make strange that which is supposedly familiar; that which, in Chambers' words again, has been said to "make sense" and thereby deployed in the construction of a "shared 'consensus' " (44).

In 1991, Prime Minister John Major "made sense" of Trollope, appropriating him as the preferred author of Downing Street, and suggesting to the Archbishop of Canterbury that Trollope be given recognition in Poets' Corner at Westminster Abbey. The only thing missing from this anecdote is the master of an Oxford college, and we have a scene worthy of Trollope himself. But this is just one instance of attempted ideological rewriting of the past, leading to various forms of cultural domination. Chambers' talk of ideological domination, and the formation through culture and nationality of a historical cultural bloc, rewrites in broader terms what Spivak alerts us to above with regard to the "role of literature in the production of cultural representation." John Major's comments constitute a single example of the way in which a familiar and domesticated Trollope is constructed. This domesticated Trollope is a particular figure belonging to a particular set of texts and discourses which constitute a "history," an ideological fiction, to which bourgeois-right literary culture has had the "proper access code" (Ronell, 273).

This Trollope is conventionally represented as an author of gently humorous, safe depictions of the everyday. This Trollope is accorded a position in the second division of Victorian authors; not as imaginative as Dickens, nor as philosophical as Eliot; safe ultimately, because he seems to be a mere documentary narrator, more easily—i.e., less troublingly—comprehensible in terms of conservative values.

There are other readings, other Trollopes however, that are, and must be, retrievable. Trollope's texts are our texts, displaced across a field of cultural, political, and semantic play. They are crucial to any analysis of the modern palimpsest of national identity, not because they are objects for study that reveal an other('s) epoch but because their "ubiquitous signs" drawn from English culture and identity perform the "illusion and the aesthetization of the world that . . . *is also us*" (Chambers 88; my emphasis). These texts can be read also as one instance of a working out, an uncovering, of the construction—and the constructedness—of a supposedly dominant identity, whilst simultaneously being available as both critique and revelation of the fallacious and illusory nature of the construct.

For even as we read these texts as playing the tropes of a specific identity—for example, that of the English Gentleman, or the English Parliamentary system as the suggested collective identity figured in the lives and relationships of certain sets of characters—we can also remark the mockery of that same identity. This is because identity is understood not as the true statement of national identity, but merely as one more position within Trollope's mapping of a political and cultural center which, in Trollope's novels, is already decentred. The decentred centre is the pretext of Trollope's writing.

If we acknowledge this, we can produce a Trollope for whom politics is both "the exercise of power" and a "profoundly cultural affair" (Chambers 44). Trollope reveals that there is no heart at the heart of the British Empire, and Englishness has nothing solid, its identity being a simulacrum. National identity in the Palliser novels is constructed and given repeated performances based on an imagined threat to the self-perceived center of the upper middle class, a threat which is understood dimly by the members of this class as having something to do with social, political difference; and with this threat, and with the idea of difference itself, Trollope works to produce his decentering fictions. In order to understand this fully, and in order to intervene with Trollope's questioning of Englishness, it is important that we first consider the use of the proper name.

II

Something is always at stake, ideologically, in the proper name and its uses, in the proper name's propriety, and in the property that the name gathers to it. The name fixes a textual body, and the apparent unity of such a body; such has been the case with the domestication of "Anthony Trollope." The name is thus part of an economic question. This is true, of course, of the cultural assimilation of any novelist's name and works. But Trollope can be read as having anticipated this in the writing of *Phineas Finn*.

So I want to question a particular proper name as a way of undoing the very unity which the name supposedly assigns; I want to play the name as a type of gambit, in order to comprehend how Trollope uses the proper name in order to open up the textuality of English identity.

Phineas Finn/*Phineas Finn*. This signature is both character and title. However, in this case, it is also an agency of refusal (I shall return to this). The use of the name as title is a ploy on the part of novel-writing to locate its subject, to insinuate a center, to compose a textual body that is proper and properly defined within the limits of narrative and ideological convention that is particular to (the subject of) English writing. But Phineas is not an English subject. What then, can be read in this signature? The proper name would seem to make matters simple, announcing the limits, the propriety of that which is to be discussed. This is conventionally the case; but can we read the signature for what it hides? We can perhaps read it for the excesses and the transgressions that the propriety of the signature attempts to silence. We can also read an insertion made by this proper name, made in the name of some other for which this name stands. In such a reading, the proper name becomes somewhat improper. This name, "Phineas Finn," complicates instead of simplifying, its insertion being a breach by Trollope of the "natural order" of English identity; the name effects an incision that refuses closure.

The name of Finn is located both centrally, whilst also being a marker of the edge. As a title indicative of a fictional unity—the supposed unity of a fiction and the fictionality of the idea of unity—it is remarked as a preface, a pretext to its subject (the narrative of the novel) on the border of the text that bears its name. This text, the text that is *Phineas Finn*/Phineas Finn, is always already doubled: the name names the subject, the one to whom the proper name is assigned, and the broader textuality of a cultural artifact and narrative, within which the agent of discourse, subject(ed) to his own signature, is situated. Subject, artifact, and narrative: this, more than mere doubling and redolent of the economy of the "fictional unity" and narrative motif of the dialetic, performs a maneouvre that cannot be resolved. But listen also to what else is signed in the fantasy of this name.

With its Latinate propriety and Gaelic impropriety, the name refuses to be settled into one place. This is true of the figure to whom the name belongs. He refuses to vote according to the directive of the Cabinet over the issue of Irish reform and so resigns, resigning himself to being not subject to the authoritarian discourses and agendas of the English Government. His resignation is an affirmative refusal of English identity. It is also the mark of a signature belonging to a non-place, both politically and nationally. Ireland is a non-site in the fantasy of the English Empire; In Tory-Liberal discourse, it does not exist outside of the empire. Its autonomy can never be other, because, sitting at the border of national identity, it always speaks of otherness to English identity, an otherness on which such identity is violently founded and, without which such identity cannot maintain its existence.

The name, "Phineas Finn," like the Ireland from which Finn comes, and like the character whose name this is, exists on borderlines, socially, culturally, politically. The name also survives as a sign of movement between cultures, between dominance and subjugation, between authority and subversion. There is no accident in the choice of the last name, the name that writes over again the first syllable of the Latinized first name, offering to begin that name again, but from an Irish perspective. With this second beginning however, the supplement with its Gaelic remarking revokes the authority and propriety that the Latinate spelling confers and seeks to keep in place. Finn is a good Irish name, suggesting the Irish patriot Finn McCool, from whom the Fenians took their collective name and identity. Phineas Finn is therefore bothersome; like his name and its contexts, he refuses either to go away or be placed, sliding between meanings, between Englishness and Irishness. And Finn's provisional locutions and the slippage written in his name are denials of the simplistic, reductive dialectic that English ideology constructs in terms of itself and its neighbour.

The slippage within the structure of the name, the elision that dismantles the laws of that structure, is curiously appropriate to the subject of politics; which is also to say appropriate to the one who is subject to the political and, in this case, the subject—Finn—who is a politician. Finn is political, an Irish Catholic whose name suggests another national history and identity of resistance and refusal; one also of subversion, of *sub versions* (of dominant narratives, told otherwise). Within Finn's lifetime, Catholic emancipation has been legislated by a Protestant parliament. His voice is thus authorized by the dominant discourse, the language and law of his colonial masters; and is it not ironic that Finn, an Irishman, works at the Colonial office?

However, Phineas traces a fin-like trajectory, between English and Irish, Catholic and Protestant, inside and outside, the colonist and the colonized, self and Other. The figure of Finn charts the sometimes surfacing, sometimes submerged textualities of the mid-nineteenth-century *realpolitik* of the performance of identity, in being part of the mechanisms, structures and institutions of the political aspects of Englishness, whilst also standing at a somewhat oblique angle to that identity; which angle throws identity into relief. Finn's signature is that which for us negotiates a range of positions that are never solely his own, but always readings of a "center," an example of which is his move from the Irish to the English borough, from Loughshane to Loughton. And the connections, not specifically his own but available within the English Government's reading of Ireland and its own positions during the 1860s, are played from the possible echoes in his name, from the Fenian to the fainéant.

Here are named the possible extremes or borders of political life that we can read from the text. The Fenian and fainéant are not of course the finite limits of ideological situation, anymore than is the name of Finn. But we can read in them, as in the Irish politician's (im)proper name, the epoch of the "violent" outside, made violent by the English reading of the Fenian's "eccentricity" (yet one more position of marginality constructed from the hub of the Empire). At the other extreme, we read the "absolute" inability for any oppositional action on the part of an individual such as Finn because of his being made fainéant politically, having been taken in as a member of a Whig Cabinet. Finn is obviously dangerous enough in the minds of his masters to warrant his promotion to the "heart" of government.

Yet these are brief readings of only the "external" structures of the narrative, a translation of the surfaces of *Phineas Finn*. We need to attend to the "internal" also. The purpose of Finn is, as I have stated, to provide an insertion which is also an opening out. Finn's presence displays the "natural" as ideological, this being uncovered as he moves between the structures of exclusion which operate the fragmented formation of English identity. His presence reads an absolute lack of unity and consensus amongst the upper middle class. Trollope also uses Finn to reveal the political games that are engaged in as part of English politics and Victorian society. And this is achieved in a self-reflexive manner:

> Indeed, when he came to think of it, there appeared to him no valid reason why he should not sit for Loughton. The favour was of the kind that had prevailed *from time out of mind in England,* between the most respectable of the great land magnates, and young rising liberal politicians. Burke, Fox and Canning had all been placed in Parliament by similar influence. Of course he, Phineas Finn, desired earnestly,—longed in his very heart of hearts,—to extinguish all such Parliamentary influence, to root out for ever the last vestige of close borough nominations; but while the thing remained it was better that the thing should contribute to the liberal than to the conservative strength of the House,—and if to the liberal, how was this to be achieved but by the acceptance of such influence by some liberal candidate? And if it were right that it should be accepted by any liberal candidate,—then, why not by him? The logic of this argument seemed to him to be perfect. He felt something like a sting of reproach as he told himself that *in truth this great offer was made to him, not on account of the excellence of his politics . . .*   (319; my emphases)

This passage, Phineas' "internal" reflections on the nature of English political preference, careers across much of what is crucial ideologically to the relationships and social performances engaged in throughout the Palliser novels. I will therefore take the time to unfold this somewhat slowly.

Thought, in the first sentence, has a realist or mimetic quality to it, in that there is suggested the possibility of "appearance," as though ideas were apparitions. Phineas' mind would seem to function as a magic lantern. The grammatical structure tricks us, however. The comic gesture is finely tuned to possible, ambiguous semantic tension. We can read in the sliding between internal and external positions of thought and feeling, this being a locus that is historically determined. The statement, "there appeared to him," is suggestive of an external or metaphysical representation or vision. Not only this, but the "externality" of appearance contradicts the internal location, framed by the process of thinking in the phrase "when he came to think of it." "It," which is very important throughout this passage, posits an empirical object available for enquiry, contradicting and confounding the site of thought as being solely within the subject (Trollope's prose breaks down the limits of both inside and outside). Further, to suggest that someone can "come to it" implies a spatial orientation that, once again, posits the externality of the object of thought.

What is "external" to Phineas is not "his" thought but the textual condition of his being which, as the grammar, syntax and vocabulary make clear, is culturally, historically grounded. Thus it is that the discourse is seen to perform the subject, rather than it being the other way around. We are able to read a denial of an essentialist or humanist concept of identity: "Phineas" is not the lantern so popular in the England of the novel; he is the blank screen on which the discourses of the period are projected. He is a condition of a conceptualization which is not peculiar to him, but is comprehensible as the often contradictory shifts of Victorian bourgeois perception. It is important to insist on this specificity if we are to register the depth to which the critical insertion of Phineas cuts in the ideology of Victorian identity.

The hyperbole that is wrapped into the first clauses is let down immediately in the negation, "no valid reason," which is in fact what appears. The appearance to Phineas is that of a negation, of validity and reason, the latter intimating both excuse and logic. There is not merely an absence as a simple binary opposite to the subject's self-presence, but the implicitly visual external presentation of the image of negativity.

And as if to counter this positive erasure, what follows immediately is recourse to the texts of both myth and history, both of which are governed by the dominant discourse of Englishness. As if to compensate for the lack of a pure theoretical or abstract logical model—one that we can assume is, in this case at least, unavailable because of its contamination by the local specificity of English liberal politics—textuality attempts to recover a historically valorized moment of subjective unity through the idea of English political narrative as precedent. The phrase, "from time out of mind," implies a continuous history of conferred privilege in the donation of parliamentary seats which has its obscured origins *before* history in a mythical and, therefore, indefineable space.

This being so, such a practice predates any parliamentary or democratic system. It is instead a native tradition, part of the culture and identity of England and the English; and, and part of English consciousness also, as the use of the word "mind" implies. The parties involved in such political transactions are revealed as great magnates and rising liberal politicians. What is interesting is that, throughout the passage, "liberal" is spelt with a lower case "l," thus presenting the term as being related in the English tradition to an ideology rather than, more narrowly, a party. It is not the new money of industry and commercial enterprise that backs the young politicians. Instead, funding and other forms of backing come from those landowners who in conventional wisdom are figured in historical and fictive discourses as Tories.

Here we can read a deal being made between political situations in order to maintain a particular social order that accommodates differing ideologies in favor of a continuing social structure; and that deal is agreed on *in the name of England*. This is clearly an England of a certain group, and not all classes. There is an attempted justification of such a practice (presumably in Phineas' thoughts) by the citation of political figures such as Burke, Fox, and Canning. This meeting of the fictive and the real offers us a textual opening up to the reader of English cultural practices supposedly external to the limits of the novel. The figure of Phineas, the figure of his contaminated logic which seeks an unethical justification through a remembrance of English political history, effects an insertion into the social formation that admits to a critical questioning as to the 'nature" of the control of power in England. The control of power and the maintenance of Tory-liberal hegemony comes down to something as elusive and as hard to define as "influence" which, as we are witness to here, has little or nothing to do with either a particular part or personality.

Of course in opening up this perspective and in bringing into question the problematic of political manipulation and mediation as discourses of compromise and co-optation, Phineas himself immediately begins to close up the same structure; such is the coercive condition of a right-liberal hegemony. As we can see from this passage, the hegemonic model is effective because it is capable of convincing the majority of the reasonable and pragmatic nature of its appeals and formulations. Even those such as Phineas who initially see the corrupting nature of the system become entrapped. And we can read the effectiveness of such silent coercion in the final line of the passage quoted, where Finn hardly feels the sting at all, but only something like it. Finn's own position within the social/political world and the textual economy of the period does partially cloud his own critical insights into the nature of political compromise, even while his cultural marginality allows him to raise questions that, otherwise, would not be articulated. This drift between clouded vision and critical questioning is a vital part of the formation of identity.

Phineas is able at least to begin the enunciation of the mystified structures of political power. Should this beginning not be available to us, then the novel might well be recuperated into the positions against which this reading seeks to position it, with Phineas being merely one more romantic hero—such as Daniel Deronda, for example—unable to act in any engaged manner, his fate being sealed by some seemingly essential fault. Trollope sidesteps such an essentialist teleology to a degree however, through the performance of a range of voices from various social groups, all of which raise complicating articulations of their own ideological contexts. It is in such pronouncements that we can read the subtle control of, and resistance to, liberal hegemony; it is the function of Phineas Finn that, in being inserted into the discourses of liberal Englishness, he is used by Trollope to reveal the ideological situation of such discourses through his placement and critical understanding of events. Other characters also unfold the mysteries of the political.

III

In Chapter 32, "Lady Laura Kennedy's Headache," it is remarked that, "everyone of those Loughton tradesmen was proud of his own personal subjection to the Earl" (324). The language reveals a feudal mentality that helps maintain a cultural *status quo*. It is the same mentality that ensures Lord Silverbridge's election in *The Duke's Children*, because the tenants understand their subjection to the manorial family, rather than to a political party or ideology. The language of the sentence also reveals a specific section of the middle class—the petty-bourgeoisie in the form of "trades-men"—whose insertion into the performance of individuality ('his own personal subjection') as 'self made men' is particularly strong. This position is further enunciated by Mrs. Low, whose name and husband's status are suggestive of her location within the class system.

Commenting on a letter of Mr. Monk's read to her and her husband by Phineas (in an act of democratic feeling, Phineas takes political discourse to the "people," only to find that the "people" in the shape of the Lows reject the radical agenda), Mrs. Low says:

> It's [the letter's contents] what I call downright Radical nonsense . . . Why should we want to have a portrait of ignorance and ugliness. What we all want is to have things quiet and orderly.   (361)

Radical nonsense. Ignorance and ugliness. Quiet and orderly. The pairing of terms is telling. The first of these three pairs is an almost tautological structure, in the context of Mrs. Low's conservatism. The phase is one of those conjunctive dismissals so beloved by the bourgeois Right, where the development runs as follows: if it's Radical then it must be nonsense; and if it's nonsense then it must be radical.

However, behind this it is clear that the nonsense if not entirely nonsensical but constitutes some type of threat. This is made evident by Mrs. Low who feels the need to continue after her put down by further rhetorical amplification which questions a mimetic image of unpalatable reality—"why should we want to have a portrait of ignorance and ugliness?"—in favor of a 'reality' which is not real but an ideological construct, one which is quiet and orderly, polite and policed: in short, bourgeois. And what is under threat is the version of national identity to which Mrs. Low subscribes.

It is also of interest to note the mapping of the subject position in this extract. Initially, Mrs. Low qualifies her put down as her own. "What I call" suggests a naming process, one that is understood by the speaking subject as peculiar to herself, to her articulations. By the end of the statement, the first-person position has been superseded by the plural, liberal community of consensus, "what we all want." The use of "what" as a predicate common to both subject positions aids the easy transference from the individual to the communal. Nominalization—the indirect desiring function expressed in naming something so as to fix it as a possible possession of the speaker—is replaced by the enunciation of direct desire ("want").

The use of "all" has various effects. It reenforces the implied community; it suggests a totality and unity to that community from which "radical nonsense" is excluded; and, in the context of the phrasing, it pinpoints grammatically Mrs. Low as one of the socially mobile petty-bourgeoisie who has recently moved "up" in the class pecking order, while not having left behind the speech patterns of a lower-class group, a group represented in the novel by the Bunces. And the Bunces are represented to us through Phineas' presence as their lodger.

IV

Phineas has a certain social duality. On the one hand, he is an M.P., initially outside the Cabinet, who dines with the aristocracy and other influential political and financial figures; on the other, he is an Irishman in London, a Catholic in a world of Protestant power, not having an income compatible with his social activities. He must take lodgings with people who go unrecognized and unremarked for the most part by Phineas' professional colleagues. Thus, he moves along various boundaries, making incursions into mutually exclusive worlds.

One such world is that of the Bunces who, if not poor, do exist at the outer limits of petty-bourgeois society. Whilst Mr. Bunce does have a trade, not owning property he cannot vote. Thus Phineas is in a position to allow the reader an understanding of an other England. The representation of the Bunces and their position through Phineas is somewhat problematic however. It partakes of a traditional figure of the 'masses'. In the middle class imagination, the masses—to borrow Baudrillard's description—"drift somewhere between passivity and wild spontaneity, but always [as] a potential energy" (7). Passivity and wild spontaneity: Jane and Jacob Bunce. Trollope's text is historically recuperated through its representation of the working class couple by the Imaginary of liberal identity and its definitions of its other. In the writing of the Bunces we can read a (sometimes comic) artifice, a crude performance (the working classes are usually comic in middle-class representations of them; comedy diffuses both political threat and the nakedness of alterity), the energy of which runs the risk of dehumanizing the characters, thereby manipulating our readings.

We thus become read as bourgeois readers, in our efforts to escape the politics of dehumanization. The ideological production of our own reading practices is unveiled in the moment that we comprehend the delegitimizing agenda of making a caricature and thus seek for an alternative, more humane reading. The double bind is that, as we try to make Mrs. Bunce "more human" for example, we can do so only by reading from the text her motherly and tenderhearted qualities. In doing this we do violence to working class women by reading only their maternal, feminine energies. Trollope gives only a partial view through Phineas, a middle-class figure whose presence guides our readings of the Bunces, as we, like Finn, like Trollope, are constrained by the provisional limits of the discourses that are at work. We thus need to negotiate the various positions—of the text, of Finn, of the Bunces, and of our readings—with care. With these concerns in mind, one passage proves illuminating:

> "For myself I don't think half so much of Parliament folk as some do. They're for promising everything before they's elected; but not one in twenty of 'em is as good as his word when he gets there."
> Mr Bunce was a copying journeyman, who spent ten hours a day in Carey Street with a pen between his fingers; and after that he would often spend two

or three hours of the night with a pen between his fingers in Marlborough Street. He was a thoroughly hard-working man, doing pretty well in the world, for he had a good house over his head, and could always find raiment and bread for his wife and eight children; but, nevertheless, he was an unhappy man because he suffered from political grievances, or, I should more correctly say, that his grievances were semi-political and semi-social. He had no vote, not being himself the tenant of the house in Great Marlborough Street. The tenant was a tailor who occupied the shop, whereas Bunce occupied the whole of the remainder of the premises. He was a lodger and lodgers were not as yet trusted with the franchise. And he had ideas, which he himself admitted to be very raw, as to the injustice of the manner in which he was paid for his work. So much a folio, without reference to the way in which his work was done, without regard to the success of his work, with no questions asked of himself, was, he thought, no proper way of remunerating a man for his labours. He had long since joined a Trade Union, and for two years past had paid a subscription of a shilling a week towards its funds. He longed to be doing some battle against his superiors, and to be putting himself in opposition to his employers: —not that he objected personally to Messrs Foolscap, Margin and Vellum, who always made much of him as a useful man;—but because some such antagonism would be manly, and the fighting of some battle would be the right thing to do . . .

Mrs Bunce was a comfortable motherly woman who loved her husband but hated politics. As he had an aversion to his superiors in the world because they were superiors, so she had a liking for them for the same reason. She despised people poorer than herself . . . the world had once or twice been almost too much for her . . . but she had kept a fine brave heart during those troubles, and could honestly swear that the children always had a bit of meat, though she herself had been occasionally without it for days together.   (106–07)

The image we read of the Bunces is one that, on the surface of things, is very sympathetic, understanding, moderate. Mrs. Low would not object (except, possibly, for the "bit of meat"). But the passage is also very English; it is marked by a middle class liberal identity because of those self-same, "typically English" qualities: sympathy, moderation, understanding. Trollope's gentle prose invites us to invest these feelings in this uncomplaining, hard-working family and, in doing so, renders critical thinking on the social inequity on which the dominant model of Englishness is founded difficult by engaging our emotions.

Unlike other passages on the lower classes, such as Bunce's arrest outside the Houses of Parliament,[2] this description largely avoids comic effect. There is a touch of humour in Jane Bunce's references to "a bit of meat" for the children, but the humour is warm, designed to elicit from us a sympathy toward the mother for her valor, self-denial, "natural instincts" and "Dunkirk spirit" manifested against the world in general, and her husband's politics in particular. Like Mrs. Low, Jane Bunce respects order and social hierarchy, hating politics.

Thus the question of national identity is bound up in the narrative mediation of that identity with a question of gender, and I shall return to this issue in a moment. Notice how Bunce's fight for his rights is a "manly thing" to do. Trollope divides the Bunces through the gendered political attitudes, leaning more towards Mrs. Bunce's fuzzy conservatism, rather than towards her husband's macho radicalism (notice, though, how the sympathetic narrative direction is not present in scenes concerning Mrs. Low; Trollope's is not a blanket conservatism). However, the Bunces are united in the reading of them as a typical English couple of their class and historical period. The passage can be read as promoting that vision through the very identification of their gendered qualities, of tenaciousness, self-consciously fuzzy thinking, tender-heartedness and fortitude (remove Trollope's satirical edge and his sharp political observation, and you end up with Noel Coward). And the problem with this vision is that it is the middle class image of the working people that has survived with minor adjustments for over 150 years. Inadvertently or not, Trollope has recourse to re-present the heavily loaded image, beloved of the New Right in the 1980s and '90s, of the family-as-national-identity, an image perpetuated in the self-interest of the right-liberal ruling order.

This passage is disturbing because, though I read it as wanting to be honest and sympathetic, honest because sympathetic, it finally gives way to the dishonesty of emotional proximity and familiarity. The cultural construction of the identity of the "family" relies on the relationship between female feeling and social status quo. The woman's supposed illogicality—and, by inference, lower class women as a definable group—becomes the fictitious site of the family's stability (registered through food and respect), despite the husband's politics. Bunce's activities become somehow unpleasant because it is implied that his wife suffers as a result of them. Because the woman feels, we are susceptible to ignoring her emotional responses as a text written onto her engendered figure, a text hostile to oppositional and dissident political activity; so, the traditional reading of woman is deployed by conservative discourse, in order to displace and mystify its own political activities which are involved in keeping the husband a docile, subservient worker.

We would be wrong though, to blame Trollope for the ideological "fault" that we perceive. What happens in this passage is a result of cultural contingency, of historical and cultural situation; the passage is written, in short, by the discourses of Englishness that Trollope is seeking to interpret and question through the figure of Phineas Finn. Importantly, the passage does at least offer a limited intervention into areas of social life that are grey and to which the middle class Victorian reader might well be ignorant or hostile. While

Bunce's response to "Parliament folk" is a stock enunciation of "the common man," his "raw" thinking of the conditions under which his work is produced is more finely tuned, albeit momentarily. This becomes overwritten by the metaphor of battle that would seem to make the issue less serious for its being somewhat clichéd. We read the passage as tracing with some difficulty an issue of considerable complexity that the dominant discourses of the period gather up ultimately. What we can read, and that very clearly, is a typical instance of the bourgeois formation of national identity, and its efforts to domesticate and make safe its Other. This formation is one still being strategically deployed in the last decade. And it is such a formation against which Phineas is written as struggling.

However, before turning to Phineas, we need to look at the question of gender as Trollope uses it in relation to national identity and in the complication of ideological positions across class.

The problem of the "female position on politics" is further complicated by Glencora Palliser. While Mrs. Low and Mrs. Bunce express conservative views about society and class position, Glencora is given one of the more "progressive" or "radical" speeches in *Phineas Finn* (and we are witness to this because of Phineas' presence at Loughlinter). In Chapter 14, Glencora follows through the logical thread of certain liberal thinking, challenging the "liberalism" of Mr. Monk and Mrs. Bonteen. (163–64)

Glencora states her reading of "our political theory," which is to make "men and women all equal." This shocks Monk, the proponent of "radical nonsense," who "cries off" from the discussion. Glencora responds, 'If I were in the Cabinet myself I should not admit so much . . . there is an official discretion." Glencora's remarks illuminate the silencing that is effected by being at what is supposedly the centre of political power. From her constantly shifting position on the fringes of that centre, Glencora, like Phineas, is empowered in her relative marginality to read the unarticulated premises of English bourgeois hegemony. She goes on to spell out these premises to Mrs. Bonteen in didactic fashion. Taking Mrs. Bonteen's comments as criticism of "me and my politics"—a phrase important for its connection of the personal and/as political in any definition of identity—Glencora states that liberalism is concerned with:

> making the lower orders comfortable . . . and educated, and happy, and good . . . make them as comfortable and good as yourself . . . I am not saying that people are equal; but that the tendency of all law-making and of all governing should be to reduce the inequalities.

Glencora's speech reveals the furthest limits of a particular reformist ideology, and also its own blindness to its own order and the power it attempts to wield. The economic necessity of liberalism is to create subjects, to subject the "lower orders" to a state of control and policing through jurisdiction and governmental legislation (Glencora's belief is in a trickle-down theory of government).

Education, happiness, comfort and moral well-being are the cornerstones to the effectiveness of the hegemonic maintenance of a docile proletariat. Notice that nowhere does Glencora suggest an actual change of class position for the others of England; nor are her "radical" proposals founded on any suggestion of concrete social change. Instead she invokes a certain indirect political discourse that encompasses the working class through a range of easily changeable theoretical positions. And it is a sign of the conservatism of the liberals listening to Glencora that they think Glencora's politics "too fast and furious."

Given statements such as Glencora's, which we should always read against the grain, and the positions of women such as Mrs. Low or Jane Bunce, it is difficult, if not impossible to suggest a final position of authority at which Trollope comes to rest on the subject of women's political attitudes. Certainly Trollope complicates the issue of ranging issues across both gender and class in such a fashion that we can fix no final political position to Trollope's understanding of national identity and the political mediations of Englishness.

There is, I believe, a degree of political irony, a playful but "responsible" anarchy with which Trollope infects his text; this ironic resonance suggests the impossibility of absolute authority and the redundancy of any effort to assume such a position of mastery. This could of course be merely another ploy of liberal humanism, which states that this is the way things are, and that there are no right or wrong positions, only beliefs and collective systems of beliefs which come to be refigured in the form of identity. However, this double bind of undecideability seems to undercut itself in offering such didactically stated moments of antagonism. Trollope constructs the textual antinomies in such a way that we are forced as readers to come to a political decision based on the contradictory choices offered us by Trollope, for which we are ultimately responsible. Reading any of Trollope's fictions, we come to comprehend the necessity for continued interventions into the culture of our identity.

V

It is the problematic condition of Phineas Finn's interventions into the cultures of England which keep the text alive for us. For, although Finn's presence ultimately offers a liberal reading (which is not necessarily ours) of historical currents, against this reading's implied recuperation of social difference and antagonism (which antagonism Trollope does not resolve other than in terms of Phineas' narrative), there is always to be remembered Phineas' own otherness. If Finn coalesces, it is because he has no other choice; he is unable to interpret his contexts in any other way.

At the beginning of Chapter 25, (258–68) Phineas' return to London precedes the narration of the political troubles, involving troops, the 40–50,000 strong "mob," and the possible dissolution of the government over the issue of the Ballot. We may perhaps see Phineas' presence as the generator of events; not in the sense that he actively contributes to or causes unrest, but that, in terms of the narrative, he is placed so as to be an involved witness, moving between the "inside" and "outside" of events. His identity is constituted as a narrative performance that does not admit of fixture, but is deliberately floated so as to "read" the various events. This allows us to comprehend both the inside of the House and Mildmay's position, and the situation of the "man in the street" as performed by Bunce. Finn's articulation in the narrative, and his deployment throughout the text, is a sustained reading and writing of the tensions within English culture, subject position and the exigencies of national identity. Without Finn the foreigner, it would not be possible to encounter Bunce's activism, or his reasons for agitation.

At the request of Mrs. Bunce, Phineas tries to intervene with Bunce, in order to prevent him being involved in the political disruption. It is typical of Finn's political blindness that he identifies the working class as "all the roughs of London" (261). However, Bunce, whose interest is in getting the vote—to him a crucial factor in the constitution of his Englishness, and the recognition by the upper classes of his stake in national identity—and who is described as a "respectable member of society" prior to Phineas remark, is able to articulate his political thoughts so as to dismiss Phineas' summing up of the proletariat as "roughs":

> If everybody with a wife and family was to say so, there'd be none there but roughs, and then where should we be? What would the Government people say to us then? If every man with a wife was to show hisself in the streets to-night,

> we should have the ballot before Parliament breaks up, and if none of 'em don't
> do it, we shall never have the ballot. Ain't that so? . . . If that's so . . . a
> man's duty is clear enough. He ought to go, though he'd two wives and families.
>
> (261–62)

Turning Finn's own language against him (as Wilkie Collins points out in his preface to *Man and Wife*, the term 'rough' belongs to middle class discourse for keeping the working class in their place; at least in the bourgeois imagination; xiv–xv), Bunce makes a clear and direct appeal for political activism, and for not shying away from the political responsibility that every person has as a member of civil society.

Civil society for Bunce has, as its basis, the nuclear family. He seeks a political voice in the name of that family and every family, and regards his responsibility as common to every "man." For Bunce, the question of political responsibility is a gendered, heterosexually normative one. We may mistakenly criticize Bunce for the ideological import of his position. But we must remember that we are reading the statement of a poorly educated, working-class male of the 1870s, who holds a belief in fair democratic change, founded on the rights of workers and the systematic, legislated protection of those rights. Despite the humorous portrayals of Bunce elsewhere, commentaries such as the one above cut through the humour to make a valid and politically urgent point which, instead of being criticized, can be adapted to include the rights of all oppressed groups.

As a Tory-liberal, Trollope may well have been antipathetic to the idea of unions and reform of suffrage, but what his intentions were do not compromise the picture. As Antonio Gramsci has put it:

> [a]lthough the author's specific aims must be considered when judging his work,
> this does not mean therefore that some other real contribution of the author
> should be omitted or disregarded or depreciated, even if it is in opposition to
> the ostensible aim.   (134)

If we do not recognise this and, in recognising it, historicise the scene of writing, then we read carelessly, not seeing the valency of articulations by those who are otherwise culturally elided. Bunce's statement posits the potential for the construction of a national identity—through political action—that is positive. It is positive because it imagines the enunciation of an identity which hitherto had no voice. It is a measure of the strength of Bunce's speech that Phineas has no argument against it; indeed, he cannot even speak. Bunce carries the point, and the conversation closes with the silence of the representative of politics in the face of the powerless man.

VI

Having presented cultural structures which are prolematized by the positioning of Phineas, I want to imagine a certain crisis foregrounded by *The Prime Minister*. The crisis is not "in" the narrative in any simple way. It exists as an instance of the cultural unconscious that we can attempt to map, from this novel and across other texts. The crisis is located across issues of definition and the impossibility of translation. It is also registered between two entirely interchangeable and moveable poles, the personal and political. The personal and political are bound up with each other, each dependent on the other. Both can be questioned in the context of Trollope's writing through a questioning of Trollope's uses of the categories "Gentleman' and "Coalition."

In *The Prime Minister*, the question of Ferdinand Lopez' origins is overdetermined by the insistent dalliance around his ambiguous status as a "gentleman." If he can be read as being a gentleman then, in Abel Wharton's eyes at least, Ferdinand can also be read as being an Englishman. And herein lies the danger for Wharton's sense and conceptualization of national identity; if the foreign is admitted as being on an equal footing with Englishness, then the cultural value of English identity is debased. This is because, as Terry Eagleton has suggested, "to acknowledge someone as a subject is at once to grant them the status as oneself and to recognize their otherness and autonomy" (415). For Wharton, a "gentleman' and an "Englishman" are one and the same, the questions of breeding, heredity, and national identity being linked inextricably.

Wharton's fears, therefore, are not peculiar to him, but figure the very question of the sovereignty of the subject. But opposed to Wharton, to open a gap in the text that allows our thinking on the subject, is the remark that:

> It was admitted on all sides that Ferdinand Lopez was a "gentleman." Johnson says that any other derivation of this difficult word than that which causes it to signify "a man of ancestry" is whimsical. There are many, who in defining the term for their own use, still adhere to Johnson's dictum;—but they adhere to it with certain unexpressed allowances for possible exceptions.   (3)

In this passage, Dr. Johnson and his dictionary are invoked by Trollope in a game of cultural semantics that refuses to fix the issue. Despite the fact that Lopez' social status and performative identity is "admitted on all sides" (the passive voice of the first sentence obscures the origin of the remark, slipping it into the doxical coinage of cultural discourse), nothing could be further from definition.

Throughout the passage, indeterminacy opens up the reliability of definition to vague contradictions and gaps. As we know from reading the "all sides" of Trollope's texts, such sources are notoriously unreliable and, in some cases, redundant, because the "collectively expressed ideas of the bourgeoisie" (Keane 214) are seen to be paradoxical; This is the case with Wharton's objections to Lopez' cultural mapping and the general ambiguity surrounding Lopez' social position. This is a textual world caught up in the failure to comprehend textuality; a world where members belonging to the same club as Lopez only "pretend to read" (11) and "people don't read Pope now, or if they do they don't take the trouble to understand him" (16). And if such is the standard of comprehension amongst those who inhabit the world, then what is admitted on all sides need not be taken seriously, because the definition of a gentleman would seem to rely on the protocols of reading and interpretation.

As we see here, the skills of reading and interpretation are spectacularly absent. The only person who once read is Abel Wharton, who can no longer complete a reading, but can only "try" the novels (as he does his cases), unsuccessfully (32). When thinking of Lopez, Wharton "feels" that he must refrain from "talk in ambiguous language of what as 'gentleman' would or would not do," (26) and tells Lopez that he wants "no definitions" (25). Abel is un–Abel, unable to read and scared of the consequences of interpretation. Note that, in the passage in question, Wharton's thought is not fixed dogmatically as are his remarks, "internally," the discourses with which he presents and constructs his identity in his social context are altogether equivocal. He "feels" rather than states, recognizing his own inability to translate and define in the ambiguity of his statements on the subject of the "gentleman." The quotation marks employed by Trollope write silently the remarking of the 'gentleman' as a dubious and provisional category, which Wharton fails to assert so unsure is he in the context of his reading. He makes plain that he wants no definitions, thereby testifying to his own internal acknowledgment that his own identity is in a process of deconstruction.

Wharton's cultural identity is at stake. He is not even able to assert his own Being-as-gentleman, so called into doubt is the cultural text. Reading and, therefore, translation are faced with the threat of the foreign and new, and are passing away. The resolution of the question of "gentleman-ness" is deferred infinitely, displaced and consumed even as it is foregrounded and made excessive, something larger than and beyond translation (into English), just like the 'Englishness' that Wharton insists on as the corollary definition of the "gentleman."

In the context of politics then, which is the context of the Palliser novels, that context by which Trollope unfolds for us the question of (the crisis of) national identity, what should the Government of England be composed of, if not "gentlemen"?

VII

If the category of "gentleman" is always already placed by Trollope in the abyss of the not-read, how are "gentlemen" to read themselves in terms of their public duty to their country, given that they too are unable to read? Perhaps the possibility of a partial interpretation, an interpretation involving compromise, lies in the category of the "coalition."

We understand Trollope revealing that no one authoritative definition of the state is possible, so dispersed are the party readings—dispersed within party structures and from one party to another—of the national text. The parties in question must therefore form a "coalition" from both Tory and Whig camps, in order to re-read national identity, such is the crisis of textuality. And our readings of the crisis in Trollope as a moment of fracture is due in part to what Terry Lovell defines as "comic implausibility" and "authorial intervention" (23–24) that is perceivable as undermining the authoritarian figure of the Gentleman, as reader and writer of Englishness. Yet Tory liberal identity on which the Gentleman depends for self definition is only possible through a coalition of ideologies; this is given political form, and thereby made visible, by Trollope, through the Coalition of *The Prime Minister*. At the head of this political compromise is Plantagenet Palliser.

Palliser's name is as significant as Phineas Finn's. Palliser's first name recalls a patronymic which carries in it a founding moment for the English aristocracy. The name also suggests a narrative of that aristocracy as a particular trace in the historical formation of an exclusive and hierarchical Englishness. So, perhaps Palliser can be called "a gentleman." In his *Autobiography*, Trollope wrote of his character that, "I think that Plantagenet Palliser, the Duke of Omnium, is a perfect gentleman. If he be not, then I am unable to describe a gentleman" (361). Trollope's statement carries an implied uncertainty that the author's cultural context—that out of which Trollope brings the whole category of "gentleman" into question in his novels—will undo his effort to describe a "gentleman." This ambiguity can be read in Palliser's names and the title of Prime Minister.

Palliser is not only himself. His identity is spread across a range of public and national signatures that are always in the service of a larger identity. Not only does his first name speak a narrative of English history, but his title also denies him a private, unified subjectivity. As Prime Minister, Palliser is rewritten as the subject of Englishness, the representative of that identity and the ideologies of his party, and, as an elected figure, the property of "the people." In this issue of public names, we can begin to comprehend how "bourgeois theories of universal liberty and individualism are ideological,"

> for they conceal the property-based interests of civil society. Despite its "appearance of guaranteeing individual freedom, civil society actually guarantees merely the freedom of private property's interests to carry on a running battle to extract surplus value."   (Keane 214–215)

This "running battle" is carried out in the public and private names of Plantagenet Palliser. His names are the signs of bourgeois ideology's investment; they guarantee the continued extraction of surplus-value which, in the case of nineteenth-century literature and across the site of the "gentleman," is the continued production of (the meaning of) the ideology of Tory-liberal Englishness. The plurality of names and the confidence they are meant to inspire are a confidence trick in the service of hegemony. Trollope shows that the figure of the aristocratic gentleman as leader of and servant to his country is a political performance. Through its implicit appeals to inheritance, heredity, continuity and the maintenance of social divisions, the performance suggests a "natural" or "given" order. This in turn hides the exploitation of the concept of the individual.

Plantagenet is mobilized by Trollope in order to promote, albeit ironically, the Englishness of the English middle classes to themselves. Yet Trollope's writing refuses the invisible suturing that would suggest the natural order (and, therefore, mark Trollope's texts with an unthinking conservatism and coalescence with the dominant ideology) through devices such as those identified above by Terry Lovell. And we can read the gaps opened by the stitches in the suture. As "The Prime Minister" (the definite article erases the personal in favor of the performative personality), Palliser is a doubled body, doubly read as both leader of the two parties in the form of the Coalition, and of the English people. His other hereditary title, the Duke of Omnium, is translatable as a pun suggesting that he has command over all. This we know to be untrue. In his private life, Palliser has no command over Glencora or his children, other than that which they allow him. Certainly, he has no control over the government he supposedly leads. His titles, rather than being the signatures of centred power, are the authorization of powerlessness. He is the subject of a writing that shows his own helplessness and marginality as a fainéant politician. Yet, because he is a "gentleman," his image is supposedly invested with power; here is the internal contradiction that Trollope plays out, and which we can read as the constant paradox of bourgeois ideology, from which come the crises of right-liberalism. And the figure of the 'coalition' is merely the grouping of the powerful-helpless, of the political(ly) powerless; of gentlemen unable to read the crisis of their own identity.

The crisis is one of historical transition and epistemological discontinuity. Which is precisely why so many are unable to read; and why the Liberal club—named, ironically, the "Progress," given the political impotence Trollope reveals—to which Wharton's son and Lopez belong is unable to muster a unified front or identity for support of the party. The concept of the club, which had done "little or nothing" (10) as a unifying organization, offers a social remapping of the political failure of gentlemen in misreading the epochal transition within which they are caught, and by which, paradoxically, they are produced. These same men, who belong to the Progress Club, are also those who support the Coalition.

"Coalition" is yet one more name for a club, and speaks of the similarities and homogeneity of traditional political discourse, whatever its party stripes or ostensible differences. We can read the failure of the gentlemen of the Coalition to read their own situation. Even though they perceive something of the crisis, they are unable to perceive the crisis as of their own making; instead of turning to self-analysis, they look outwards to a metaphysics of illusory unity. Thus, they form a cabinet that takes the moderates of both parties, while attempting to avoid Church reformists, Home Rulers, and "philosophical Radicals" (107). Yet again, Palliser is typical of the failure to perceive the problem of liberal identity. Plantagenet's particular blindness to his own situation as a crisis of cultural and social making is registered in a remark to Glencora: "Cora, there are different natures which have each their own excellencies and their own defects" (102). So immersed is Plantagenet in the discourses that read and write him, that he can only find fault within himself with his running of the Government, perceiving the trouble as that of human nature. Palliser proposes a theoretical model of human existence, reliant on an atomistic and essentialist view of humanity. His view reveals to us the moment of self-unawareness in liberal humanist ideology. Thus his identity is enmeshed by liberal humanist belief, which blinkers him to comprehending the material conditions that inform the turmoil and insularity of English society in the 1870s,[3] a turmoil produced by the economic policies of successive Tory and Whig governments, and by gentlemen such as Palliser. This turmoil led to a round of ever deepening recessions, widespread unemployment and "chronic anxiety" in public opinion (Bédarida 103).

So, in *The Prime Minister* we come to read that the "heads of the parties were at a standstill" (45). Palliser feels unequal to the task of writing the list of Cabinet members, so ambivalently does he regard the power that is not his. We can comprehend from our reading of Trollope an apparent stasis and impotence. This lack of movement is Trollope's registration of an epistemic break, focused for late Victorian culture by Trollope in the problematic status of the category of "gentleman." As Trollope makes us aware, both the problem and the cultural reliance on the concept of the "gentleman" informs the ideologies of both parties in their attempts to represent the 'true' politics of national identity. And it is this incestuous, familial resemblance between ostensibly different party-political positions that constitutes the momentary ends of a particular form of paternal authoritarianism that, during the 1870s and 1880s, found itself unable to stand before or against the strategies of the slowly emergent petty-bourgeois hegemony which it had helped to produce. Trollope's governments shuffle from one muddle to another, as did the governments of Trollope's England, and as is the current administration of John Major, unable to effect change in the face of social problems comparable to those in the 1880s.

VIII

If Trollope does not offer us a clear political position in opposition to the dominant Tory-liberal model of his time, this does not mean a retreat from politics on Trollope's part. Rather, we should read Trollope's resistance to position as an engaged play, the inconclusiveness of which is, to quote James R. Kincaid, "characteristic of the ironic form" (175). Such open-endedness determines the possibility of hope for a new and fairer politics of Englishness, a politics of the margin and other Englishnesses.

Reading Trollope is a small enough beginning in the attempted determination of rethinking national identity. But from reading Trollope's complications of Victorian culture, we may be able to comprehend our own performed and performative functions, and so start to interfere with the political processes that mediate our identities. These suppositions are not necessarily hopelessly utopian or naively idealist. It is, after all, out of a desire for articulation through the figure of an alternative political community looking after the interests of the marginal that Jacob Bunce joins a trade union, the idea of which was, in the 1860s and 70s not that much more fanciful than Septimus Harding's imaginary 'cello.

We need to imagine an articulation as a reaction to the discursive re-runs of the "Victorian" epoch that the authoritarian ideology of the New Right has financed and invested in, in the name of national identity. This "normative Victoriana" is a phantasm of our own culture, rather than being some truth of a bygone age. That which is presented to us is really the work of a political economy desirous of maintaining its power through the tyranny of a fictive unity.

This tyranny, manifested as the evocation of the previous century's identity, belongs to an effort on the part of the New Right to deal with the paradoxes of its own corporate-liberal beliefs. In Alan Sinfield's words:

> Margaret Thatcher's calls for a return to 'Victorian' values are intended to deal with this difficulty by evoking a time when aggressive competition co-existed with tradition, family, religion, responsibility and deference . . . New-right economic policy encourages selfish social attitudes, but community feeling cannot be invoked or acknowldged because it is likely to sound like social-ism . . . Thatcher's difficulty in specifying the right kind of individualism makes it all the more necessary to harp on about Englishness, respectability, family and nation.   (296–97)

Finn cannot build a "family" of his own in England, his nation and religion held at arm's length as just one more barely tolerated property of the English. His first Irish wife dies in childbirth and he cannot marry into the society around which he hovers, at times despairingly. At the center of that society is Plantagenet Palliser, who is just as caught as Finn. Both men foreground the problems of liberal ideology, rather than celebrating it. Economic compet-itiveness, selfishness and aggressive individualism are the direct consequences of Palliser's political philosophy, and it is these same negative aspects of Tory-liberalism that undo Palliser, and not "human nature" as he seems to think.

But more importantly, what Trollope can be read as unraveling are the subtly written protocols that hide their ideological chicanery underneath the speculative concepts such as "family," "nation," and "gentleman," which are still the stock in trade of the New Right's polemic. Trollope can make us laugh at the deadpan earnestness of the Right, as he writes its figures larger than life. Nationalist liberalism is made farcical; and the political value of farce in our reading is that an alternative "reality" is not offered. Trollope leaves things up in the air as the structures and institutions are revealed as shaken. The margins are opened to us. Those who inhabit the margins seek to articulate their identities beyond the Tory-liberal ethos. Whether or not they realise their desire is not important, for to understand this would be to read one more closure; and closure is still closure the conservative recuperation of the other effected, the old order re-established. Trollope "lets go" of control. In doing so, he intimates to us that there is always another story, others' stories, to be told.

NOTES

This essay is dedicated, with affection and grateful thanks, to James Kincaid.
1. As I write, this has been expressed most strongly in the Government's nefarious dealings with miners and the National Union of Mineworkers, and the attempted illegal closure of over thirty pits in 1992. This is just one narrative of Tory self-interest and power-brokerage, going back to 1984.
2. Bunce's arrest is described somewhat farcically. This does tend to delegitimize worker's rights. We can speculate that the scene is farcical because the "threat" of an organised proletariat is too great a challenge psychically to the middle class. Also, Trollope focuses on the individual, whose character we are already familiar with. Such a focus tends towards depoliticizing the scene which also, again denies the potential power of the workers.
3. On the crisis in Victorian values see, for example, Bédarida 1991, 99–109.

WORKS CITED

Baudrillard, Jean. *In the Shadow of the Silent Majorities or, the End of the Social and Other Essays*. Trans. Paul Foss, John Johnston, and Paul Patton. New York: SemioTexte, 1983.

Bédarida, François. *A Social History of England 1851–1990*. Trans. A. S. Forster and Jeffrey Hodgkinson. London: Routledge, 1991.

Chambers, Iain. *Border Dialogues: Journeys into Postmodernity*. London: Routledge, 1990.

Collins, Wilkie. *Man and Wife*. Stroud: Alan Sutton, 1990.

Eagleton, Terry. *The Ideology of the Aesthetic*. Oxford: Blackwell, 1990.

Gramsci, Antonio. *Selections from Cultural Writings*. Trans. William Boelhower, David Forgacs and Geoffrey Nowell Smith. Cambridge: Harvard UP, 1985.

Keane, John. *Democracy and Civil Society: On the Predicaments of European Socialism, the Prospects for Democracy, and the Problem of Controlling Political Power*. London: Verso, 1988.

Kincaid, James R. *The Novels of Anthony Trollope*. Oxford: Clarendon, 1997.

Lovell, Terry. *Consuming Fiction*. London: Verso, 1987.

Ronell, Avital. *The Telephone Book: Technology, Schizophrenia, Electric Speech*. Lincoln: U of Nebraska P, 1989.

Sinfield, Alan. *Literature, Politics, and Culture in Postwar Britain*. Berkeley: U of California P, 1989.

Spivak, Gayatri Chakravorty. "Three Feminist Texts and a Critique of Imperialism," *A Feminist Reader*, ed. Catherine Belsey and Jane Moore Oxford: Blackwell, 1989.

Trollope, Anthony. *An Autobiography*. Ed. Michael Sadleir and Michael Page. Oxford: Oxford UP, 1987.

———. *The Duke's Children*. Ed. Hermione Lee. Oxford: Oxford UP, 1983.

———. *Phineas Finn. The Irish Member*. Ed. John Sutherland. Harmondsworth: Penguin, 1975.

———. *Phineas Redux*. Ed. John C. Whale. Oxford: Oxford UP, 1990.

———. *The Prime Minister*. Ed. Jennifer Uglow. Oxford: Oxford UP, 1983.

Recent Dickens Studies:1991

William J. Palmer

"Round up the usual suspects," Louis Reynaud (Claude Raines), Casablanca's bribe-taking *roué* Prefect of Police, orders twice in the most romantic of all classic American movies. "Who *are* those guys?" Butch Cassidy (Paul Newman) asks the equally quizzical Sundance Kid (Robert Redford) in another quite romantic American film. Both of these immortalized movie lines could serve as an epigraph to 1991's *DSA* review of Dickens Studies. This year a number of the prominent "usual suspects" in Dickens scholarship and criticism, such as Richard Altick and J. Hillis Miller, turned up like good, well-burnished pennies while a number of new and relentless "guys" pursuing new trails of understanding our "Inimitable," such as Claire Tomalin, Audrey Jaffe, Pam Morris, and Doris Alexander, rode over the horizon to quicken our whole approach to the chase after the intricacies, mysteries, and magic of Dickens' life, world, art, and artifice. Rounding up "the usual suspects" and introducing "those guys" who have recently taken up the chase is the ongoing function of *DSA*'s annual omnibus review of Dickens Studies, which ends each year's volume and presents to each member of the Dickens family "an offer he can't refuse."

Famous movie lines notwithstanding, the omnibus reviewer of the year's work in Dickens Studies must ultimately disembark from his omnibus, wrestling down his large portmanteau, and set up shop on some busy London streetcorner, "unbox his puppets" so to speak, as Thackeray does at the gateway to *Vanity Fair*, and put them in some sort of order. Perhaps first he will extract the Charlie and Nellie puppets who dance such a provocative dance, followed by the pitiful puppets of poverty who stagger off over the curbstones to collapse in the gutter, or the muscular, mustachioed, militarily uniformed puppets of Imperialism who put on such a dashing and barbaric

331

show, or the postmodernist puppets of pedagoguery who, like Bradley Headstone, pound their heads against the solid barrel of the Dickens canon. Nineteen ninety-one was indeed a vigorous year for the biographers, scholars, and
critics all casting their diverse spells over the life, the world, and the works
of Charles Dickens. They are far from being "usual" in their suspicions and,
as ever, they are relentless in their pursuit of Victorian England's most exciting literary outlaw.

BIOGRAPHY

One of the two major events in Dickens Studies in 1991 was the aftershock
of the American publication of Peter Ackroyd's biography, *Dickens*, in December 1990. Perhaps owing to its late arrival on the scene or to its daunting
rhetorical complexity, which combines a number of different though complementary types of discourse, Ackroyd's biography is dismissed rather cava-
lierly in one brief paragraph by Chris R. Vanden Bossche in his "The Year
in Dickens Studies:1990" in *DSA:1991*. Vanden Bossche finishes: "In his
defense, it should be said that Ackroyd is a novelist and this biography has
certain literary pretensions and so may not be concerned with the scholarly
audience; I will leave the discussion of its literary merits, however, to other
reviewers." The pretensions in that statement seem more the reviewer's than
the biographer's. The implications that a novelist cannot write a credible
biography, that a novelist's biography would certainly not be of interest to
scholars, and that a scholar, especially a postmodernist one, should leave the
discussion of such a work's "literary merits" to other, presumably less serious, reviewers are rather too inclusive and presumptive.

In fact, Ackroyd's biography is perhaps most interesting expressly because
it is written by a novelist. In his prologue, Ackroyd clearly takes up the
challenge of literary biography. "For this is the challenge," he writes, "to
make biography an agent of real knowledge. To find in a day, a moment, a
passing image or gesture, the very spring and source of his creativity; and to
see in these details, too, the figure of the moving age" (xvi). Thus, Ackroyd
early declares that he is writing both a romantic biography, concerned with
the wellsprings of his subject's imagination, and a historicist biography,
concerned not only with the "history," as Henry Fielding would put it, of a
great man, but also with the history of an exciting age. But beyond both these
intentions, Ackroyd's *Dickens* is very much a novelistic biography. Yes, it
has a few interludes which are indulgences in a clearly fictional stream of

consciousness, the stuff of novels not biographies, but those playful little chapters are not the most interesting novelistic characteristics of Ackroyd's work. His biography, in its thematic concerns and language patterns, is structured novelistically.

Romantic biography, historicist biography, novelistic biography: these are the three clearest strains which pipe through the pages of Ackroyd's *Dickens*.

The romanticism of Ackroyd's approach to the imagination of the "Inimitable" lies in his consistent probing for the correspondent breeze which inspires Dickens' fiction. "The art of fiction was for him the art of memory" (16), Ackroyd begins, and he goes on to paint and explore "the primary landscapes of his imagination" (20). Often the landscape was itself an imaginary one, formed out of the books Dickens read both in his nightmarish childhood and all through his writing career. "His childhood reading became for him a living presence," Ackroyd writes, "almost a magical presence which he could summon . . . by rubbing 'that wonderful lamp within him' " (45). Ackroyd's (and Dickens') image for the imagination (from *The Arabian Nights*) is also M. H. Abrams' famous image for the romantic impulse in literature. Trading the mirror of the senses for the lamp of imagination was perhaps Dickens' greatest contribution to the genre, and Ackroyd meticulously tracks the growth of the novelist's mind, tracing the journey of his imagination from his childhood to his crowning fictions where the lamp burns brightest.

Like Keats and Byron, Dickens was always involved in "writing himself" (61), and Ackroyd is at his best in this biography when noting and describing and analyzing those places and people and events from which Dickens, like Jay Gatsby, created his art out of "a platonic conception of himself." For Ackroyd is in constant pursuit of those "usual suspects" who are "deeply implicated in the process of Dickens' imagination" (83). Those suspects may be other writers and their works, contemporary events, or the people in Dickens' life, but most often the major rub on that "wonderful lamp" is Dickens' own complex psyche. How romantic biography, the retracing of Dickens' footsteps on the journey of imagination, verges into psychobiography, the analysis of how the events of Dickens' life formed his inner life and thus inspired his work, becomes one of Ackroyd's most interesting attendant concerns. He presents the major psychobiographical events—the blacking factory, Mary Hogarth's death, Ellen—journalistically, but then connects them ingeniously to the fictional events created out of Dickens' "wonderful lamp" of imagination.

However, if Ackroyd's biography is initially concerned with the processes of Dickens' imagination, it soon finds a corresponding interest in Dickens as a man of his age, a player in the complex and exciting game of Victorian social history. Ackroyd's is a historicist biography in its evocation of the world, and the events and people of that world of the Victorian Age in which Dickens lived, for which Dickens wrote, and to change which Dickens polemicized his art. "London. The Great Oven. The Fever Patch. Babylon. The Great Wen," Ackroyd writes in a feverish moment trying to capture the sensual confusion of the Dickens World much as Dickens himself did (much better) in the opening of *Bleak House*. Yes, Ackroyd describes the real landscape of Victorian England in the sensual ways that novelists do, but he is also adept at fixing the historicist temper of the age in all its social, political, cultural dimensions.

"The streets were a breeding ground not only for disease but also for all forms of sexual licence; that Dickens's wanderings in London coincided with the onset of his own sexuality and puberty suggests that he must have been profoundly affected by the far from decorous world he saw around him. Alleys and bushes were used as lavatories; sexual intercourse in the streets with prostitutes was not uncommon . . . sex was free and was, as one historian put it, 'the only pleasure of the poor' " (89). Ackroyd's colorful evocation of Victorian England's byways, mores, and morals doesn't stop with the social. It can only include political philosophy: "only in the late eighteenth and early nineteenth centuries," he writes, "a real sense of nationhood developed. That nationalism, and a sense of national identity (in contrast to simple patriotism), became a potent force. Typically, this was a middle-class phenomenon, rooted in part in instinctive dislike of the Europeanized upper class. . . . But nationalism took its strength, too, from the increase of literacy among the middle-class, from the growth of industrialism and from a belief in the need for the moral regeneration of the nation" (198). Thus, Ackroyd is not averse to assuming the voice of the social historian to accompany the voice of the romantic psychobiographer. But always his departures into cultural speculation find their way back into biographical motive. For example, at a number of points Ackroyd manages to fold a sociohistorical observation into a biographical conclusion. "Certainly the passage of the railway was to figure largely both in his life and in his fiction," Ackroyd writes, "although his attitude towards it remained somewhat ambiguous—resembling, as it did, his later attitude toward the industrial age itself, compounded both of admiration and distrust, realization of a need for progress and nostalgia for the recent past, a worship of speed and a hatred of the destruction which it wrought'' (274).

For Ackroyd, the making of history and the making of art seem to be two inseparable, parallel responsibilities of the biographer. His technique is reminiscent of the prestructuralist Geneva School ''consciousness of consciousness'' illusion which J. Hillis Miller received from George Poulet and temporarily shopped to appreciative Dickensians. But if Ackroyd is a romantic biographer and a historicist biographer, he is also very much a novelist writing a biography of a novelist, a metabiographer.

The most obvious novelistic trait of Ackroyd's *Dickens*, the author's regular sailing out in a differing typeface upon a metafictional stream of consciousness, is also the least interesting. More novelistic (and useful) is Ackroyd's structuring of his arguments and the patterning of his language in terms of novelistic concerns. For example, Ackroyd's is a symbolic biography of Charles Dickens. He organizes the events of Dickens' life in terms of the symbols which pattern Dickens' work. ''We might use the imagery of the seascape,'' Ackroyd writes, such as the most dramatic scene of *David Copperfield*, to represent ''how Dickens seemed to live in the storm'' (xv). Writing of Dickens' funeral, Ackroyd analyzes the crowds who gathered to pay him homage as ''registering in symbolic sense the end of an age of which he was the single most visible representative; more so than Palmerston, now dead, more so than Gladstone, who stood in uneasy relation to the period yet to come, and more so than the Queen herself who had not, like Dickens, seen all the transitions of the century. He had more than seen them; he had felt them, had experienced them, had declared them in his fictions'' (xv). Ackroyd consistently sees Dickens' life and motives in symbols: the sea and ships, old clothes (''an interesting symbol, this, for the changes that were taking place within the culture itself'' [23]), the city, wooden legs, the cross on St. Paul's, the prison, boot blacking, the railway, fire and fire-watchers, the play. All of these were ''the figures he carried in his head, and the figures he transposed to his fiction'' (98). But for Ackroyd, the symbols of Dickens' biography are not simply tools to construct fictions, but rather ''over all social and political matters Dickens erected a vast shadowy symbolic structure'' (304). In his biography, Ackroyd serves his readers well as a guide to that ''vast shadowy symbolic structure'' that was the life, the world, and the art of Charles Dickens.

Dickensians have been fortunate in the biographers who have opened out the life and art of their ''Inimitable.'' From the myth-making protectiveness of Forster to the radical politicization of Jack Lindsey to the brilliant research

and critical sensitivity of Edgar Johnson to the eloquent humanizing of Fred
Kaplan and now Peter Ackroyd, Dickensian biography has always explored
the magic and the mystery, the commitment and the coincidence of that
wonderful act of romantic alchemy whereby life and reality are transmuted
into art and artifice. In a sense, like Jerry Cruncher, all biographers are
"resurrectionists" with rusty fingers and nighttime habits. Peter Ackroyd's
latest reinvigoration of the Dickens life and myth is a noble and creative one.
It is by no means perfect. Its style tends too much to parades of rhetorical
questions and a rhetorical tentativeness that fathers such unwieldy phrases as
"it may be unwise to suggest" (229) and "but perhaps one might pick out"
(1029), which along with those destructive departures into fictional stream of
consciousness make the reader squirm and ultimately bark "good god, man,
get on with it!" It is precisely because of the cluttered quality of Ackroyd's
style as compared to the purity and eloquent directness of Fred Kaplan's style
that makes Kaplan's biography the much more useful and manageable work
for Dickens scholars. Every serious Dickensian must read Ackroyd's biography, and will find that it brings the hero of his own life vividly back to life,
but when it is time to recommend a Dickens biography to our students, it
must be Fred Kaplan's.

If the reading and discussion of Peter Ackroyd's biography was the major
event in Dickens studies in the winter of 1991, then Claire Tomalin's *The
Invisible Woman* was the sultriest beach reading for serious Dickensians that
year. Its title promised the sort of revealing, provocative, polemic, biographical revelations which surely deserve a place in Dickensians' beach bags right
alongside the suntan lotion and the latest completion of *The Mystery of Edwin
Drood*. As Ada Nisbet in *Dickens and Ellen Ternan* in 1952 spackled up the
biggest hole in both Forster's and Edgar Johnson's biographies of Dickens,
Claire Tomalin strips away the whitewash applied by all of Dickens' previous
male biographers and presents a meticulously researched, eloquently reasoned, understated feminist view of the relationship of the young actress Ellen
Ternan and the much older but not tamer literary lion Charles Dickens.

Where Ackroyd's biography of Dickens is extravagant, ambitious, and
creative in its psychoanalytic forays, in its novelistic imagery and narrative
structures, in its romantic speculations on the sources from life of the people,
places, scenes, and moods of Dickens' art, Tomalin's biography, which is as
much about Dickens as it is about Ellen Ternan, is none of these things. Ellen
is no Zelda Fitzgerald, and *The Invisible Woman* is no anguished psychobiographical howl, as was Nancy Mitford's *Zelda*. Tomalin honestly and objec-
tively lays out the facts of two fascinating intertwined lives. She tells their

story straightforwardly, and rarely embellishes her narrative with creative touches or purple prose. She rarely speculates either on events that might have happened in the lives of her subjects or on the ebbings and flowings of their inner lives. When she is forced to speculate, even on strong circumstantial evidence, she does it with a respectful reticence that refuses to pander to the impulses of sensation or gossip. For example, here is how careful she can be in describing one of the juiciest, most controversial, periods in the affair of Dickens and Ternan:

> This chapter has tried to make some sense of the known facts of the years between 1861 and 1865, and suggested a simple outline of a narrative to fit them: that Nelly became pregnant by Dickens and that to minimize the possibility of scandal he moved her to France, probably somewhere in the Paris area; that she had her baby there, with her mother in attendance, some time in 1862; that the baby died, probably during the summer of 1863; and that she then stayed on in France or spent most of her time abroad until June 1865, when the Staplehurst accident occurred. (147–48)

Unlike in Ackroyd's biography, in Tomalin's *The Invisible Woman* Dickens and Ellen are always subjects of biography, not characters in a novelistic narrative.

There is a factual power, a documentariness, in Tomalin's prose. Her straightforward, often simple, sentences collect and order the meticulous scholarship which she has hunted down, captured, and put on trial for our judgment. This power emanates not from the artifice of style but from the art of biographical research clearly presented. Tomalin's narrative moves swiftly along its track toward its story's crises like that Victorian railway train speeding toward the Staplehurst bridge. Why were the Ternan women rendered invisible? "Nelly and Fanny Ternan were written out for two reasons," Tomalin writes with her customary directness. "The first and obvious one is that Nelly was a blot on the good name of Dickens, and the Dickens machinery for public relations was unrivalled . . . This leads us to the other reason for the blotting out of the name of Ternan. The Ternans were a theatrical clan. Nelly, her two sisters, her mother, her aunt and her grandmother, were all on the stage, mostly from infancy upwards. They were part of a subculture of British life which, throughout the nineteenth century, was viewed by the rest of society with at best equivocal feelings, at worst alarm" (6). As clearly as she can write it, Tomalin thus states the reason why her book needed to be written.

But there are other reasons as well. Dickens was "so successful in imposing his version of what happened on the world" (9) that this interesting, talented, independent, and enterprising family of Victorian women was literally rendered invisible because "in the scale of things Nelly is not an important person. No one would have begun to think about her were it not for Dickens, standing like a giant over the Victorian age" (10). And that Victorian age is also an important part of the central subject of Tomalin's book. Like Ackroyd's, Tomalin's is a historical biography. The basic focus of its historical vision is the definition of how actresses (and other women of indeterminate social class) were situated in the world of Victorian England. "Nelly's story," Tomalin writes, "casts light over a whole area of nineteenth-century life which is still very shadowy: first the world of professional actresses, then the world of women who knew themselves to be bad and were condemned by respectable people" (11). But the social history themes of *The Invisible Woman* are also closely linked to the uncovering of a buried feminist consciousness within a brutishly antifeminist society. "Nelly's history begins with a matriarchy," Tomalin argues. "Mother and grandmother were women who earned their own livings, organized their own careers and managed to bring up their families without the help of husbands, brothers or sons . . . The stage was virtually the only profession in which this sort of independence was possible for women at this time" (13).

Though Tomalin's title, and her focus upon the sociohistorical lot of classless women in the Victorian age, may seem to signal a polemic feminist bias bearing down on the reader like that relentless packet boat at the end of *Great Expectations*, that signal is deceiving. *The Invisible Woman's* feminist message is scrupulously understated, subtly implied, consistently freed to reveal itself in the facts of the case rather than having to be prosecuted by the author. But Claire Tomalin's feminist argument doesn't have to be pushed. She has done her research (both biographical and historical) so well, ordered her material so intelligently, told her story so honestly and directly, that the polemic embedded in the material is immediately evident to the reader. For example, "the truth is that, to succeed as an actress, you needed to be a woman of exceptional courage, intelligence and self-reliance. You had to be prepared to work yourself to the bone, to ignore sickness, pregnancy, and childbirth as well as bereavement and any other personal distress. You had to be tough enough to endure the harsh opinion of the world as well as homelessness and discomfort" (21). And, beyond all those obstacles to overcome, you had to be intelligent and have talent. The sheer force of detail and accuracy in Tomalin's arguments replaces any need for rhetorical polemics. What emerges from her book is not a feminist whine that invisibility was the result of the oppression of a great man upon a helpless woman, but that invisibility was an ingeniously accomplished necessity of survival in an oppressive age.

In *The Invisible Woman*, Dickens is never a melodramatic, mustachioed, male villain. Rather, like everyone else in this book, he is a fully dimensioned and sympathetically offered human being. One thing which rings utterly clear throughout Tomalin's book is how devoted Dickens truly was to Ellen. "Collins could take a mistress lightly enough—he could take two, still lightly," Tomalin writes in one of her more jocular moments, "but Dickens was cut to a different pattern . . . his 'magic circle' consisted of one member only" (132). Yet Dickens was no choir boy either. Tomalin shows how "even in the early years of his marriage his interest in the sexual underworld may not have been purely that of an observer." In a letter, he urges his friend the painter Maclise "to join him in Broadstairs for a break, promising 'conveniences of *all kinds* at Margate (do you take me?) and I know where they live' " (84).

Yet, notwithstanding (and despite) the even tone, the meticulous scholarship, and the refusal to indulge in psychological or lurid physical speculation, the real fun of *The Invisible Woman* still lies in its potential for generating juicy Dickensian gossip. Juiciest are the seeing through of all the elaborate subterfuges that Dickens choreographed to be with his mistress Ellen and to keep anyone else from knowing he was with her: forcing Collins to accompany him on a walking tour in order to stalk his actress in Doncaster; sending Nelly's mother and older sister to France so that he would have access to her without the inconvenience of chaperones; sending her off to France to have their love child. This is all *National Enquirer* material which Tomalin handles with all the sensationalism of a *PMLA* article. Even a year after *The Invisible Woman* was published, new revelations continued to surface. As a coda to her book Tomalin announced to the world the discovery of new evidence that Dickens, à la Nelson Rockefeller, didn't die in his study under the road from Gad's Hill but in the arms of his mistress Nelly. No matter how fine the scholarship, in biography gossip ultimately will out.

One excellent addendum to Tomalin's book which appeared soon after it in 1991 is Tracy C. Davis' *Actresses As Working Women: Their Social Identity in Victorian Culture*. Neither Dickens nor Ellen Ternan is ever mentioned in this book, but Davis describes in great detail the same world of the Victorian Theatre through which Tomalin's subjects move. Informed by Marxist and feminist theory, *Actresses As Working Women* is a much more polemic, much more overtly sexual portrayal of gender exploitation in the Victorian age. In its discussions of the Victorian double standard, of Victorian theatre and pornography, of voyeurism and sexual licence, it reminds us of Steven Marcus' *The Other Victorians*. Perhaps its most interesting chapter is titled ''The Geography of Sex in Society and Theatre.'' That chapter reads in its descriptions like sections out of both Mayhew and Dickens. What is most interesting about reading Tomalin's *The Invisible Woman* and Davis' *Actresses As Working Women* is the corroboration each gives the other. They have both captured the dark underside of the world of the Victorian Theatre with shocking accuracy.

SOCIAL CRITICISM

London. From Wordsworth's ''monstrous ant-hill on the plain'' to Dickens' looming, brooding, corrupting dust heaps, the city of London, the urban myth, the confusion of metropolitan society, hangs over nineteenth-century life and letters like a suffocating cloud, a fog of obscuring, alienating, dislocating, and obliterating forces which make existence within its social confines not just uncomfortable but unbearable, with meaning and understanding not even a possibility.

In the nineteenth century, the city appropriates literature, forces the novel genre especially to deal with its scandals, mysteries, indignities, injustices, corruptions, and all manner of social presumptions and problems which were not a major concern of a more rural, less chaotic eighteenth-century literature. In 1991, for some inexplicable reason, perhaps celebrating the twentieth anniversary of Alexander Welsh's *The City of Dickens*, a cluster of critical works appeared, all focused upon the representations of the city in Dickens' work.

Late in *The Celebration of Scandal: Toward the Sublime in Victorian Urban Fiction*, Carol Bernstein writes: ''After exploring texts of James, Wordsworth and George Eliot, we come finally to focus on Dickens, whose early sketches mark an entrance to narrative fiction and whose late novels, especially *Our Mutual Friend*, trace a more fully developed aesthetics of the city'' (171). Bernstein's book begins and ends with Dickens while in between exploring the narrative and characterizational rhetorics of dealing with the Victorian urban experience. Informed thoroughly by George Lukács, Michel Foucault, and Walter Benjamin, Bernstein's attempts to capture the wraiths of representation of the Victorian city result in an exceedingly elusive and insubstantial aesthetic, one of mystery, sublimity, and ultimately immateriality. And she is right. The very reason that the Victorian city, as it is represented in the literature of that time, is so fascinating, so mind-engaging, is that it is so elusive, so ungraspable, like John Fowles' *deus absconditus* of this story "The Enigma," so other and undefined and protean.

Bernstein is constantly throwing concept words at the shape-shifting presence of the Victorian city to see if they will stick, but what happens is that her attempts serve to prove one of her major points, that the Victorian city defies representation in words and that the only words capable of representing the Victorian city are words which stress its immateriality, its unreachableness, its powers of other-ness, words, in other words, of sublimity, but an idiosyncratic urban sublimity much different from its gothic, Romantic predecessor. "The novels of Dickens, Eliot, Hardy and Gissing concur, then, in several assumptions about the role of the city" (183), she writes, and then proceeds to fire a volley of concept words at her subject. The city exists in "doubleness," is "mystifying," emanates "confusion," and creates what she calls an "urban sublime" whereby "the city is transformed into apparitions, ruins, confusion, into lights itself" (184).

Bernstein's applications of deconstructive theory to the reading of the text of the city with emphasis on its representational, characterizational, and narratological strategies, while rather heavily jargoned (which all such studies can hardly resist being), is both ingenious and compelling. "This study of the representation of the city," she opens, "originates in two observations: that the growth of the nineteenth-century city was as mythical as it was undeniable, and that any representation of the city, any gesture of the verbal toward the material, is perforce a contradiction in terms" (1). Contradiction though it may be, Bernstein nonetheless does not hesitate to collect and analyze a whole century of such literary gestures which examine the city, "celebrate its mysteries" (2), define how the city's "social practices" dictate a writer's "descriptive procedures," and analyze the distortions which occur when "grammatical structures are not sufficient to maintain the disparity between word and city" (3). But Bernstein goes further, takes an even bigger risk. Riding boldly into the theoretical valley of death in which so many have perished before, one part of her study focuses on that old shibboleth, character. She convincingly defines "urban character" in the nineteenth-century novel as accomplished "in modes of negative figuration" by which the idealities of characters in novels are always dissolving, fragmenting, veritably going up in smoke and turning into dust.

Two concepts, of "scandal" and of "sublimity," govern Bernstein's attempts to fix a mobile meaning on her reading of the text of the city in Victorian fiction. Both materially and conceptually, the city is a "scandal"

when examined according to any social rubric. "Urban scandals have generally been understood as sociably caused and thus comprehensible, all the
more shocking for their clarity," Bernstein argues, "the slums that lie at the
heart of the city and contradict its myths of progress, the corruption that
festers in self-celebrating governments, the secrets and betrayals that belie
bourgeois as well as aristocratic solidarities. All these scandals are only
intensified in certain methods of representation" (2). One means of ameliorat-
ing such scandals is to sublimate them:

> Since cities have always figured as the polar opposite to the natural . . . they
> would seem imperious at least to the scandal that crosses nature and culture.
> Yet urban writers, whether from a culturally induced nostalgia, or a desire to
> control the city by distancing it, or an ideological denial of the city's material
> pressures, have often invoked the natural. Nature is a sublime metaphor that
> links cities with forests and floods, with anything vast and threatening.   (4)

What Bernstein is so avidly pursuing is "an urban sublime," a "contradiction in terms, a theoretical scandal" (10). In the novels of the nineteenth
century, she finds this "scandal," this "urban sublime," in the complex
deconstruction of the representation of the city.

For Dickensians, Bernstein's book offers challenging new readings of
works from all phases of the canon of the "Inimitable." She begins with an
examination of the anthropomorphic "storehouse of images" (32) in *Sketches
by Boz*, images that create an "immersion, that tolerance of mystery, that
recognition of language's displaced relation to the object-world of the city"
which "can be seen as the very factors that allowed the urban novel to come
into being" (45). She touches on *Oliver Twist* and uses *Bleak House* as an
ongoing exemplar, but she ends her book with successively brilliant readings
of *Little Dorrit* and *Our Mutual Friend*, a clear case of saving the best 'til
last. Her reading of *Little Dorrit* defines urban characterization as captured
in Dickens' image of the "go-betweens" that Arthur Clennan observes after
having accidentally spent a night in debtor's prison. These beings "emblema-
tize the relation between prison and city: urban existence is a continuing
transaction between inside and outside" (157). Her reading of *Our Mutual
Friend* is a curiously old-fashioned one which, nonetheless, employs new,
postmodernist tools. She focuses on a single controlling trope, "surfaces and
depths" (191), as a way of defining Dickens' attempt to penetrate the persistent opaqueness of the "urban sublime." Bernstein's book is a model for
deconstructive readings both of a social text like the city and of literary texts
of the sort that an urban novelist like Dickens proffers. Its own rhetorical

strategies propel the reader into the most useful exercises of critical and theoretical thought. It is an excellent workout.

Similarly empowered by the theoretical work of Walter Benjamin, similarly focused on the elusiveness of a coherent urban myth, similarly historicist in its study of a subgenre within the Victorian novel, Anne Humpherys, in her essay "And Urban Twists: The Victorian Mysteries Novel," accompanies Bernstein into the labyrinth of the Victorian city and arrives at exactly the same deconstructed destination, a destination, one might add, at which J. Hillis Miller also arrived, though by somewhat different conveyance, more than thirty years ago. As Humpherys makes her major points,

> This is the "mysteries" novel, a fictional response to urbanization and its institutions in the mid-nineteenth century, and a bridge between two more well-known genres, the Newgate novel of the 1830s and the sensation novel of the 1860s. (455)
> The mysteries novel negotiates the shift between these two genres, reflecting an unstable border in the mid-nineteenth century between the public and private spheres. (455)
> "Mysteries" refers linguistically to the fragmented and hence incoherent experience of the modern city as well as to the resulting feelings of disconnectedness. (456)
> The primary focus of the mysteries narratives, moreover, like that of the Newgate novel but unlike that of either the traditional detective or sensation novel, is an exposé of institutions . . . These institutions evolved to counter the effects of urban fragmentation and loss of connection, but ironically they have themselves in many cases added to the sense of modern alienation.   (457)

she proves a clear fellow traveler with both Bernstein and Miller into the confusing maze of the Victorian city. Like Bernstein's book, Humpherys' essay explores the evils of Victorian urbanization in both their material and their rhetorical aberrance. Both writers emphasize how the literature of the urban experience stresses instability, fragmentation, incoherence, disconnection, and alienation as the results of the human inability to cope with the mysteriousness, the incomprehensibility of the Victorian city. Humpherys' arguments, based on the readings of three urban "mysteries" texts—*Les Mystères de Paris* by Eugene Sue, *The Mysteries of London* by G. W. M. Reynolds, and Dickens' *Bleak House*—are made equally convincingly on the same linguistic and rhetorical grounds that Bernstein uses. For both writers, the language, the scenes, and the characters which their respective subjects employ to attempt representation of the urban experience itself mirror that experience in all its sublime intractableness. Thus, Bernstein's book and Humpherys' essay are natural theoretical complements to each other, and should be read together. Together they present an overwhelming argument for the city as the most prominent deconstructing force in Victorian literature.

For Dickensians, Humpherys' essay is not as satisfying or useful as Bernstein's book. Humpherys concentrates on Sue's and Reynolds' novels, which are given full treatment in their own sections of the essay, while the brief comments on *Bleak House* are diffused throughout, usually to illuminate the more specific points made in the discussion of the other two works.

As Bernstein focused on the motifs of "surfaces and depths" in her reading of *Our Mutual Friend*, Humpherys fixes on "fog and fever" as a supposed "set of linguistic and literary connections which serve as both a foreshadowing and cohering force" (465). But she immediately qualifies, as any true deconstructor must, the "tendency to overdetermine linguistic connection" which "leads in some cases to a strain manifested by hyperbole and extended metaphor which is evident in all the novels and which in *Bleak House* probably contributed to contemporary criticisms of the text as overwrought" (465). As Bernstein also argues, the controlling imagery is there, but it can't control. The Victorian city is too fragmented, too disconnected, for language to find a successful unity.

This failure of language and representation accounts for the tentativeness about meaning which Bernstein and Humpherys share. "The mysteries novel," Humpherys writes, "thus marks a short moment when it seemed at least possible that narrative might not only represent the totality of modern urban life but even contribute to the reform of its institutions" (470). But, as Humpherys and Bernstein clearly realize, the chaos of the Victorian city is much too powerful in its resistance to such attempts.

A far more pedestrian exercise in the social critique of the institutions which make up the Victorian city is James Boasberg's essay "Chancery as Megalosaurus: Lawyers, Courts and Society in *Bleak House*." Published in an interdisciplinary literary journal, Boasberg's article is addressed to lawyers not literary critics, and is much more intent on preaching legal ethics than on examining the meaning or style of *Bleak House*. It reads like a legal brief, with quotations from *Bleak House* cited as nineteenth-century precedents for the author's case against some of the contemporary prevailing attitudes of the late-twentieth-century legal profession and court system.

A serious (or even a frivolous) Dickensian would find Boasberg's essay a methodical trudge through the obvious. It opens by quoting the opening of *Bleak House*, a not unknown passage for most Dickensians, and proceeds to state that "Charles Dickens' *Bleak House* is also one of the longest and most significant fictionalized treatments of the law in the English language" (38).

What follows is a succession of equally unoriginal statements of the obvious. He tells Dickensians nothing which they do not already know (and have known for a long time) about *Bleak House*. The question is: Are the lawyers whom he is supposedly addressing in this literary journal (Do lawyers read literary journals?) as uninformed and imperceptive as his rudimentary summary of the themes and characterizations of Dickens' novel presumes?

In a brief meditation on language, Boasberg does, however, make one point which brings together the professions of the law and postmodernist literary criticism, the pretentions of both lawyers and critics. "The manners of Kenge and Guppy illustrate the emptiness and lack of passion in the rhetoric of the law," he writes. "Their conduct epitomizes how lawyers can shrink behind a wall of convoluted language, never coming forth to respond to their client's concerns" (44). That indictment could serve just as easily for postmodernist literary critics as for the lawyers on whom it is passed down. But whereas Bernstein and Humpherys rigorously examined the representation of the Victorian city and the institutions of the urban experience, like the law, Boasberg methodically rehashes decades of received opinion and builds up such a stack of redundancies that they rival the workings of Dickens' Chancery itself.

Richard Altick's *The Presence of the Present* is an altogether different sort of social history from the language-based, postmodernist social histories of Bernstein and Humpherys. Altick was an instinctive New Historicist before Hayden White, Dominick LaCapra, and their theoretical spawn ever surfaced out of the philosophical depths of Derrida and Foucault. Were it not for Altick's graceful, witty, clear, unjargoned prose style, were it not for his copious and meticulous research so ingeniously ordered and argued and analyzed, were it not for the sheer weight of his long career of being the best, most widely read Victorian scholar of us all, *The Presence of the Present* would be an overlong compendium of interesting sociohistorical details, the ultimate trivia book of the Victorian age, a reading experience akin to walking into Brian Moore's *The Great Victorian Collection*. But that is exactly what Altick's book sets out to be and that is exactly what it is, except that it is so well done, so interesting, offers the opportunity to learn so much, that it is worth the long trek because you are always in such good company. Altick's is a voice from another age of criticism, an age that fell somewhere between the Formalists and the Structuralists, and still refuses to acknowledge the gymnastic acts of the Postmodernists. It is the voice of good, old-fashioned, up-to-the-elbows scholarship, coupled with an acute sociohistorical consciousness. It is an older voice, but a solid, vigorous voice still well worth listening to and heeding.

The Presence of the Present is subtitled "Topics of the Day in the Victorian Novel" and is about what Altick, employing a critical term of his own coinage, calls "topicalities." Altick's point of departure is a statement of purpose from the first page of the first issue of *Punch* in 1841, and he employs it as the theme statement for his book on that Victorian genre which "makes the most of the present, regardless of the past or future." He sees this temporal consciousness as "the spirit that dominated Victorian fiction" (1).

"Topicalities in the strict sense," Altick defines, "are references to people, events or places that were present in the public consciousness, usually but not always as news items at the time a novel was published or within recent memory. The word . . . also includes what might be called physical topicalities—objects and scenes which were new presences in the contemporary view, the visible results of change" (2). As Altick makes his bow to New Historicism, topicalities, "to adopt a term current in present-day historiography . . . show how the Victorian *mentalité*—the common fund of information, opinions, assumptions, and idea- and value-structures—was manifested in the product the novelists set before their public" (2). These "topicalities" are the "experiences of everyday life in a rapidly changing world and a sprinkling of large events" which "provided the novelists with the materials that would most satisfy their readers' insatiable interest in the contemporary scene" (1). What Altick is, in more romantic terms, actually exploring is that magical alchemy whereby a wizard like Dickens or Thackeray or Eliot or Hardy could transmute the ordinary events of everyday contemporary life into the stuff of novelistic art.

But Altick's cataloguing of the "topicalities" of Victorian fiction is more complicated in its sociohistorical intents. He is interested in collecting, describing, analyzing, and, both textually and extratextually, interpreting those "time-specific details" which are so often in great literature overshadowed by those "time-neutral details" and themes which carry more universal, mythic meanings. In fact, that may be the major attraction of Altick's book and of Altick himself as a critic—he still believes in meaning; he still believes that the smallest detail, the most obscure reference in a massive Victorian novel (like *Bleak House*) can be the key that unlocks the meaning of the text. And, as a critic writing in an increasingly aliterate, electronic media-distracted age, Altick still exudes a refreshing optimism. "An awareness of the topicalities that its first readers discovered and responded to," he gushes, "enables us to read, with greater understanding than is otherwise possible, the living book of Victorian fiction" (4).

Altick's *The Presence of the Present* is about the Victorian age (as well as
the Victorian novel)—its feel, its tastes, its world-changing events as well as
its bric-a-brac—in the same way that J. H. Buckley's *The Victorian Temper*
and Walter Houghton's *The Victorian Frame of Mind* and Basil Willey's
Nineteenth-Century Studies were back in the Fifties and Sixties. It constantly
gives off that wonderful sense of "being there," of walking leisurely through
the world that Dickens would bring to life in his novels. He characterizes the
Victorian age as an age of "communal narcissism" (9), an age which was
constantly looking at itself. The self-consciousness of the Victorian age studied and evaluated and morally judged all its actions and events and social
trends. In turn, "the kind of literature that was most in demand was the kind
that somehow reflected, as newspapers did, the world . . . its readers knew
best" (10). This type of literature was the novel, and Altick's book examines
how Victorian novels both held the mirror up to Victorian "topicalities" but
also expanded on them, interpreted them, turned them into social symbols,
transmuted them into myths.

Across the length and breadth of *The Presence of the Present*, Altick
examines the relationships between the novels of the day—those of the
"great" novelists like Dickens and Thackeray, the sensation novelists like
Wilkie Collins, and the lesser writers and downright hacks who also were
widely read—and the "topicalities" which fed those novels' need for conte-
mporaniety. Topicality superseded the historical novels of Sir Walter Scott's
day so that "by the middle of the century, a novel was virtually assumed to
be a story of the present day" (38). In fact, the self-consciousness of the age
became so strong that publishers (in contracts) began to demand "novels the
scenes of which are to be descriptive of contemporary English life, society
and manners" (39). Altick orders his "topicalities" in chapters which focus
on a single or a few related sources for topical influences on Victorian novels.
For example, he examines the ways in which new forms of transportation,
the expansions of popular entertainments, and the new stress on advertising
all inspired scenes, metaphors, even social commentaries within the novels of
the day. One chapter, intriguingly titled "The Favorite Vice of the Nineteenth
Century," focuses solely on smoking as it appears and is used symbolically
in Victorian fiction. Other chapters deal with the topical exploitability of
London landmarks, modes of male and female fashion, political monuments,
and the whole financial world of speculation and bankruptcy proceedings.
Altick does not forget the roman à clef possibilities that Victorian fiction was
always exploiting. He provides a fascinating scorecard whereby all the players
who appear under assumed names in the novels can be identified. Most

interesting, however, are his early, more general chapters. In "Forms and Sources," he discusses how the very method of publication, serialization, forced topicality upon the Victorian novel. He also discusses how the rise of newspapers, the novel genre's major competition for reading time, both forced and provided fodder for the topical necessity in the Victorian novel.

For Dickensians, *The Presence of the Present* is a veritable treasure chest of material. Clearly aligned with the earlier sociohistorical approaches of Dickensians like Humphry House, Phillip Collins, Trevor Blount, and Alexander Welsh, Altick refers to Dickens on almost every page, canvasses the text of every Dickens novel for its numerous topicalities, and elevates Dickens above all the other writers of his day as the paradigm, the leader in the novel's realization of and reaction to the overwhelming topical consciousness of the day. Some of Altick's Dickens readings are new, many are well known, but all are presented with Altick's acute sociohistorical, critical perception which, in his clear prose, makes all the right connections. Especially for Dickensians, but for all students of the Victorian novel, *The Presence of the Present* is a delightfully useful book which never loses sight of its goal of showing how the spirit of the Victorian age was minutely embedded in the novels which were the age's most representative literary documents.

CULTURAL CRITIQUE

Pam Morris, author of *Dickens's Class Consciousness*, in her earliest reading of Dickens' novels noticed an "insistent picking out of the servants and leaving unmentioned their masters" which signaled "within Dickens's texts, a consciousness . . . a way of seeing which belongs to the experience of marginalization—of both class and sex" (ix). Morris' subtitle, "A Marginal View," and the title of her introduction, "From Margin to Centre," also signal the subject of her cultural critique: how Dickens was consistently conscious of the antagonistic relation between on the one hand the society he criticized for having marginalized many of his readers, and on the other the readers themselves. A "model of identification with alienation," Morris writes, "offers a means of understanding the nature and mechanisms of class marginalization, the patterns of which, psychological and social, inscribe themselves upon Dickens's texts" (5). In order to understand the conflict between the texts and subtexts of margin and center within Dickens' master texts, "a dialogic reading practice is essential for the accentuation of these complex internal polemics. A dialogic approach also allows for some redistribution of critical focus from the central characters, at times the least imaginatively compelling, towards those at the margin of the text'' (14).

For Morris, the perception of dialogic tension between margin and center in social class terms is essential to the understanding of Dickens' novels. "Dickens himself acknowledged when he suggested readers should substitute classes for his individual fictitious characters'' that this sort of dialogic reading was apposite, but Morris also argues that "the resolution of the main story is often implicitly challenged by values asserted in the subtext. This intrinsic dialogism is most clearly demonstrated at the level of plot structure'' (10). Her ongoing critical technique is to tie the controlling image structures of the novels to this dialogic confrontation between the classes, between the margin and the center within Victorian society itself. For example, that "the structuring motifs of illegitimacy and illicit love in Dickens's texts provide a powerfully emotive image by which to express the fundamentally exploitative nature of class relations'' (12) and that there is "a pattern of doomed circular flight, in which illicit love and illegitimacy centre increasingly upon the impossibility of escape from one's past, from shame, guilt, and the physical force of sexual desire'' (13) are two such imagistic departure points.

Just as in Bernstein's book, Morris's focus on plot, image, and character reveal 'the way Dickens' texts express, explore, and challenge the social and psychological effects of interpellation of margin to centre in a class formation with the resulting constitution of individuals as class subjects'' (14). But Morris also grounds her arguments in a historicist refutation of decades of traditional critical attitude towards Dickens' polemic topicality. "Far from challenging such rules of exclusion,'' Morris argues, "a long tradition of Dickens criticism contributed the sanction of scholarship to the view that his political thought was impressionistic and unrigorous and, depending on the critic, either benevolent but naive, or naive and reactionary'' (2). She, on the other hand, using *Martin Chuzzlewit* as an example, argues that "far from following in the wake of social movement, Dickens's text registers an initial moment of historical change. In 1844, as *Martin Chuzzlewit* was published, speculative activity in railways and other commercial projects was about to explode'' (41). In this sense, *Dickens's Class Consciousness* parallels the stronger topical emphasis which Altick also attributes to Dickens' fiction. Morris' invocation to a dialogic cultural critique mode of reading Dickens, then, is underpinned by a historicist reading of the texts of Victorian society as well in terms of the religious (read Evangelical) and social (read Utilitarian) marginalization of the lower classes as exploitable and expendable objects outside the social power of the center, the governing Victorian middle class. As she writes, the ''Victorian middle class constructed its identity upon an absolute opposition between its respectability and the moral unfitness of the working class'' (11).

Rigorously informed by the theoretical social and cultural models of Bakhtin, Lacan, Althusser, Said, and Freud, *Dickens's Class Consciousness* is a careful melding of theory and criticism, both formal and historical, which not only challenges past readings of the Dickens vision, but offers new interpretations and reading strategies which greatly enhance the perception of Dickens as a writer of the streets, the common people, the disenfranchised of Victorian society. One of the drawbacks of such a wide-ranging theoretical base for an applied critical text is that, at times, Morris' book is jargon-heavy, difficult to translate because of the succession of specific-meaning theoretical terms heavily laden with referential cargo. But difficult though the reading sometimes is, the payoff is substantial. New definitions of the dynamics at work in a selection of Dickens' novels—*The Pickwick Papers, David Copperfield, Bleak House, Great Expectations, Our Mutual Friend*—offer a fresh and politically invigorating view both of Dickens the engagé novelist and of those individual works. Morris reads *David Copperfield*, for example, as a novel in which the ''heroes of David's life . . . are revealed as identical in their will to power and repression, despite external differences of manner. The gentlemanly Steerforth is shown to be as brutal as either Murdstone or Creakle, and it is his discourse, especially, which images the most callous class oppression'' (78). Morris' conclusion—

> what the text confesses to, most poignantly, is the inability to disengage imaginative desire from the romantic Absolute Subject signified in the social encodement of ''gentleman.'' Despite an unveiling of a pernicious reality underlying the myth, David's love for Steerforth, even after the seduction of Em'ly and destruction of the Yarmouth home, is the most strongly registered desire of the text.   (79)

—shows the manner in which Dickens, through his imperceptive first-person narrator, is exposing the betrayal of the naive Romantic illusion of class patronage.

Similarly politicized, socialized, and historicized readings of *Bleak House, Great Expectations*, and *Our Mutual Friend* both revise and polish traditional readings of those novels as well as commenting on the consistently lower-class sympathetic political allegiances of their author. Morris' readings carefully explore the growing complexity of relation and the deepening alienation between the English social classes throughout Dickens' career. Morris' final major theme in stressing the dialogic reading strategy and analyzing Dickens' lower class, "street" characters is to stress that "these characters' language asserts . . . not any overt political programme, but a set of oppositional values, a subversive, nonhegemonic view of human life which challenges the hegemonic validity of dominant culture" (26). The result of this class confrontation was debilitating for English culture and society as both Morris and Matthew Arnold (in *Culture and Anarchy* or "Dover Beach") would surely agree. "So, by the 1850's," Morris writes, "began a slow ebbing away of energy and life force within British culture, disguised but not checked by the rise of empire" (79).

It is, specifically, that "rise of empire" which fuels (as it has other cultural critics such as Said, Dierdre David, Patrick Brantlinger, and Peter Hulme) Suvendrini Perera's study of the nineteenth-century British novel *Reaches of Empire: the English Novel from Edgeworth to Dickens*. Like Pam Morris in *Dickens's Class Consciousness* (as well as Altick in a less obvious way) Perera is touting a new strategy of critical reading rather than simply offering a series of critical readings for a reader's enlightenment. Quoting Rosemary Hennessy and Rojeswari Mohan, who campaign for a "global reading strategy"—"reading is a material practice contributing to the construction of the social real; any reading of any text of culture is first of all an intervention in the available ways of making sense of 'history' in the subject's historical present" (x)—Perera makes it clear that her essay is "a strategy for reading empire" (x) rather than just another collection of readings of selected British "great novels."

Perera also, like Morris, is utterly dependent on the center vs. margin argument. Stepping off from Jonah Raskin's *The Mythology of Imperialism*, which subdivides the British Empire into "metropolis" and "hinterland," Perera enters into an argument quite similar to Morris': "by designating center and margins, charting the limits of alien and natural elements, inimical land and life-giving sea, the novel maps the boundaries between self and other, grounding each in specifically constituted locations. The project of *Reaches of Empire* is to read those peripheral spaces as they appear at the edges of early and mid-ninteenth-century texts" (3). Echoing Morris's subtitle, Perera's is also a marginal view. She is revealing the margins and the marginalized of early empire as they appear in the margins and between the lines of the "Great Tradition" English novels of the pre-Empire (before 1870) period.

"This book reads the great cultural texts of English literature as they work to construct empire at the primary levels of vocabulary, image, character, place, plot, narrative'' (x), Perera announces early on. Compared to Morris's wide-ranging cultural critique, her objectives are somewhat modest, but her diction and argument are much clearer, much easier to follow, and thus equally powerful. There is, or should be, something to be said for minimalist clarity as a viable alternative to the jargon-heavy, often Byzantine, opacity of much academic theoretical criticism.

Perera confronts some interesting genre concerns as well. She temporally redefines the historicity of empire criticism by arguing that ''imperial ideology, far from being an incidental intrusion of the late Victorian period, was throughout a major factor in the English novel'' (2) because ''empire is not simply expressed or reflected in the novel; . . . it is rather processed and naturalized by it'' (7). In other words, empire may have been a theme in English fiction, but English fiction actually advertised and legitimized the British Empire to a whole century of readers.

Perera's marginalized strategy for reading the text of empire is perhaps best expressed in an interrogation of narrative critics by Mineke Schipper:

> Who is *not* speaking? Who has *no* right to speak? Who does *not* see? Whose view is *not* expressed? Who does *not* act? Who has been deprived of the right to act? Who is powerless to act?   (14)

These are the questions that the selected texts within which Perera reads the text of empire must answer.

As does Altick in *The Presence of the Present*, Perera pays more attention to Dickens than to any of the other nineteenth-century novelists considered: Maria Edgeworth, Jane Austen, Elizabeth Gaskell, Charlotte Brontë, Thackeray. Dickens gets two chapters, one on *Dombey and Son* and one on *The Mystery of Edwin Drood*. Perera's goal, ''to situate'' *Dombey and Son* ''in relation to a discourse of empire'' (61), is pursued through the doorways of imagery and dialogic reading. The polarization of mercantile imperialism and innocent, well-meaning romanticism, ''based on the conflict between Florence and Dombey, is most often characterized by a symbolism of the sea as natural fluid and cyclical as opposed to the rigid industrial realities of man-made progress'' (64). Perera's reading carefully and perceptively parallels historical events and documents of the time of *Dombey and Son* to the dialogic imperialist discourse of the novel, thus echoing the ''topicalities'' method of Altick's book. She describes ''Dickens' cartography'' in the novel as an opposition between ''the House of Dombey and the Wooden Midshipman's shop—the one signifying money and destructive pride, the other romance and childlike love—on the meeting ground of the East India Docks'' (62). Thus, the novel ''participates in contradictory discourses of expansion'' (63). In the end, ''the triumphant regeneration of expansionist mercantilism in *Dombey and Son* cannot dismiss the costly returns of empire'' (77).

The domestic and the exotic, the cartography of the English countryside and an Orientalist underworld, also orchestrate ''the central concerns of empire'' (103) in *The Mystery of Edwin Drood*. The conflict of empire is embodied in the tension between Rosa Budd and Edwin Drood. Rosa ''hates'' both the people of the East and the ''archaeologists and engineers'' who ''in their penetration'' (sexual?) ''of colonized earth or of colonized history'' are ''all equally the paraphernalia of imperial conquest and progress.'' Edwin ''also embodies a particular sexual thrust; his will to change the whole condition of an undeveloped country'' thus projecting his ''proprietary assurance'' (104–05) in his rights to Rosa. Perera reads *The Mystery of Edwin Drood* as a ''racially charged novel of symbolic sexual imperialism.'' The ''power relations'' between the characters in the novel are ''a casual indication of the complicated imperial and sexual tensions in their increasing complexity'' which finally accounts for the narrative inconclusiveness of *Edwin Drood* (107). One might venture to add, however, that Dickens' death also had somewhat to do with it!

Perhaps the most interesting section of Perera's essay on *The Mystery of Edwin Drood* deals with the Victorian drug trade and compares the novel to De Quincey's *Confessions of an English Opium Eater*. Like the opium addict, the imperialist is incurably addicted, as will be Conrad's Kurtz later, to the possibilities for power endemic in the adventure of empire. Perera's readings of Dickens are ingenious, provocative, and adept applications of New Historicist thought to the discourse of culturally informed texts. Her arguments are consistently convincing.

REVISIONIST GENDER CRITICISM

Gender criticism informs and speaks as subtext both in Pam Morris' discussions of types of marginalization in Dickens' fiction and in Suvendrini Perera's symbolic discussions of empire. ''Deeply indicated in the representation of cultural difference is also the representation of gender'' (8), Perera asserts. Claire Tomalin's biography of Ellen Terman is, of course, a major primary document of all sorts of gender issues. Lynda Zwinger's *Daughters, Fathers and the Novel* is a clearly focused, Freudian-based, primary-text, gender study of one of the touchier story problems in literature. Subtitled "The Sentimental Romance of Heterosexuality," it examines the complexly ambivalent character type that Zwinger designates "the daughter of sentiment" in five major novels: Richardson's *Clarissa*, Dickens' *Dombey and Son*, Alcott's *Little Women*, James's *The Golden Bowl*, and Pauline Réage's *The Story of O*. In these novels, as in the mythic fairy tale "The Beauty and the Beast" which serves as the opening invocation of her book, the central female character "is a father's daughter . . . constructed . . . to the very particular specifications of an omnipresent and unvoiced paternal desire." As two of the major participants in the four-sided Freudian family romance, the "fictional daughter and her father are, in fact, two of the most compelling and problematic figures in the history of heterosexuality and its attendant/engendering stories" (4). Zwinger's "daughter of sentiment" is a classically Victorian figure, a woman caught between two worlds, both defined by her ambivalent relationship to her father as an object of unfulfillable desire and a paradigm of romanticized hope. She sees the daughter figure in literature as a critically torn object, torn between "critical scorn" for her submissions to patriarchal power and popular approval for "her (admittedly daunting) collection of virtues" (5).

Dombey and Son is perhaps Zwinger's best template for proving her theories of the cultural myth of the daughter of sentiment and the contradictive dilemma of the father of such a "good woman" daughter. Dombey "insists upon exaggerated homage from those around him, yet rejects the one character who consistently and genuinely offers it to him—his own daughter, who ought to be a comfort and solace to him, but instead embodies for him a persistent and mysterious dread" (6). Zwinger's reading of *Dombey and Son* is predicated on the great man's (and father's) inexplicable fear of his daughter, which is a cultural fear, "one man's doomed resistance" to having his family firm's future in the hands of a daughter rather than a son. Zwinger gives Dickens more credit than most critics do when she acknowledges that like "Agnes Wickfield, Lizzie Hexam and Esther Summerson, Florence is not merely ornamental" (30). She describes this succession of Dickens heroines as self-reliant, intelligent, and resourceful while also embodying all the sentimental and loving "virtues of the house angel" (30). This is a slightly revisionist view of the traditional judgments of ineptitude made against Dickens's characterization of women.

Dombey the father is different from all other Dickens fathers of daughters, however, because, owing to his mercantile, patriarchial obsession with "Dombey and Son," his great "House," he cannot accept her filial love and attentions, and instead actually becomes her tormentor. Early in the novel

Dombey is indifferent to his daughter, but his indifference is really fear, because he, "hoarding his son to his heart, wants no rivals for his son's attentions" (32). Ignored, Florence is an unrecognized rival of his son. After Paul dies, however, Dombey's hostility toward Florence is compounded by his reading her as, simply because she is still alive and so vengefully healthy, the successful rival. Out of fear of the threat to his eminence that Florence poses, Dombey possesses himself of Edith Skewton Granger to serve as a buffer between himself and his loving daughter. But, unfortunately, Edith proves an independent wife unwilling to reject the daughter that Dombey so fears. Faced with his impotence within the dynamics of the family romance, Dombey drives his daughter out into the streets.

Going against the grain of most Dickens critics who talk about the women in his fiction, Zwinger offers a new and powerful reading of *Dombey and Son* which opens a frightening box of sexual demons which the novel harbors. Dickens is the most psychological of novelists and Zwinger's reading of *Dombey and Son* is brilliant in its sympathy and its analyst's patience with the tormented and confused sexual relationship between father and daughter. Her discussions of the other novels included in this study are equally incisive, intelligent, and sympathic to the interior torments of their characters. Lynda Zwinger is a gender critic of the highest caliber.

Thus, whereas conventional wisdom has always portrayed Dickens as not having a very sensitive, or radical, way with women characters in his novels, recent revisionist thinking on gender issues, by critics like Zwinger and Robert Newsom in his essay "*Villette* and *Bleak House*: Authorizing Women," argues that Dickens is neither the antifeminist villain nor the confused benevolent despot nor the exploitative patriarch which, in the past, he has so often been painted to be. Newsom's is a model of postmodernist comparative criticism. Though his repeated first-person intrusions make Newsom the critic much too present in his criticism, still his comparative essay on the treatment of the heroines Lucy Snowe of Charlotte Brontë's *Villette* and Esther Summerson of Dickens' *Bleak House* is convincingly argued and thought-provoking in the most constructive ways. His even-handed approach to both the gender politics and the thematic realities of these novels could be taken right into the classroom as a model not only for the reading of these two novels but for the reading of all novels from a gender perspective.

Newsom's opening point—"*Villette* and *Bleak House* occupy the unusual position of having been able to influence one another" (54)—places his whole argument on an unusually solid footing. "Is the first number of *Bleak House*

generally admired?'' Newsom quotes tellingly from a letter written by Charlotte Brontë in March 1853, only weeks after the novel began serial publication. ''I liked the Chancery part, but when it passes into the autobiography
form, and the young women who announces that she is not 'bright' begins
her history, it seems to me too often weak and twaddling; an amiable nature
is caricatured, not faithfully rendered, in Miss Esther Summerson'' (55).
Obviously, Charlotte Brontë wasn't very impressed with Dickens' characterization of this woman, but Newsom, who has read the whole book whereas
Brontë had read only the first serial number when she wrote her letter, sees
both Dickens' characterization of Esther and Brontë's characterization of
Lucy Snowe as rather more complex and rather more similar than past critics
(including Brontë herself) have noticed. He may be guilty of being a revisionist gender critic as well as an apologist for Dickens, but Newsom is utterly
clear-sighted as to what he is doing. As Morris and Perera did in their books,
Newsom recognizes the dialogic opposition between margin and center as
present in the past gender considerations of the two writers. ''Brontë created
heroines that are nothing if not spirited and angry,'' he writes, ''while Dickens's seem to be models of contentment—busy little bodies, endlessly and
happily bustling about in the service of their households. Thus Brontë has
been assumed to speak for the dominated margins and Dickens for the dominating center'' (56). But Newsom is unhappy with this ''easy opposition of
margin and center'' when comparing Charlotte Brontë and Dickens because
''they are each extraordinarily ambivalent about the position of women, in
different ways blurring conventionally defined gender roles and positing radical redefinitions of gender equality at the same time that they remain ostensibly content with the formal arrangements of power in mid-Victorian culture''
(56).

What follows is a to-the-point comparative study of the two novels which
places their social texts and their gender subtexts in invigorating relation to
one another. Newsom defines both novels as batteries aimed at monolithic
Victorian institutions, the Court of Chancery and the Roman Catholic Church,
but after the smoke clears, they are ''equally interested in exploring the
complications of gender roles and in promoting gender equality'' (78). Newsom's essay is one to be taken right into the classroom in any Victorian novel
course to prove how closely the novelists of this period monitored each other's
work and thought, but it is also an excellent paradigm for how not to get
carried away in the application of postmodernist critical theories.

POSTMODERNIST NARRATIVITY

In his essay "Dickens and the Genealogy of Postmodernism," Jay Clayton begins with a head fake. In "any traditional history of postmodernism, Charles Dickens would play no role at all," he writes. In fact, in almost every case, the nineteenth-century British novelists (as opposed to their European counterparts: "Balzac in Roland Barthes, Hölderlin in Michel Foucault") are seen as "benighted, old-fashioned" when compared to "the exciting fictionists of our time" (181). Yet Clayton's is not a "traditional history," but a Foucault-inspired "genealogy" which "points to what has been left out, what is conspicuous by its absence" (182). Clayton considers this omission of Dickens even more eccentric when Dickens has been so valuable to earlier theorists, such as J. Hillis Miller in phenomenology and deconstruction. Clayton's major point, of course, is that Dickens should not have been left out.

"So why was Dickens left out of the discourse of postmodernism?" (184), Clayton asks, and his essay fast-breaks from there as a knowledgeable apologia for the excluding theorists and an ingenious arbitration for the excluded novelist. That he "does not fit neatly in either the sixties or eighties version of postmodernism" (185) is acknowledged, but that does not deter Clayton from attempting a messier alignment. Dickens is postmodern in his willingness to exploit "undervalued narrative conventions," in his "eccentric characters," in his "postmodern fascination with the circuit of communication, the medium of the message" (187), in "the disturbingly mobile nature of his desire" (188). "We must recognize," Clayton concludes his curiously static essay, "that postmodernism is not the dawning of a new age but the realization of certain possibilities within Western society that were salient even in the time of Charles Dickens" (195).

Clayton is interested in why Dickens was banished by contemporary theorists (which he has not been at all), but Audrey Jaffe in her *Vanishing Points: Dickens, Narrative and the Subject of Omniscience* attempts to understand a different sort of vanishing act. Taking as her *point de départ* Roland Barthes' often rather difficult to answer question "Who is speaking?" (1), she explores the elusive mobility of Victorian omniscience especially as practiced by Charles Dickens. The postmodernist problem has become that "if earlier critics tended to find the 'authorial' narrator's voice intrusive, for more recent critics that voice hardly exists at all. Or, rather, it refers not to individuals but to institutions" (3). Because of the elusiveness of that narrative voice, critics must choose how to handle a novel's omniscient narrator—as presence or personification? as impersonal technique? as implied author? or a character? as simply "'writing''?—in order ever to understand the novel's, the author's, the narrator's motives. Jaffe's answer to this exploding question is to throw the responsibility back on the narrator, the text itself. "Rather than naturalize omniscience, we can understand ourselves precisely in the way in which it naturalizes or refuses to naturalize itself," she writes, thus defining her book as the Ellis Island of Dickensian narrative criticism. Empowered to accept Dickens' huddled masses of narrators, she processes them through and sets them free to invigorate out readings of the familiar novels of the Dickens canon. Thus, her "rereading of Dickens" is also "a rereading of narrative conventions" in which "omniscience is understood to be a fantasy about knowledge" (7), which makes every omnisciently narrated novel an epistemo- logical mystery story in which the narrator attempts to track down his or her own self-realization, understand his or her own motives. Moving from *Sketches by Boz* to *Our Mutual Friend*, she engages in "tracing the disappear- ance of the personified narrator" (21). But her interest is in comparing per- sonified with disembodied narrators, rather than simply tracking the extinction of a species.

For Audrey Jaffe, the narrators of Dickens (like those longing-to-be-natu- ralized immigrants through Ellis Island) are a widely diverse lot, a rather motley assortment of dialects and social classes and political loyalties and schemes for both self-improvement and self-agrandizement. For instance, the narrator of *Sketches by Boz* is a "shadow" which can "loom as a fanciful thing all over London" while the narrator of *The Old Curiosity Shop* evolves in his own curiosity in some quite self-reflexive ways while the omniscient voice in *Dombey and Son* is that of either a narrative peeping Tom or a narrative private eye, someone who either spies on or exposes those things which the "characters wish to keep secret" (71) while the narrators of *David Copperfield* and *Bleak House* strive to couple the displaced first-person narra- tor with the sometimes but not always disembodied omniscient narrator while the shape-shifting narrator of *Our Mutual Friend*, "generally regarded as the most modern of Dickens's works because of the absence of a prominent omniscient voice and a clear omniscient perspective" (150), is a mischievous agent of surprise. The great strengths of Jaffe's *Vanishing Points: Dickens, Narrative and the Subject of Omniscience* (and this is a very strong book) are its versatility in defining the differences between the Dickens narrators and its patience in exploring the causes, motives, techniques, and effects of a dogged evolution of narrative style which powerfully argues for Dickens as a fulcrum between the empowerment of Victorian omniscience and the rebellion of Modernism. Jaffe should be credited for crediting Dickens with a narrative intelligence which, in the light of his special effects, too many critics overlook.

The first truly postmodernist critic of the works and the "consciousness of consciousness" of Charles Dickens was, of course, J. Hillis Miller. Miller's *Charles Dickens: The World of His Novels* changed forever both the discourse (and the rhetoric in which it was couched) of Dickens criticism. *Victorian Subjects* is a collection of thirty-five years of Miller essays, predominantly about Dickens' works, but also dealing with Hopkins, Balzac, Trollope, George Eliot, Thackeray, and Carlyle. For Dickens critics weaned in the Sixties on Miller's "ambience bubbles" and "intersubjective looks," much of this anthology of one critic's criticism will be not merely familiar but, in the case of "the disappearance of God" and "the ethics of reading," part of their everyday lexicon. Ten of the twenty essays included in this collection are Dickens studies, the most recent of which was originally published in 1971. Thus, much of what is included here will be quite recognizable to established Dickensians and confirmed Millerites. But the real value of *Victorian Subjects* is its utility for introducing a new generation of Dickens critics and interpreters of Victorian literature to the Miller way and the Miller style.

Miller's title for his collection, *Victorian Subjects*, carries the same multivalent allusiveness that has marked his long career in criticism. Certainly, the essays deal with "topics within Victorian literature," but all are also concerned with Victorian subjects "in the sense of subjectivity, consciousness, or selfhood as it was expressed in Victorian literature," by authors "who were subject to Queen Victoria, that is, subject to the reigning ideologies of the time, among them the prevalent ideologies about subjectivity" (vii). Those are the three senses of Victorian subjects which Miller is playing with in these essays, but he is quite careful to warn the reader of trying "to find some teleological unity in these essays, for example a movement from a phenomenological 'criticism of consciousness' to a deconstructive rhetorical criticism, and, beyond that, to the premonitory signs of a criticism focusing on a performative, positional ethics of writing and reading" (viii). Interestingly enough, in that one sentence of warning Miller has managed to rather specifically characterize the progress and the way stations of his own constantly changing, developing, exploring critical journey. Miller has always been an evolutionary critic, the innovator of the species, the first to naturally select the next step along the critical scale.

Like all books of this sort, staples of university presses hungry for name-recognition prestige, Miller's collection is efficient, Utilitarian. The graduate student need only make one stop in the library to pick up all these diverse items of Miller criticism, sort of a supermarket approach. The essays herein are excellent and provocative, but a young Dickensian intent on one-stop shopping would be much better served by picking up *Charles Dickens: The World of His Novels*. The difference is one of fast food versus a gourmet meal.

CHARACTER CRITICISM

Richard Altick in *The Presence of the Present* and Doris Alexander in *Creating Characters with Charles Dickens* are essentially playing to the same audience. Altick, however, is playing on a much bigger stage, raising the curtain on grand opera rather than on a Punch and Judy show. Altick's stage is the whole field of the Victorian novel plus all of the politics, social history and public personalities out of which the genre's characters, plots, themes, objects of satire, and allusions are drawn. Alexander focuses on the "real" originals for about forty of Dickens's characters—"Dickens lovers have always felt impelled to hunt down real persons who might have sat for his characters" (1)—and along the way tells some pretty good stories, reveals some interesting social history, makes some perceptive interpretations of both Dickens' style of characterization and his intentionality. The only question that arises is whether anyone cares. The old-fashionedness of Altick's critical endeavor is ameliorated by the breadth and depth of his political and sociohistorical savvy. Alexander's criticism, which identifies and describes before speculating on Dickens's intentionality, is simply old-fashioned in a critical age dominated by postmodernist thought and theory. "Why hunt originals?" is the title of Alexander's introductory chapter, and the answer may well be "why indeed?"

The rest of her chapters, all bearing cute Fieldingesque chapter titles—"Bad Old Men in *Bleak House*: On How Dickens Transformed Real Persons into Villains" or "Role Players in *Bleak House*: On How Dickens Made Role Players Play Their Roles Fictionally" or "Copperfield Reincarnate: On How Dickens's Life Story Brought in a Novel's Configuration of Characters and Shaped Them"—focus on individual characters in individual novels in hopes of "determining factually just how accurately Dickens penetrated the psychology of his originals and their effect on their world" (2).

Alexander claims a great deal for her detective work into the identification of these originals of Dickens' characters. She claims that "these identifications will demand changes in Dickens biography, for biographers have usually modeled their conception of important persons in Dickens' life on certain of his characters under the mistaken belief that those characters were portraits of them" (4). John Forster, Edgar Johnson, Fred Kaplan, and Peter Ackroyd would probably protest that biography is not quite that inexact a science. She also claims that her investigation into character originals "suggests that many conventional assumptions about Dickens's best known characters, about his life story, and even about his personality and creative method must be revised and reinterpreted" (4). Not only does Alexander claim too much for her detective work, but she protests too much in its defense.

Nonetheless, her anecdotal accounts of her detective work in pursuit of Dickens' originals for some of his more interesting characters are fun to read and provide some interesting addenda to the trivia of the Dickens world. Alexander writes beautifully and researches well. The book itself is 150 pages of witty reading followed by 68 more pages of scholarly notes. There is an irony in all those pages of notes, however, because Alexander's *Creating Characters with Charles Dickens* is itself but a footnote to both past and contemporary Dickens criticism.

Alexander is quite right about one thing, however. The fascination Dickens critics have for analyzing the symbolic, thematic, psychological, political, topical, genealogical, rhetorical, cultural, and mythical dimensions of Dickens' characters is ongoing. A single character, or perhaps a couple, seems just the right size for a scholarly article, and battalions of such articles march through the pages of scholarly journals every year. As Altick did for all the Victorian novelists, Shifra Hochberg in "Mrs. Sparsit's Coriolanian Eyebrows and Dickensian Approach to Topicality" tries to do for one character in *Hard Times*. Mirroring Altick's attitudes toward "topicalities," she argues that for Dickens' topical caricaturing "the intention is always the same: immediacy, instant recall, and frequently, striking pictorial detail" (32). She goes on to argue a Shakespearean influence on characterization which is used "to underscore Dickens's economic and sociopolitical concerns" (34).

Phillip V. Allingham also writes about the characters in *Hard Times*. His essay "Theme, Form, and the Naming of Names in *Hard Times for These Times*" asks whether the book is a "fable" or rather a "novel in the modern sense" (17). Somehow, in the nineties, that question isn't as immediate or even necessary as it was to F. R. Leavis back in the forties because the answer is so inconclusive and, in postmodernist theoretical terms, so meaningless and even unnecessary. *Hard Times* is both and neither, and, in fact, fable or novel, who cares? "The key to the story's theme would then seem to lie in the characters' names," Allingham argues, but name games in literature are rarely more than that, games, little in-jokes, which are rarely capable of hoisting the full cargo of thematic meaning. It may be interesting to know that the "origins of the names of the twenty-three characters tend to be biblical, topical, historical, and colloquial" (17), and it may be true that "for Dickens, names were truly magical; they concealed and revealed identity" (17), but no matter how intricate a novel's genealogy, themes, especially in a novel as socially involved as *Hard Times*, usually turn on much larger issues.

While all of these articles about individual characters feed fairly familiar critical fires, Charles Forsyte in "Dickens and Dick Datchery" may be roasting the oldest chestnut of all. Like Alexander's question "Why hunt originals?" Forsyte's question "Who is Dick Datchery?" has been asked and answered many times in the past, and perhaps is deserving of being given a rest. In fact, penetrating the literary disguise, unmasking Dick Datchery, has always been one of the favorite Dickensian parlor games. There are almost as many Dick Datcherys around as there have been Elvis sightings. Datchery has been identified as "Dickens himself," as a "private detective," as almost every other character in the novel at one time or another, yet Forsyte tries mightily to convince that Bazzard, the professional actor, is really Dick Datchery in disguise. Which is all well and good, and is supported by excellent arguments, but to what real purpose? The trouble with books like Alexander's and articles like Hochberg's, Allingham's, and Forsyte's is that all they ultimately do is identify. Unfortunately, as the beleagured policeman at the beginning of *Our Mutual Friend* would be the first to agree, identification is only the first step in a much more complicated process and isn't always accurate to boot.

Richard Currie, employing a much more current theoretical model based on psychoanalysis, in his essay " 'As if she had done him a wrong': Hidden Rage and Object Protection in Dickens's Amy Dorrit" nonetheless also focuses very narrowly on one character from one novel. Though his arguments are original and perceptive, he never draws any conclusion(s) which illuminate either the novel as a whole or the thematic concerns in which the characterization of the title character so centrally participate. His conclusion that "the quiet, self-effacing way Amy conducts herself is a facade. Underneath the unassuming attitude we see anger functioning as a narcissistic wound while self-attack and protection of the object constitute the central features of her personality'' (375) never attempts to be any more than a psychoanalysis of her behavior, never concerns itself with the contexts of her existence or the larger meanings of the novel in which she exists. Currie's arguments are extremely well formulated and supported, but they just don't go anywhere.

Wilfred Dvorak's essay about another character in that same novel, ''The Misunderstood Pancks: Money and the Rhetoric of Disguise in *Little Dorrit*,'' while also focusing on a single, though multidimensional, character, is much more expansive in its contextualizing and thematicizing, with the result that the essay is really about the novel rather than simply about an isolated character. Arguing that the metaphor and rhetoric of disguise control the meaning of *Little Dorrit*, Dvorak reads the novel as a halucinatory and deceptive journey through the ''nothing is ever as it seems'' world of 1850s capitalism. Again, Altick-like, Dvorak shows how the rhetoric of disguise centered in Pancks ''directs the reader to a set of important topical issues'' which allow Dickens ''to very effectively express his views about the state of his times'' (339), topicalities such as the Sadleir speculative bubble scandal. What Dvorak is arguing is that *Little Dorrit*, through Pancks Wemmick-like rhetoric of disguise ''is presenting a quite subtle argument about getting and spending in the fifties'' (344) and that Panck's heroism in doffing his own disguise and cutting off the false disguise which the rapaciousness of Victorian capitalism hides behind is Dickens' comment on how men must break the control which a corrupt economic system holds over them. What is salutary about Dvorak's character criticism is its ability to analyze a fully realized character within the context of the whole novel. Character never exists for character alone, but as part of a community of characters within a world of a novel.

Two other essays by Doris Alexander, overflow perhaps from her book of character originals, appeared elsewhere in 1991. ''Benevolent Sage or Blundering Booby?'' tracks down the original of Christopher Casby in *Little Dorrit* and forms a nice triptych with the articles of Currie and Dvorak. These three essays, while all enlightening, illuminate to much different degrees. Alexander identifies, Currie psychoanalyzes, but only Dvorak accomplishes true character criticism which places the character within the context of the book. Alexander's other essay, '' 'Seven Hundred Thousand Imprecations' by Charles Dickens,'' corners ''the real Pecksniff of *Martin Chuzzlewit*'' (95). Perhaps that phrase signals the most basic problem of Alexander's character criticism. If Pecksniff is a fictional character, can he have a reality? If he can have a fictional reality, then how can a topically real person be that reality? If that real person is really Pecksniff, then who is the fictional Pecksniff? If the topically real person and the fictionally real person are the same,

then why don't they have the same name? It is a critical dilemma that deserves
to end up in the Circumlocution Office, but it is also a critical fascination that
proliferates. Elisabeth Gitter in "Laura Bridgeman and Little Nell" also
nominates an original, but acknowledges the differences between the real
person and the fictional reality, something that Alexander often fails to do.

READINGS

Always the most popular kind of Dickens criticism is the focused interpretation of a chosen one of Dickens's novels. 1991 was *Barnaby Rudge*'s 150th
Anniversary year in *Dickens Quarterly*. The March issue was devoted solely
to that novel. David Paroissien's excellent introduction to the number not
only details the composition and publication history of *Barnaby Rudge* but
also locates the novel within a number of relevant contexts. Though a survey
has shown that *Barnaby Rudge* "is both the least read and the least loved"
(5) of all of Dickens' novels, Paroissien offers good reasons for renewing
critical interest in it, as do the other articles in this collection.

Michael Hollington's "Monstrous Faces: Physiognomy in *Barnaby
Rudge*" focuses on "a rather seriously neglected" stylistic and thematic
aspect of all of Dickens' novels, physiognomy, "the art or science of reading
character through the face" (6). Nineteenth-century fiction, from Franken-
stein to Heathcliff to Quilp to Mr. Hyde, is densely populated with monsters
whose faces customarily twist into horrible visages, and Holington offers
a thorough and authoritative definition of Dickens' system of countenance
psychology. Two other essays, Joel Brattin's " 'Secrets inside . . . to strike
to your heart': New Readings from Dickens's Manuscript of *Barnaby Rudge*,
Chapter 75" and Barbara Stuart's "The Centaur in *Barnaby Rudge*," both
deal with the "centaur" significances from very different perspectives. Brattin's textual criticism is really character criticism, the revelation of Sir John
Chester's villainous character by way of Dickens' vision and revision of it in
both manuscript and finished text. Stuart's is more conventional imagistic
criticism which analyzes the meaning of the animal imagery in *Barnaby
Rudge* as it underscores "the social injustice at the heart of the novel" and
"the complacent or callous neglect of human responsibility in public as well
as private life" (29). The essay focuses on Hugh "the Centaur," the leader
of the riots, and on how the evolution of his character from animality to
mobility to execution forms an elaborate matrix of social comments. The final
essay, Iain Crawford's " 'Nature . . . drenched in blood': *Barnaby Rudge*

and Wordsworth's 'The Idiot Boy' " is both an influence study and a piece of character criticism quite similar to both Brattin's and Stuart's. Crawford examines the origins and meanings of Dickens' title character to arrive at the conclusion that as a "Dickensian Child of Nature" (39) among many (Oliver, Smike, Nell) Barnaby is not only a Wordsworthian figure but also a figure whose "own imaginative disorder is then hardly unique in a novel where the construction of fictitious versions of reality is widespread, and his limitations may be seen as a paradigm of the failings which afflict individuals and households, and finally threaten the stability of the very nation itself" (46).

Alternating with essays on *Jane Eyre*, captivity novels, H. G. Wells' *Time Machine*, sensation fiction, *Mary Barton*, and Gissing's *The Odd Woman*, *The Dickens World* published single novel studies of *Bleak House, Little Dorrit, David Copperfield*, and *Great Expectations* in 1991. Michael Kent's "Henry Gowan's Masterpiece: Art in *Little Dorrit*" and Keith Todd's "The Hearth and the Bench: Implications of Family Law Reform in *Great Expectations* and *What Maisie Knew*" both cross-examine particular symbolic scenes, image patterns, and language matrices which illuminate one of Dickens' themes. Kent perceptively examines "Dickens's conception of the true role of the artist in society" in *Little Dorrit*, which he sees as Dickens' "most complex and complete analysis in fiction of Victorian culture—its art, its technology, its government, and its business" (61). Todd goes back to one of Dickens' own favorite subjects, the law and lawyers, in his comparative study of *Great Expectations* and *What Maisie Knew*. There is a great deal of information about the law in this essay, but not much that is useful about *Great Expectations* except that perhaps Mrs. Joe isn't that horrible a mother-figure and that what seem the "brutal realities" (101) of Dickens' portrayal of the plights of Victorian children were not really as brutal as the real realities of child exploitation and abuse in that age. Based on Foucault and offering an alternative to D. A. Miller's recent deconstructive reading of the novel, Jon Anderson's "Dickens's 'Pathologic Labour': Madness and Moral Management in *Bleak House*" is the most exciting essay in this collection and a most thought-provoking reading of that great novel. For Anderson, *Bleak House* is a novel which concerns "ways of seeing society as a whole, but that seeing is not so important, ultimately, to Dickens as it is a way of feeling symbolized by an alternative discourse to the law, that of medicine" (3). He wants to offer "a thesis which contradicts what everyone knows to be true about *Bleak House*," that "the central concern in this novel is rendered not in legal but in medical terms" (4). His argument is utterly convincing and ought to be consulted by every teacher of the novel. Because *David Copperfield* is about "how hard it is to tell your own story and be your own hero" (82), Dona Budd's title "Double-Talk in *David Copperfield*" is obviously appropriate. Dickens' most overt metafiction, his only novel where the protagonist-narrator is also a novelist, his most self-reflexive novel not only about himself but about his novel-writing, *David Copperfield* is especially receptive to the narrativist reading which Budd gives it. Narrative anxiety is her theme and she argues it well.

"Usual suspects," and "those guys," and "offers" we "can't refuse" are all part of the year 1991 in Dickens studies. What a rich year it was!

WORKS CITED

Ackroyd, Peter. *Dickens*. New York: Harper, 1990.

Alexander, Doris. *Creating Characters with Charles Dickens*. University Park: Pennsylvania State UP, 1991.

———. " 'Seven Hundred Thousand Imprecations' by Charles Dickens." *The Dickensian* 87. 2 (Summer 1991):95–101.

———. "Benevolent Sage or Blundering Booby." *Dickens Quarterly* 8. 3 (September 1991):120–27.

Allingham, Philip V. "Theme, Form and the Naming of Names in *Hard Times for These Times*." *Dickensian* 87. 1 (Spring 1991):17–31.

Altick, Richard. *The Presence of the Present: Topics of the Day in the Victorian Novel*. Columbus: Ohio State UP, 1991.

Anderson, Jon B. "Dickens's 'Pathologic Labour': Madness and Moral Management in *Bleak House*." *Dickens World* 7 (Summer 1991):3–16.

Bernstein, Carol. *The Celebration of Scandal: Toward the Sublime in Victorian Urban Fiction*. University Park: Pennsylvania State UP, 1991.

Boasberg, James. "Chancery as Megalosaurus: Lawyers, Courts and Society in *Bleak House*." *University of Hartford Studies in Literature* 21 (1989):38–60.

Brattin, Joel J. " 'Secrets inside . . . to strike your heart': New Readings from Dickens's Manuscript of *Barnaby Rudge*, Chapter 75." *Dickens Quarterly* 9. 1 (March 1991):15–28.

Budd, Dona. "Doubletalk in *David Copperfield*." *Dickens World* 7 (Summer 1991):82–91.

Buckley, Jerome Hamilton. *The Victorian Temper*. Cambridge: Harvard UP, 1951.

Clayton, Jay. "Dickens and the Genealogy of Postmodernism." *Nineteenth-Century Literature* 46. 2 (September 1991):181–95.

Crawford, Iain. " 'Nature . . . drenched in blood': *Barnaby Rudge* and Wordswroth's 'The Idiot Boy.' " *Dickens Quarterly* 9. 1 (March 1991):38–47.

Currie, Richard A. " 'As if she had done him a wrong': Hidden Rage and Object Protection in Dickens's Amy Dorrit." *English Studies* 72. 4 (August 1991):368–76.

Davis, Tracy C. *Actresses as Working Women: Their Social Identity in Victorian Culture*. London and New York: Routledge, 1991.

Dvorak, Wilfred P. "The Misunderstood Pancks: Money and the Rhetoric of Disguise in *Little Dorrit*." *Studies in the Novel* 23. 3 (Fall 1991):339–47.

Forster, John. *The Life of Charles Dickens*. New York: Doubleday, 1928.

Forsyte, Charles. "Dickens and Dick Datchery." *Dickensian* 87. 1 (Spring 1991):50–57.

Gitter, Elisabeth. "Laura Bridgeman and Little Nell." *Dickens Quarterly* 8. 2 (June 1991):75–79.

Hochberg, Shifra. "Mrs. Sparsit's Coriolanian Eyebrows and Dickensian Approach to Topicality." *Dickensian* 87. 1 (Spring 1991):32–36.

Hollington, Michael. "Monstrous Faces: Physiognomy in *Barnaby Rudge*. *Dickens Quarterly* 9. 1 (March 1991):7–15.

Houghton, Walter. *The Victorian Frame of Mind*. New Haven: Yale UP, 1957.

Humpherys, Anne. "And Urban Twists: The Victorian Mysteries Novel." *Victorian Studies* 34. 4 (1991):455–72.

Jaffe, Audrey. *Vanishing Points: Dickens. Narrative and the Subject of Omniscience*. Berkeley: U of California P, 1991.

Johnson, Edgar. *Charles Dickens: His Tragedy and Triumph*. New York: Simon and Schuster, 1952.

Kaplan, Fred. *Dickens: A Biography*. New York: Morrow, 1988.

Kent, Michael. "Henry Gowan's Masterpiece: Art in *Little Dorrit*." *Dickens World* 7 (Summer 1991):61–66.

Lindsey, Jack. *Charles Dickens: A Biographical and Critical Study*. New York: Dakers, 1950.

Marcus, Steven. *The Other Victorians*. New York: Basic Books, 1966.

Miller, J. Hillis. *Victorian Subjects*. Durham: Duke UP, 1991.

————. *Charles Dickens: The World of His Novels*. Cambridge: Harvard UP, 1958.

Mitford, Nancy. *Zelda: A Biography*. New York: Harper and Row, 1970.

Morris, Pam. *Dickens's Class Consciousness: A Marginal View*. New York: St. Martin's, 1991.

Newsom, Robert. "*Villette* and *Bleak House*: Authorizing Women." *Nineteenth-Century Literature* 46. 1 (June 1991):54–81.

Nisbet, Ada. *Dickens and Ellen Ternan*. Berkeley: U of California P, 1952.

Paroissien, David. Preface. *Dickens Quarterly* 9. 1 (March 1991):3–6.

Perera, Suvendrini. *Reaches of Empire*. New York: Columbia UP, 1991.

Stuart, Barbara. "The Centaur in *Barnaby Rudge*." *Dickens Quarterly* 9. 1 (March 1991):29–37.

Todd, Keith. "The Hearth and the Bench: The Implications of Family Law Reform in *Great Expectations* and *What Maisie Knew*." *Dickens World* 7 (Summer 1991):98–107.

Tomalin, Claire. *The Invisible Woman: The Story of Nelly Ternan and Charles Dickens*. New York: Knopf, 1991.

Vanden Bossche, Chris R. "The Year in Dickens Studies:1990." *Dickens Studies Annual* 20 (1991).

Welsh, Alexander. *The City of Dickens*. Oxford: Clarendon Press, 1971.

Willey, Basil. *Nineteenth-Century Studies*. New York: Columbia UP, 1949.

Zwinger, Lynda. *Daughters, Fathers, and the Novel: The Sentimental Romance of Heterosexuality*. Madison: U of Wisconsin P, 1991.

Index